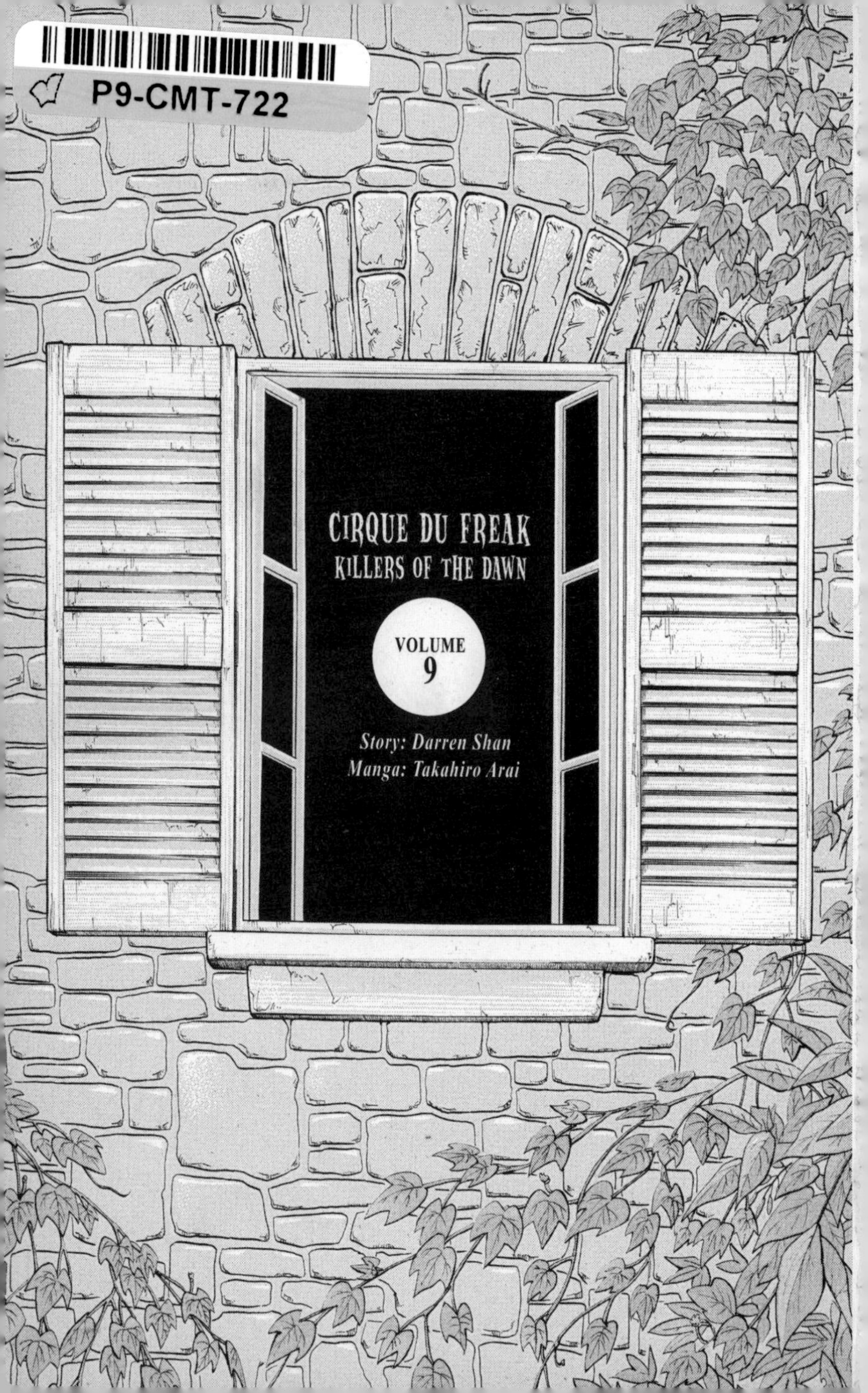
CIRQUE DU FREAK
KILLERS OF THE DAWN
VOLUME 9
Story: Darren Shan
Manga: Takahiro Arai

A SUMMARY OF ALLIES OF THE NIGHT:

ON HIS QUEST TO DEFEAT THE VAMPANEZE LORD, DARREN STOPS IN A FAMILIAR TOWN AND MEETS NOT ONLY HIS OLD GIRLFRIEND, DEBBIE, BUT HIS ONE-TIME FRIEND, STEVE, NOW A GROWN VAMPANEZE HUNTER. ONE DAY WHILE SEARCHING FOR THE ENEMY IN THE SEWERS WITH HIS RE-UNITED FRIENDS, DARREN AND HIS GROUP ARE TAKEN BY SURPRISE AND SURROUND-ED. IT WAS ACTUALLY A TRAP SET BY STEVE, WHO IS IN FACT A HALF-VAMPANEZE. DEBBIE IS KIDNAPPED, AND DESPITE BEING IN THE PRESENCE OF THE VAMPANEZE LORD, DARREN HAS NO CHOICE BUT TO RETREAT...

CIRQUE DU FREAK 9
CONTENTS

CHAPTER 75: ESCAPE

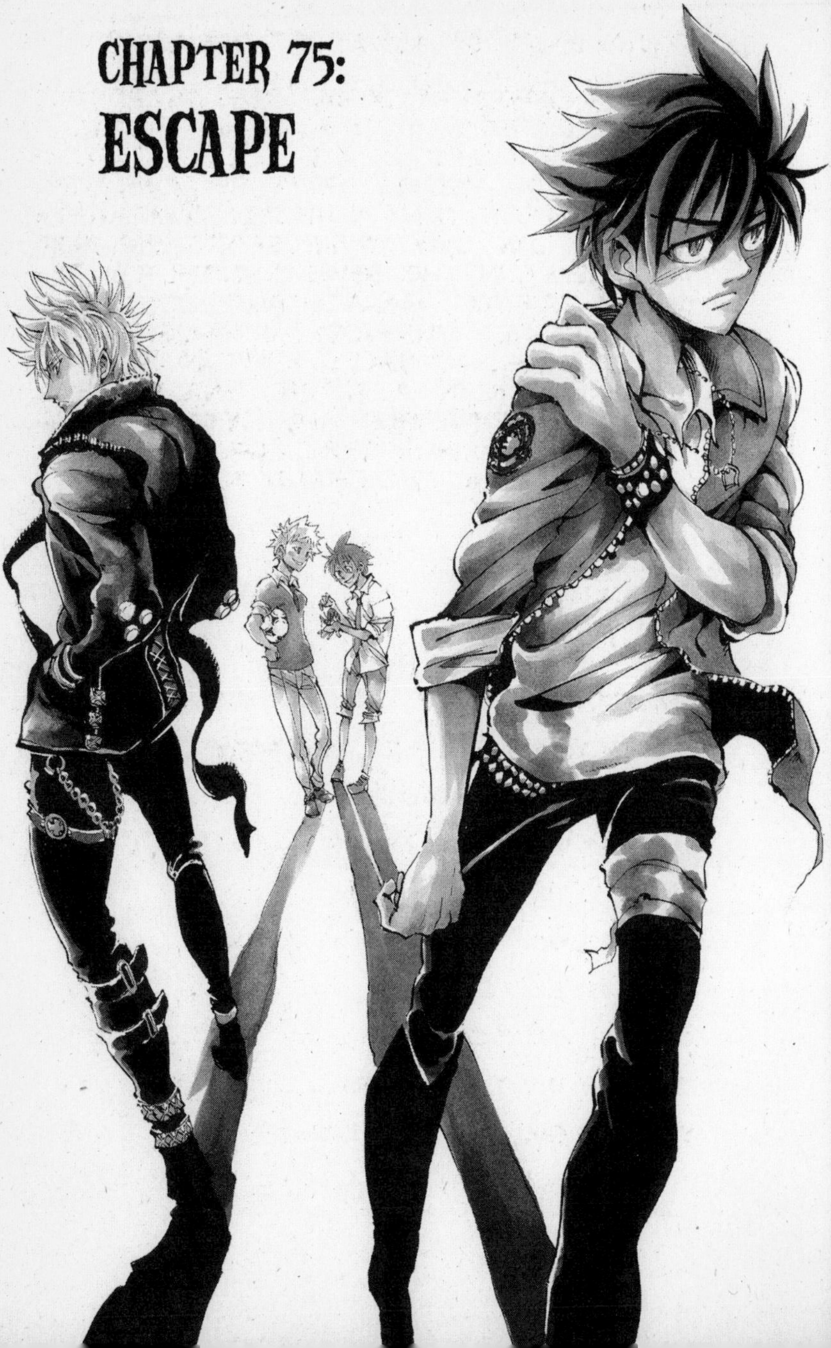

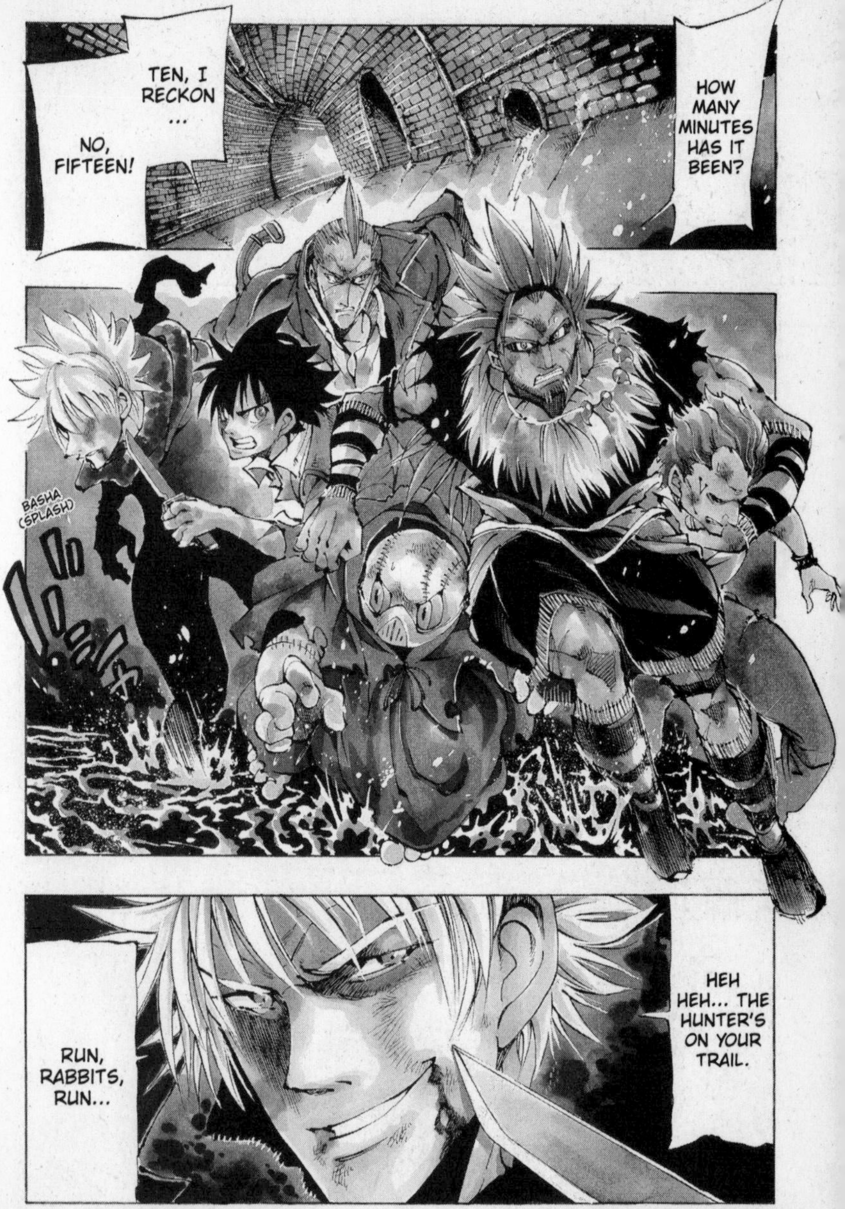
HOW MANY MINUTES HAS IT BEEN?
TEN, I RECKON ...
NO, FIFTEEN!
BASHA (SPLASH)
HEH HEH... THE HUNTER'S ON YOUR TRAIL.
RUN, RABBITS, RUN...

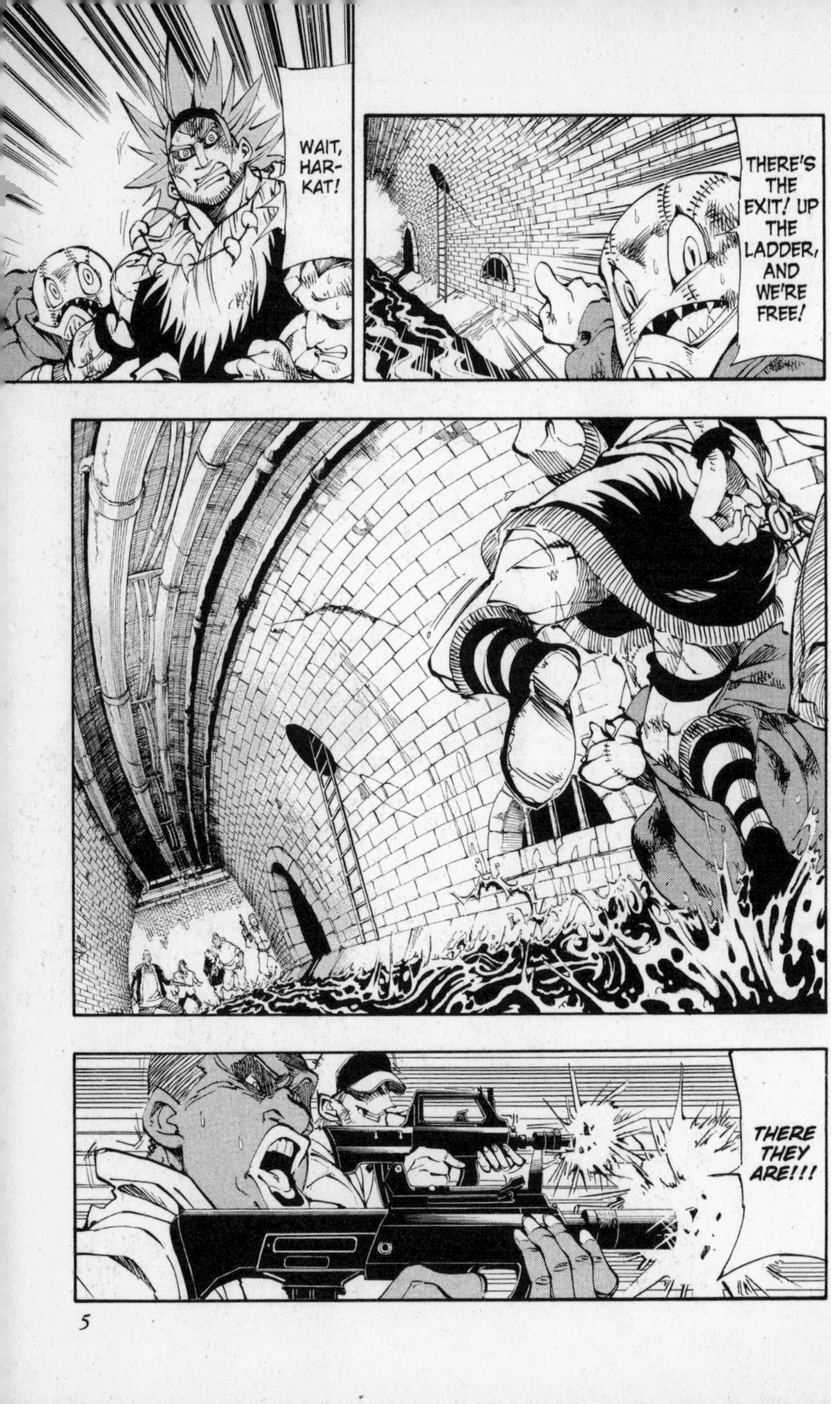
THERE'S THE EXIT! UP THE LADDER, AND WE'RE FREE!
WAIT, HAR-KAT!
THERE THEY ARE!!!

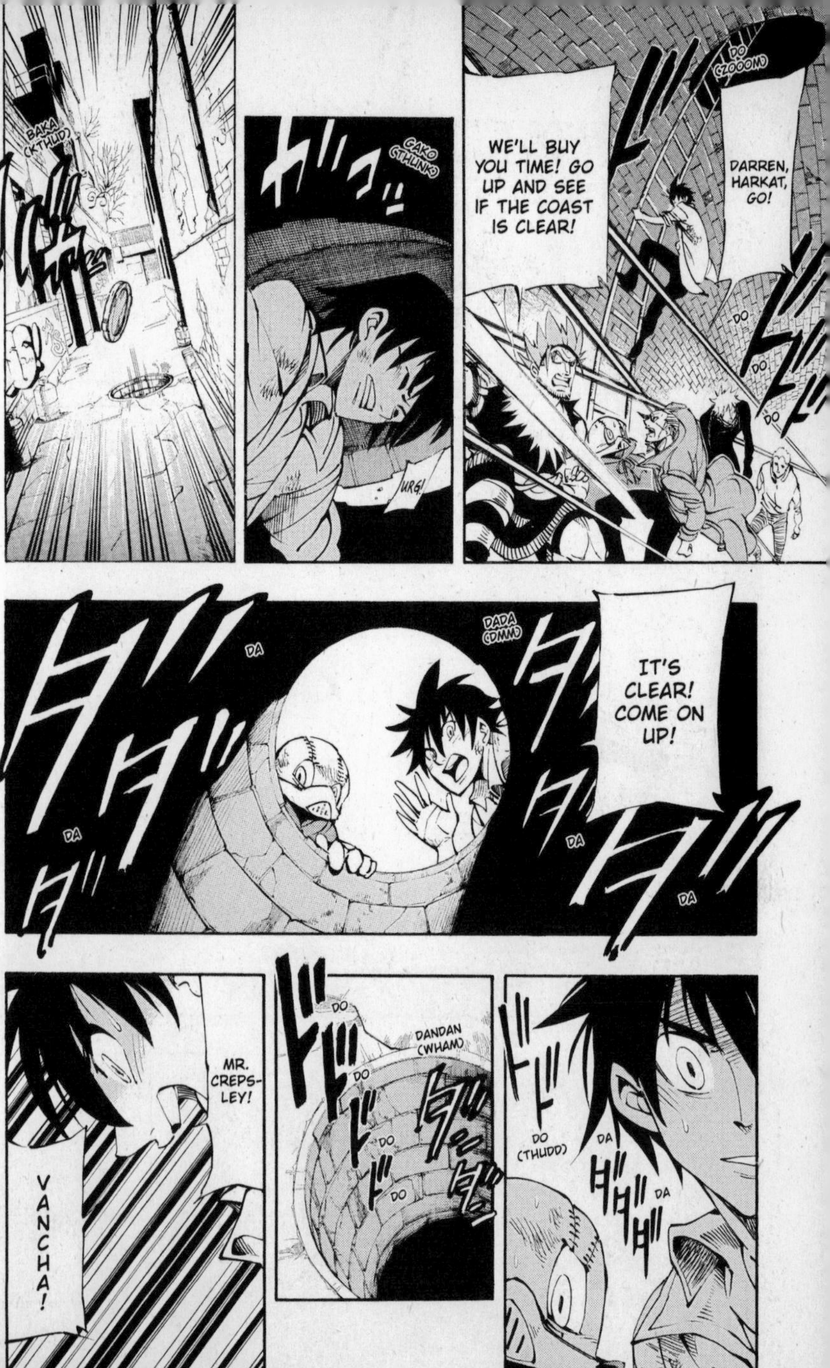
DO (ZOOOM)
DARREN, HARKAT, GO!
WE'LL BUY YOU TIME! GO UP AND SEE IF THE COAST IS CLEAR!
DO
DO
DO
GAKO (THUNK)
URG!
BAKA (KTHUD)
DADA (DMM)
IT'S CLEAR! COME ON UP!
DA
DA
DA
DA
DO (THUDD)
DA
DA
DO
DANDAN (WHAM)
DO
DO
MR. CREPSLEY!
VANCHA!

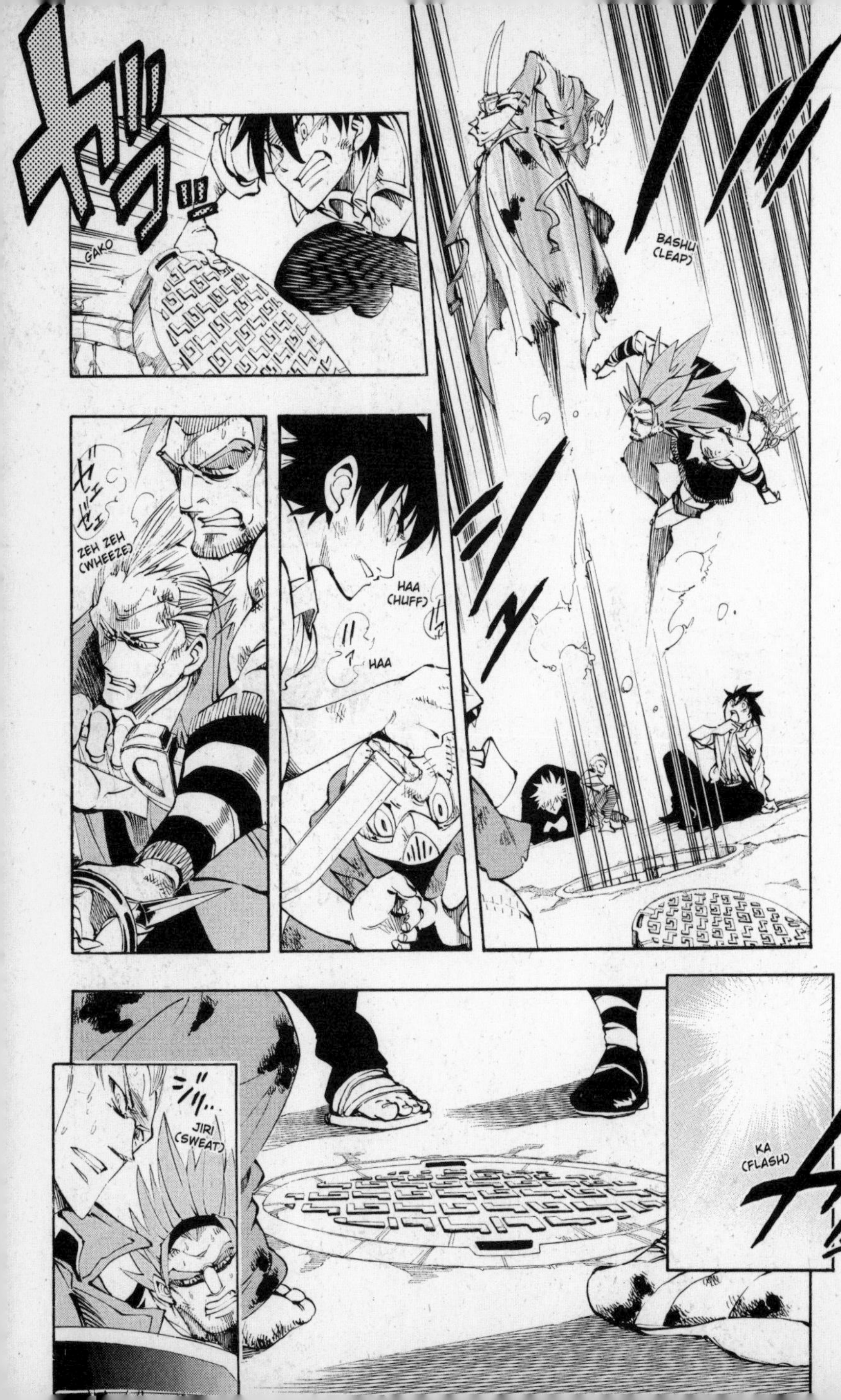
BASHU
(LEAP)
GAKO
HAA
(HUFF)
HAA
ZEH ZEH
(WHEEZE)
KA
(FLASH)
JIRI
(SWEAT)

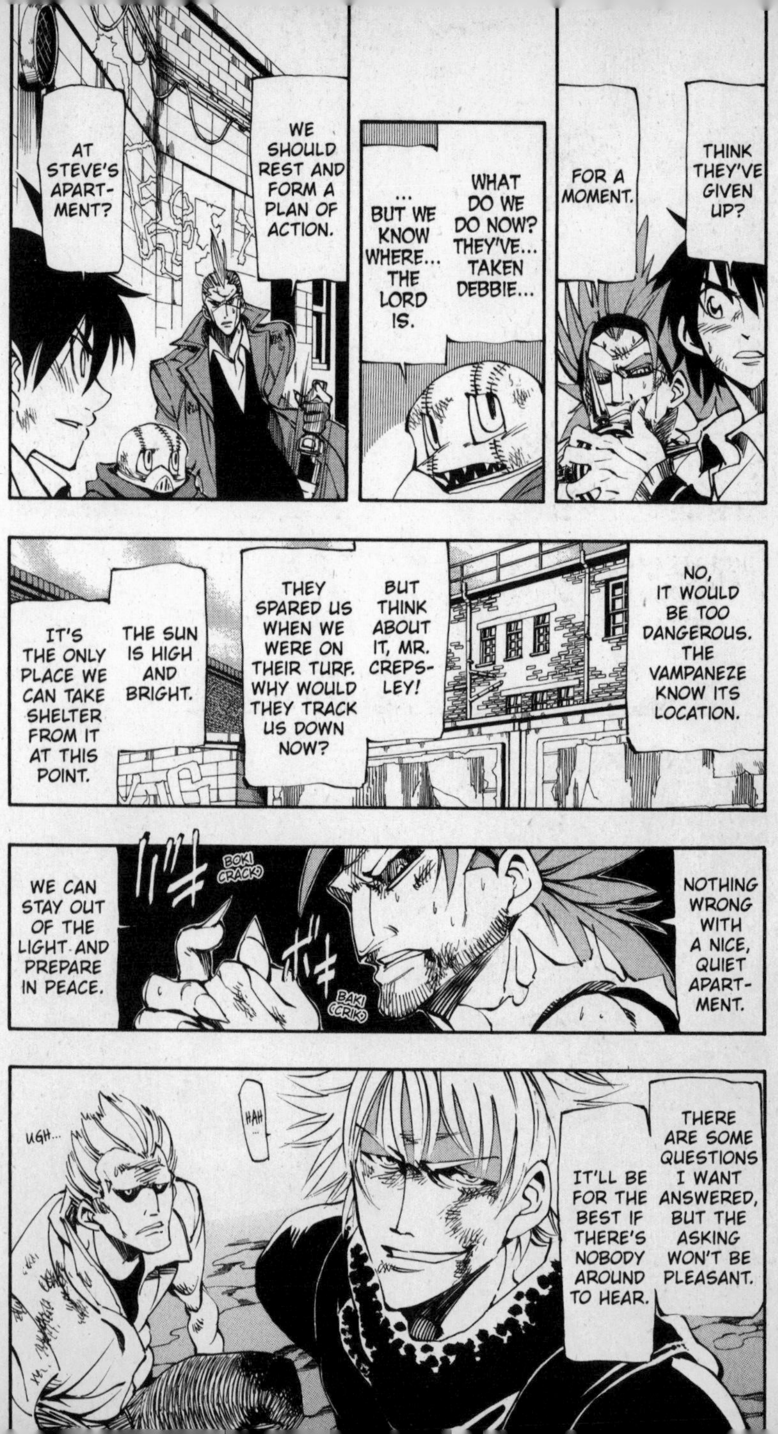
THINK THEY'VE GIVEN UP?
FOR A MOMENT.
WHAT DO WE DO NOW? THEY'VE... TAKEN DEBBIE...
... BUT WE KNOW WHERE... THE LORD IS.
WE SHOULD REST AND FORM A PLAN OF ACTION.
AT STEVE'S APART-MENT?
NO, IT WOULD BE TOO DANGEROUS. THE VAMPANEZE KNOW ITS LOCATION.
BUT THINK ABOUT IT, MR. CREPS-LEY!
THEY SPARED US WHEN WE WERE ON THEIR TURF. WHY WOULD THEY TRACK US DOWN NOW?
THE SUN IS HIGH AND BRIGHT.
IT'S THE ONLY PLACE WE CAN TAKE SHELTER FROM IT AT THIS POINT.
NOTHING WRONG WITH A NICE, QUIET APART-MENT.
BOKI (CRACK)
BAKI (CRIK)
WE CAN STAY OUT OF THE LIGHT AND PREPARE IN PEACE.
THERE ARE SOME QUESTIONS I WANT ANSWERED, BUT THE ASKING WON'T BE PLEASANT.
IT'LL BE FOR THE BEST IF THERE'S NOBODY AROUND TO HEAR.
HAH ...
UGH...

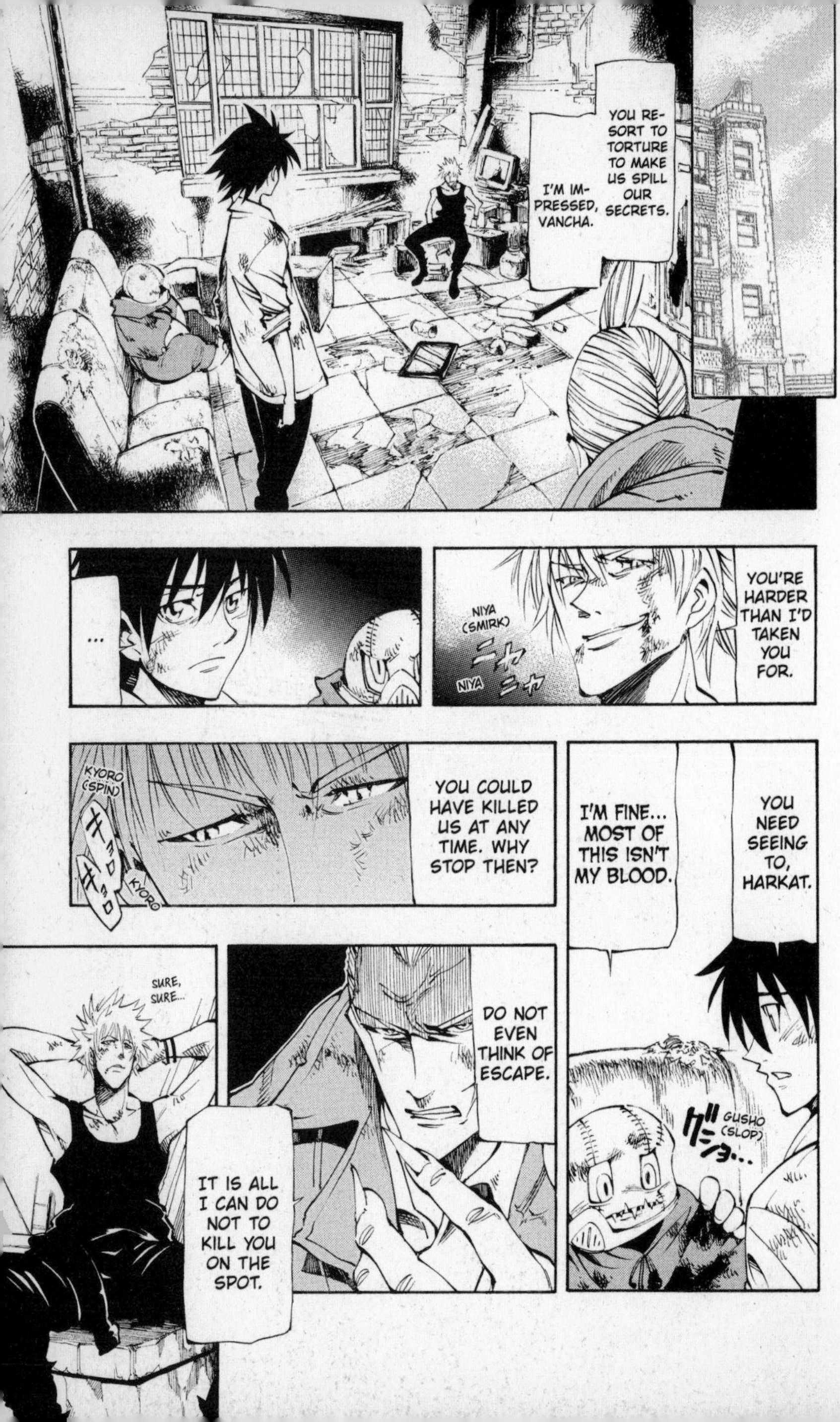

YOU RE-SORT TO TORTURE TO MAKE US SPILL OUR SECRETS.
I'M IM-PRESSED, VANCHA.
YOU'RE HARDER THAN I'D TAKEN YOU FOR.
NIYA (SMIRK)
ニヤ
NIYA
ニヤ
...
YOU NEED SEEING TO, HARKAT.
I'M FINE... MOST OF THIS ISN'T MY BLOOD.
GUSHO (SLOP)
グショ...
YOU COULD HAVE KILLED US AT ANY TIME. WHY STOP THEN?
KYORO (SPIN)
キョロ
KYORO
キョロ
DO NOT EVEN THINK OF ESCAPE.
IT IS ALL I CAN DO NOT TO KILL YOU ON THE SPOT.
SURE, SURE...

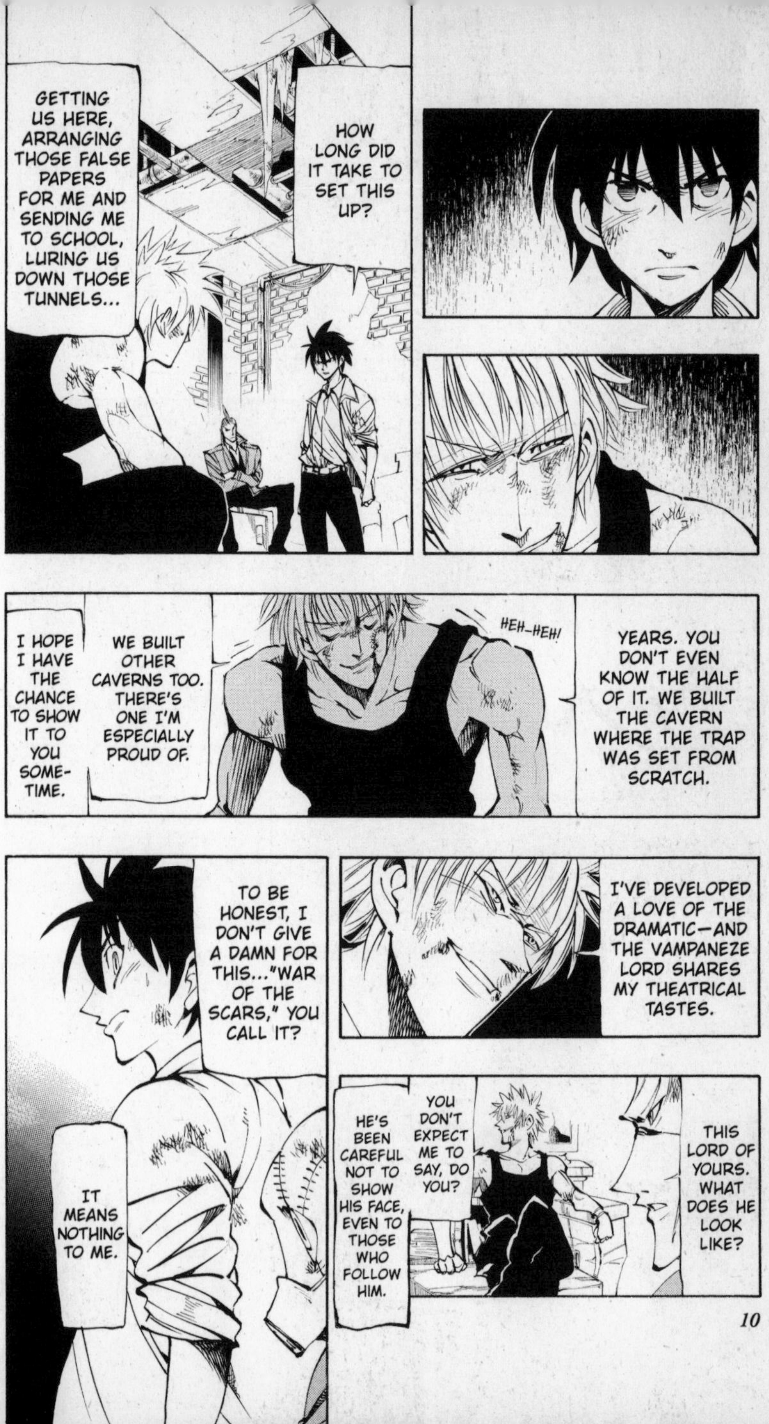
HOW LONG DID IT TAKE TO SET THIS UP?
GETTING US HERE, ARRANGING THOSE FALSE PAPERS FOR ME AND SENDING ME TO SCHOOL, LURING US DOWN THOSE TUNNELS...
YEARS. YOU DON'T EVEN KNOW THE HALF OF IT. WE BUILT THE CAVERN WHERE THE TRAP WAS SET FROM SCRATCH.
HEH-HEH!
WE BUILT OTHER CAVERNS TOO. THERE'S ONE I'M ESPECIALLY PROUD OF.
I HOPE I HAVE THE CHANCE TO SHOW IT TO YOU SOME-TIME.
I'VE DEVELOPED A LOVE OF THE DRAMATIC—AND THE VAMPANEZE LORD SHARES MY THEATRICAL TASTES.
THIS LORD OF YOURS. WHAT DOES HE LOOK LIKE?
YOU DON'T EXPECT ME TO SAY, DO YOU?
HE'S BEEN CAREFUL NOT TO SHOW HIS FACE, EVEN TO THOSE WHO FOLLOW HIM.
TO BE HONEST, I DON'T GIVE A DAMN FOR THIS..."WAR OF THE SCARS," YOU CALL IT?
IT MEANS NOTHING TO ME.

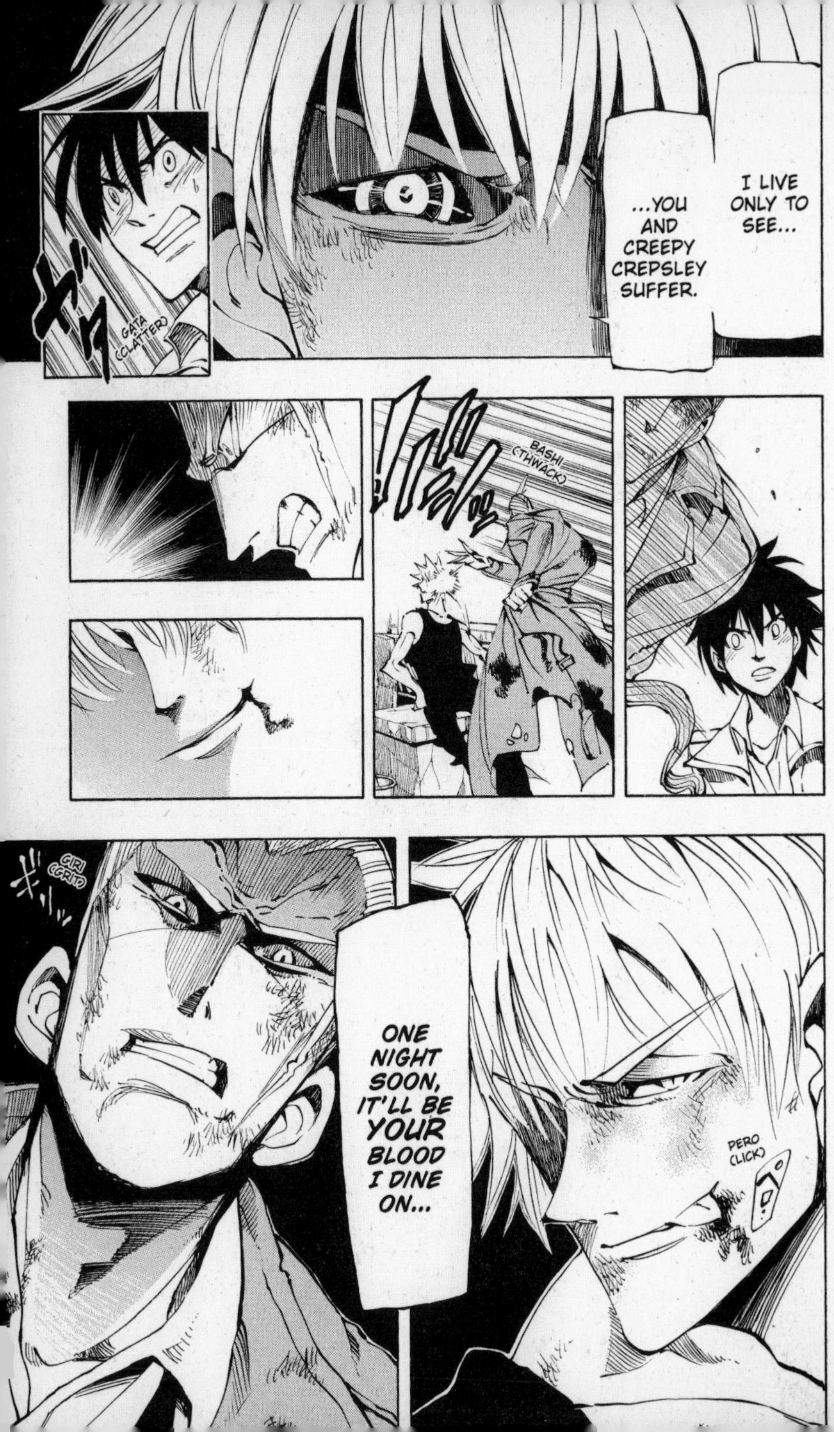
I LIVE ONLY TO SEE...
...YOU AND CREEPY CREPSLEY SUFFER.
GATA (CLATTER)
BASHI (THWACK)
ONE NIGHT SOON, IT'LL BE YOUR BLOOD I DINE ON...
PERO (LICK)
GIRI (GRIT)

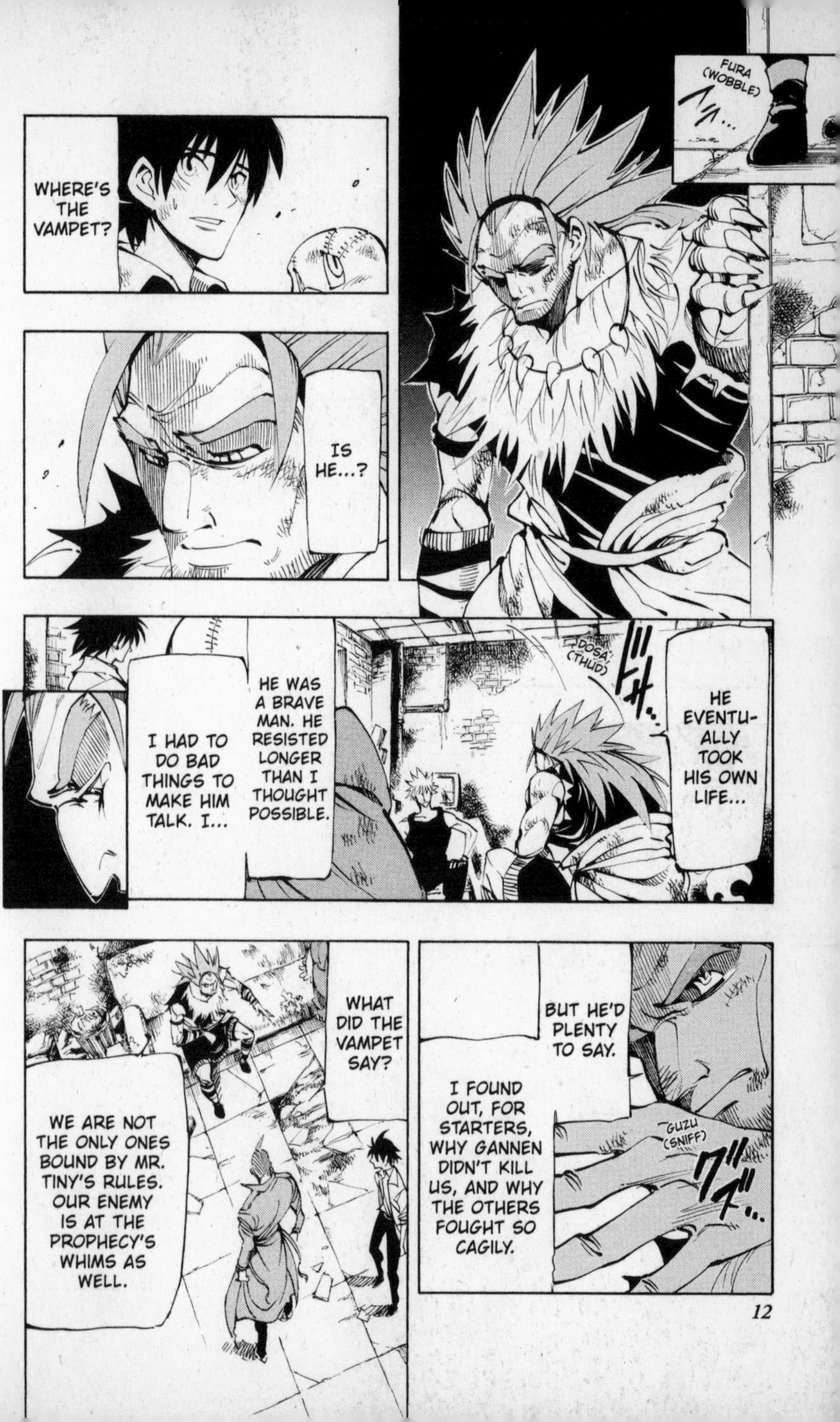
FURA (WOBBLE)
WHERE'S THE VAMPET?
IS HE...?
DOSA (THUD)
HE EVENTU-ALLY TOOK HIS OWN LIFE...
HE WAS A BRAVE MAN. HE RESISTED LONGER THAN I THOUGHT POSSIBLE.
I HAD TO DO BAD THINGS TO MAKE HIM TALK. I...
BUT HE'D PLENTY TO SAY.
I FOUND OUT, FOR STARTERS, WHY GANNEN DIDN'T KILL US, AND WHY THE OTHERS FOUGHT SO CAGILY.
GUZU (SNIFF)
WHAT DID THE VAMPET SAY?
WE ARE NOT THE ONLY ONES BOUND BY MR. TINY'S RULES. OUR ENEMY IS AT THE PROPHECY'S WHIMS AS WELL.

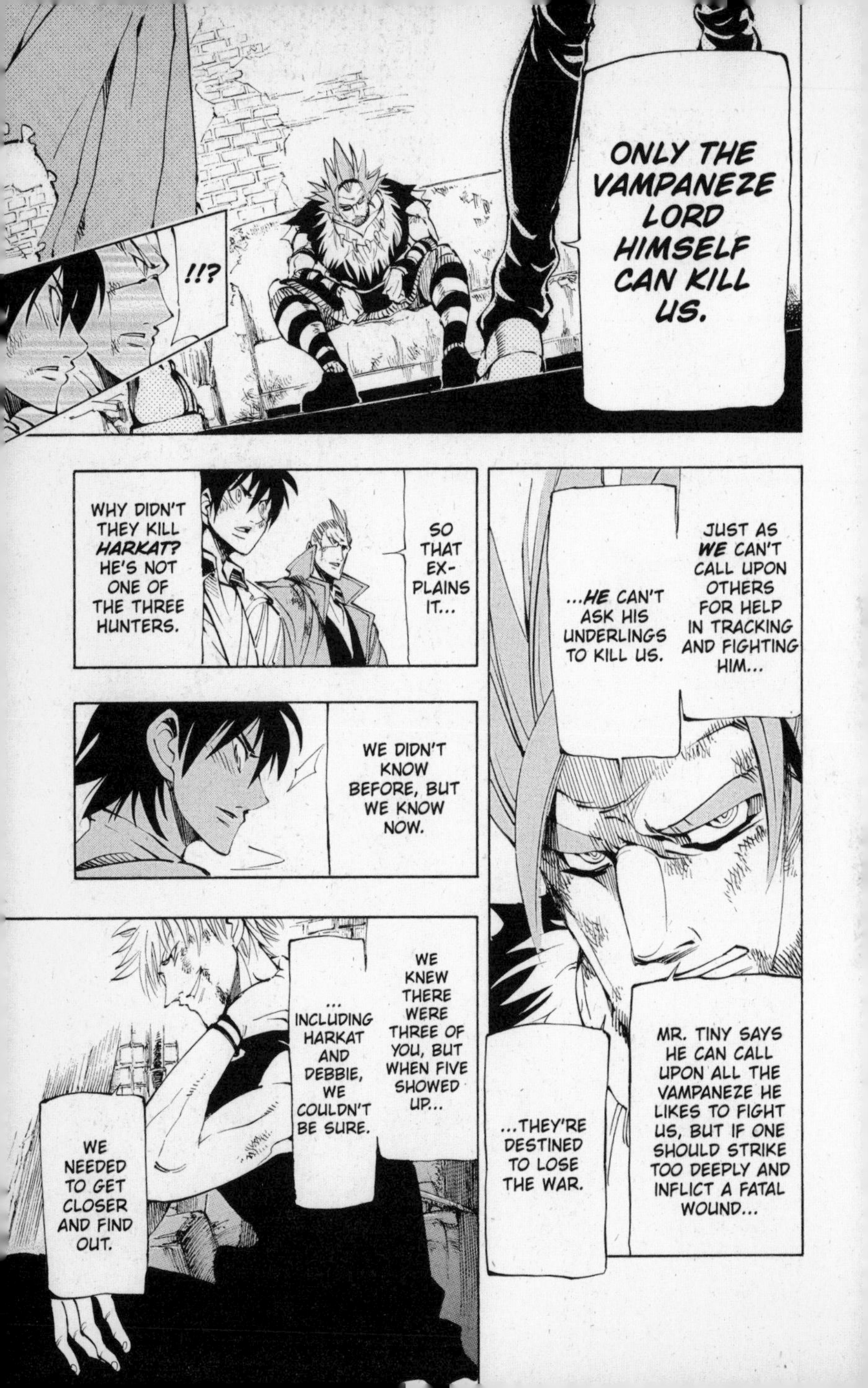
ONLY THE VAMPANEZE LORD HIMSELF CAN KILL US.
!!?
JUST AS WE CAN'T CALL UPON OTHERS FOR HELP IN TRACKING AND FIGHTING HIM...
...HE CAN'T ASK HIS UNDERLINGS TO KILL US.
MR. TINY SAYS HE CAN CALL UPON ALL THE VAMPANEZE HE LIKES TO FIGHT US, BUT IF ONE SHOULD STRIKE TOO DEEPLY AND INFLICT A FATAL WOUND...
...THEY'RE DESTINED TO LOSE THE WAR.
SO THAT EX-PLAINS IT...
WHY DIDN'T THEY KILL HARKAT? HE'S NOT ONE OF THE THREE HUNTERS.
WE DIDN'T KNOW BEFORE, BUT WE KNOW NOW.
WE KNEW THERE WERE THREE OF YOU, BUT WHEN FIVE SHOWED UP...
...INCLUDING HARKAT AND DEBBIE, WE COULDN'T BE SURE.
WE NEEDED TO GET CLOSER AND FIND OUT.

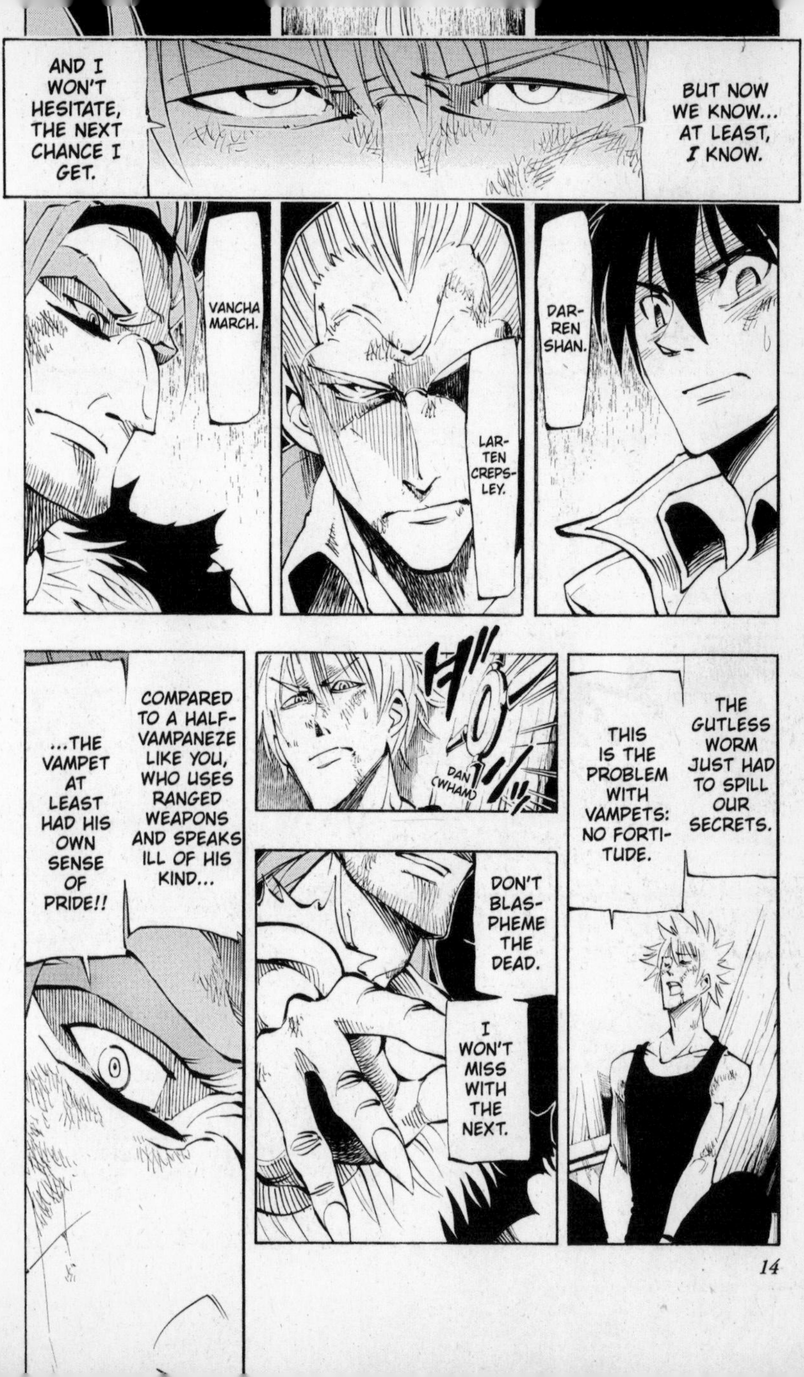
BUT NOW WE KNOW... AT LEAST, I KNOW.
AND I WON'T HESITATE, THE NEXT CHANCE I GET.
DARREN SHAN.
LARTEN CREPSLEY.
VANCHA MARCH.
THE GUTLESS WORM JUST HAD TO SPILL OUR SECRETS.
THIS IS THE PROBLEM WITH VAMPETS: NO FORTITUDE.
DAN (WHAM)
DON'T BLASPHEME THE DEAD.
I WON'T MISS WITH THE NEXT.
COMPARED TO A HALF-VAMPANEZE LIKE YOU, WHO USES RANGED WEAPONS AND SPEAKS ILL OF HIS KIND...
...THE VAMPET AT LEAST HAD HIS OWN SENSE OF PRIDE!!

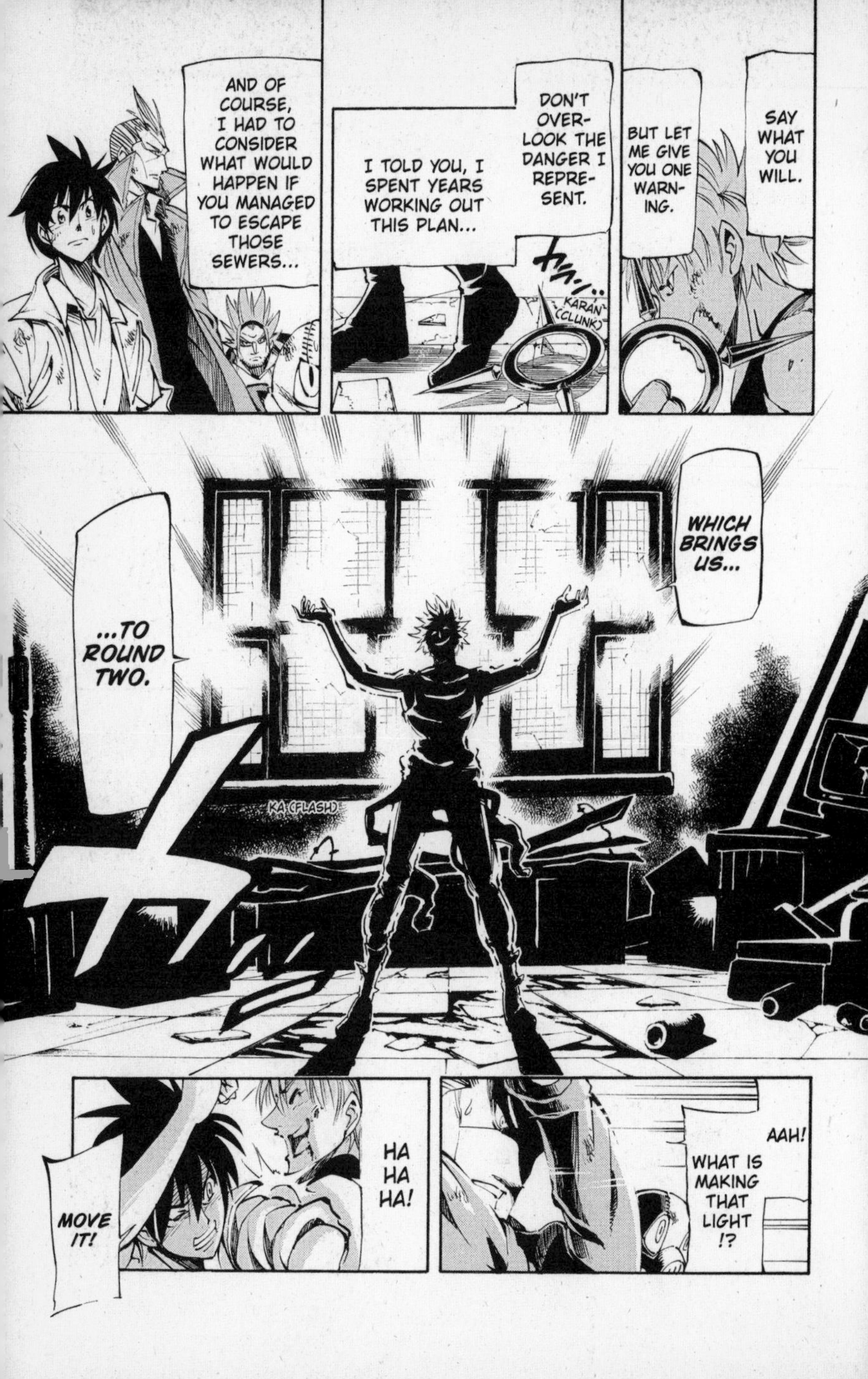
SAY WHAT YOU WILL.
BUT LET ME GIVE YOU ONE WARNING.
DON'T OVERLOOK THE DANGER I REPRESENT.
I TOLD YOU, I SPENT YEARS WORKING OUT THIS PLAN...
KARAN (CLUNK)
AND OF COURSE, I HAD TO CONSIDER WHAT WOULD HAPPEN IF YOU MANAGED TO ESCAPE THOSE SEWERS...
WHICH BRINGS US...
...TO ROUND TWO.
KA (FLASH)
AAH!
WHAT IS MAKING THAT LIGHT!?
HA HA HA!
MOVE IT!

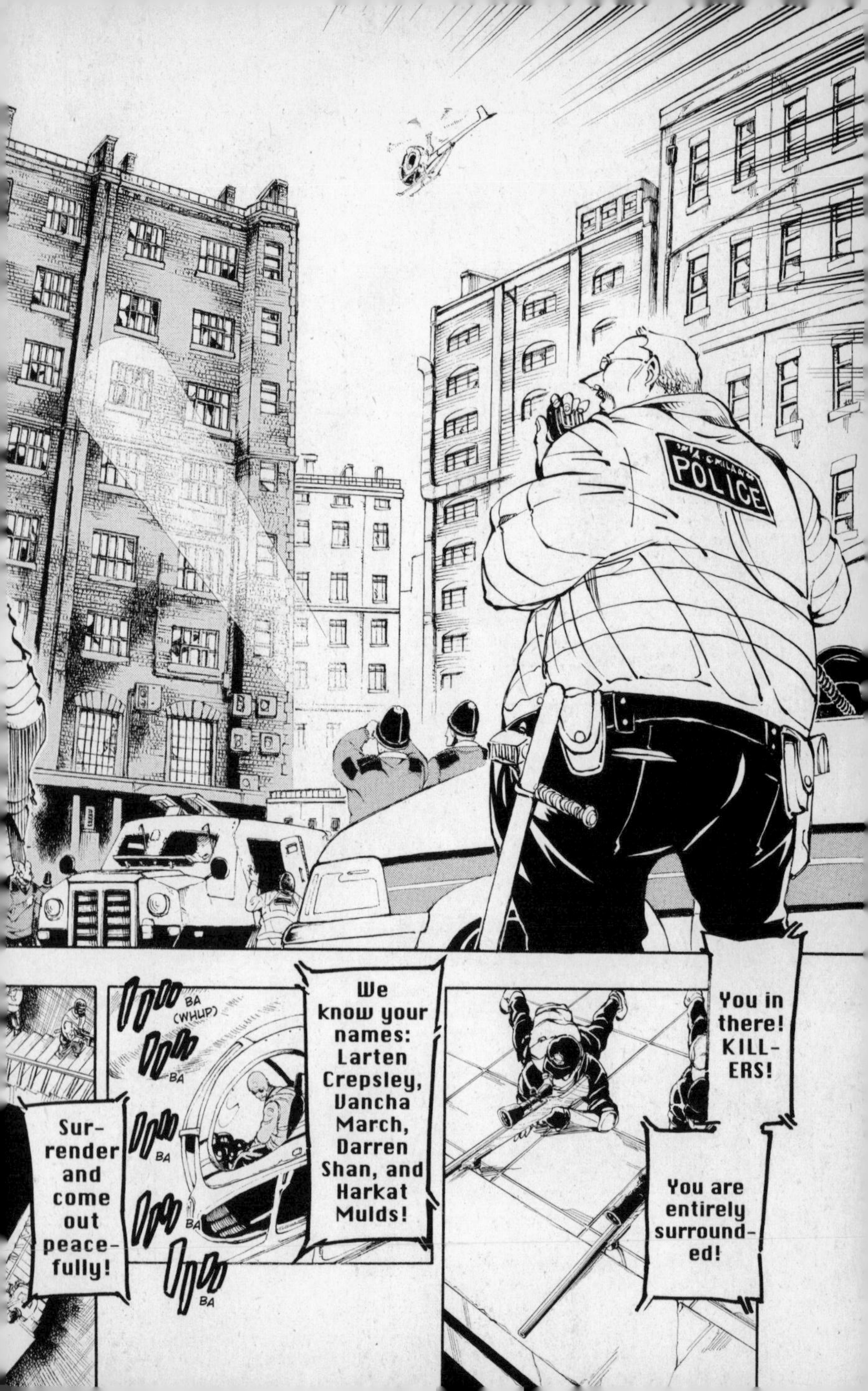

POLICE
BA (WHUP)
BA
BA
BA
BA
Surrender and come out peacefully!
We know your names: Larten Crepsley, Vancha March, Darren Shan, and Harkat Mulds!
You in there! KILLERS!
You are entirely surrounded!

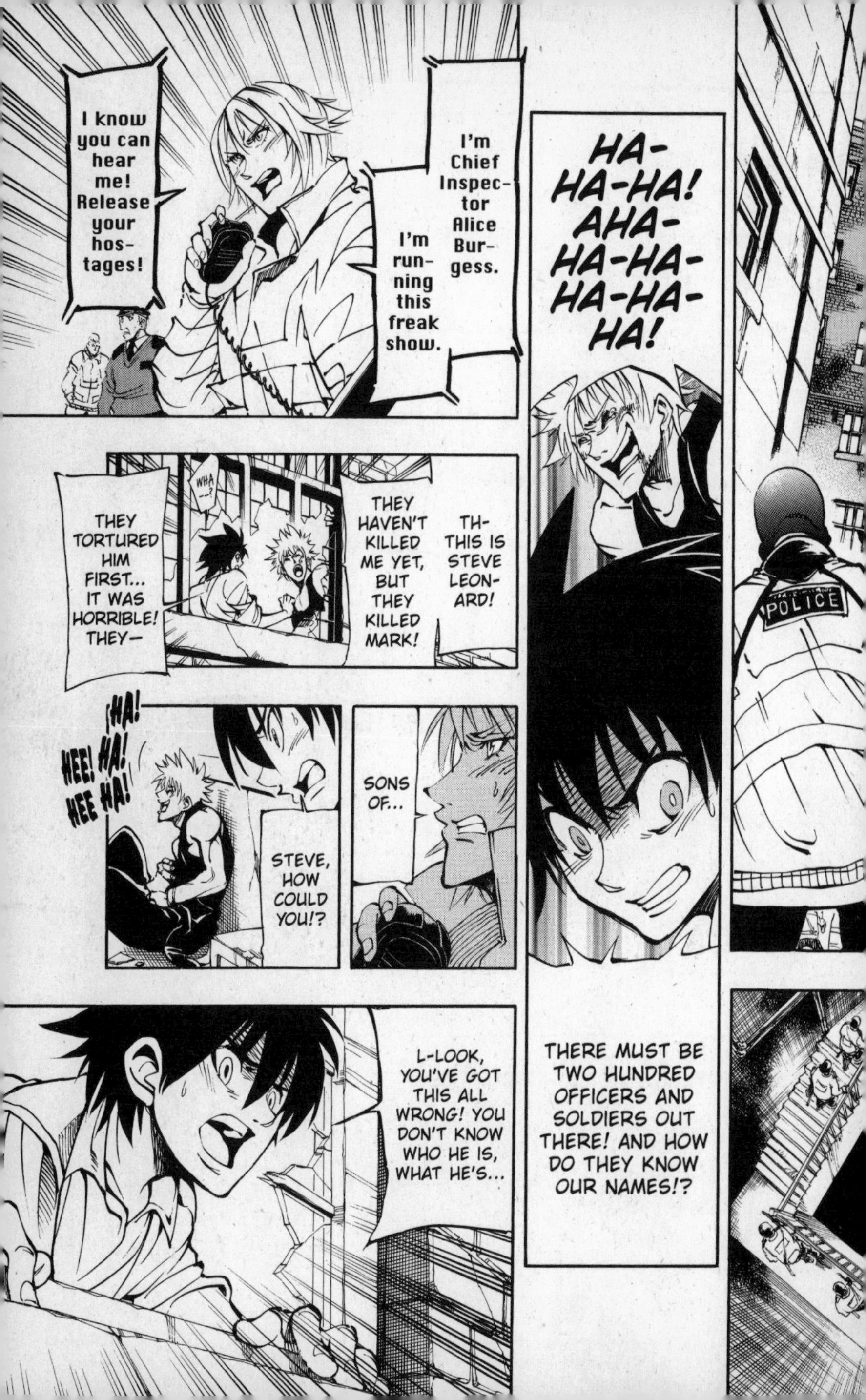
HA-HA-HA! AHA-HA-HA-HA-HA-HA-HA!
THERE MUST BE TWO HUNDRED OFFICERS AND SOLDIERS OUT THERE! AND HOW DO THEY KNOW OUR NAMES!?
I'm Chief Inspector Alice Burgess.
I'm running this freak show.
I know you can hear me! Release your hostages!
TH-THIS IS STEVE LEONARD!
THEY HAVEN'T KILLED ME YET, BUT THEY KILLED MARK!
WHA--?
THEY TORTURED HIM FIRST... IT WAS HORRIBLE! THEY—
SONS OF...
STEVE, HOW COULD YOU!?
HA!
HEE! HA!
HEE HA!
L-LOOK, YOU'VE GOT THIS ALL WRONG! YOU DON'T KNOW WHO HE IS, WHAT HE'S...

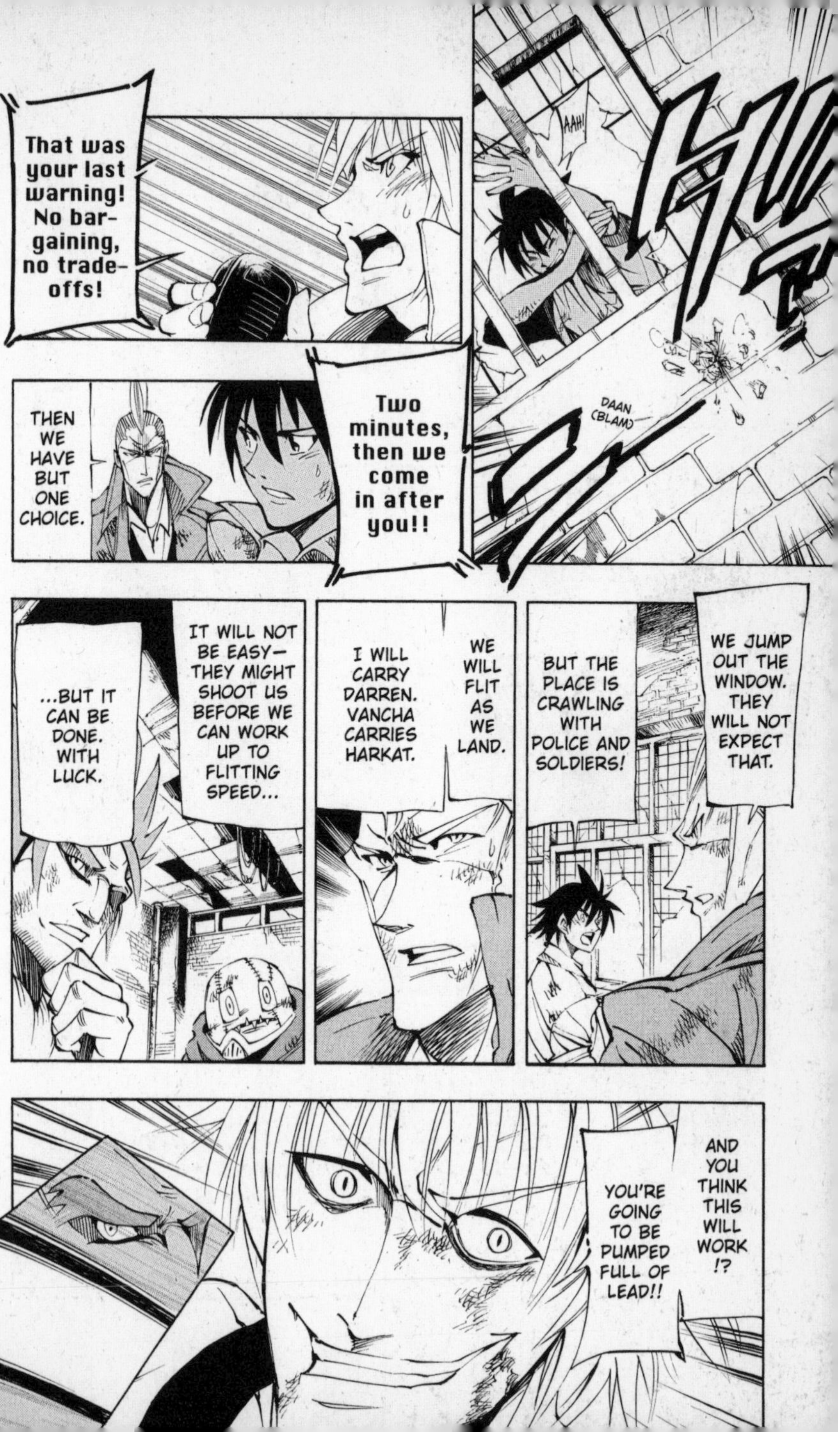
AAH!
DAAN (BLAM)
That was your last warning! No bar-gaining, no trade-offs!
Two minutes, then we come in after you!!
THEN WE HAVE BUT ONE CHOICE.
WE JUMP OUT THE WINDOW. THEY WILL NOT EXPECT THAT.
BUT THE PLACE IS CRAWLING WITH POLICE AND SOLDIERS!
WE WILL FLIT AS WE LAND.
I WILL CARRY DARREN. VANCHA CARRIES HARKAT.
IT WILL NOT BE EASY— THEY MIGHT SHOOT US BEFORE WE CAN WORK UP TO FLITTING SPEED...
...BUT IT CAN BE DONE. WITH LUCK.
AND YOU THINK THIS WILL WORK!?
YOU'RE GOING TO BE PUMPED FULL OF LEAD!!

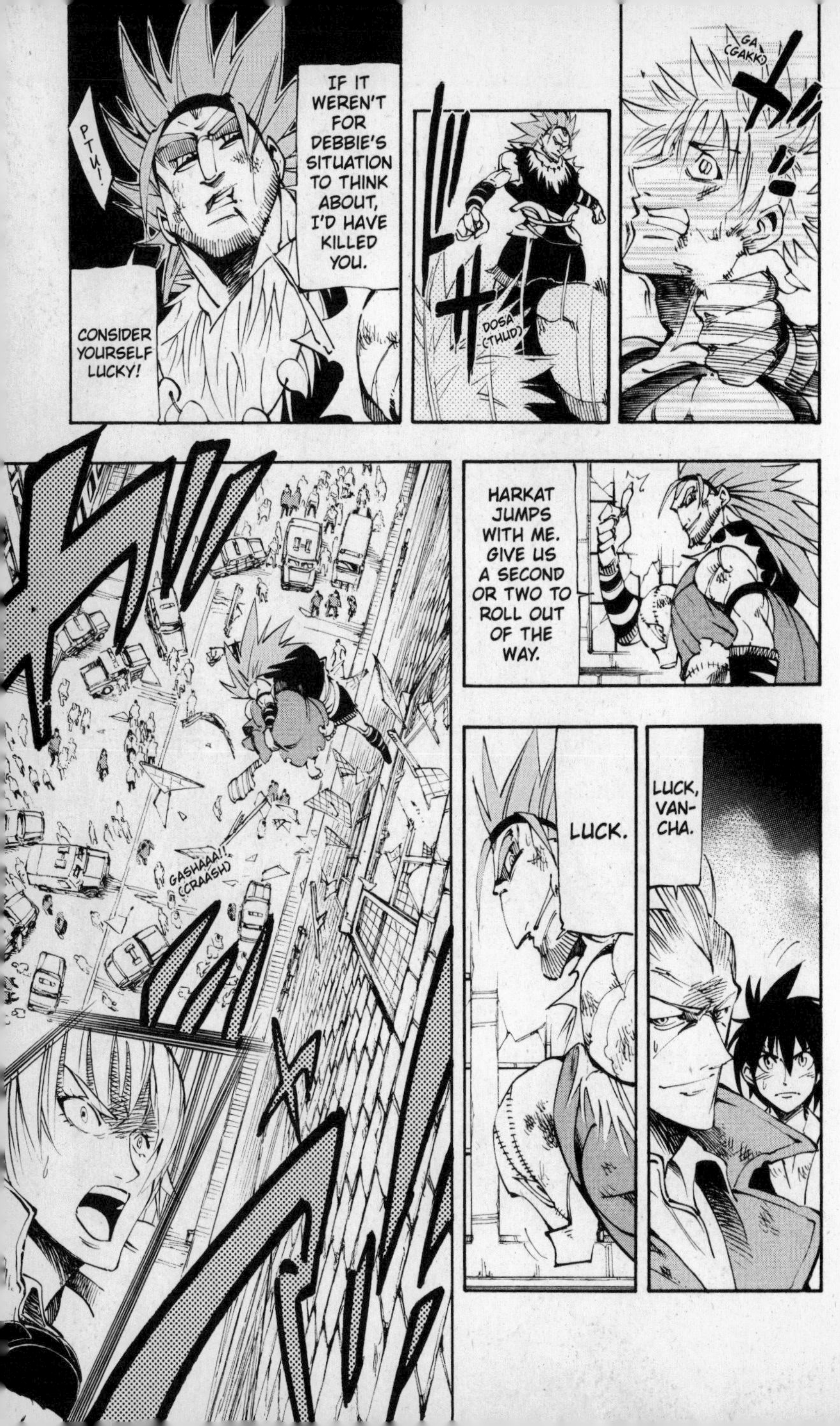
GA
(GAKK)
DOSA
(THUD)
IF IT WEREN'T FOR DEBBIE'S SITUATION TO THINK ABOUT, I'D HAVE KILLED YOU.
PTUI!
CONSIDER YOURSELF LUCKY!
HARKAT JUMPS WITH ME. GIVE US A SECOND OR TWO TO ROLL OUT OF THE WAY.
LUCK, VAN-CHA.
LUCK.
GASHAAA!!
(CRAASH)

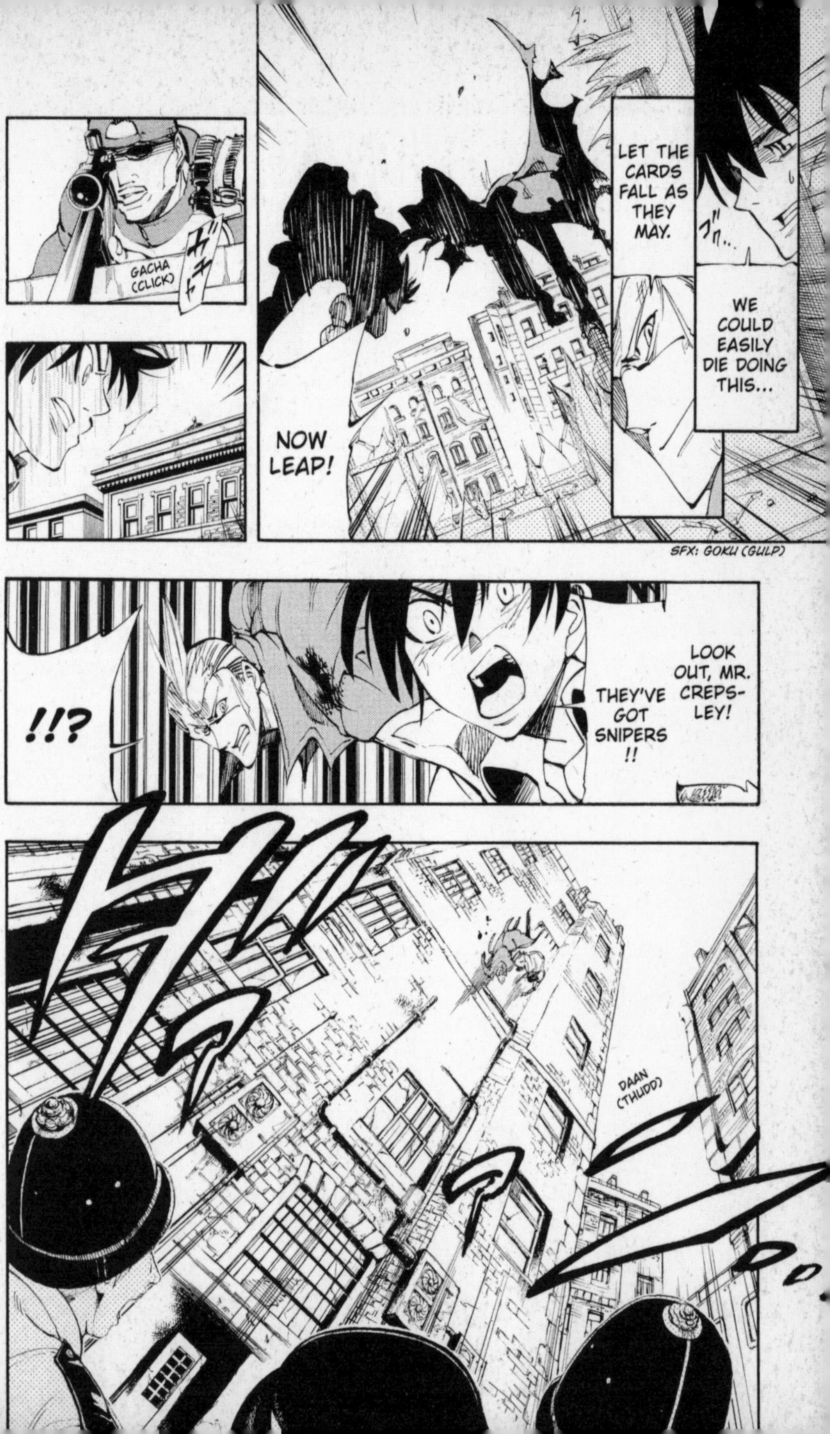
LET THE CARDS FALL AS THEY MAY.
WE COULD EASILY DIE DOING THIS...
NOW LEAP!
GACHA (CLICK)
SFX: GOKU (GULP)
LOOK OUT, MR. CREPSLEY!
THEY'VE GOT SNIPERS!!
!!?
DAAN (THUDD)

THE QUESTIONING ROOM

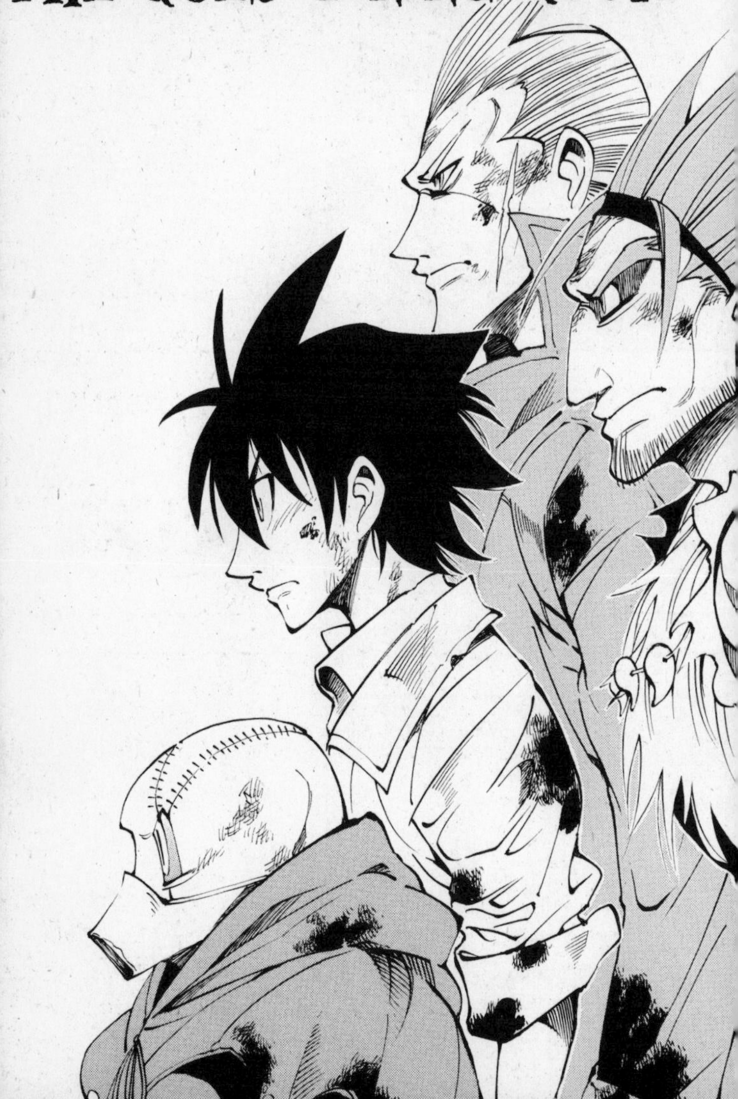

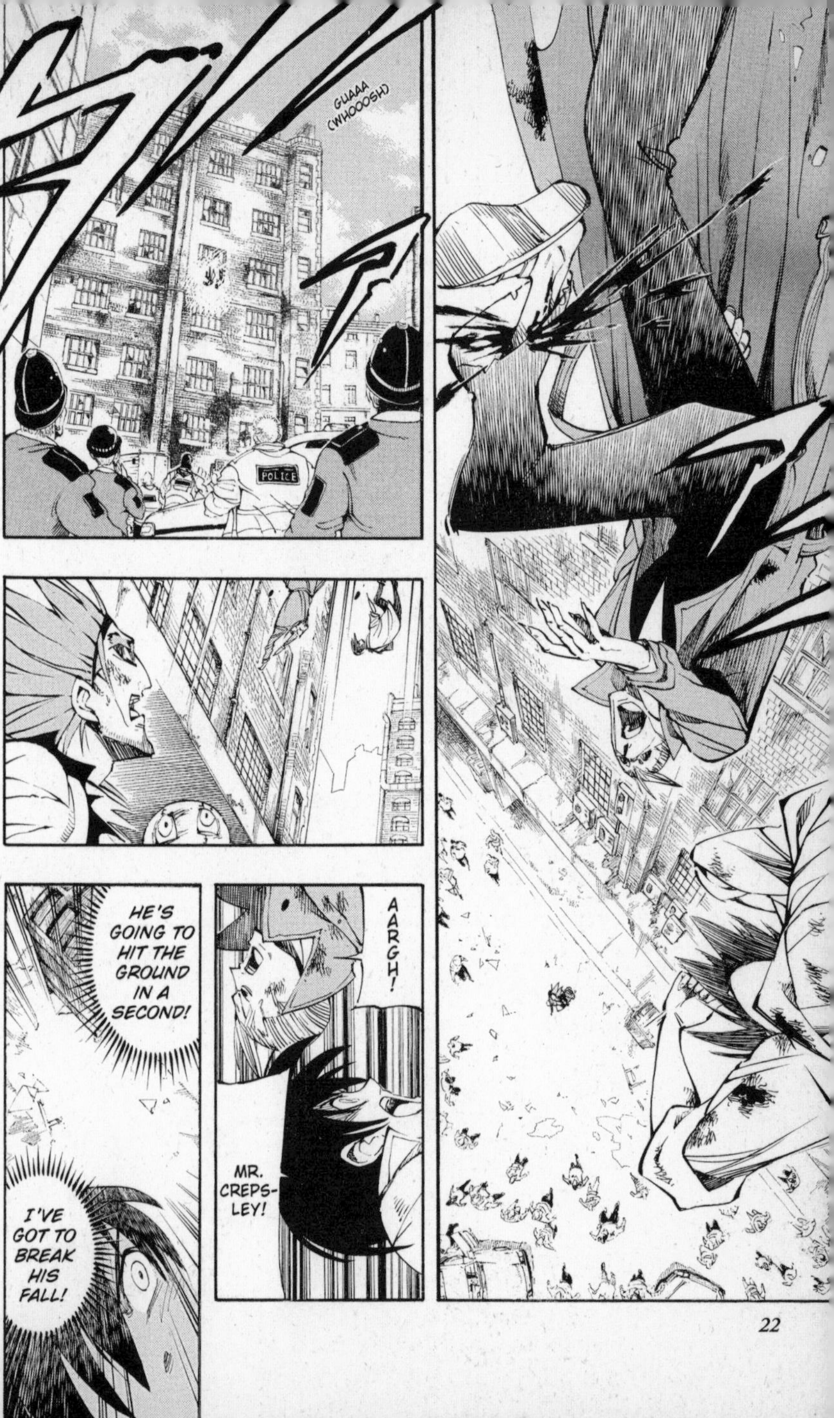
GUAAA (WHOOOSH)
AARGH!
MR. CREPSLEY!
HE'S GOING TO HIT THE GROUND IN A SECOND!
I'VE GOT TO BREAK HIS FALL!

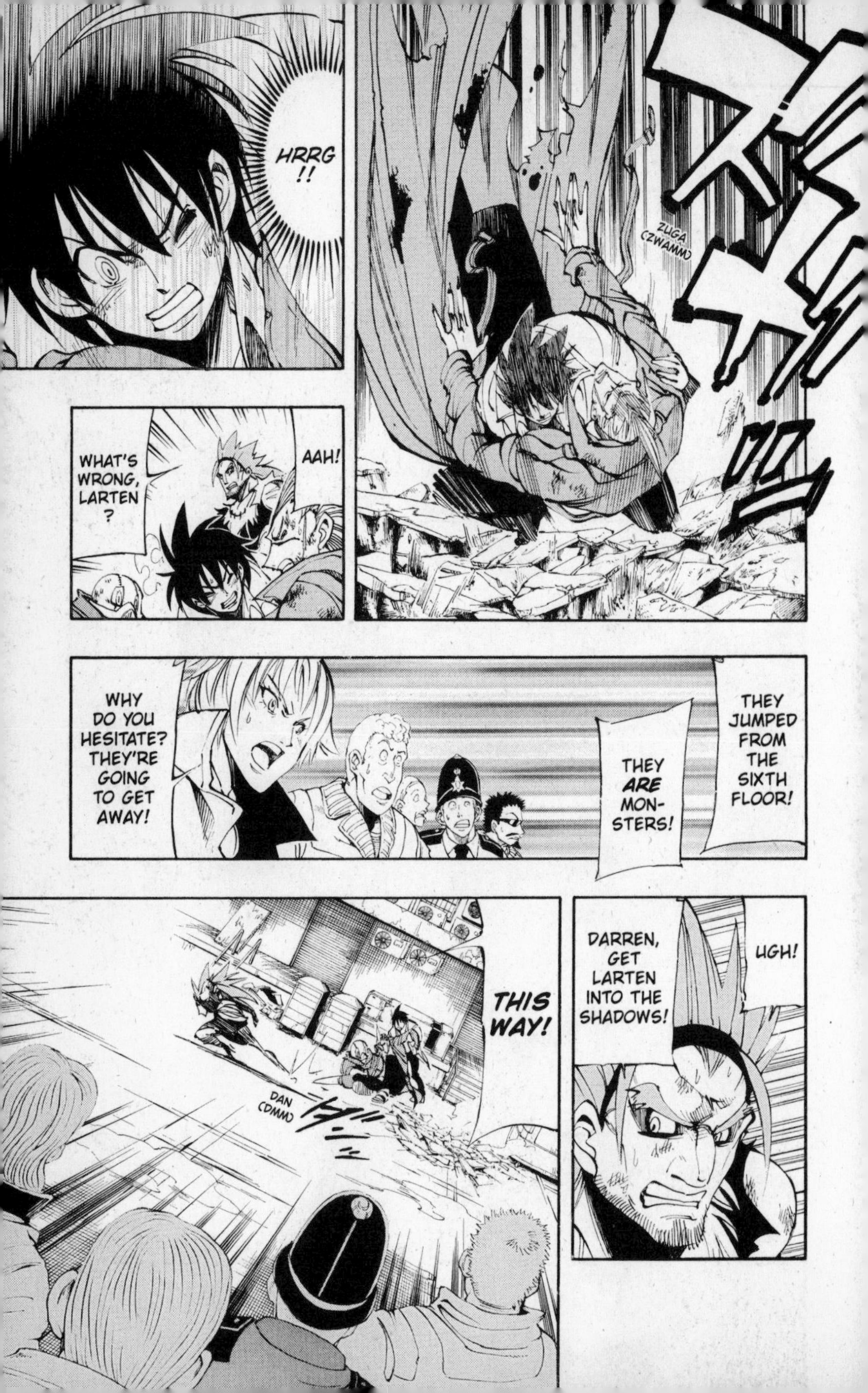
ZUGA (ZWAMM)
HRRG !!
AAH!
WHAT'S WRONG, LARTEN?
THEY JUMPED FROM THE SIXTH FLOOR!
THEY *ARE* MONSTERS!
WHY DO YOU HESITATE? THEY'RE GOING TO GET AWAY!
UGH!
DARREN, GET LARTEN INTO THE SHADOWS!
THIS WAY!
DAN (DMM)

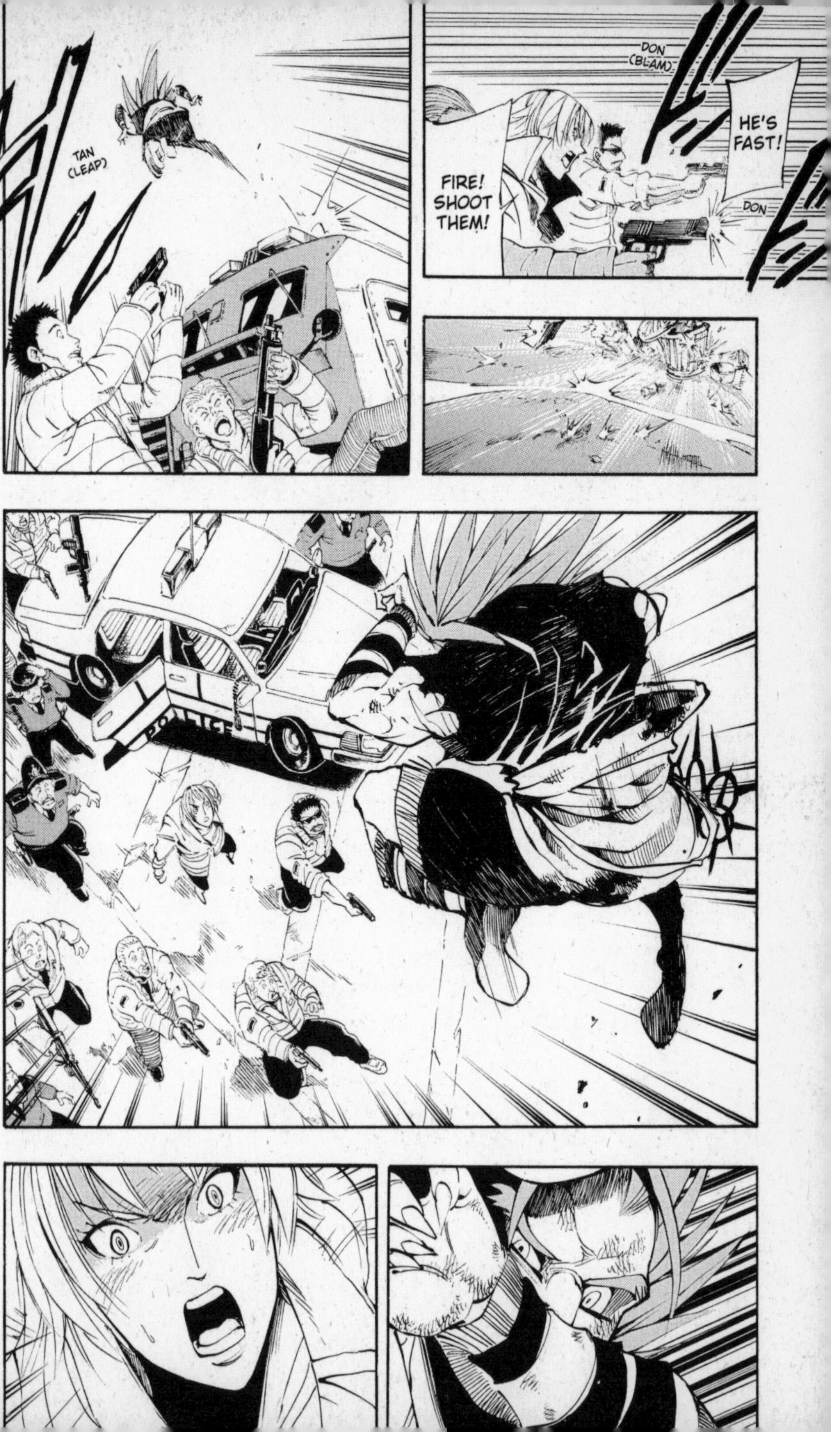
DON (BLAM)
HE'S FAST!
FIRE! SHOOT THEM!
DON
TAN (LEAP)

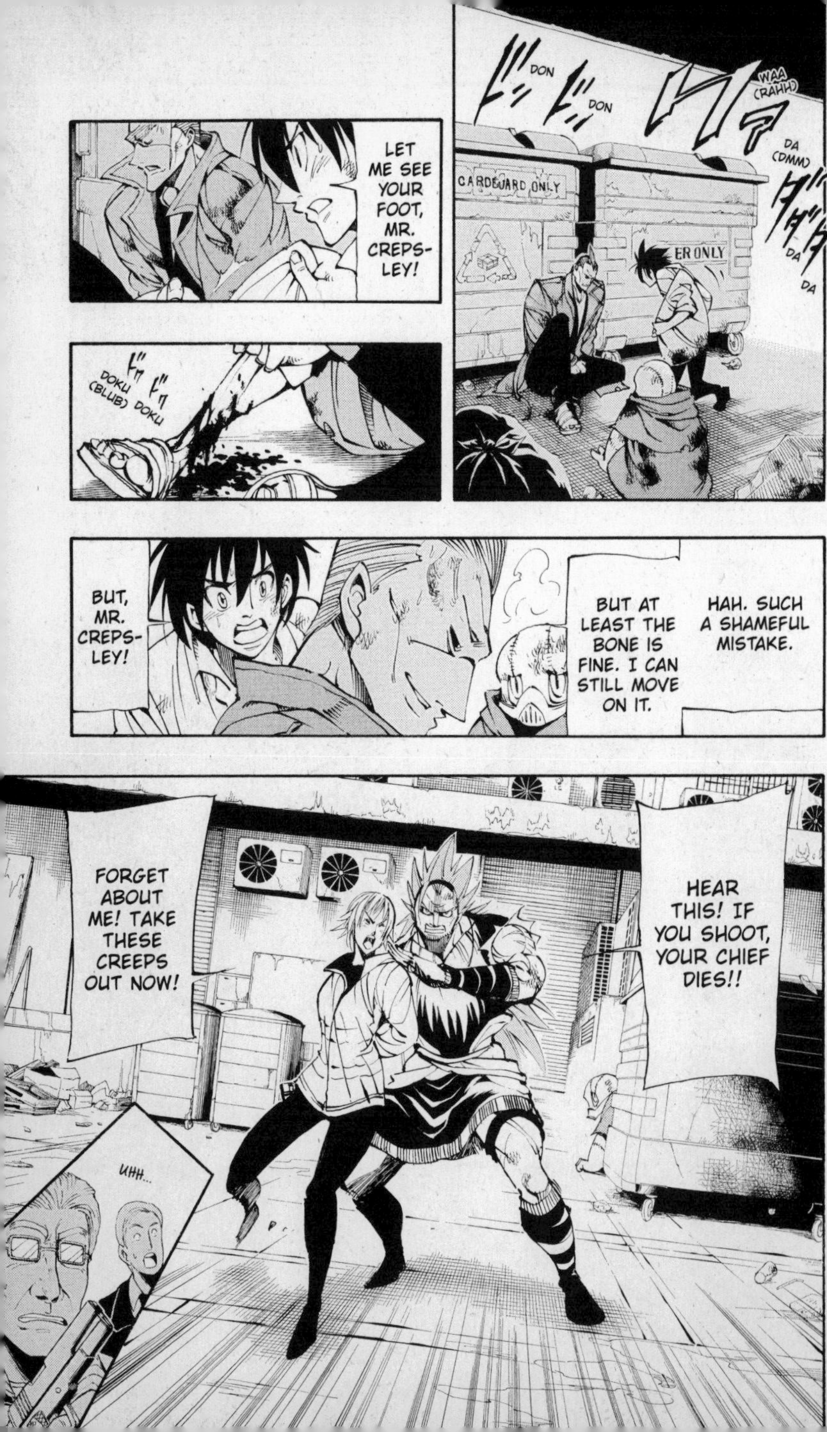
DON
DON
WAA (RAHH)
DA (DMM)
DA
DA
CARDBOARD ONLY
ER ONLY
LET ME SEE YOUR FOOT, MR. CREPSLEY!
DOKU (BLUB) DOKU
HAH. SUCH A SHAMEFUL MISTAKE.
BUT AT LEAST THE BONE IS FINE. I CAN STILL MOVE ON IT.
BUT, MR. CREPSLEY!
HEAR THIS! IF YOU SHOOT, YOUR CHIEF DIES!!
FORGET ABOUT ME! TAKE THESE CREEPS OUT NOW!
UHH...

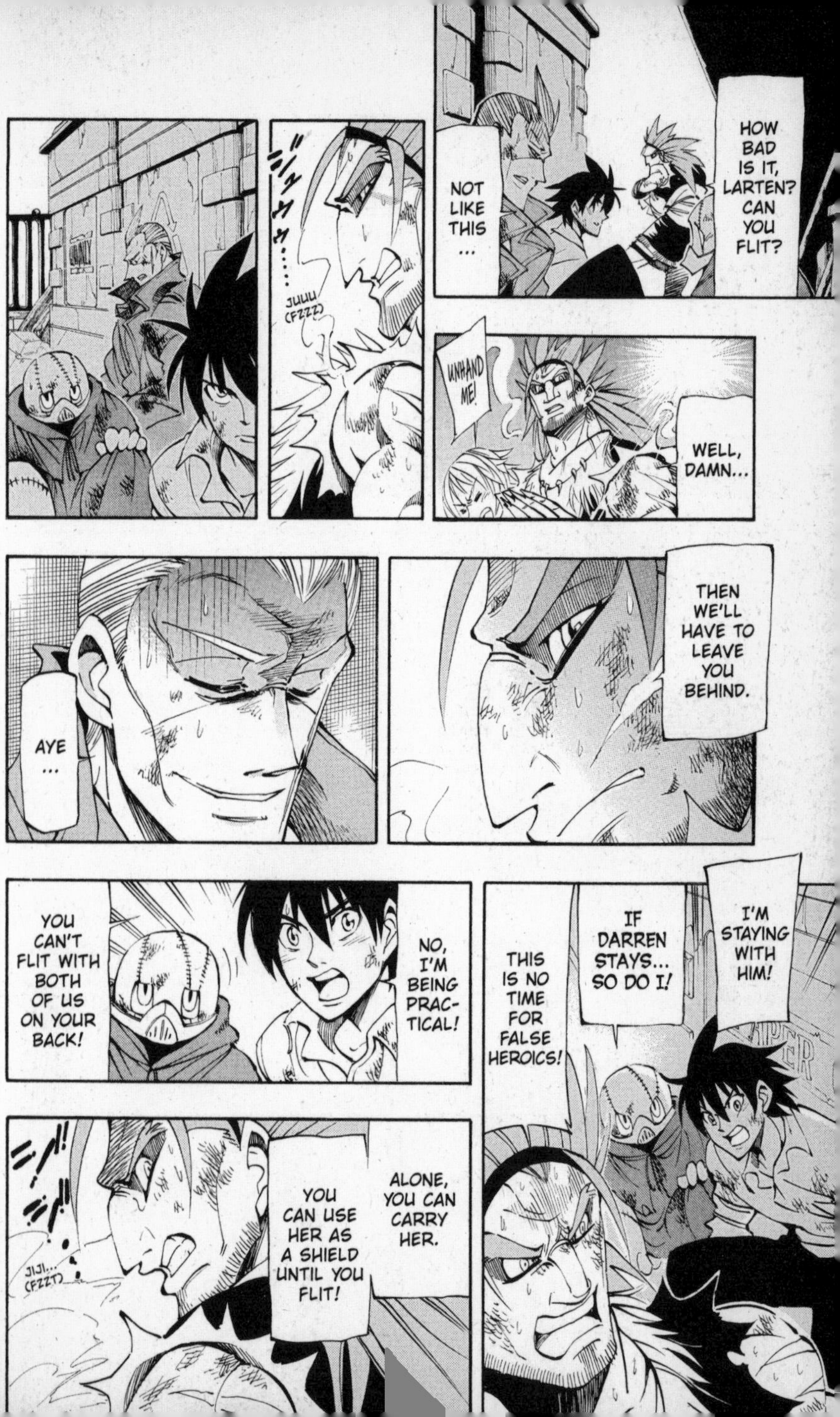
HOW BAD IS IT, LARTEN? CAN YOU FLIT?
NOT LIKE THIS ...
WELL, DAMN...
UNHAND ME!
JUUU (FZZZ)
THEN WE'LL HAVE TO LEAVE YOU BEHIND.
AYE ...
I'M STAYING WITH HIM!
IF DARREN STAYS... SO DO I!
THIS IS NO TIME FOR FALSE HEROICS!
NO, I'M BEING PRAC-TICAL!
YOU CAN'T FLIT WITH BOTH OF US ON YOUR BACK!
ALONE, YOU CAN CARRY HER.
YOU CAN USE HER AS A SHIELD UNTIL YOU FLIT!
JIJI... (FZZT)

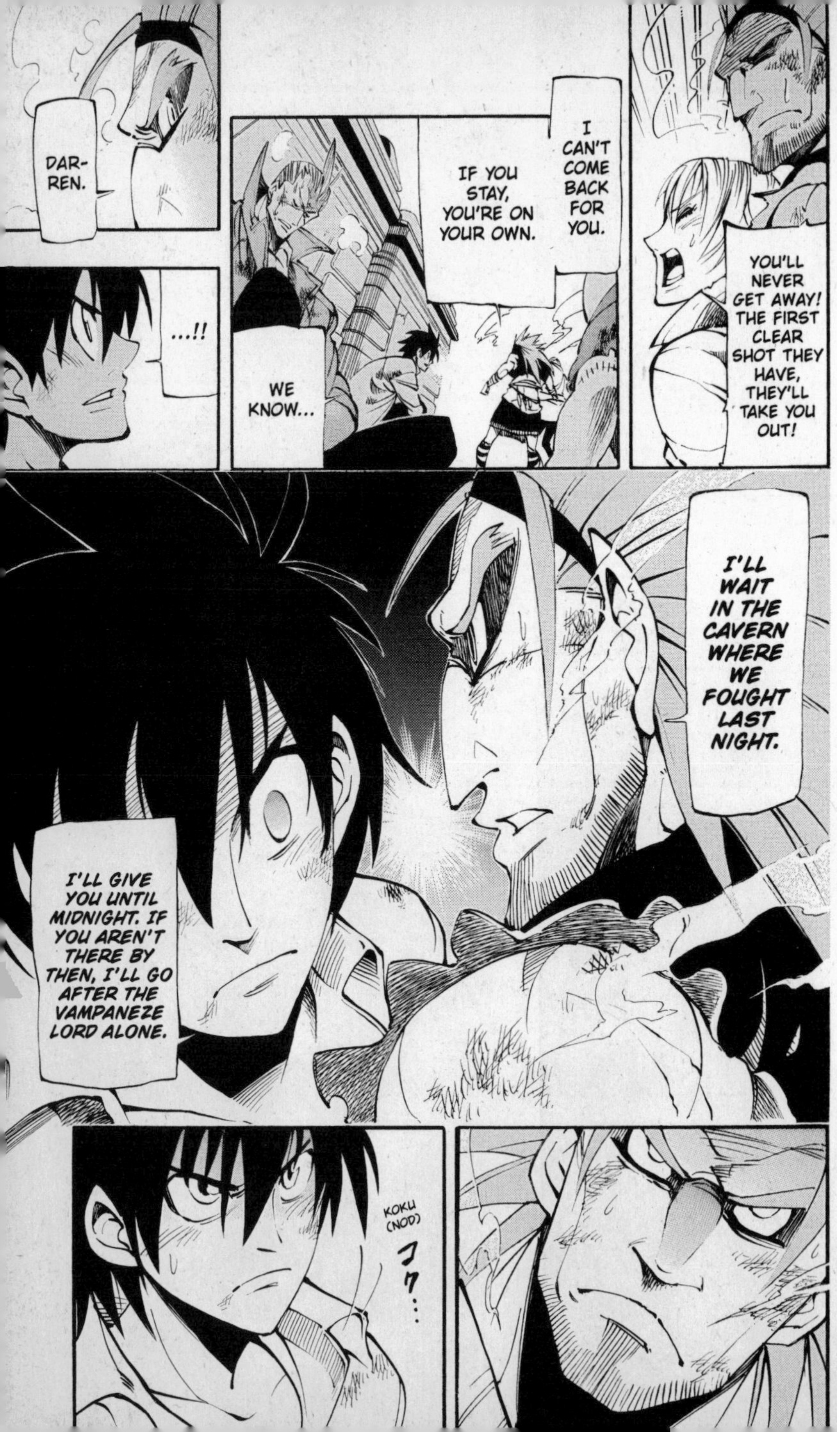
YOU'LL NEVER GET AWAY! THE FIRST CLEAR SHOT THEY HAVE, THEY'LL TAKE YOU OUT!
I CAN'T COME BACK FOR YOU.
IF YOU STAY, YOU'RE ON YOUR OWN.
WE KNOW...
DAR-REN.
...!!
I'LL WAIT IN THE CAVERN WHERE WE FOUGHT LAST NIGHT.
I'LL GIVE YOU UNTIL MIDNIGHT. IF YOU AREN'T THERE BY THEN, I'LL GO AFTER THE VAMPANEZE LORD ALONE.
KOKU (NOD)
コク…

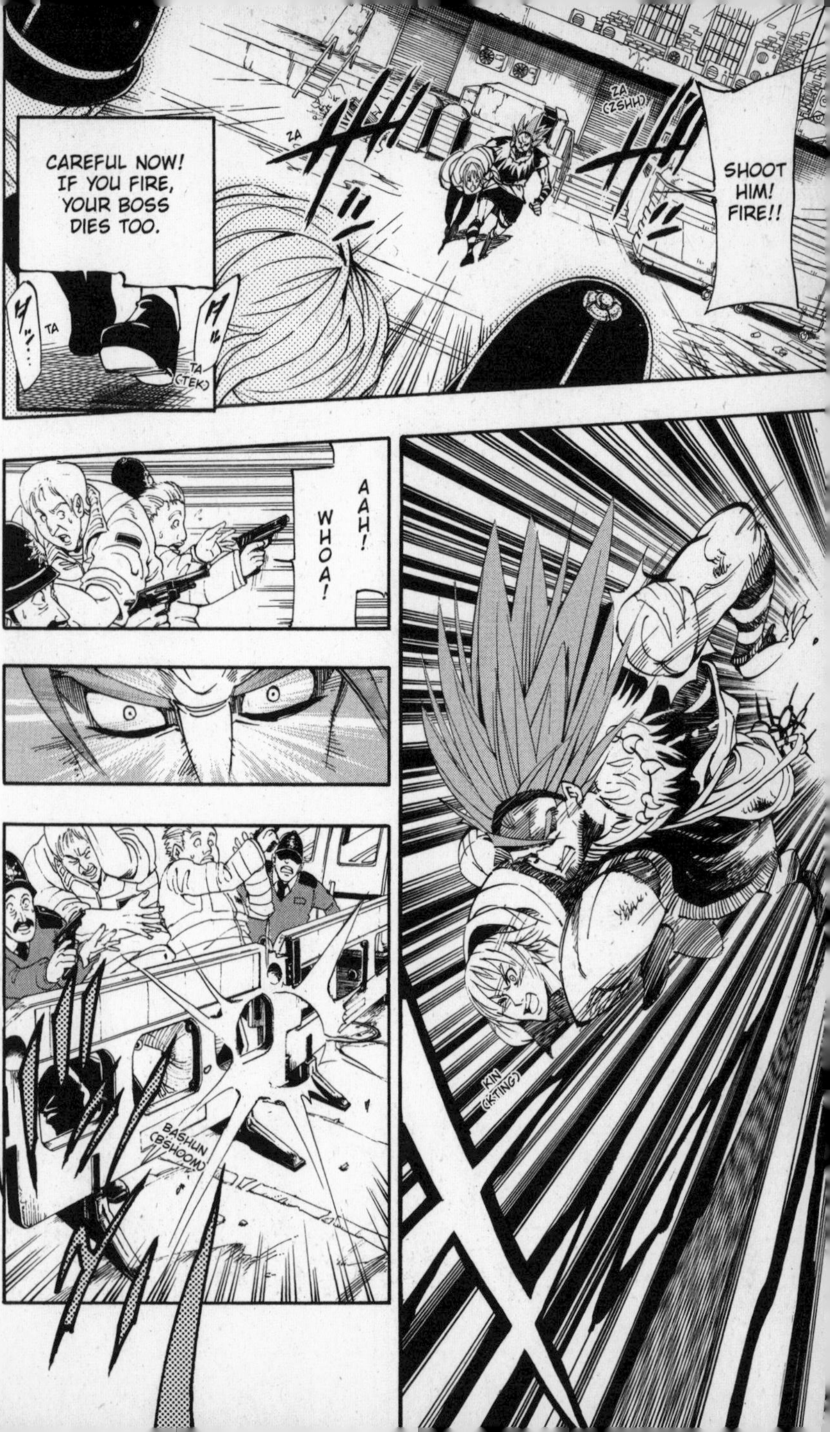
SHOOT HIM! FIRE!!
ZA (ZSHH)
ZA
CAREFUL NOW! IF YOU FIRE, YOUR BOSS DIES TOO.
TA (TEK)
TA
KIN (K'TING)
AAH!
WHOA!
BASHUN (BSHOOM)

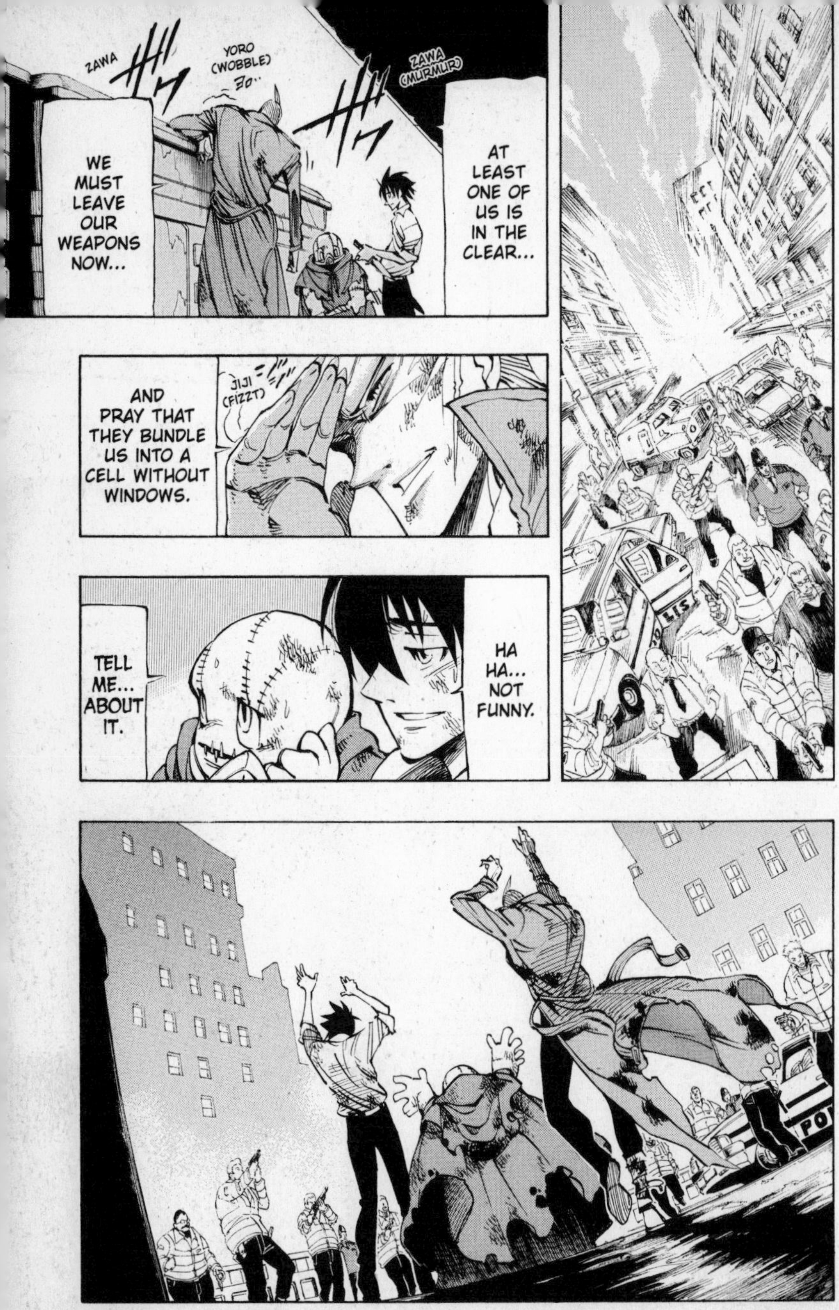
ZAWA (MURMUR)
AT LEAST ONE OF US IS IN THE CLEAR...
YORO (WOBBLE)
ZAWA
WE MUST LEAVE OUR WEAPONS NOW...
JIJI (FIZZT)
AND PRAY THAT THEY BUNDLE US INTO A CELL WITHOUT WINDOWS.
HA HA... NOT FUNNY.
TELL ME... ABOUT IT.

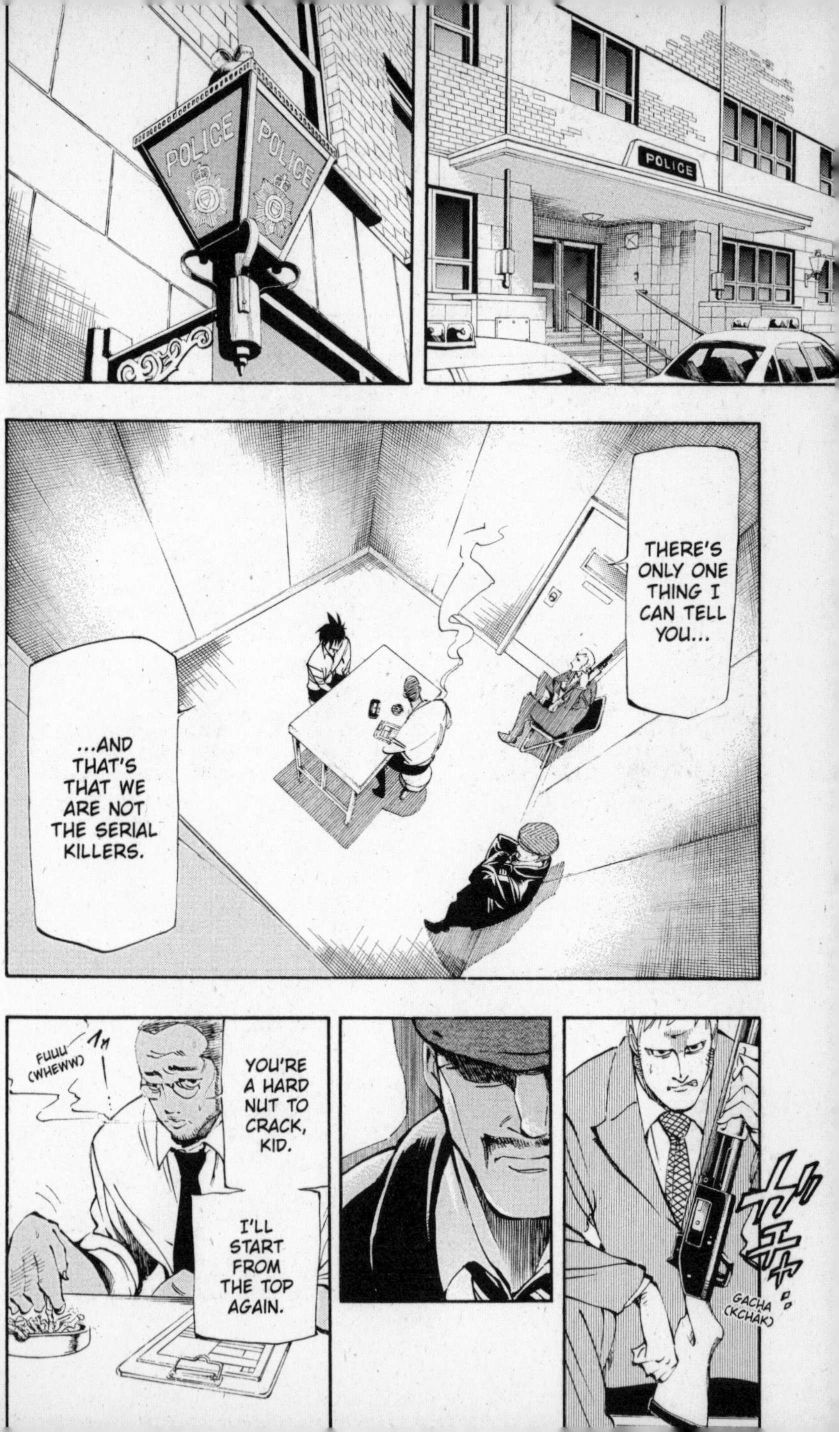
POLICE
POLICE
POLICE
THERE'S ONLY ONE THING I CAN TELL YOU...
...AND THAT'S THAT WE ARE NOT THE SERIAL KILLERS.
GACHA (KCHAK)
YOU'RE A HARD NUT TO CRACK, KID.
FUUU (WHEWW)
I'LL START FROM THE TOP AGAIN.

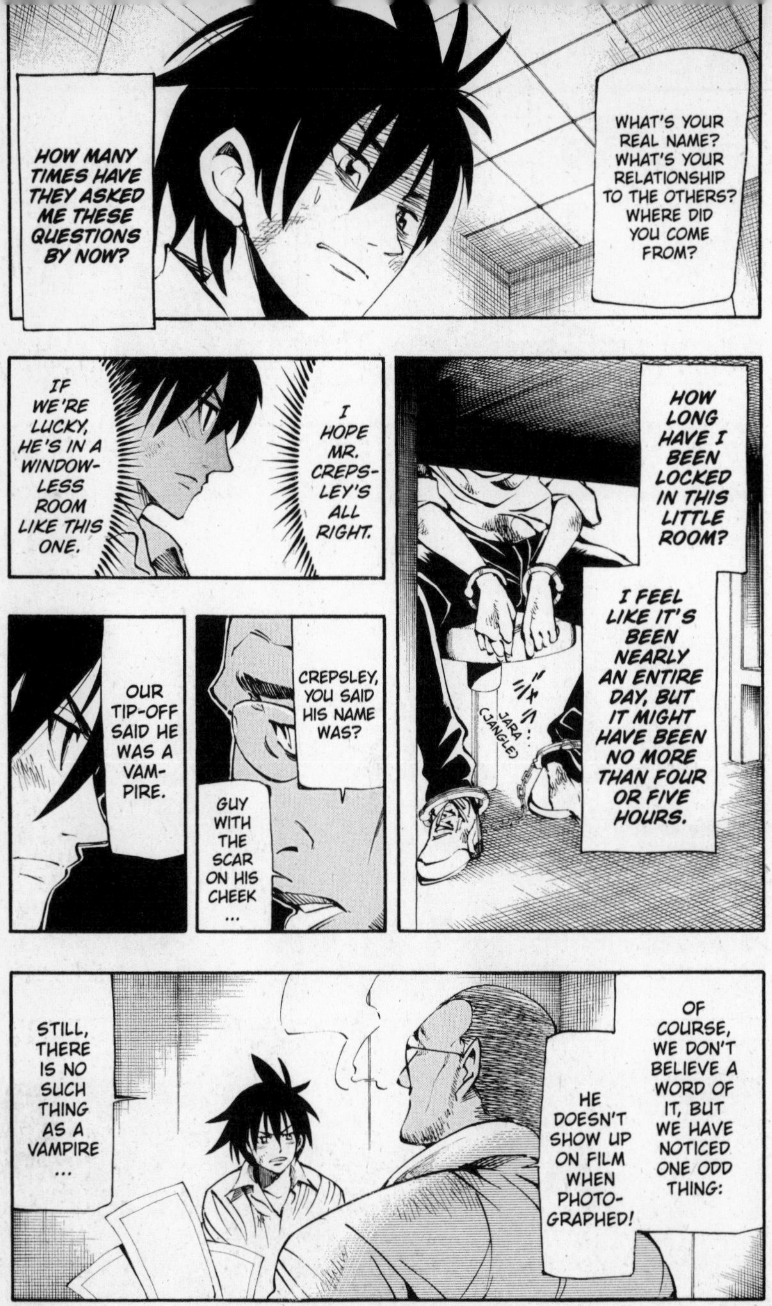
WHAT'S YOUR REAL NAME? WHAT'S YOUR RELATIONSHIP TO THE OTHERS? WHERE DID YOU COME FROM?
HOW MANY TIMES HAVE THEY ASKED ME THESE QUESTIONS BY NOW?
HOW LONG HAVE I BEEN LOCKED IN THIS LITTLE ROOM?
I FEEL LIKE IT'S BEEN NEARLY AN ENTIRE DAY, BUT IT MIGHT HAVE BEEN NO MORE THAN FOUR OR FIVE HOURS.
JARA (JANGLE)
I HOPE MR. CREPSLEY'S ALL RIGHT.
IF WE'RE LUCKY, HE'S IN A WINDOWLESS ROOM LIKE THIS ONE.
CREPSLEY, YOU SAID HIS NAME WAS?
GUY WITH THE SCAR ON HIS CHEEK...
OUR TIP-OFF SAID HE WAS A VAMPIRE.
OF COURSE, WE DON'T BELIEVE A WORD OF IT, BUT WE HAVE NOTICED ONE ODD THING:
HE DOESN'T SHOW UP ON FILM WHEN PHOTOGRAPHED!
STILL, THERE IS NO SUCH THING AS A VAMPIRE...

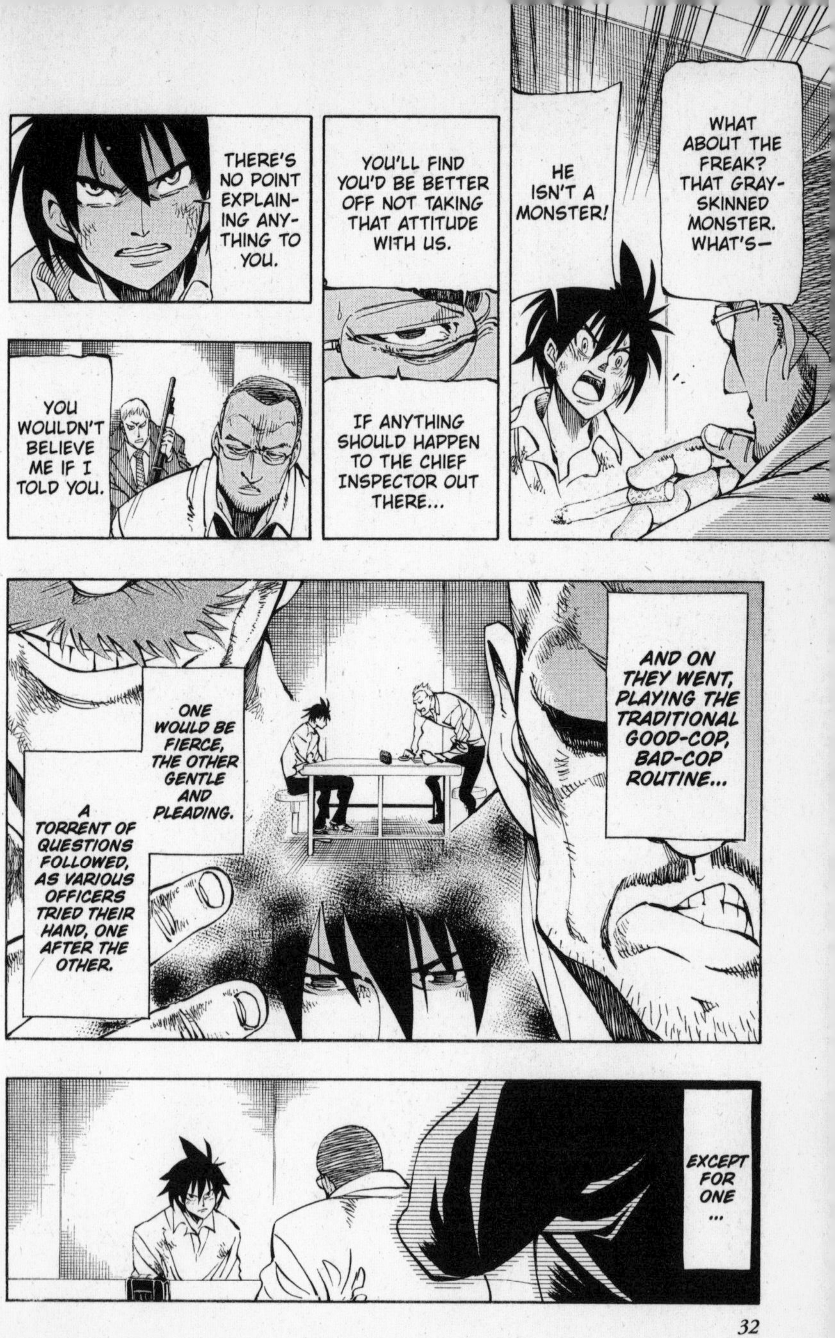
WHAT ABOUT THE FREAK? THAT GRAY-SKINNED MONSTER. WHAT'S—
HE ISN'T A MONSTER!
YOU'LL FIND YOU'D BE BETTER OFF NOT TAKING THAT ATTITUDE WITH US.
IF ANYTHING SHOULD HAPPEN TO THE CHIEF INSPECTOR OUT THERE...
THERE'S NO POINT EXPLAIN-ING ANY-THING TO YOU.
YOU WOULDN'T BELIEVE ME IF I TOLD YOU.
AND ON THEY WENT, PLAYING THE TRADITIONAL GOOD-COP, BAD-COP ROUTINE...
ONE WOULD BE FIERCE, THE OTHER GENTLE AND PLEADING.
A TORRENT OF QUESTIONS FOLLOWED, AS VARIOUS OFFICERS TRIED THEIR HAND, ONE AFTER THE OTHER.
EXCEPT FOR ONE ...

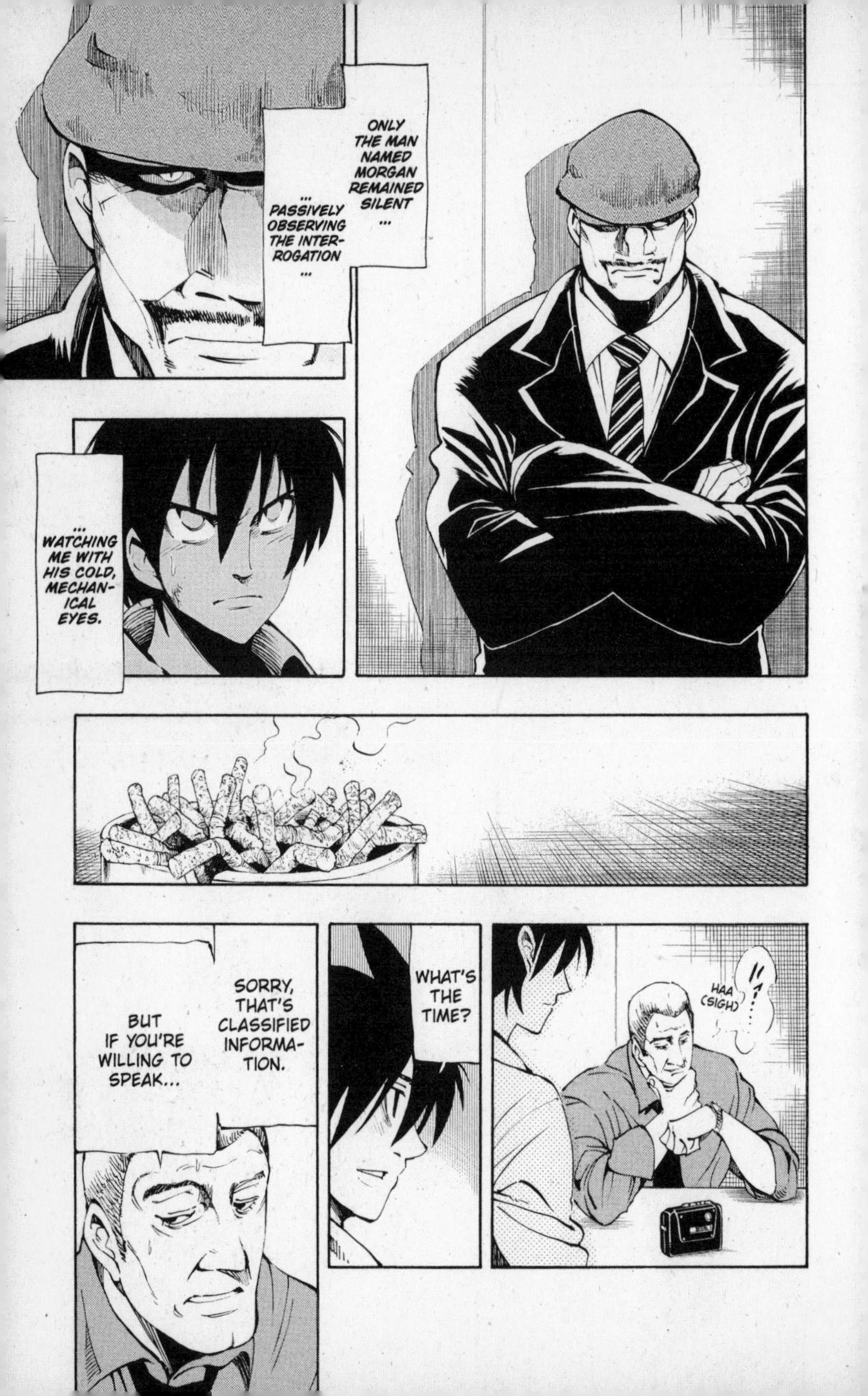
ONLY THE MAN NAMED MORGAN REMAINED SILENT ...
... PASSIVELY OBSERVING THE INTER-ROGATION ...
... WATCHING ME WITH HIS COLD, MECHAN-ICAL EYES.
HAA (SIGH)
WHAT'S THE TIME?
SORRY, THAT'S CLASSIFIED INFORMA-TION.
BUT IF YOU'RE WILLING TO SPEAK...

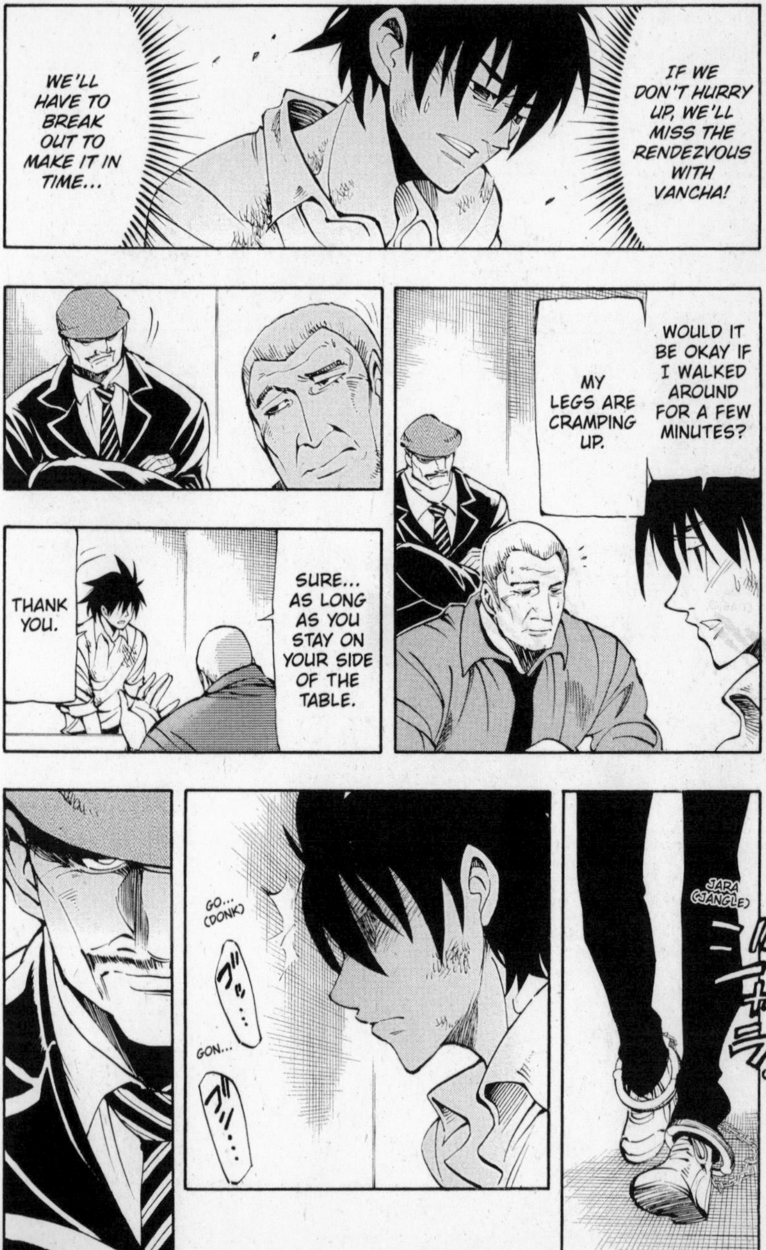
IF WE DON'T HURRY UP, WE'LL MISS THE RENDEZVOUS WITH VANCHA!
WE'LL HAVE TO BREAK OUT TO MAKE IT IN TIME...
WOULD IT BE OKAY IF I WALKED AROUND FOR A FEW MINUTES?
MY LEGS ARE CRAMPING UP.
SURE... AS LONG AS YOU STAY ON YOUR SIDE OF THE TABLE.
THANK YOU.
JARA (JANGLE)
GO... (DONK)
GON...

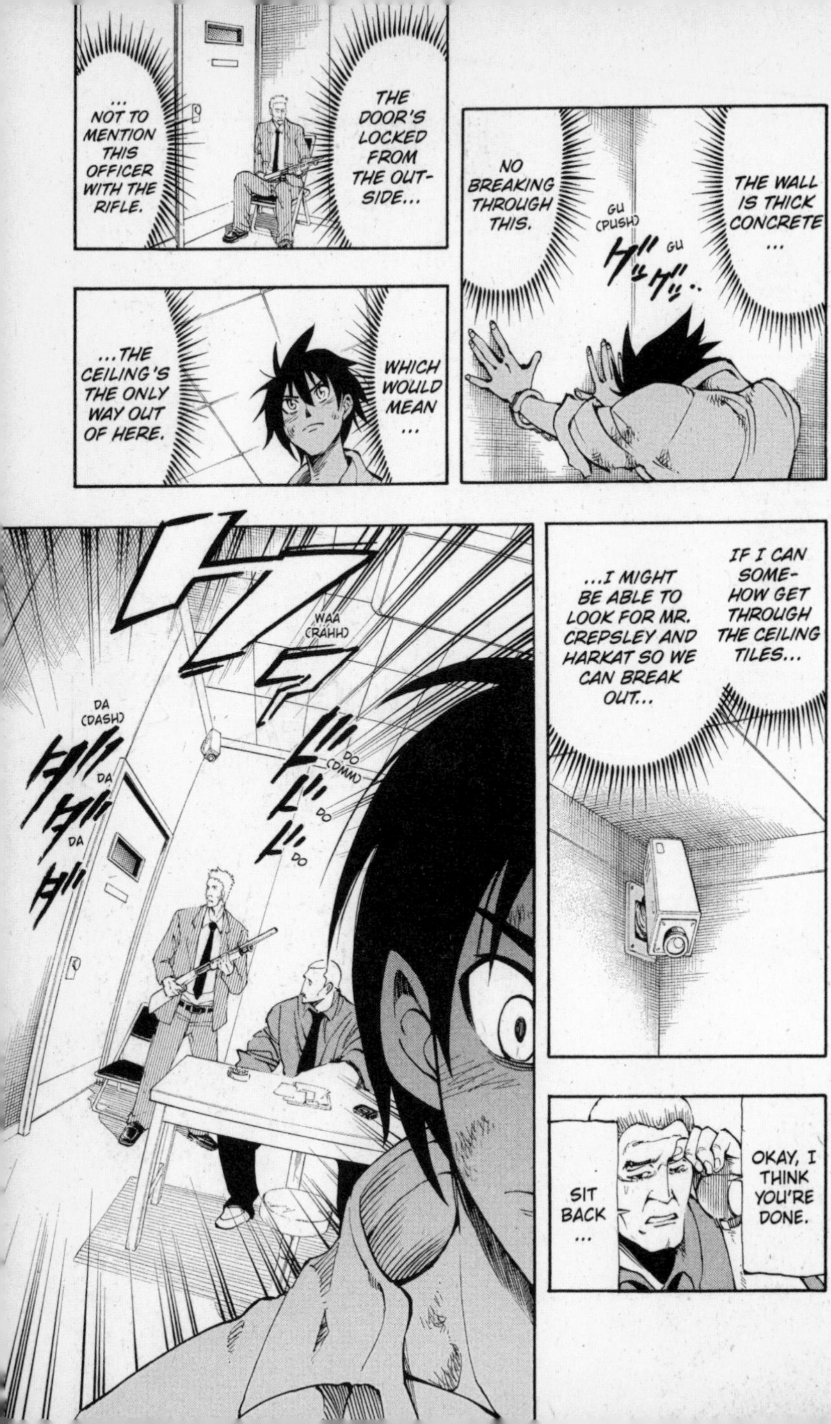
THE WALL IS THICK CONCRETE ...
NO BREAKING THROUGH THIS.
GU (PUSH)
GU
THE DOOR'S LOCKED FROM THE OUT-SIDE...
... NOT TO MENTION THIS OFFICER WITH THE RIFLE.
WHICH WOULD MEAN ...
...THE CEILING'S THE ONLY WAY OUT OF HERE.
IF I CAN SOME-HOW GET THROUGH THE CEILING TILES...
...I MIGHT BE ABLE TO LOOK FOR MR. CREPSLEY AND HARKAT SO WE CAN BREAK OUT...
OKAY, I THINK YOU'RE DONE.
SIT BACK ...
WAA (RAHH)
DO (DMM)
DO
DO
DA (DASH)
DA
DA

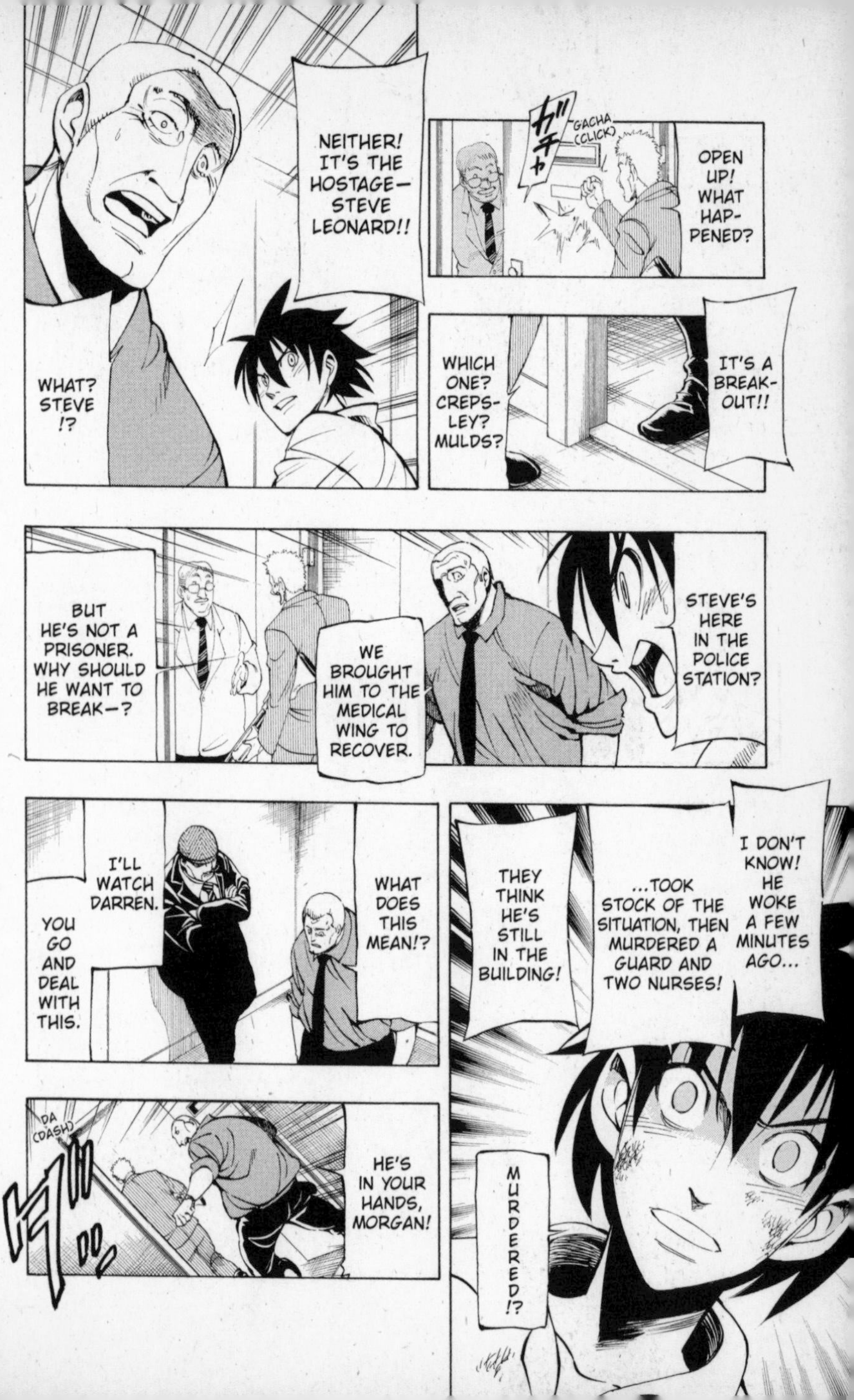
GACHA (CLICK)
OPEN UP! WHAT HAP-PENED?
IT'S A BREAK-OUT!!
WHICH ONE? CREPS-LEY? MULDS?
NEITHER! IT'S THE HOSTAGE—STEVE LEONARD!!
WHAT? STEVE!?
STEVE'S HERE IN THE POLICE STATION?
WE BROUGHT HIM TO THE MEDICAL WING TO RECOVER.
BUT HE'S NOT A PRISONER. WHY SHOULD HE WANT TO BREAK—?
I DON'T KNOW! HE WOKE A FEW MINUTES AGO...
...TOOK STOCK OF THE SITUATION, THEN MURDERED A GUARD AND TWO NURSES!
THEY THINK HE'S STILL IN THE BUILDING!
MURDERED!?
WHAT DOES THIS MEAN!?
I'LL WATCH DARREN.
YOU GO AND DEAL WITH THIS.
HE'S IN YOUR HANDS, MORGAN!
DA (DASH)

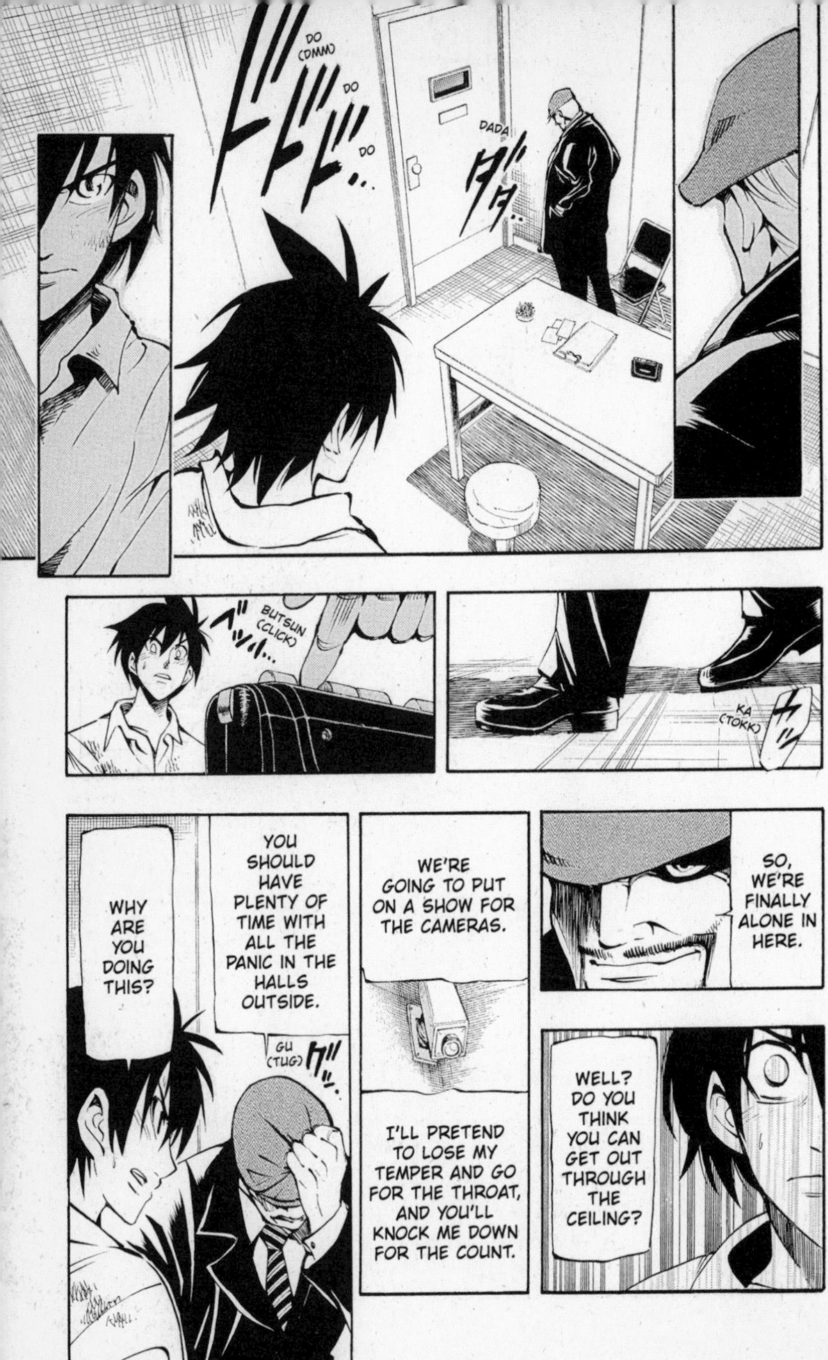
DADA
DO (DMM)
DO
DO
KA (TOKK)
BUTSUN (CLICK)
SO, WE'RE FINALLY ALONE IN HERE.
WELL? DO YOU THINK YOU CAN GET OUT THROUGH THE CEILING?
WE'RE GOING TO PUT ON A SHOW FOR THE CAMERAS.
I'LL PRETEND TO LOSE MY TEMPER AND GO FOR THE THROAT, AND YOU'LL KNOCK ME DOWN FOR THE COUNT.
YOU SHOULD HAVE PLENTY OF TIME WITH ALL THE PANIC IN THE HALLS OUTSIDE.
WHY ARE YOU DOING THIS?
GU (TUG)

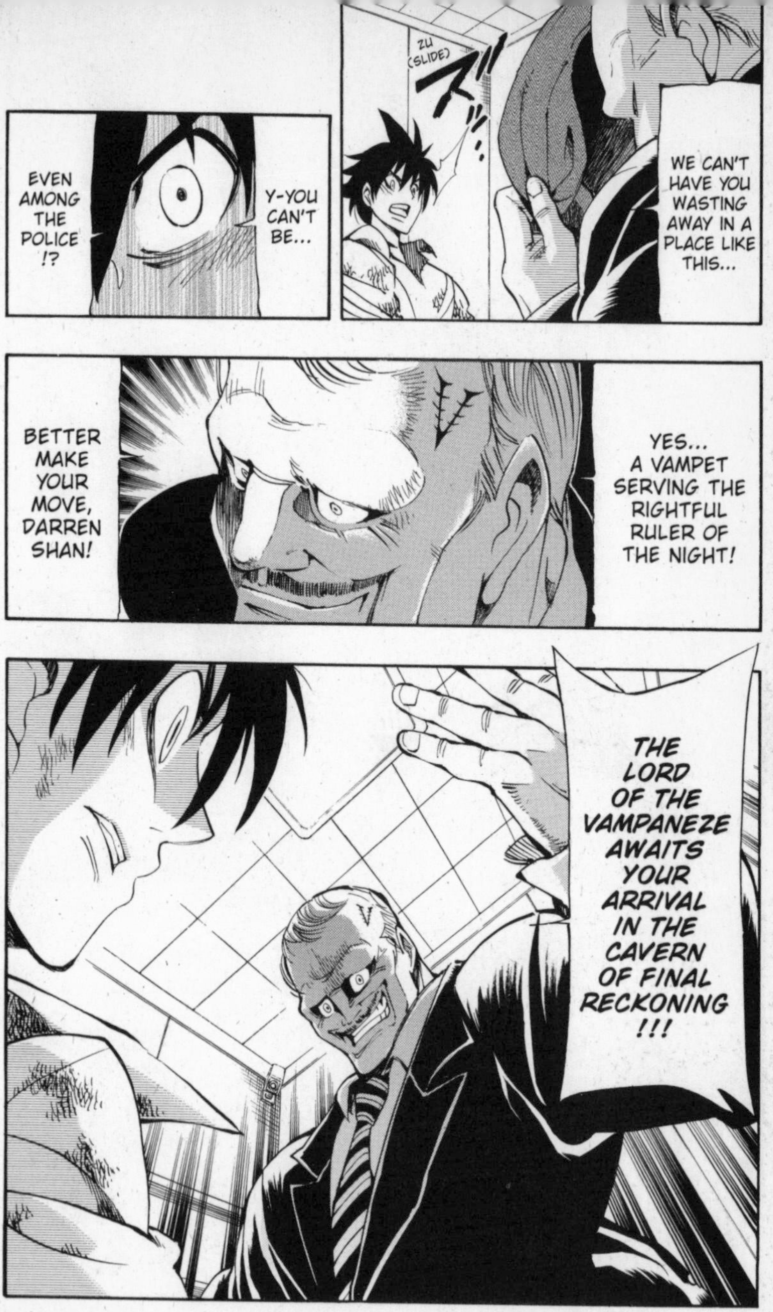
ZU (SLIDE)
WE CAN'T HAVE YOU WASTING AWAY IN A PLACE LIKE THIS...
Y-YOU CAN'T BE...
EVEN AMONG THE POLICE !?
YES... A VAMPET SERVING THE RIGHTFUL RULER OF THE NIGHT!
BETTER MAKE YOUR MOVE, DARREN SHAN!
THE LORD OF THE VAMPANEZE AWAITS YOUR ARRIVAL IN THE CAVERN OF FINAL RECKONING !!!

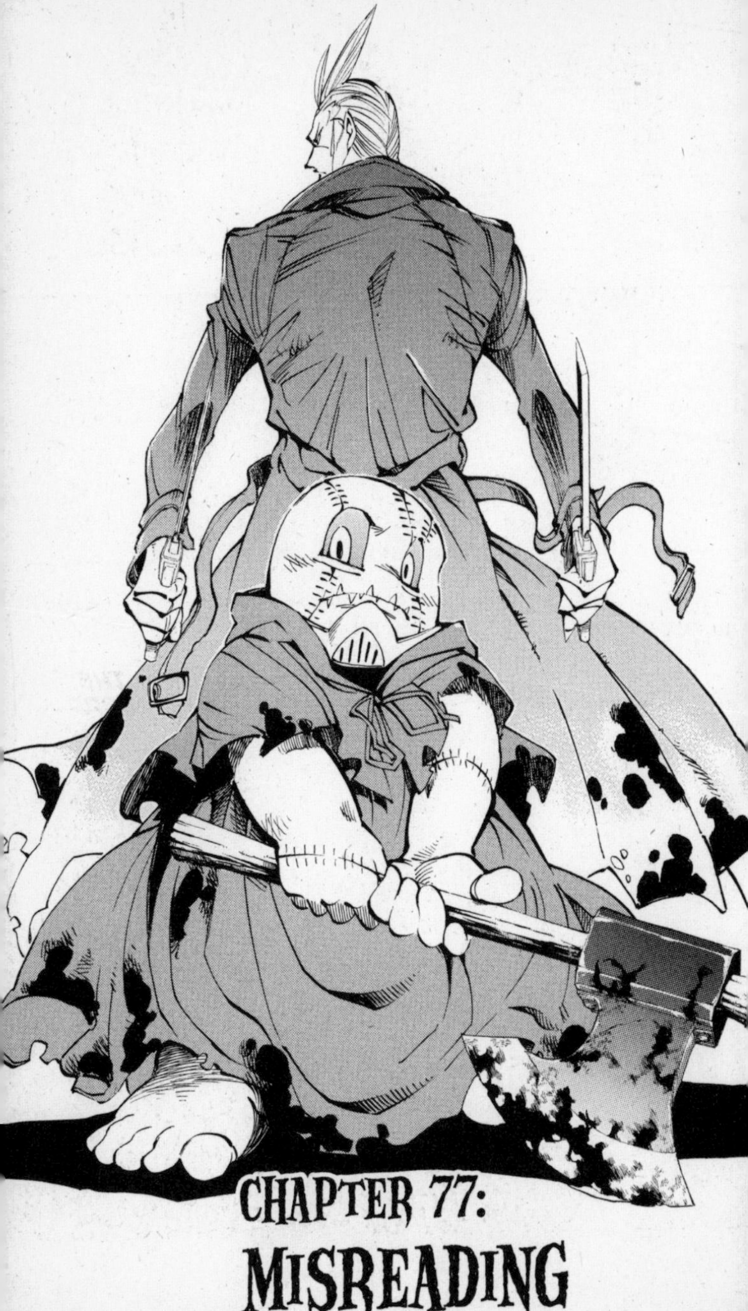
CHAPTER 77:
MISREADING

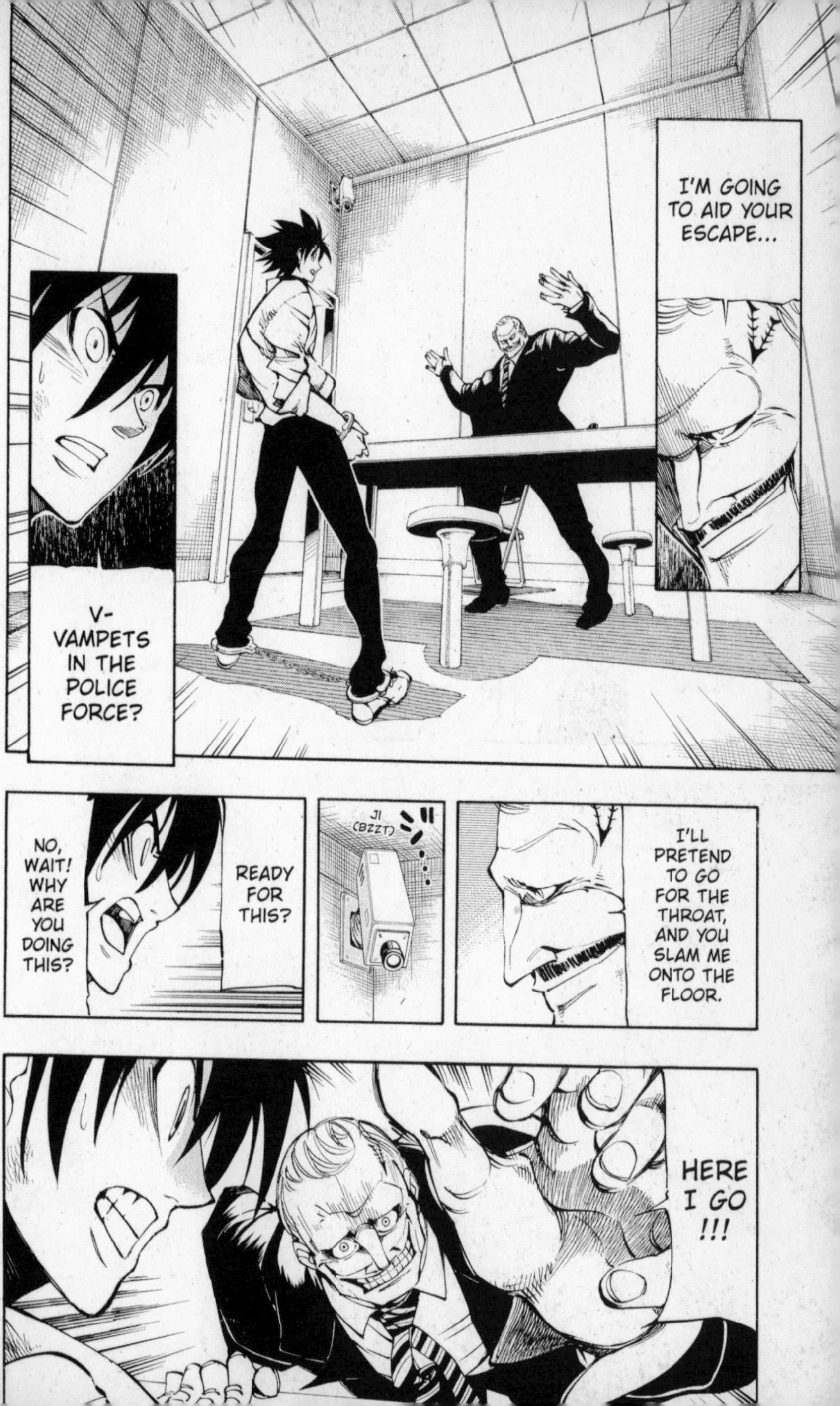
I'M GOING TO AID YOUR ESCAPE...
V-VAMPETS IN THE POLICE FORCE?
I'LL PRETEND TO GO FOR THE THROAT, AND YOU SLAM ME ONTO THE FLOOR.
JI (BZZT)
READY FOR THIS?
NO, WAIT! WHY ARE YOU DOING THIS?
HERE I GO !!!

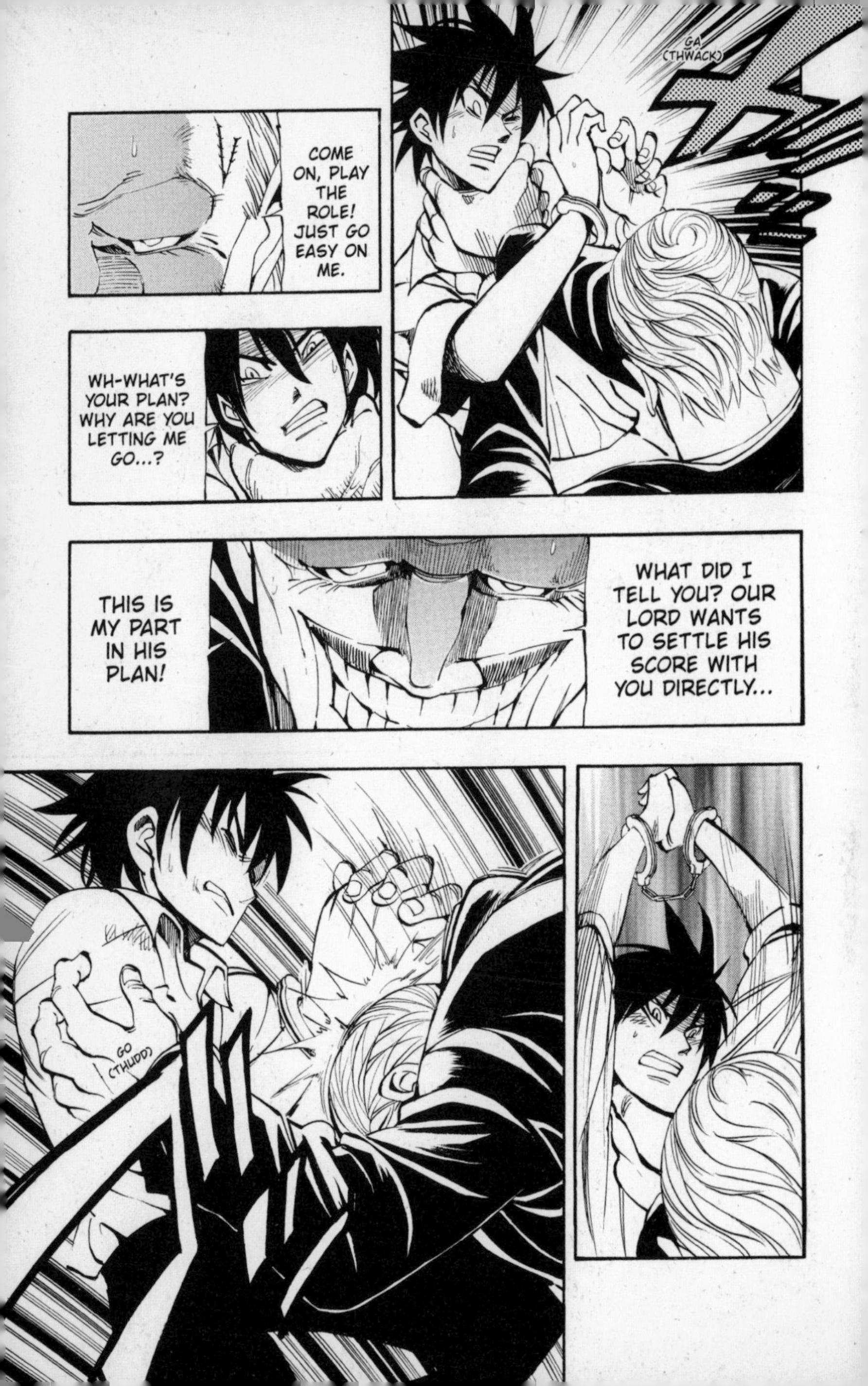
GA (THWACK)
COME ON, PLAY THE ROLE! JUST GO EASY ON ME.
WH-WHAT'S YOUR PLAN? WHY ARE YOU LETTING ME GO...?
WHAT DID I TELL YOU? OUR LORD WANTS TO SETTLE HIS SCORE WITH YOU DIRECTLY...
THIS IS MY PART IN HIS PLAN!
GO (THUDD)

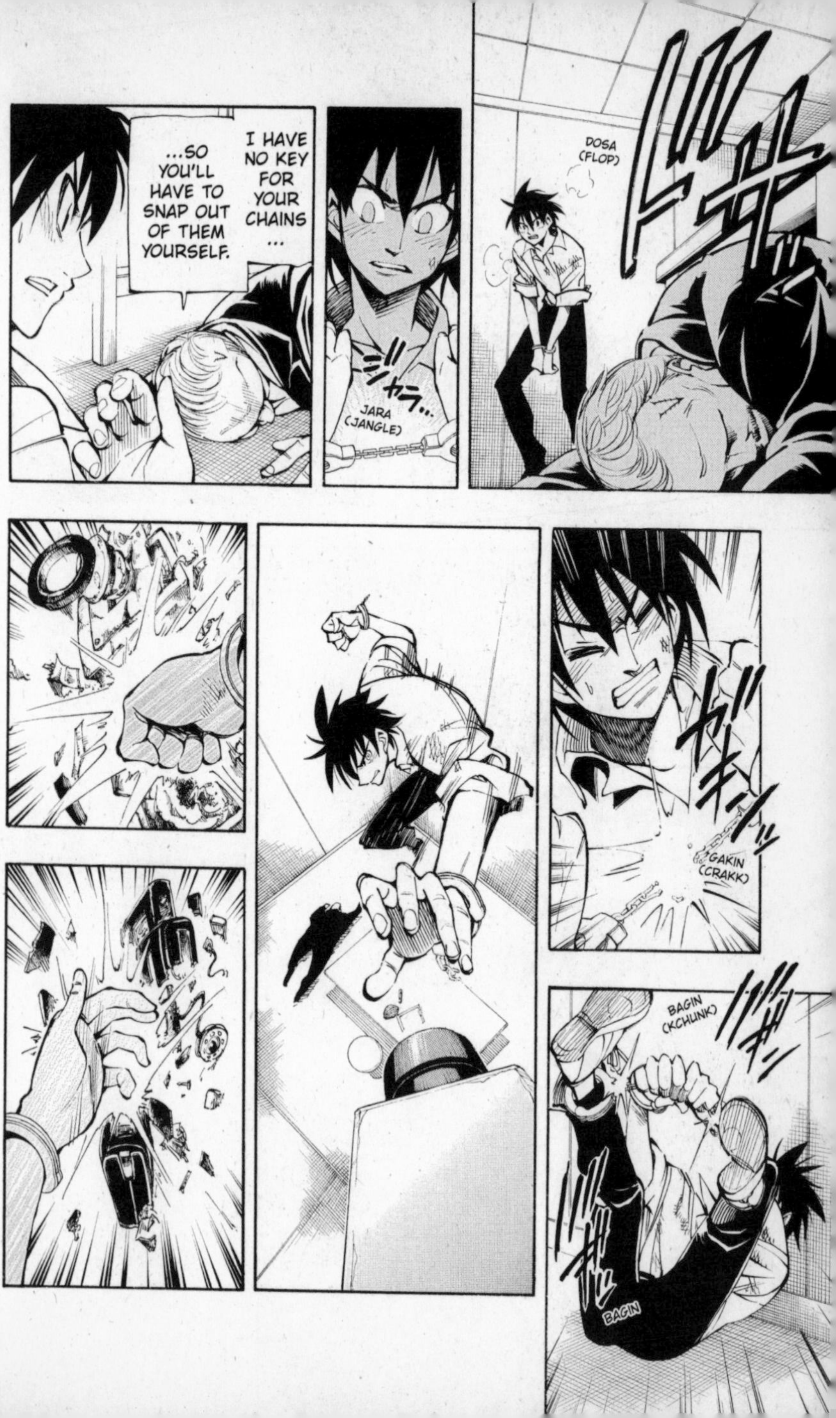

DOSA (FLOP)
I HAVE NO KEY FOR YOUR CHAINS ...
...SO YOU'LL HAVE TO SNAP OUT OF THEM YOURSELF.
JARA (JANGLE)
GAKIN (CRAKK)
BAGIN (KCHUNK)
BAGIN

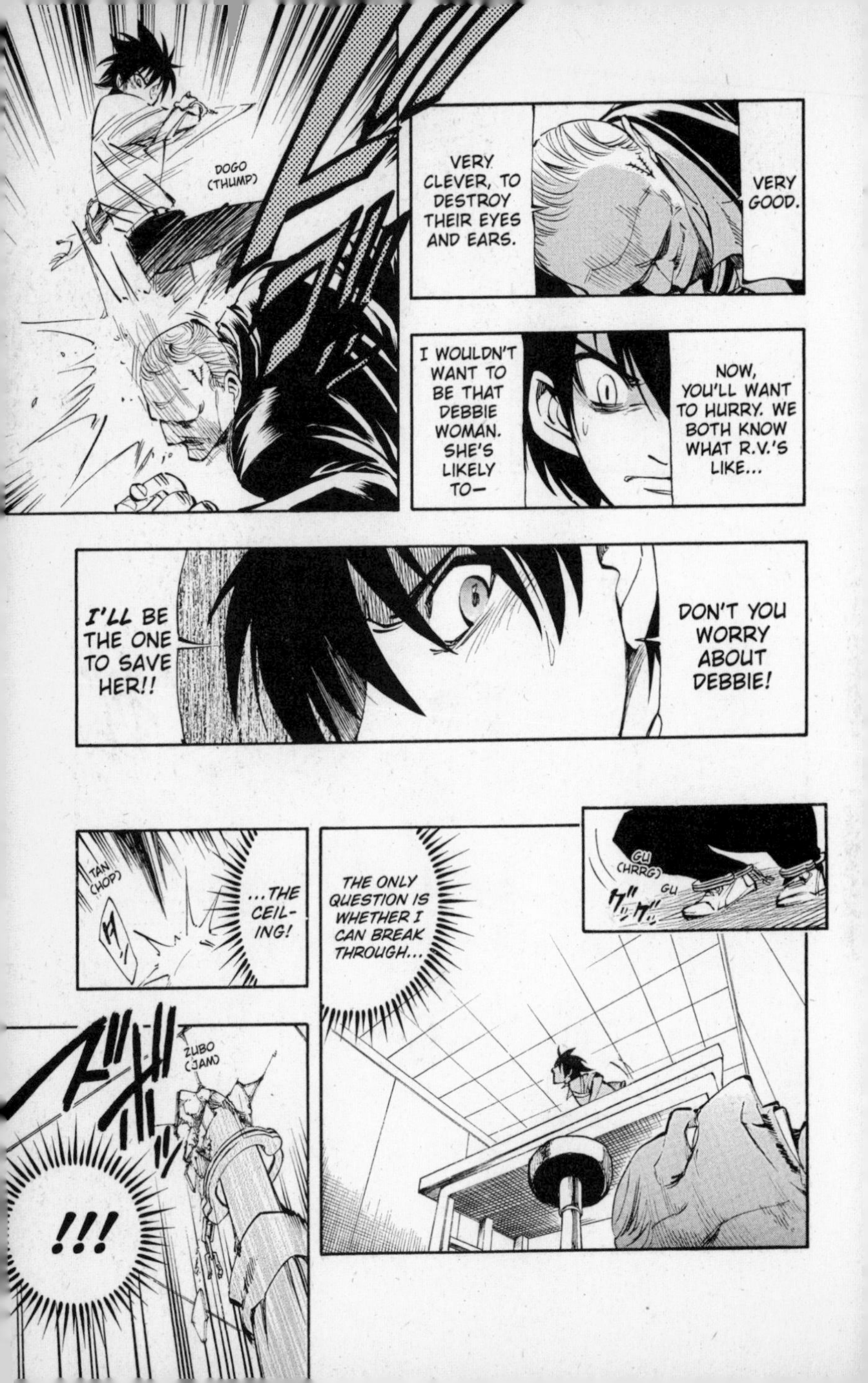
VERY GOOD.
VERY CLEVER, TO DESTROY THEIR EYES AND EARS.
NOW, YOU'LL WANT TO HURRY. WE BOTH KNOW WHAT R.V.'S LIKE...
I WOULDN'T WANT TO BE THAT DEBBIE WOMAN. SHE'S LIKELY TO—
DOGO (THUMP)
DON'T YOU WORRY ABOUT DEBBIE!
I'LL BE THE ONE TO SAVE HER!!
GU (HRRG) GU
THE ONLY QUESTION IS WHETHER I CAN BREAK THROUGH...
...THE CEIL- ING!
TAN (HOP)
ZUBO (JAM)
!!!

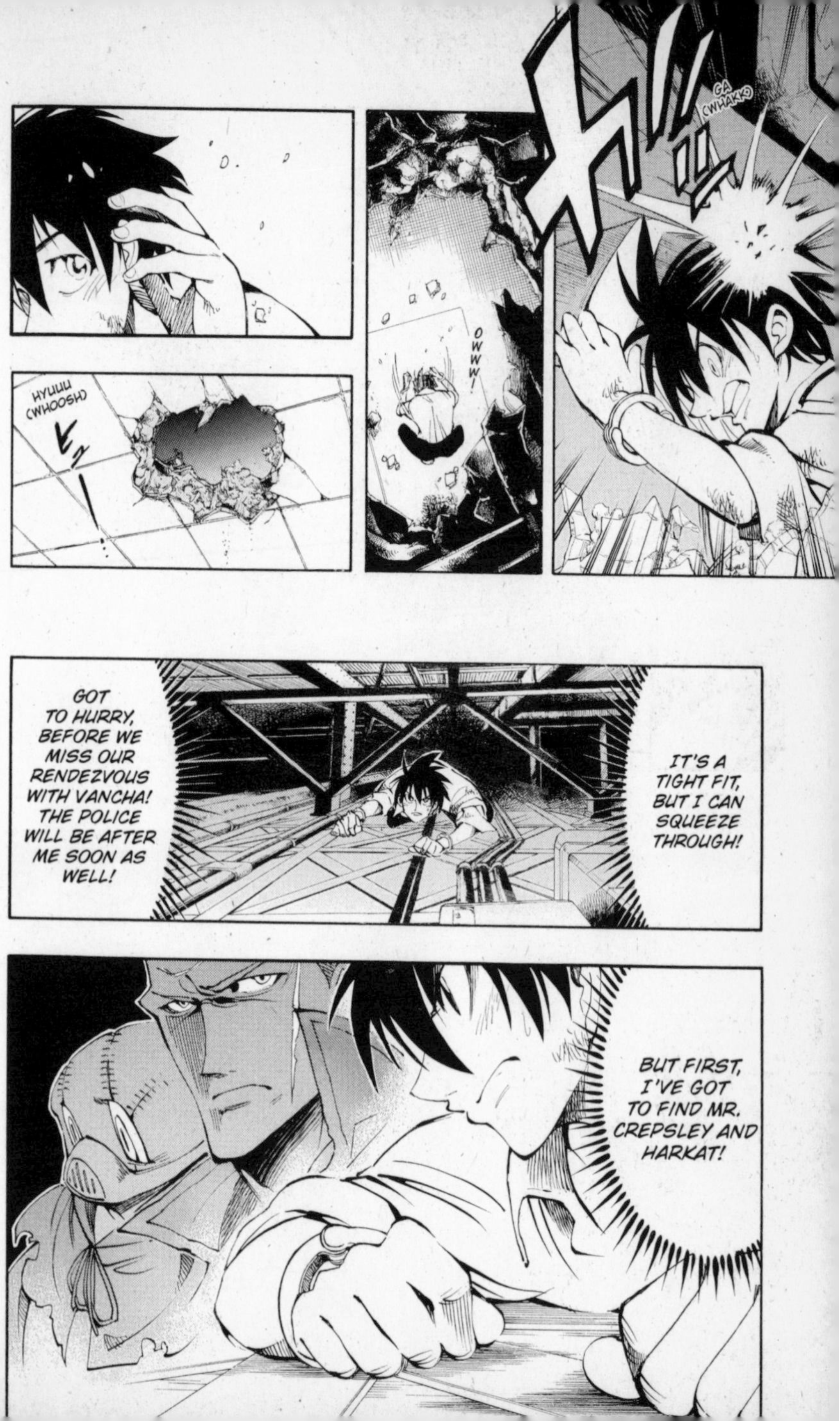
GA (WHAKK)
OWWW!
HYUUU (WHOOSH)
IT'S A TIGHT FIT, BUT I CAN SQUEEZE THROUGH!
GOT TO HURRY, BEFORE WE MISS OUR RENDEZVOUS WITH VANCHA! THE POLICE WILL BE AFTER ME SOON AS WELL!
BUT FIRST, I'VE GOT TO FIND MR. CREPSLEY AND HARKAT!

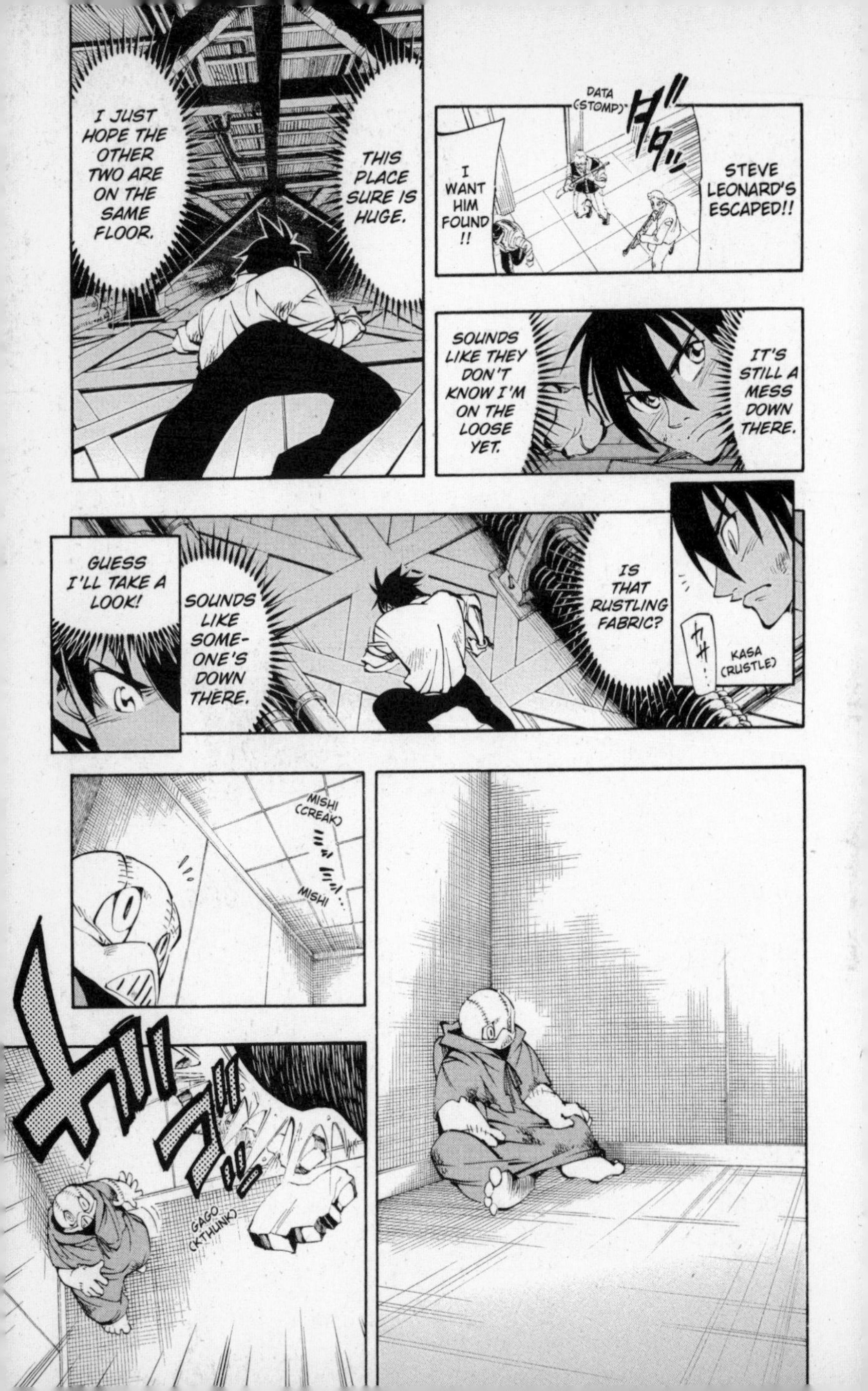
STEVE LEONARD'S ESCAPED!!
DATA (STOMP)
I WANT HIM FOUND!!
IT'S STILL A MESS DOWN THERE.
SOUNDS LIKE THEY DON'T KNOW I'M ON THE LOOSE YET.
THIS PLACE SURE IS HUGE.
I JUST HOPE THE OTHER TWO ARE ON THE SAME FLOOR.
KASA (RUSTLE)
IS THAT RUSTLING FABRIC?
SOUNDS LIKE SOME-ONE'S DOWN THERE.
GUESS I'LL TAKE A LOOK!
MISHI (CREAK)
MISHI
GAGO (KTHUNK)

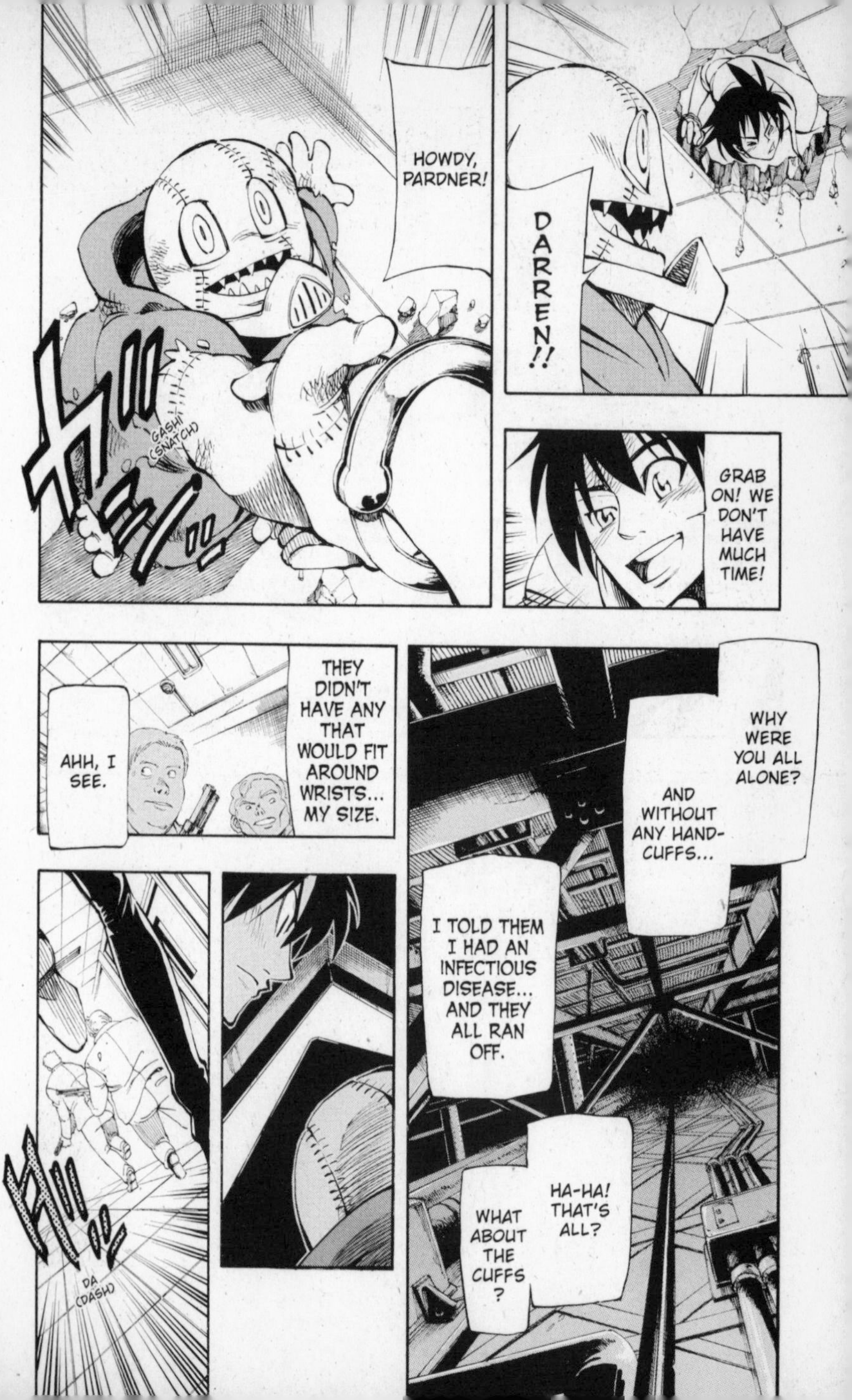
DARREN!!
HOWDY, PARDNER!
GASHI (SNATCH)
GRAB ON! WE DON'T HAVE MUCH TIME!
WHY WERE YOU ALL ALONE?
AND WITHOUT ANY HAND-CUFFS...
I TOLD THEM I HAD AN INFECTIOUS DISEASE... AND THEY ALL RAN OFF.
HA-HA! THAT'S ALL?
WHAT ABOUT THE CUFFS?
THEY DIDN'T HAVE ANY THAT WOULD FIT AROUND WRISTS... MY SIZE.
AHH, I SEE.
DA (DASH)

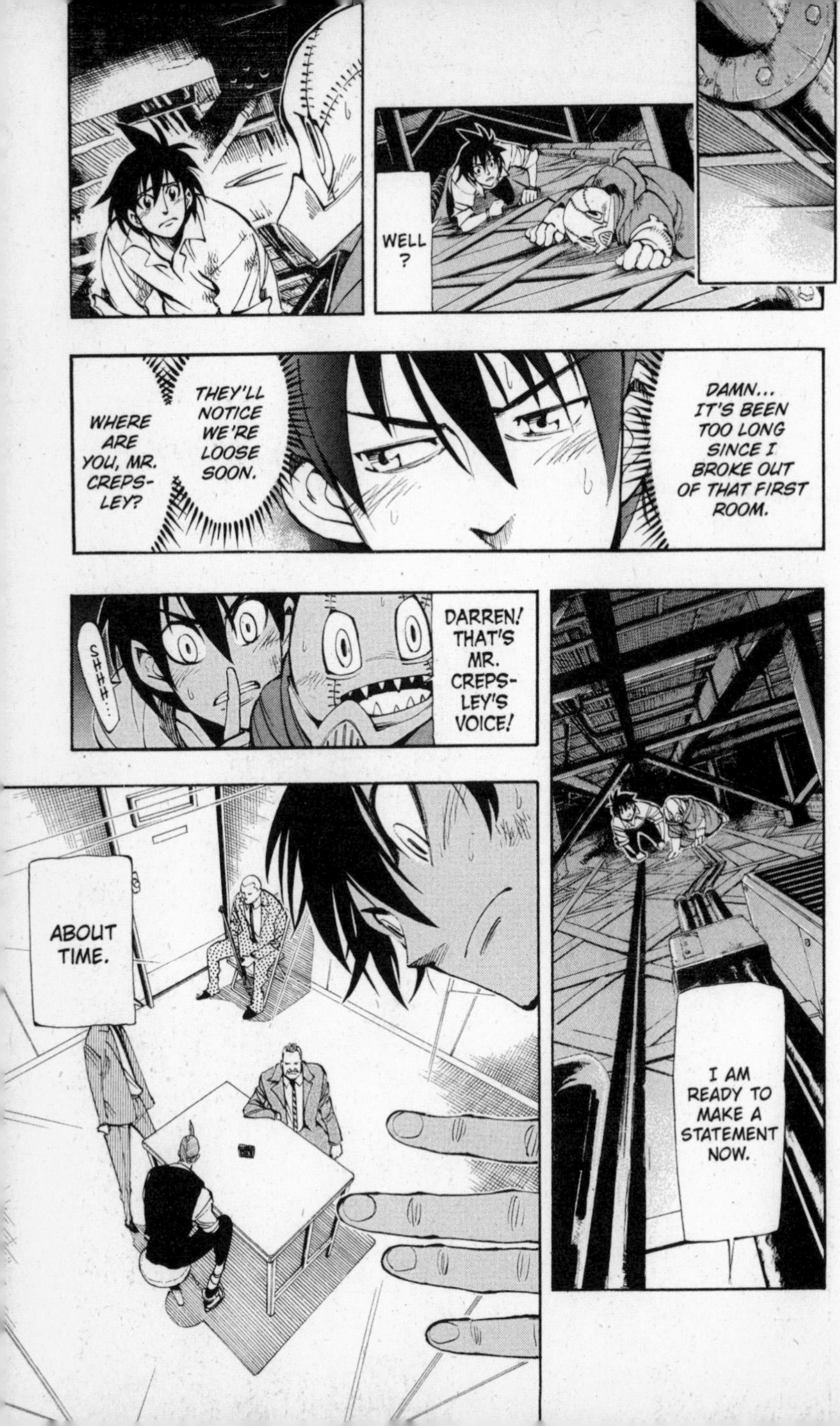
WELL?
DAMN... IT'S BEEN TOO LONG SINCE I BROKE OUT OF THAT FIRST ROOM.
THEY'LL NOTICE WE'RE LOOSE SOON.
WHERE ARE YOU, MR. CREPS-LEY?
I AM READY TO MAKE A STATEMENT NOW.
DARREN! THAT'S MR. CREPS-LEY'S VOICE!
SHHH...
ABOUT TIME.

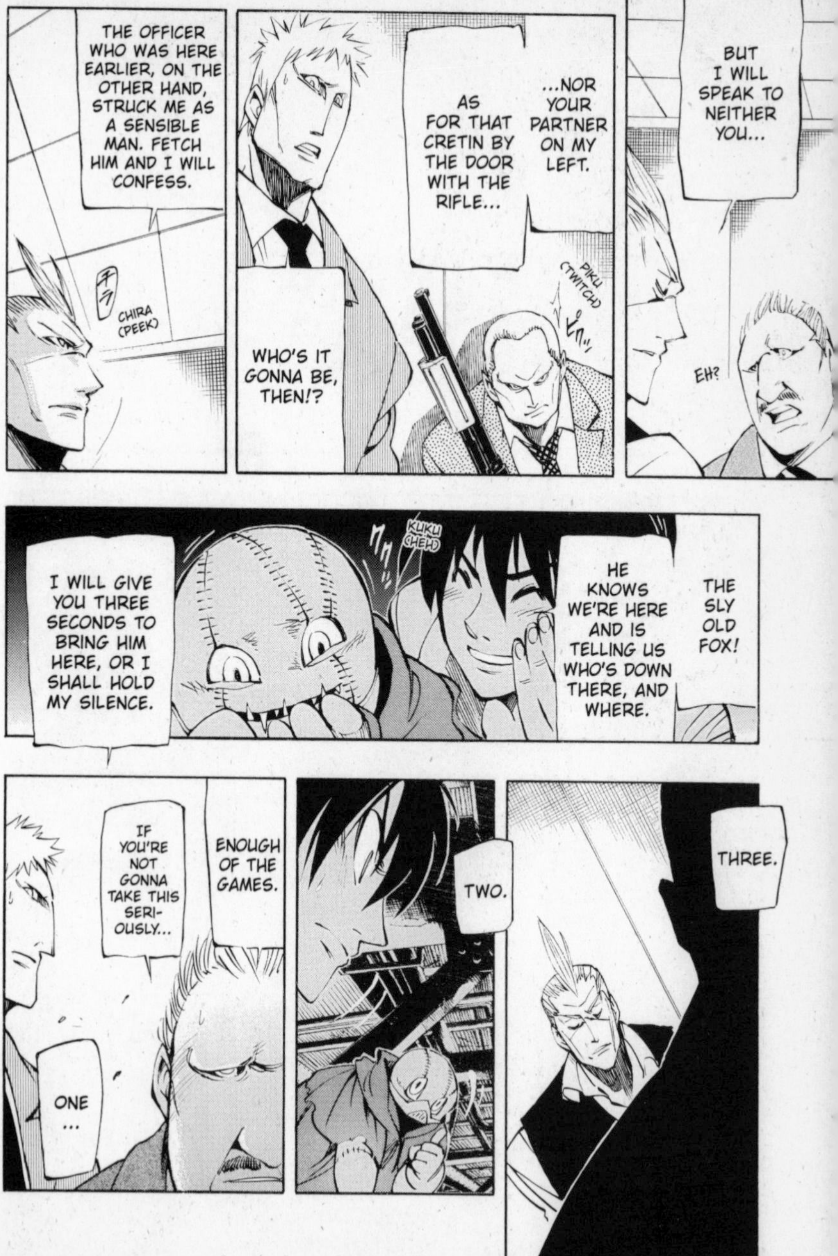
BUT I WILL SPEAK TO NEITHER YOU...
EH?
...NOR YOUR PARTNER ON MY LEFT.
AS FOR THAT CRETIN BY THE DOOR WITH THE RIFLE...
PIKU (TWITCH)
WHO'S IT GONNA BE, THEN!?
THE OFFICER WHO WAS HERE EARLIER, ON THE OTHER HAND, STRUCK ME AS A SENSIBLE MAN. FETCH HIM AND I WILL CONFESS.
CHIRA (PEEK)
THE SLY OLD FOX!
HE KNOWS WE'RE HERE AND IS TELLING US WHO'S DOWN THERE, AND WHERE.
KUKU (HEH)
I WILL GIVE YOU THREE SECONDS TO BRING HIM HERE, OR I SHALL HOLD MY SILENCE.
THREE.
TWO.
ENOUGH OF THE GAMES.
IF YOU'RE NOT GONNA TAKE THIS SERIOUSLY...
ONE...

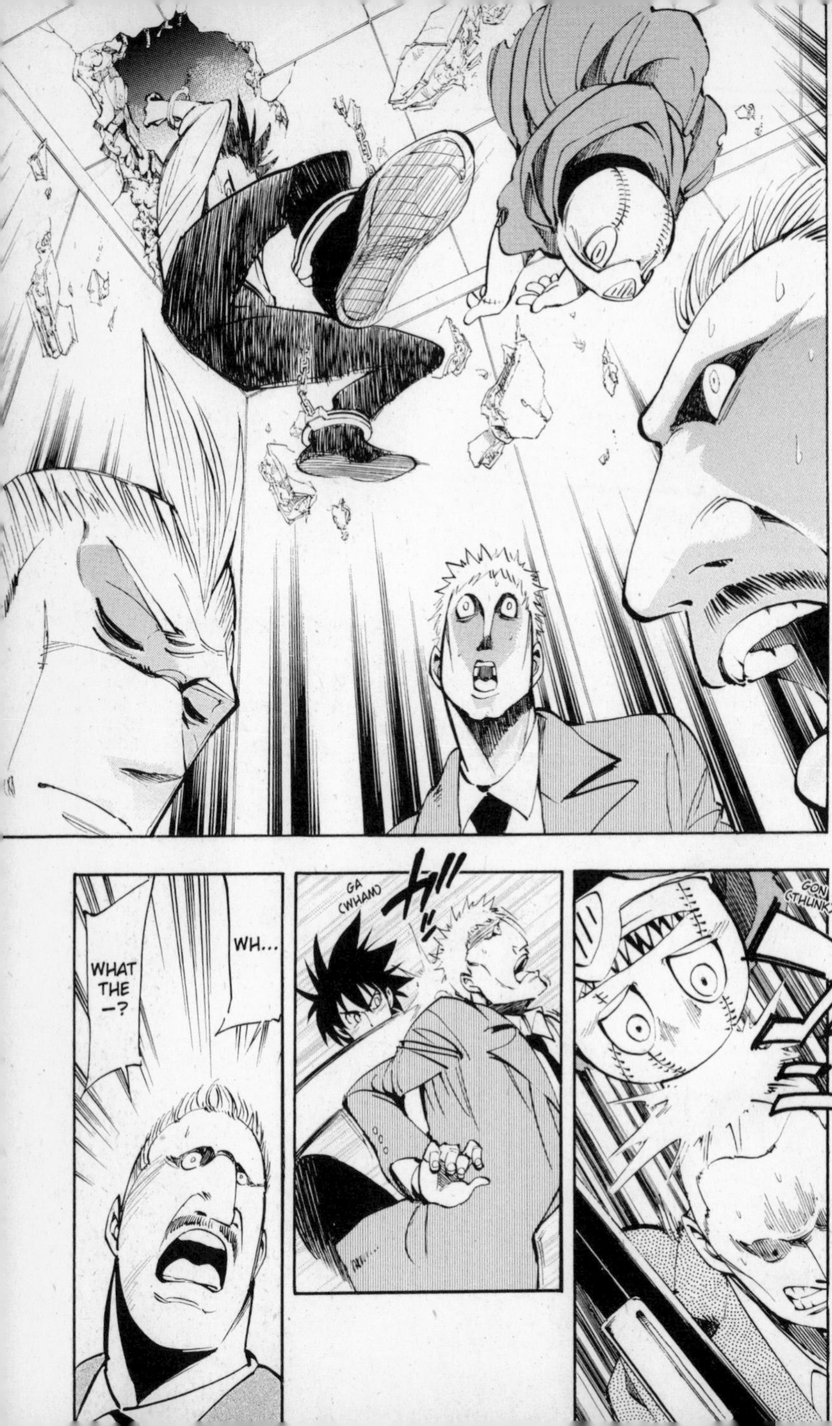
GON (THUNK)
GA (WHAM)
WH...
WHAT THE —?

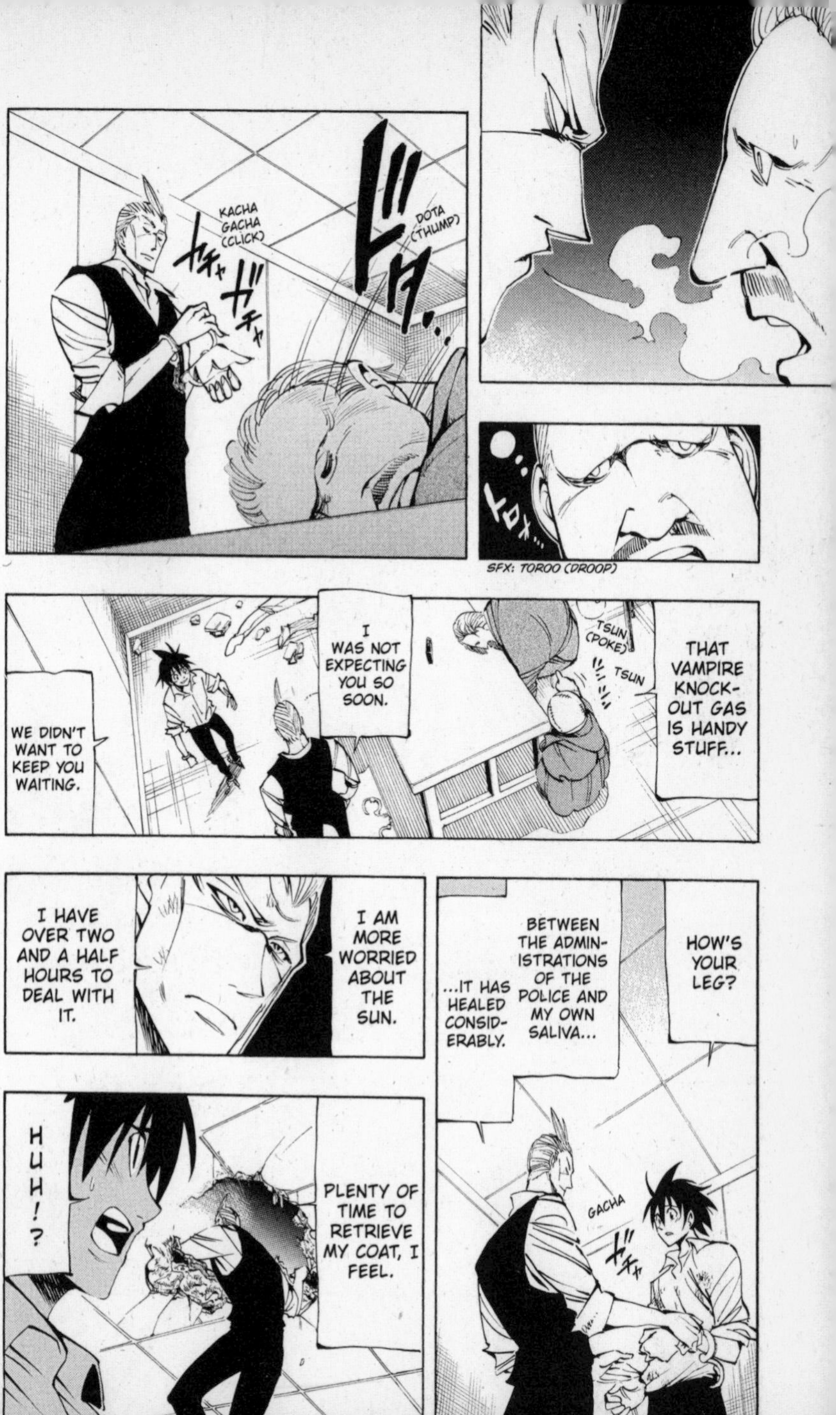

SFX: TOROO (DROOP)
KACHA GACHA (CLICK)
DOTA (THUMP)
THAT VAMPIRE KNOCK-OUT GAS IS HANDY STUFF...
TSUN (POKE)
TSUN
I WAS NOT EXPECTING YOU SO SOON.
WE DIDN'T WANT TO KEEP YOU WAITING.
HOW'S YOUR LEG?
BETWEEN THE ADMINISTRATIONS OF THE POLICE AND MY OWN SALIVA...
...IT HAS HEALED CONSIDERABLY.
GACHA
I AM MORE WORRIED ABOUT THE SUN.
I HAVE OVER TWO AND A HALF HOURS TO DEAL WITH IT.
PLENTY OF TIME TO RETRIEVE MY COAT, I FEEL.
HUH!?

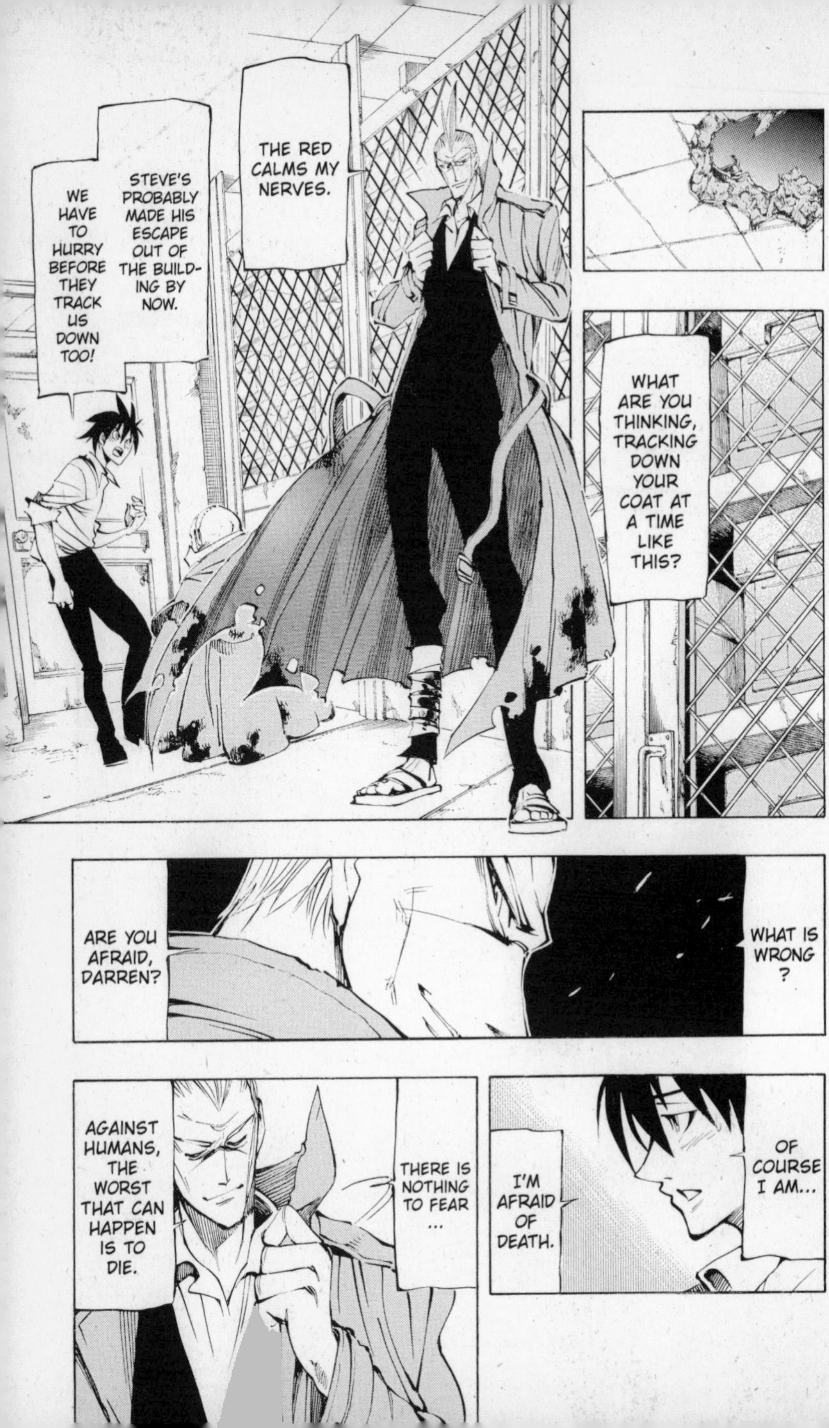
WHAT ARE YOU THINKING, TRACKING DOWN YOUR COAT AT A TIME LIKE THIS?
THE RED CALMS MY NERVES.
STEVE'S PROBABLY MADE HIS ESCAPE OUT OF THE BUILD-ING BY NOW.
WE HAVE TO HURRY BEFORE THEY TRACK US DOWN TOO!
WHAT IS WRONG ?
ARE YOU AFRAID, DARREN?
OF COURSE I AM...
I'M AFRAID OF DEATH.
THERE IS NOTHING TO FEAR ...
AGAINST HUMANS, THE WORST THAT CAN HAPPEN IS TO DIE.

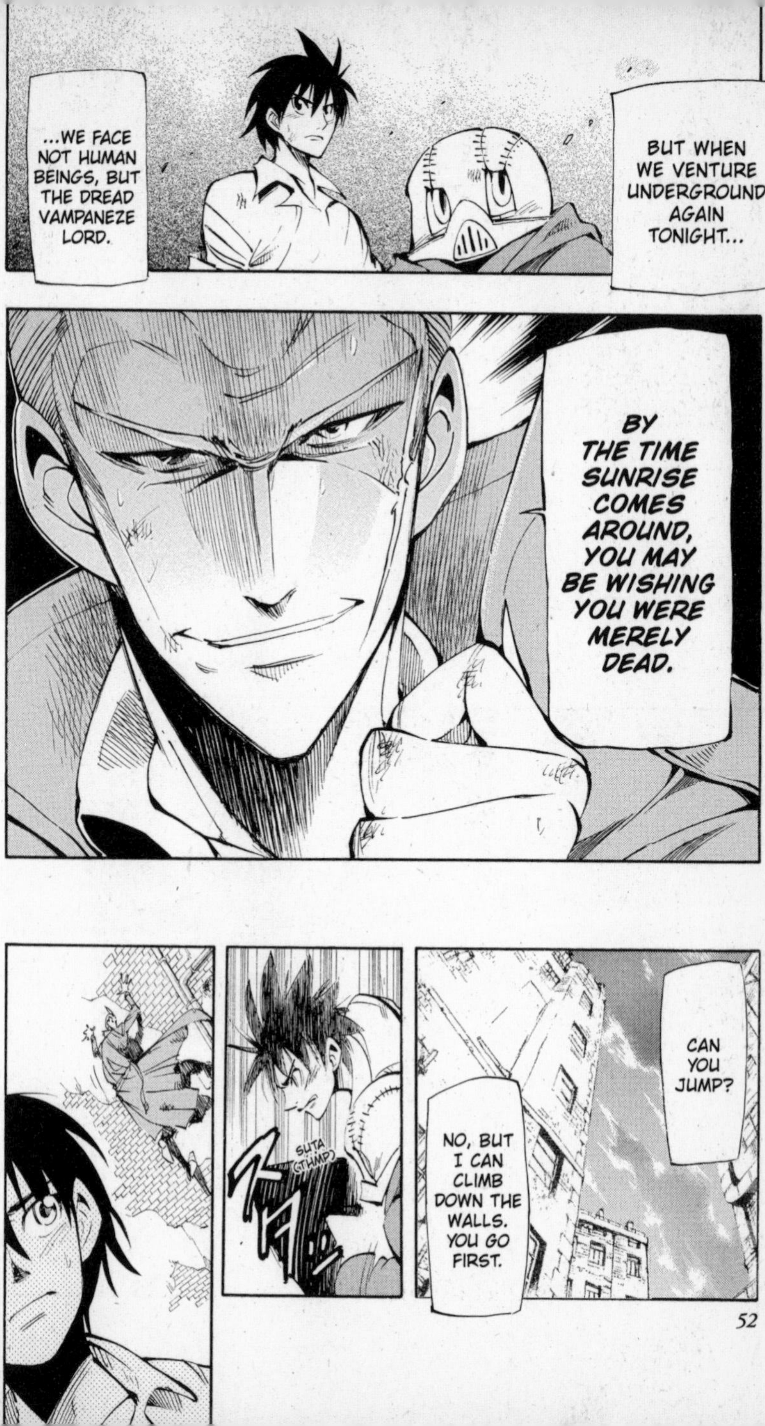
BUT WHEN WE VENTURE UNDERGROUND AGAIN TONIGHT...
...WE FACE NOT HUMAN BEINGS, BUT THE DREAD VAMPANEZE LORD.
BY THE TIME SUNRISE COMES AROUND, YOU MAY BE WISHING YOU WERE MERELY DEAD.
CAN YOU JUMP?
NO, BUT I CAN CLIMB DOWN THE WALLS. YOU GO FIRST.
SUTA (STHMP)

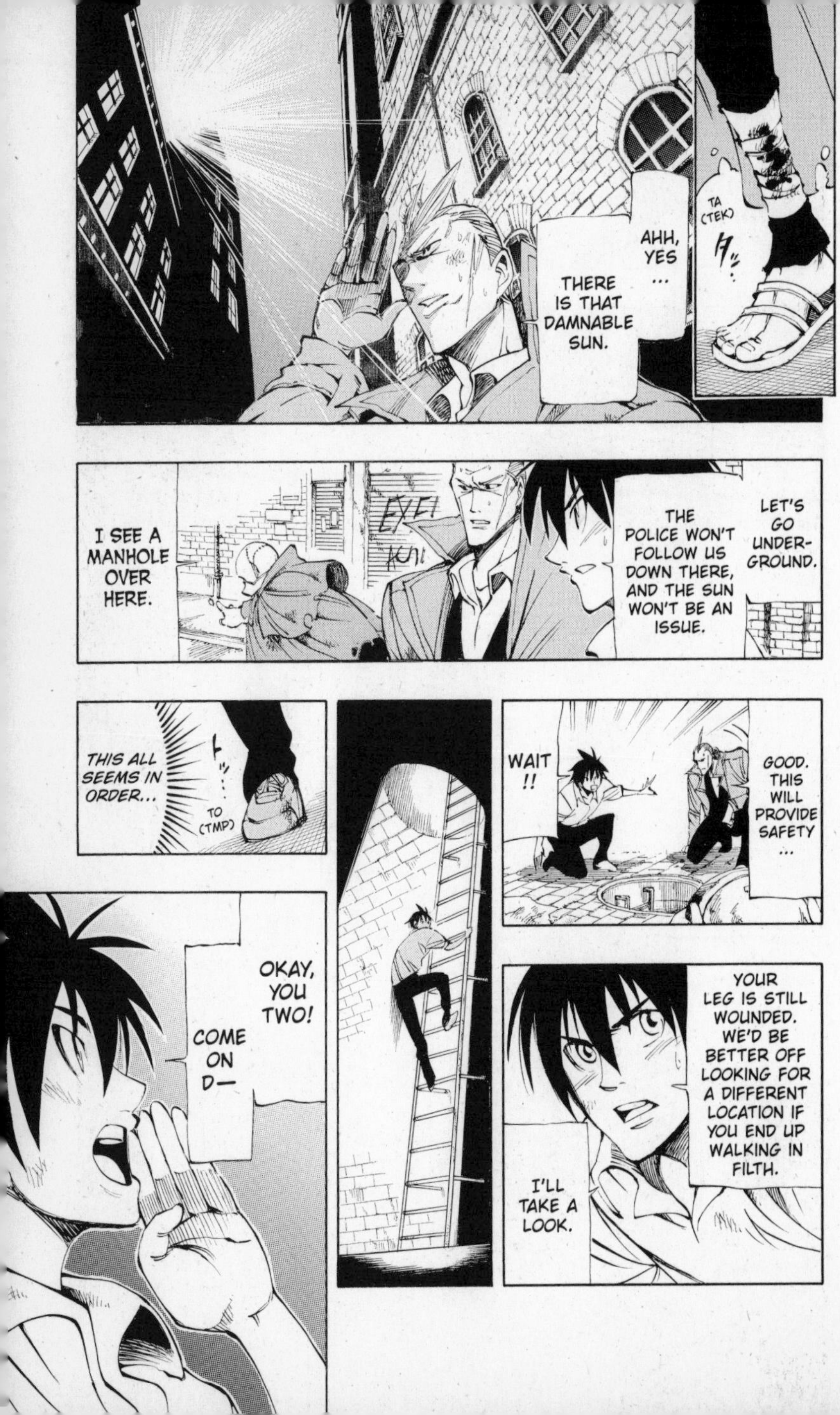
TA (TEK)
AHH, YES ...
THERE IS THAT DAMNABLE SUN.
LET'S GO UNDER-GROUND.
THE POLICE WON'T FOLLOW US DOWN THERE, AND THE SUN WON'T BE AN ISSUE.
I SEE A MANHOLE OVER HERE.
GOOD. THIS WILL PROVIDE SAFETY ...
WAIT !!
YOUR LEG IS STILL WOUNDED. WE'D BE BETTER OFF LOOKING FOR A DIFFERENT LOCATION IF YOU END UP WALKING IN FILTH.
I'LL TAKE A LOOK.
THIS ALL SEEMS IN ORDER...
TO (TMP)
OKAY, YOU TWO!
COME ON D—

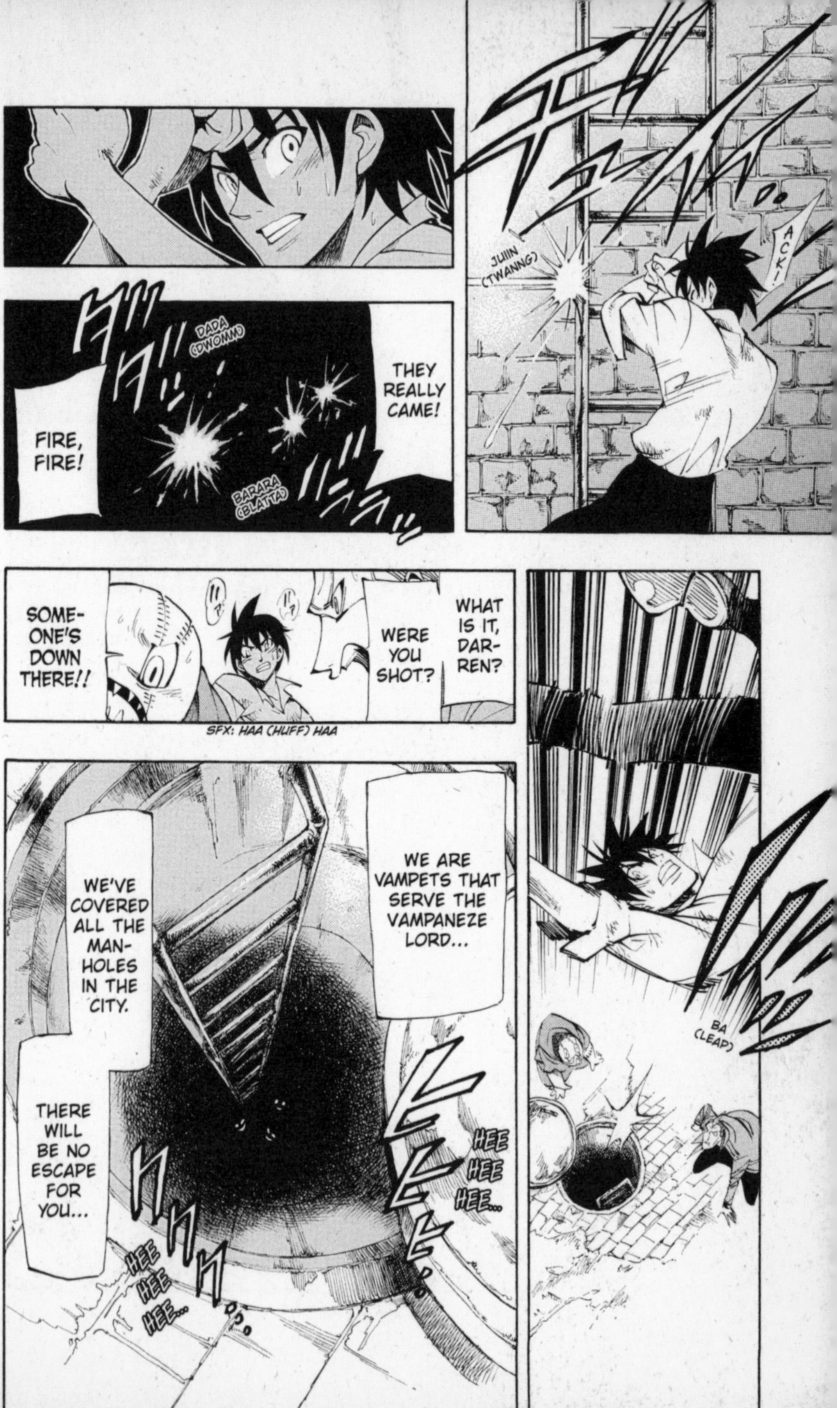
ACK!
JUIN (TWANNG)
DADA (DWOMM)
THEY REALLY CAME!
FIRE, FIRE!
BARARA (BLATTA)
BA (LEAP)
WHAT IS IT, DARREN?
WERE YOU SHOT?
SOME-ONE'S DOWN THERE!!
SFX: HAA (HUFF) HAA
WE ARE VAMPETS THAT SERVE THE VAMPANEZE LORD...
WE'VE COVERED ALL THE MAN-HOLES IN THE CITY.
HEE HEE HEE...
THERE WILL BE NO ESCAPE FOR YOU...
HEE HEE HEE...

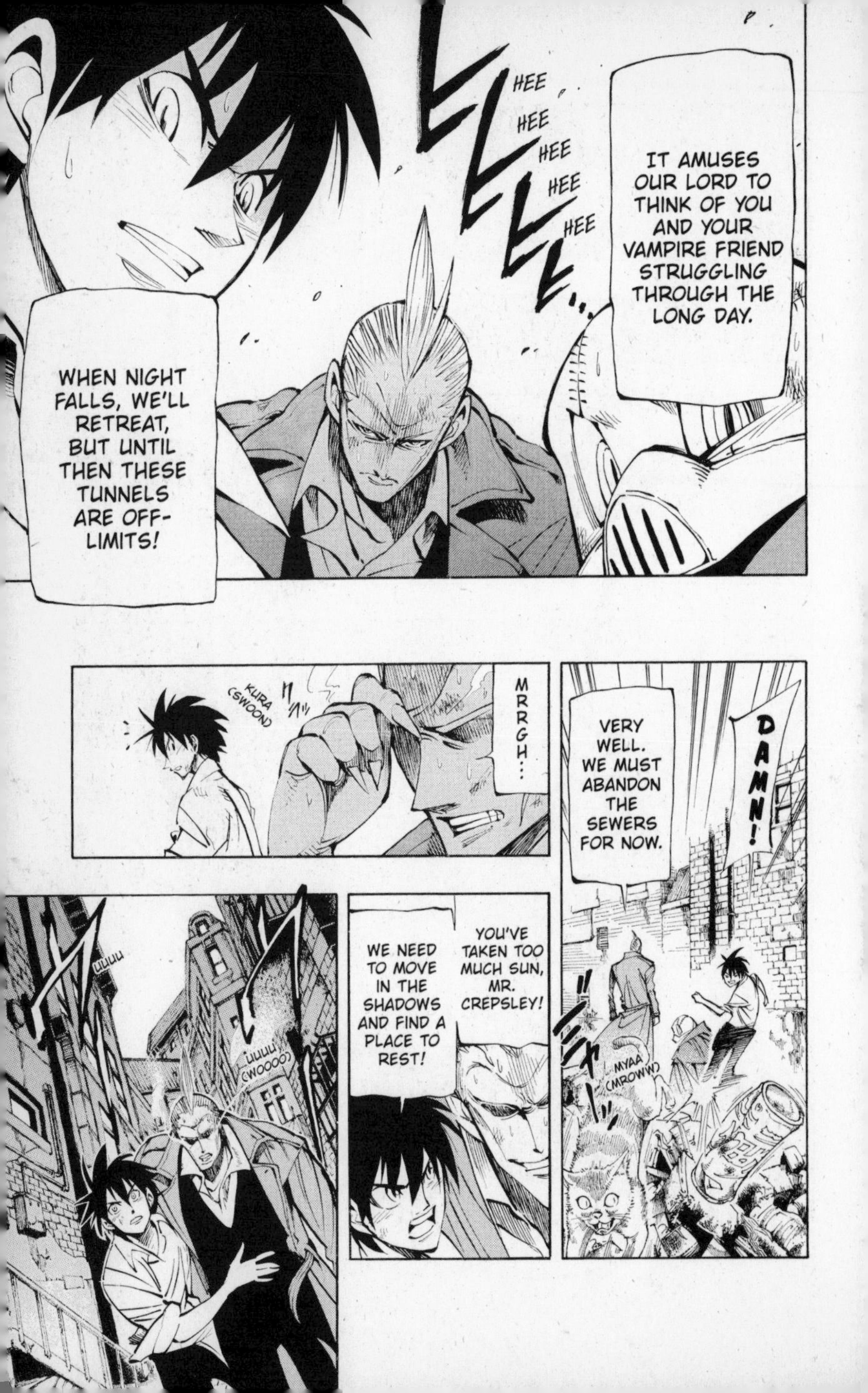
IT AMUSES OUR LORD TO THINK OF YOU AND YOUR VAMPIRE FRIEND STRUGGLING THROUGH THE LONG DAY.
HEE HEE HEE HEE HEE
WHEN NIGHT FALLS, WE'LL RETREAT, BUT UNTIL THEN THESE TUNNELS ARE OFF-LIMITS!
VERY WELL. WE MUST ABANDON THE SEWERS FOR NOW.
DAMN!
MYAA (MROWW)
MRRGH...
KURA (SWOON)
YOU'VE TAKEN TOO MUCH SUN, MR. CREPSLEY!
WE NEED TO MOVE IN THE SHADOWS AND FIND A PLACE TO REST!
UUUU
UUUU (WOOOO)

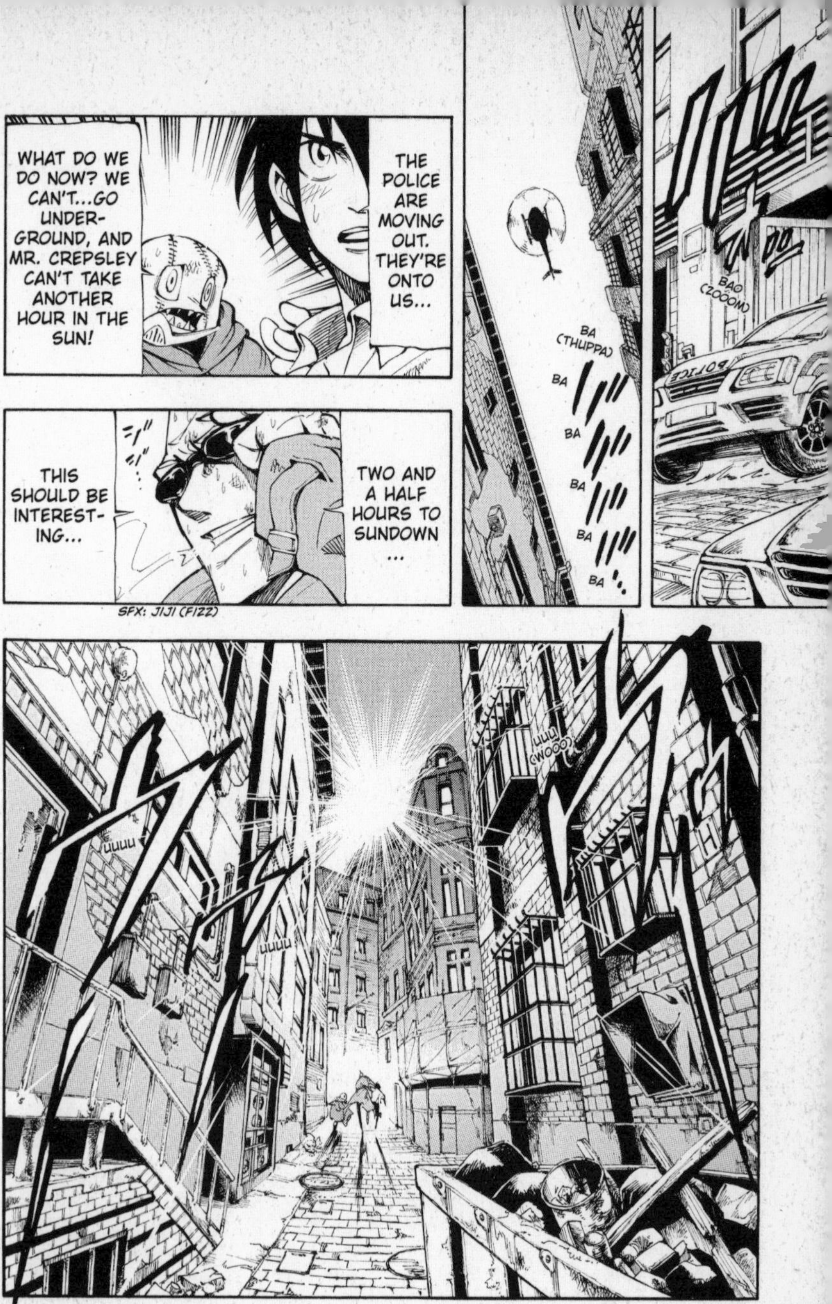
BAO (ZOOOM)
BA (THUPPA)
BA
BA
BA
BA
BA
THE POLICE ARE MOVING OUT. THEY'RE ONTO US...
WHAT DO WE DO NOW? WE CAN'T...GO UNDER-GROUND, AND MR. CREPSLEY CAN'T TAKE ANOTHER HOUR IN THE SUN!
TWO AND A HALF HOURS TO SUNDOWN ...
THIS SHOULD BE INTEREST-ING...
SFX: JIJI (FIZZ)
uuu (WOOO)
uuuu
uuuu

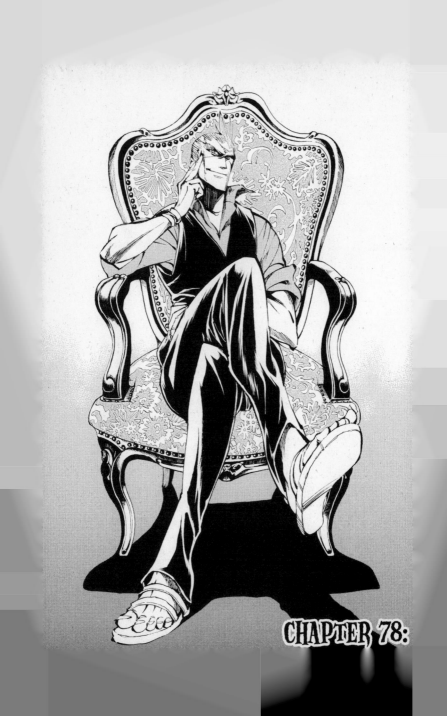

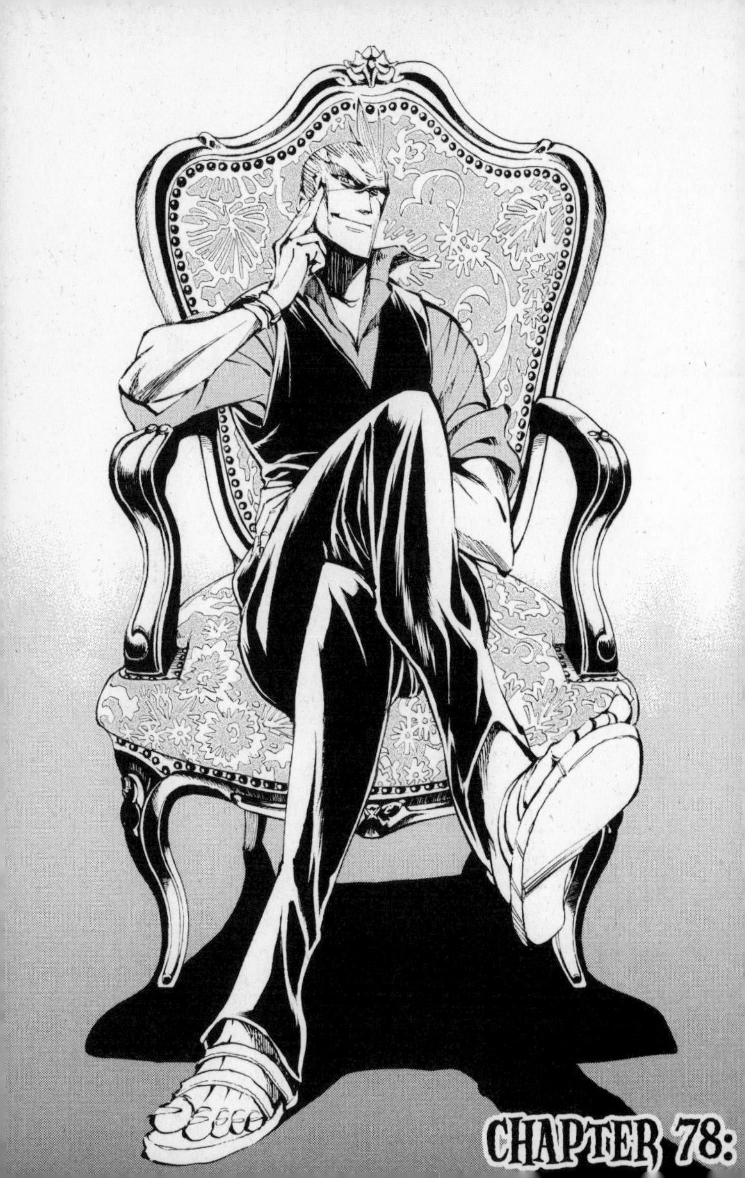
CHAPTER 78:

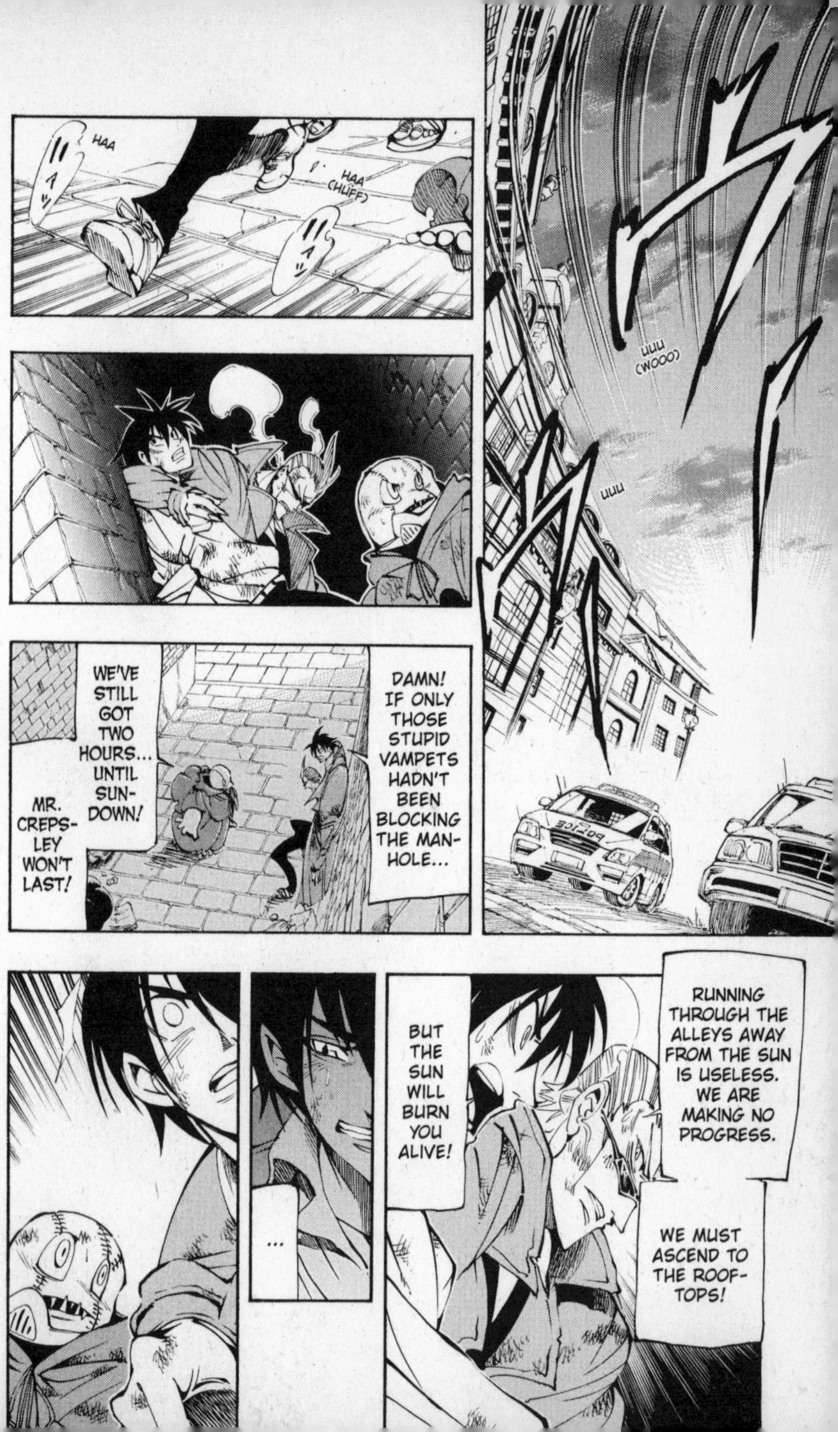
uuu (WOOO)
uuu
HAA
HAA (HUFF)
DAMN! IF ONLY THOSE STUPID VAMPETS HADN'T BEEN BLOCKING THE MAN-HOLE...
WE'VE STILL GOT TWO HOURS... UNTIL SUN-DOWN!
MR. CREPS-LEY WON'T LAST!
RUNNING THROUGH THE ALLEYS AWAY FROM THE SUN IS USELESS. WE ARE MAKING NO PROGRESS.
WE MUST ASCEND TO THE ROOF-TOPS!
BUT THE SUN WILL BURN YOU ALIVE!
...

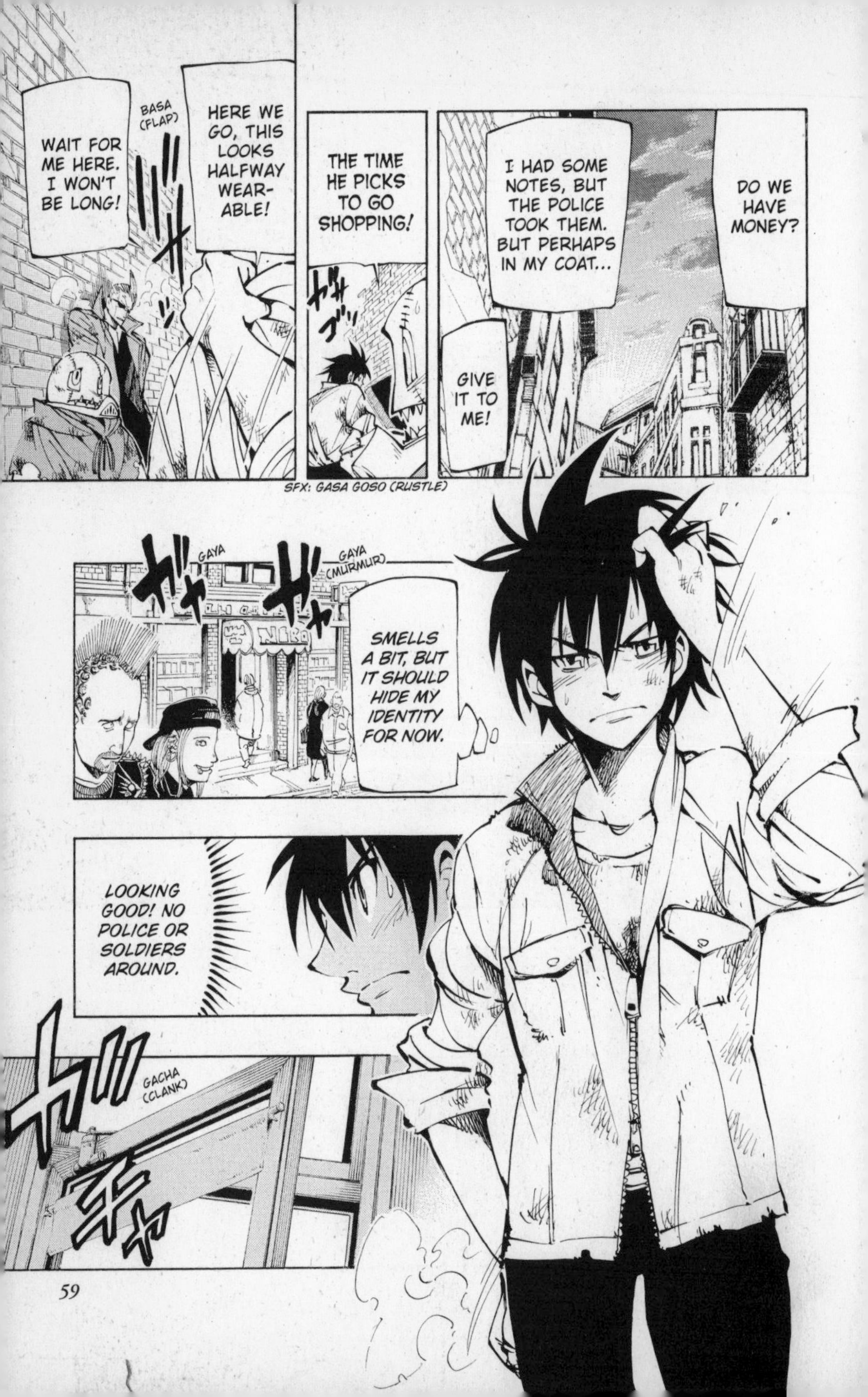
DO WE HAVE MONEY?
I HAD SOME NOTES, BUT THE POLICE TOOK THEM. BUT PERHAPS IN MY COAT...
GIVE IT TO ME!
THE TIME HE PICKS TO GO SHOPPING!
SFX: GASA GOSO (RUSTLE)
HERE WE GO, THIS LOOKS HALFWAY WEARABLE!
BASA (FLAP)
WAIT FOR ME HERE. I WON'T BE LONG!
GAYA
GAYA (MURMUR)
SMELLS A BIT, BUT IT SHOULD HIDE MY IDENTITY FOR NOW.
LOOKING GOOD! NO POLICE OR SOLDIERS AROUND.
GACHA (CLANK)

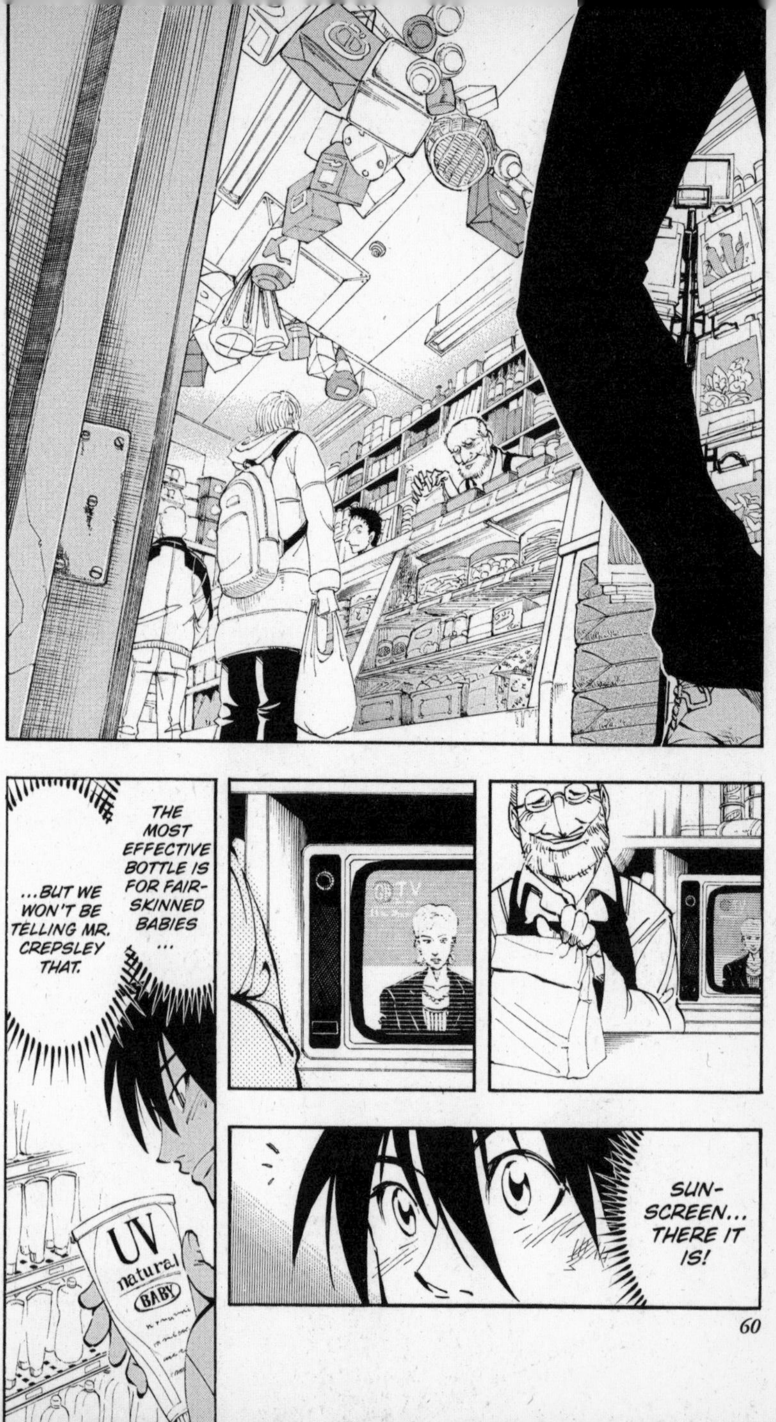
SUN-SCREEN... THERE IT IS!
THE MOST EFFECTIVE BOTTLE IS FOR FAIR-SKINNED BABIES...
...BUT WE WON'T BE TELLING MR. CREPSLEY THAT.
UV
natural
BABY

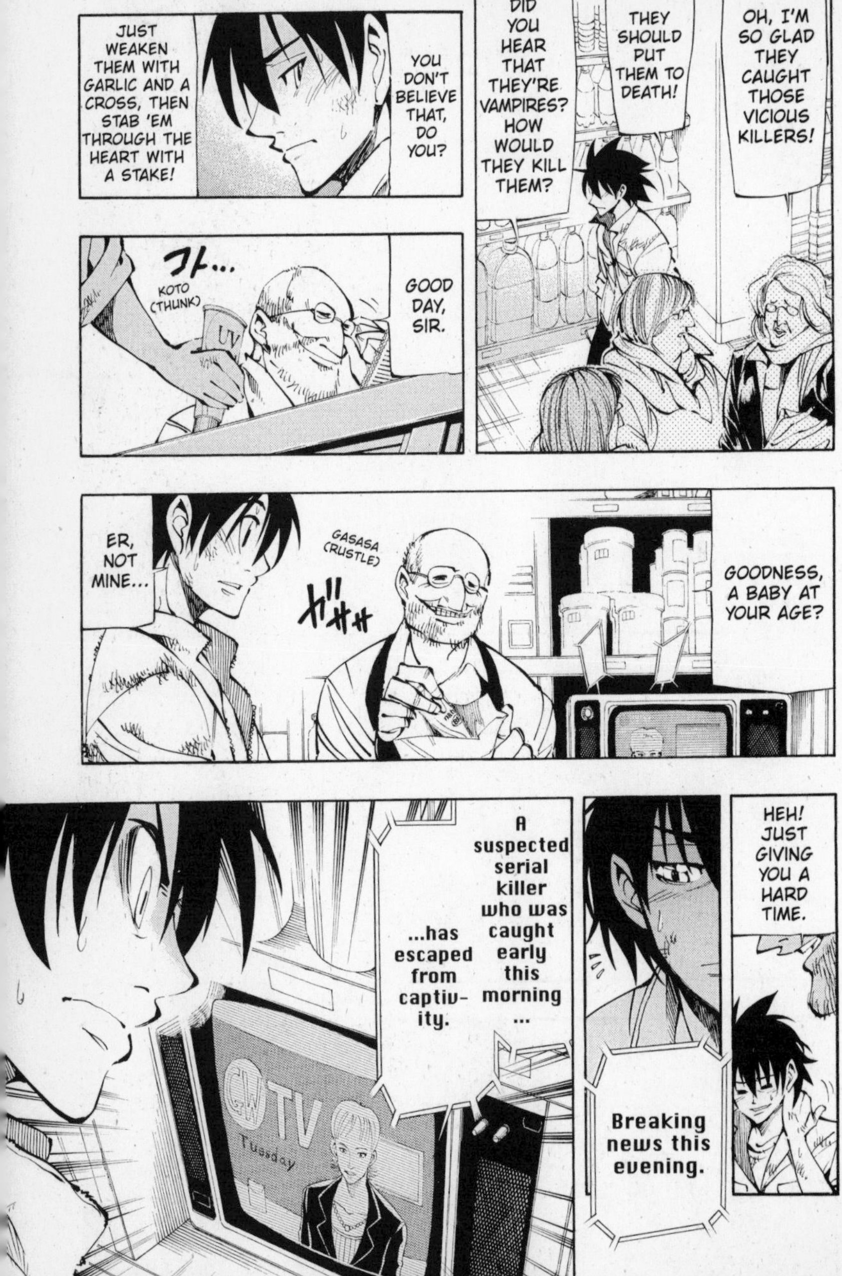
OH, I'M SO GLAD THEY CAUGHT THOSE VICIOUS KILLERS!
THEY SHOULD PUT THEM TO DEATH!
DID YOU HEAR THAT THEY'RE VAMPIRES? HOW WOULD THEY KILL THEM?
YOU DON'T BELIEVE THAT, DO YOU?
JUST WEAKEN THEM WITH GARLIC AND A CROSS, THEN STAB 'EM THROUGH THE HEART WITH A STAKE!
GOOD DAY, SIR.
KOTO (THUNK)
UV
GOODNESS, A BABY AT YOUR AGE?
GASASA (RUSTLE)
ER, NOT MINE...
HEH! JUST GIVING YOU A HARD TIME.
Breaking news this evening.
A suspected serial killer who was caught early this morning...
...has escaped from captivity.
GW TV
Tuesday

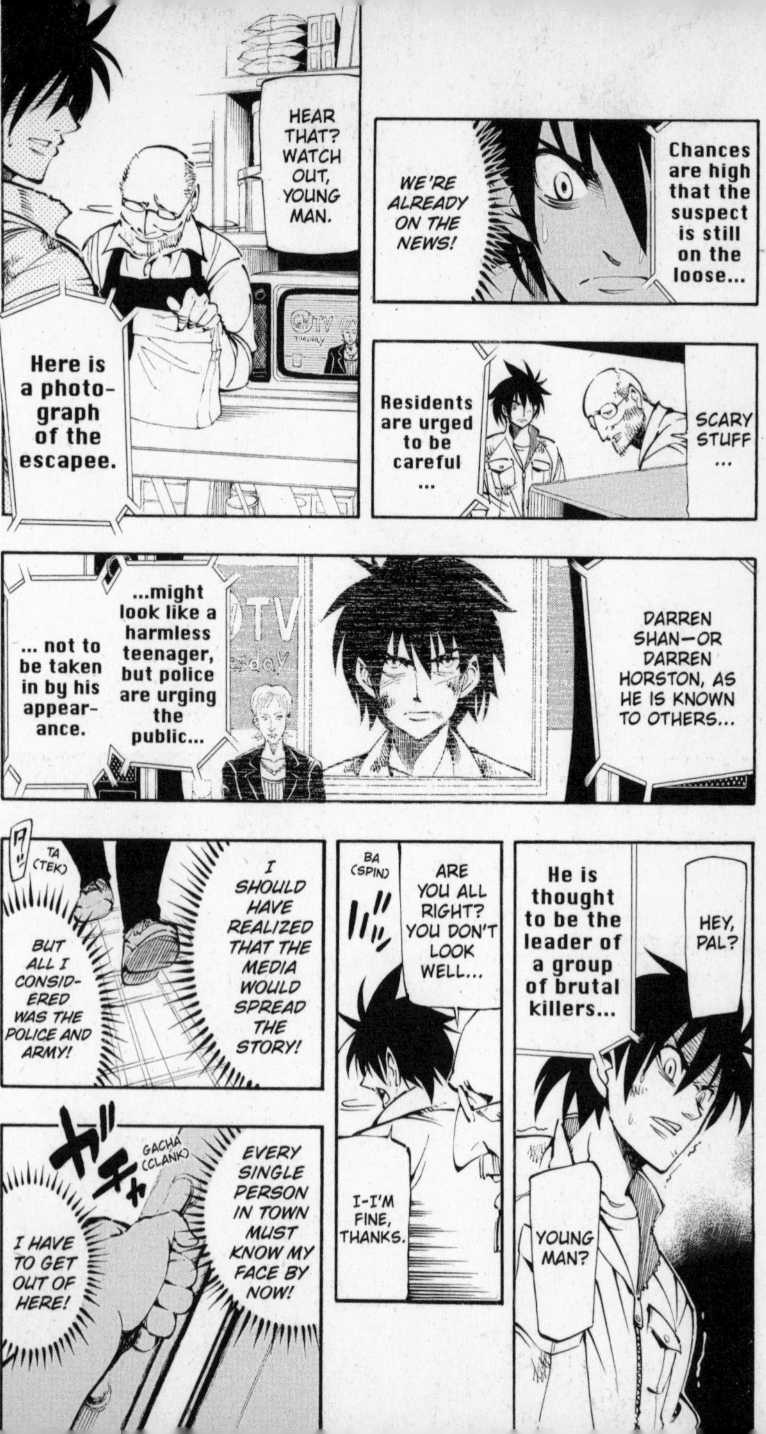
Chances are high that the suspect is still on the loose...
WE'RE ALREADY ON THE NEWS!
SCARY STUFF ...
Residents are urged to be careful ...
HEAR THAT? WATCH OUT, YOUNG MAN.
Here is a photograph of the escapee.
DARREN SHAN—OR DARREN HORSTON, AS HE IS KNOWN TO OTHERS...
...might look like a harmless teenager, but police are urging the public...
... not to be taken in by his appearance.
HEY, PAL?
He is thought to be the leader of a group of brutal killers...
YOUNG MAN?
ARE YOU ALL RIGHT? YOU DON'T LOOK WELL...
BA (SPIN)
I-I'M FINE, THANKS.
I SHOULD HAVE REALIZED THAT THE MEDIA WOULD SPREAD THE STORY!
TA (TEK)
BUT ALL I CONSIDERED WAS THE POLICE AND ARMY!
EVERY SINGLE PERSON IN TOWN MUST KNOW MY FACE BY NOW!
GACHA (CLANK)
I HAVE TO GET OUT OF HERE!

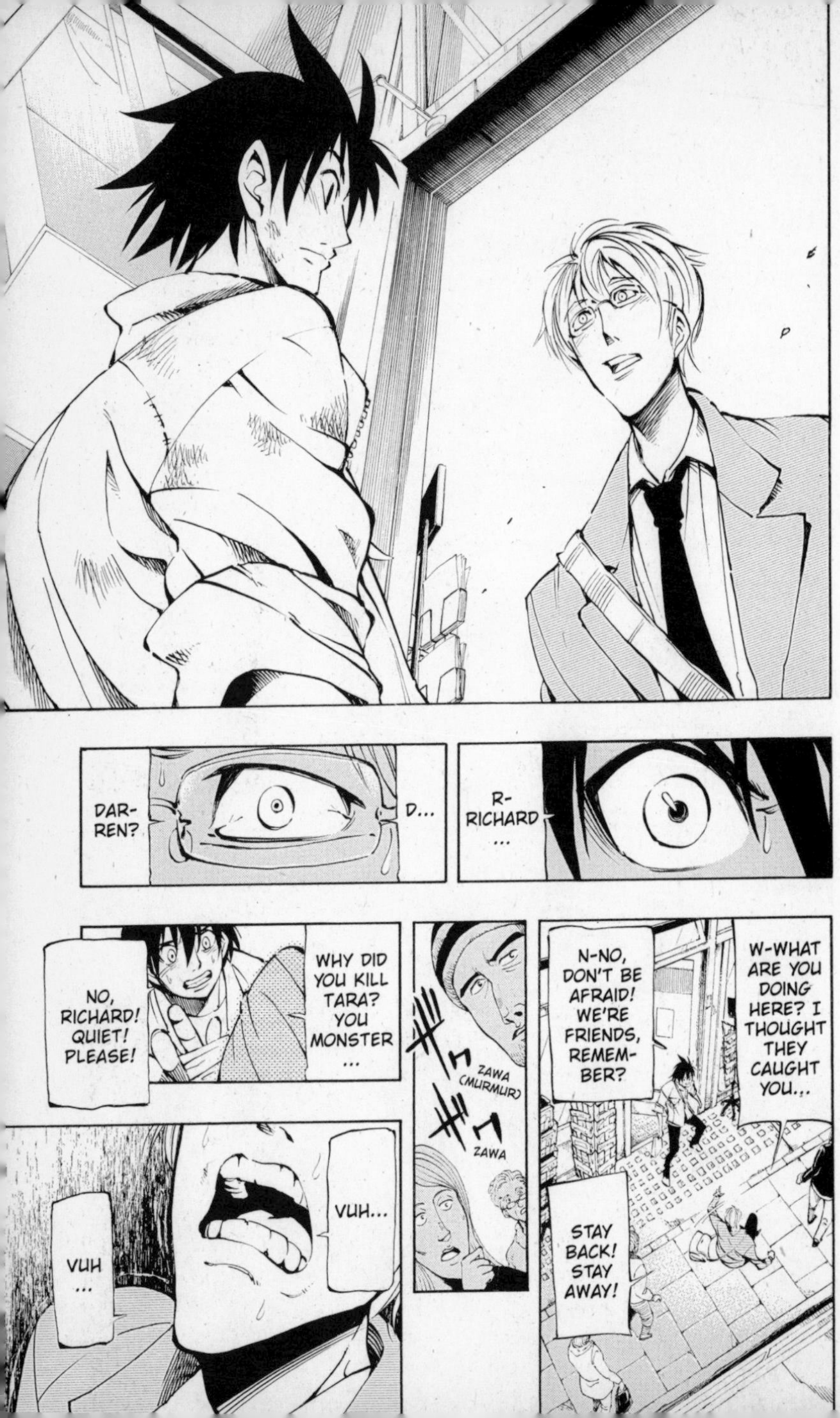
R-
RICHARD
...
D...
DAR-
REN?
W-WHAT ARE YOU DOING HERE? I THOUGHT THEY CAUGHT YOU...
N-NO, DON'T BE AFRAID! WE'RE FRIENDS, REMEMBER?
STAY BACK! STAY AWAY!
ZAWA (MURMUR)
ZAWA
WHY DID YOU KILL TARA? YOU MONSTER ...
NO, RICHARD! QUIET! PLEASE!
VUH...
VUH ...

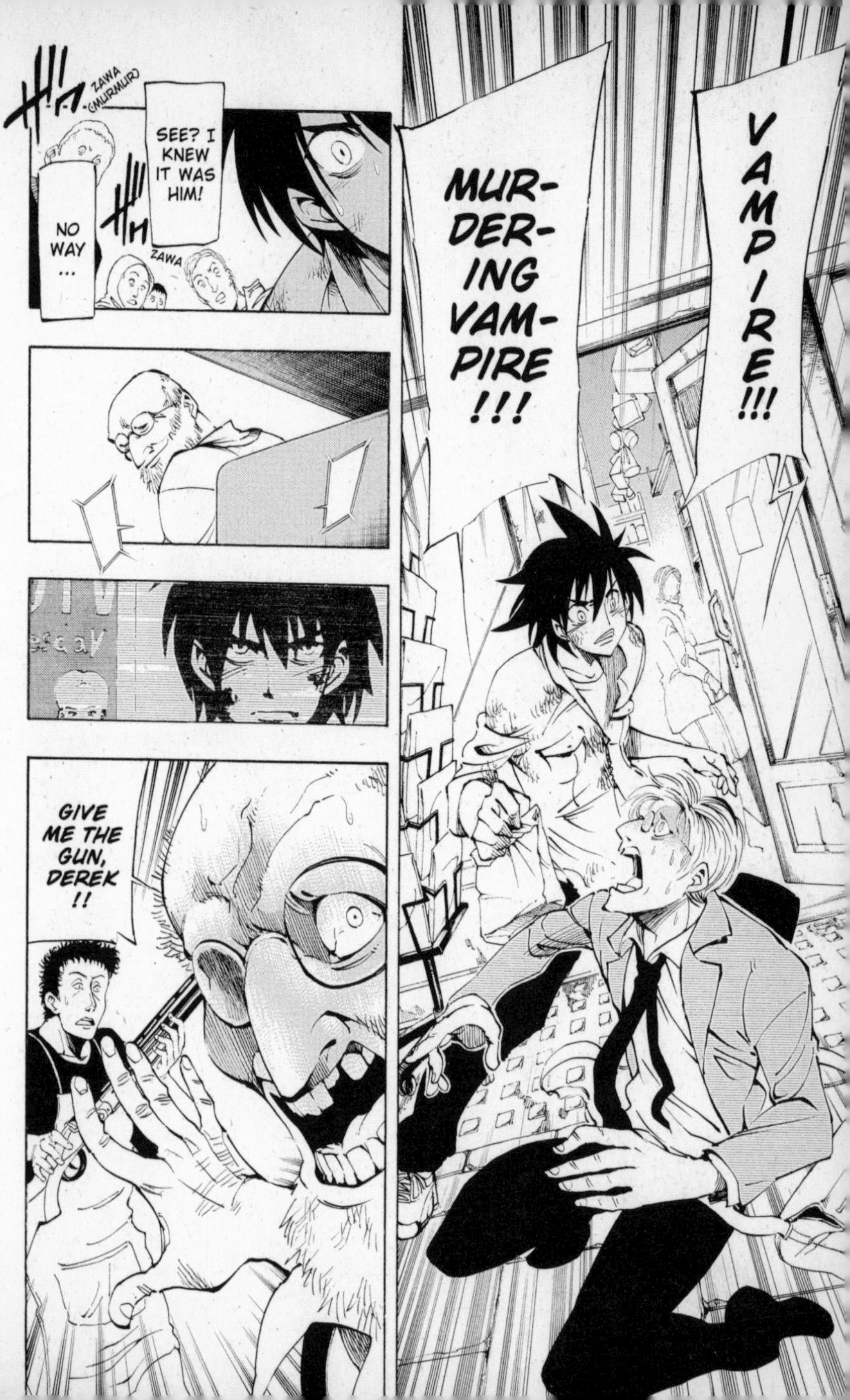
VAMPIRE!!!
MUR-DER-ING VAM-PIRE!!!
ZAWA (MURMUR)
SEE? I KNEW IT WAS HIM!
NO WAY ...
ZAWA
GIVE ME THE GUN, DEREK!!

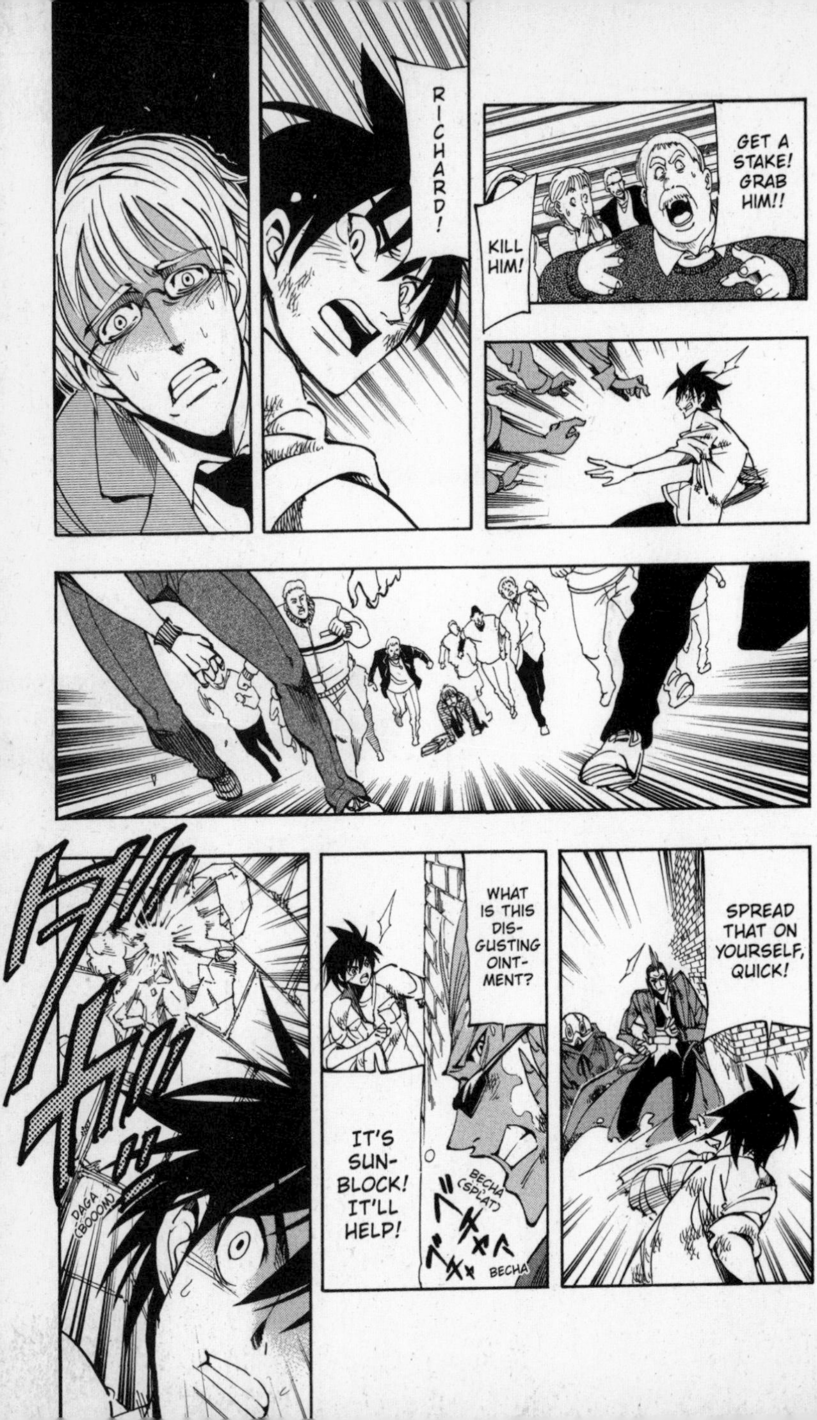
GET A STAKE! GRAB HIM!!
KILL HIM!
RICHARD!
SPREAD THAT ON YOURSELF, QUICK!
WHAT IS THIS DIS-GUSTING OINT-MENT?
BECHA (SPLAT)
BECHA
IT'S SUN-BLOCK! IT'LL HELP!
DAGA (BOOOM)

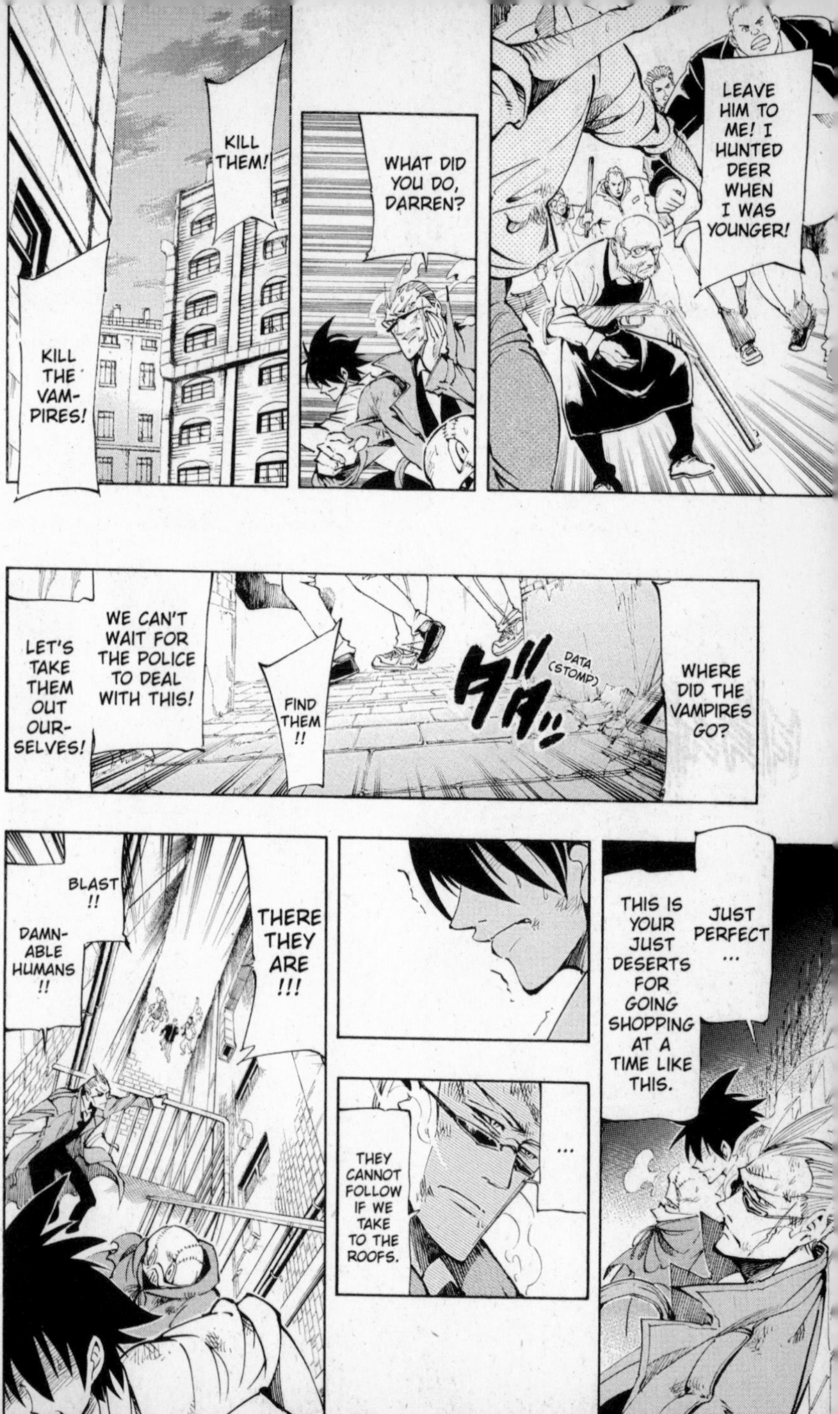
LEAVE HIM TO ME! I HUNTED DEER WHEN I WAS YOUNGER!
WHAT DID YOU DO, DARREN?
KILL THEM!
KILL THE VAMPIRES!
WHERE DID THE VAMPIRES GO?
DATA (STOMP)
FIND THEM !!
WE CAN'T WAIT FOR THE POLICE TO DEAL WITH THIS!
LET'S TAKE THEM OUT OURSELVES!
JUST PERFECT ...
THIS IS YOUR JUST DESERTS FOR GOING SHOPPING AT A TIME LIKE THIS.
...
THEY CANNOT FOLLOW IF WE TAKE TO THE ROOFS.
THERE THEY ARE !!!
BLAST !!
DAMNABLE HUMANS !!

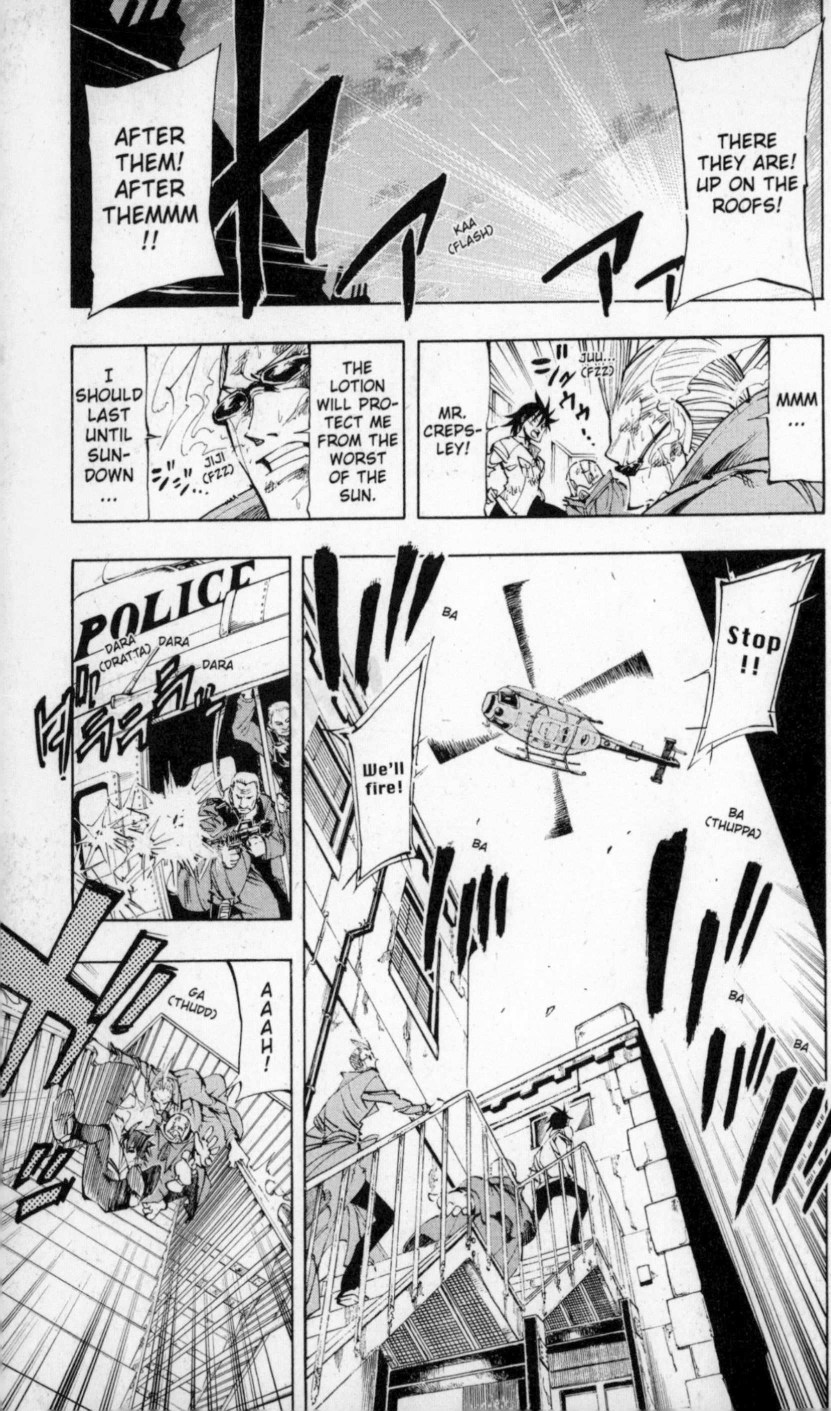
THERE THEY ARE! UP ON THE ROOFS!
KAA (FLASH)
AFTER THEM! AFTER THEMMM!!
MMM...
JUU... (FZZ)
MR. CREPS-LEY!
THE LOTION WILL PRO-TECT ME FROM THE WORST OF THE SUN.
JIJI (FZZ)
I SHOULD LAST UNTIL SUN-DOWN...
Stop!!
BA
We'll fire!
BA (THUPPA)
BA
BA
BA
BA
POLICE
DARA (DRATTA) DARA DARA
GA (THUDD)
AAAAH!

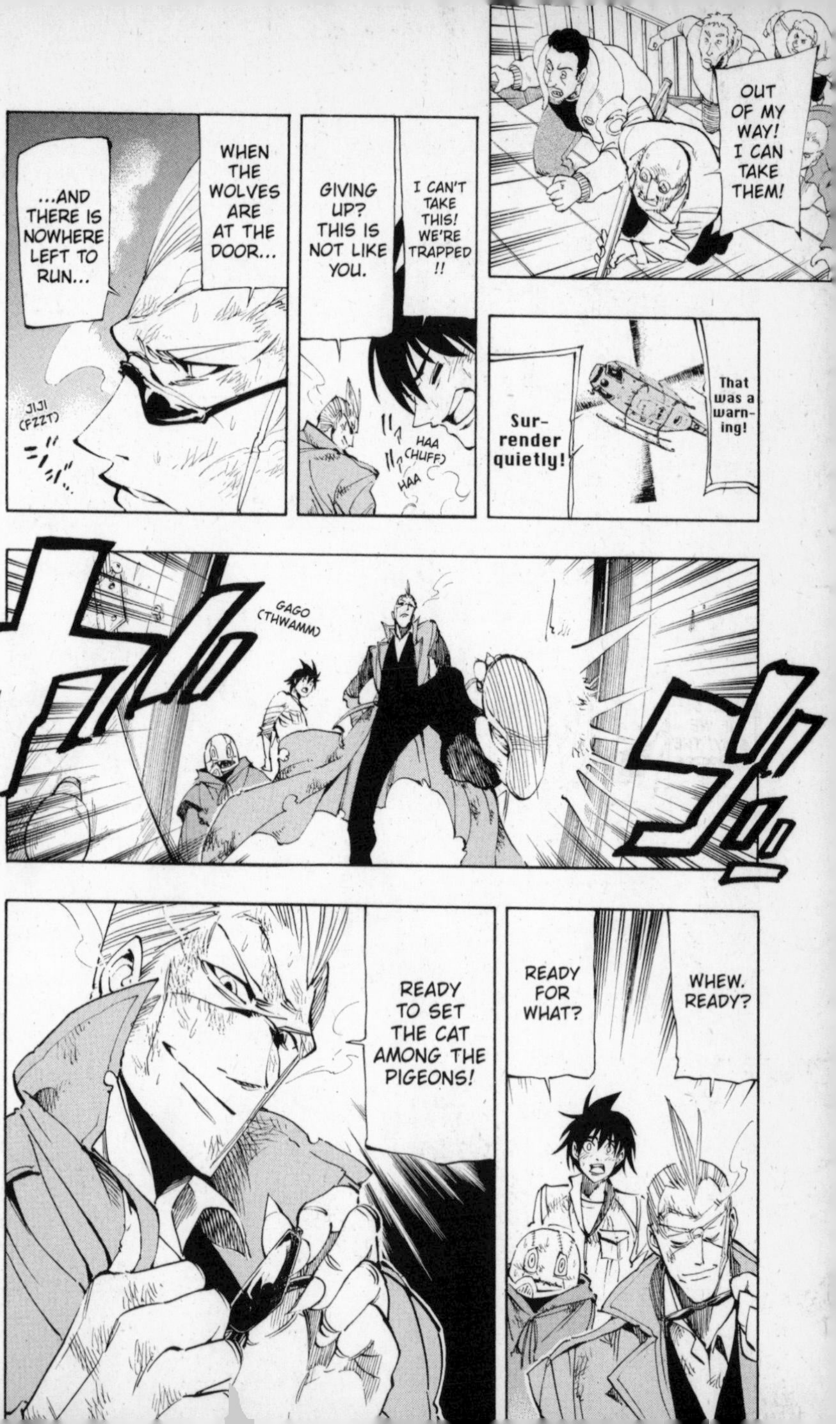
OUT OF MY WAY! I CAN TAKE THEM!
That was a warning!
Surrender quietly!
I CAN'T TAKE THIS! WE'RE TRAPPED!!
GIVING UP? THIS IS NOT LIKE YOU.
HAA (CHUFF) HAA
WHEN THE WOLVES ARE AT THE DOOR...
...AND THERE IS NOWHERE LEFT TO RUN...
JIJI (FZZT)
GAGO (THWAMM)
WHEW. READY?
READY FOR WHAT?
READY TO SET THE CAT AMONG THE PIGEONS!

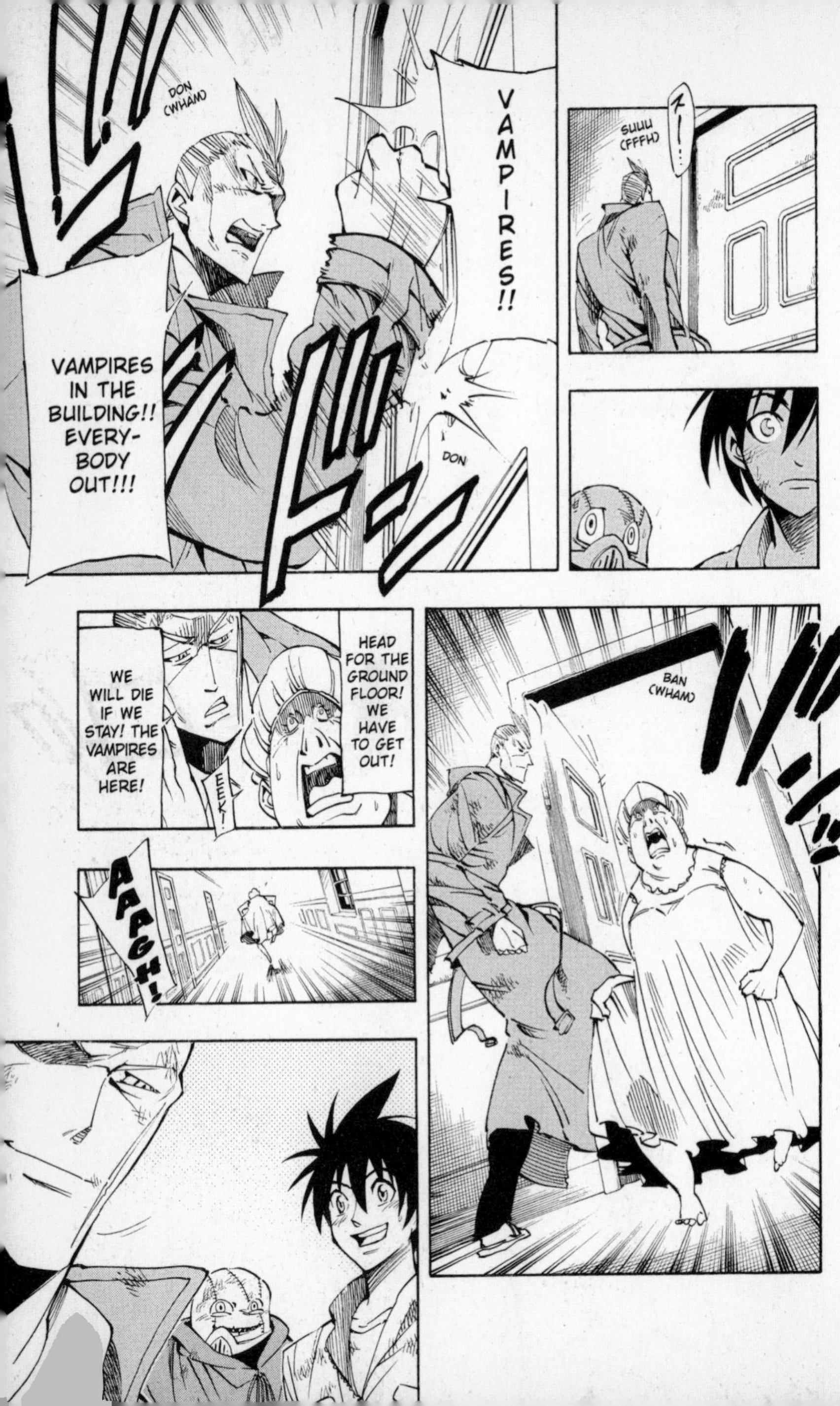
SUUU (FFFH)
スー…
VAMPIRES!!
DON (WHAM)
DON
VAMPIRES IN THE BUILDING!! EVERY-BODY OUT!!!
BAN (WHAM)
HEAD FOR THE GROUND FLOOR! WE HAVE TO GET OUT!
WE WILL DIE IF WE STAY! THE VAMPIRES ARE HERE!
EEK!
AAAGH!

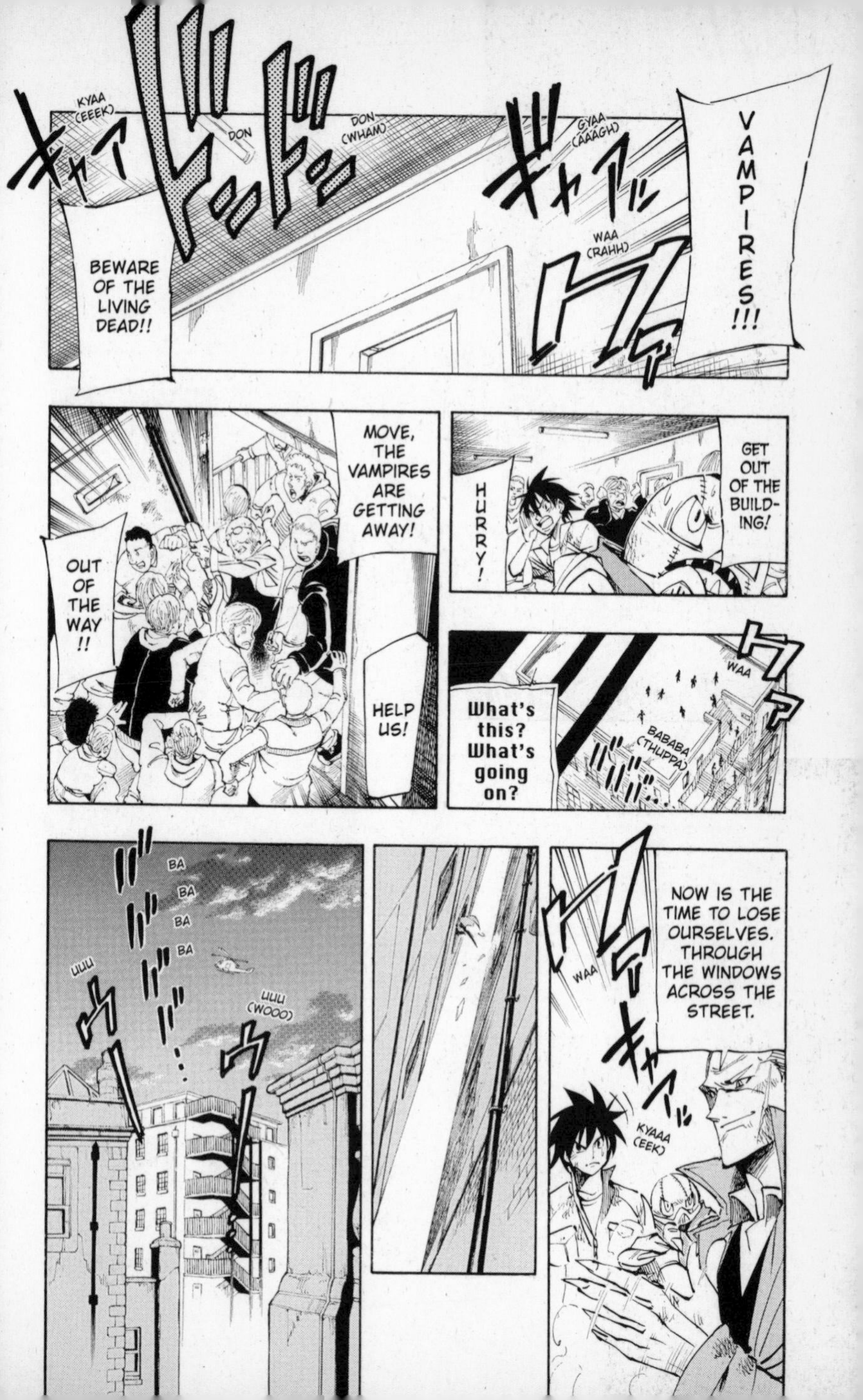
VAMPIRES!!!
GYAA (AAAGH)
WAA (RAHH)
DON (WHAM)
DON
KYAA (EEEK)
BEWARE OF THE LIVING DEAD!!
GET OUT OF THE BUILD-ING!
HURRY!
WAA
BABABA (THUPPA)
What's this? What's going on?
MOVE, THE VAMPIRES ARE GETTING AWAY!
OUT OF THE WAY!!
HELP US!
NOW IS THE TIME TO LOSE OURSELVES. THROUGH THE WINDOWS ACROSS THE STREET.
WAA
KYAAA (EEK)
BA
BA
BA
BA
UUU
UUU (WOOO)

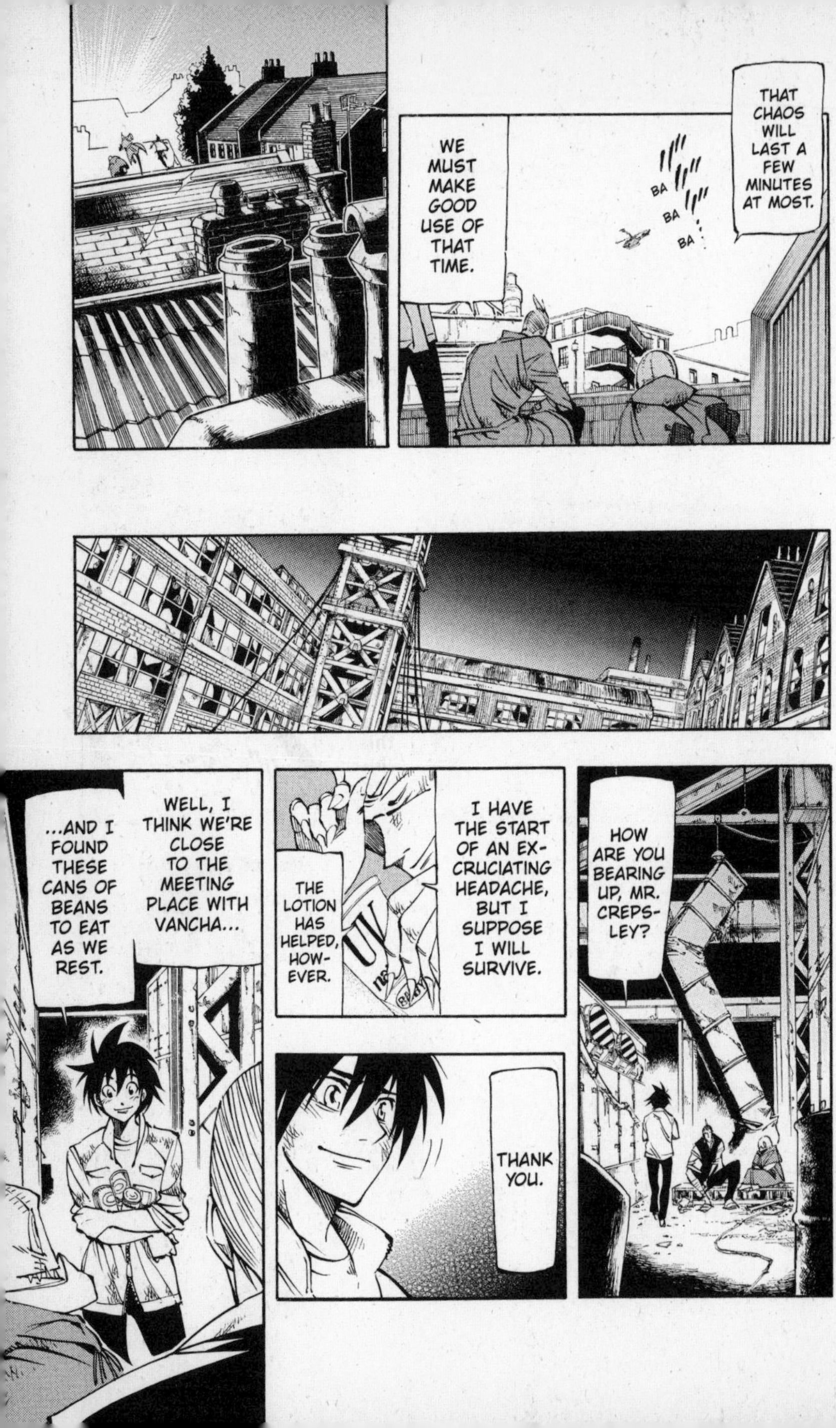
THAT CHAOS WILL LAST A FEW MINUTES AT MOST.
BA BA BA
WE MUST MAKE GOOD USE OF THAT TIME.
HOW ARE YOU BEARING UP, MR. CREPSLEY?
I HAVE THE START OF AN EXCRUCIATING HEADACHE, BUT I SUPPOSE I WILL SURVIVE.
THE LOTION HAS HELPED, HOWEVER.
UV
THANK YOU.
WELL, I THINK WE'RE CLOSE TO THE MEETING PLACE WITH VANCHA...
...AND I FOUND THESE CANS OF BEANS TO EAT AS WE REST.

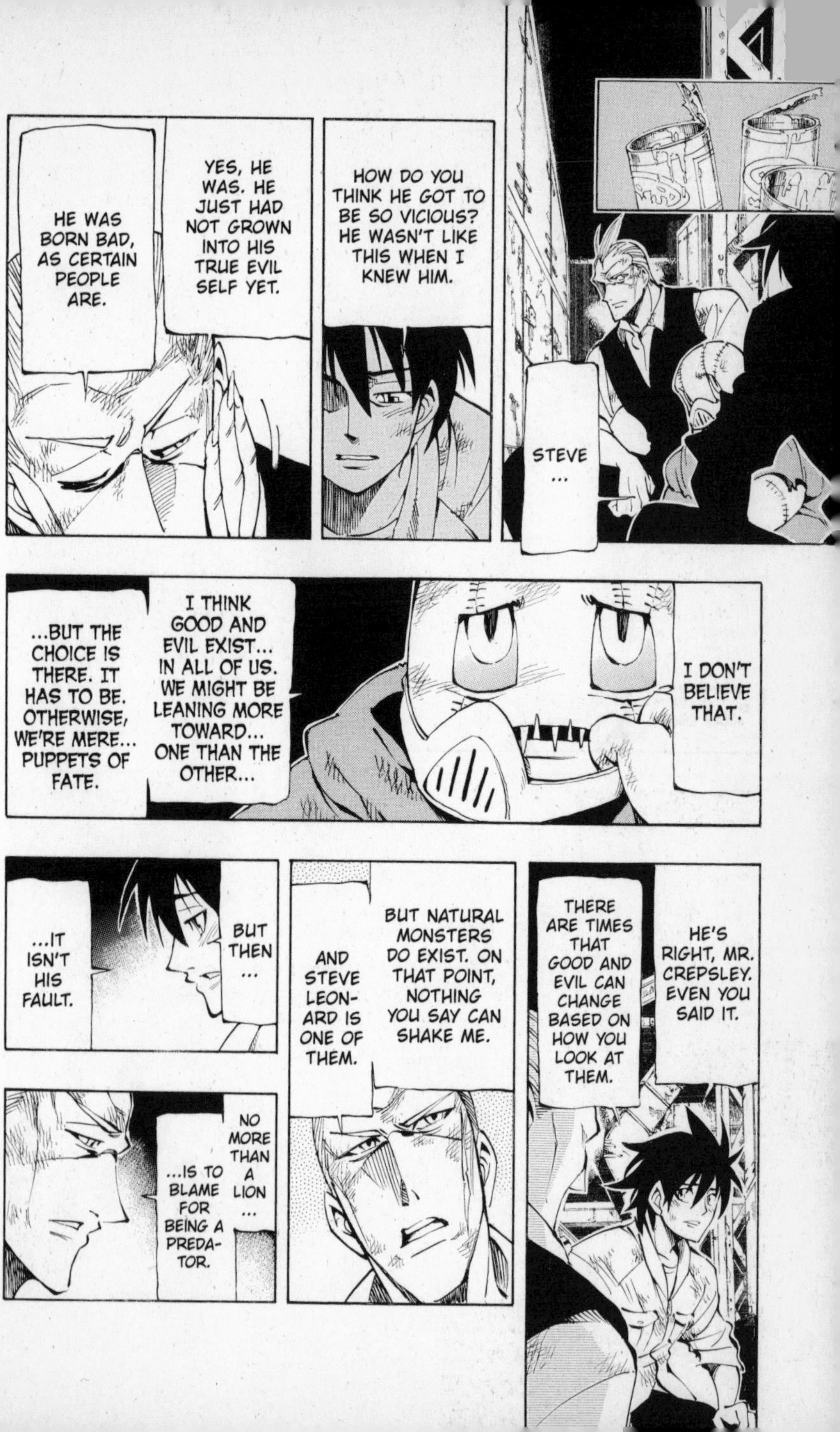
STEVE ...
HOW DO YOU THINK HE GOT TO BE SO VICIOUS? HE WASN'T LIKE THIS WHEN I KNEW HIM.
YES, HE WAS. HE JUST HAD NOT GROWN INTO HIS TRUE EVIL SELF YET.
HE WAS BORN BAD, AS CERTAIN PEOPLE ARE.
I DON'T BELIEVE THAT.
I THINK GOOD AND EVIL EXIST... IN ALL OF US. WE MIGHT BE LEANING MORE TOWARD... ONE THAN THE OTHER...
...BUT THE CHOICE IS THERE. IT HAS TO BE. OTHERWISE, WE'RE MERE... PUPPETS OF FATE.
HE'S RIGHT, MR. CREPSLEY. EVEN YOU SAID IT.
THERE ARE TIMES THAT GOOD AND EVIL CAN CHANGE BASED ON HOW YOU LOOK AT THEM.
BUT NATURAL MONSTERS DO EXIST. ON THAT POINT, NOTHING YOU SAY CAN SHAKE ME.
AND STEVE LEON-ARD IS ONE OF THEM.
BUT THEN ...
...IT ISN'T HIS FAULT.
NO MORE THAN A LION ...
...IS TO BLAME FOR BEING A PREDA-TOR.

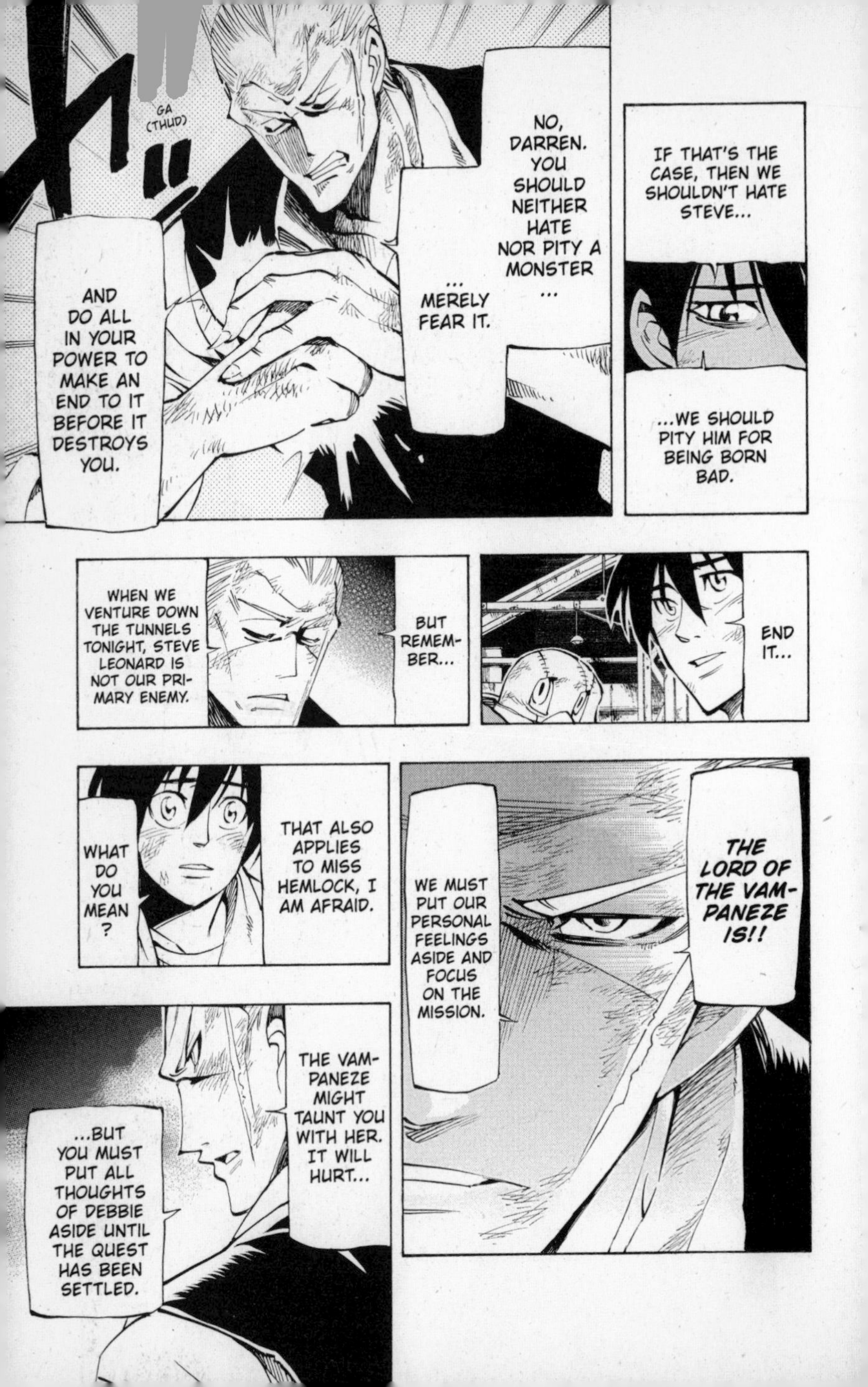
IF THAT'S THE CASE, THEN WE SHOULDN'T HATE STEVE...
...WE SHOULD PITY HIM FOR BEING BORN BAD.
NO, DARREN. YOU SHOULD NEITHER HATE NOR PITY A MONSTER ...
... MERELY FEAR IT.
GA (THUD)
AND DO ALL IN YOUR POWER TO MAKE AN END TO IT BEFORE IT DESTROYS YOU.
END IT...
BUT REMEMBER...
WHEN WE VENTURE DOWN THE TUNNELS TONIGHT, STEVE LEONARD IS NOT OUR PRIMARY ENEMY.
THE LORD OF THE VAMPANEZE IS!!
WE MUST PUT OUR PERSONAL FEELINGS ASIDE AND FOCUS ON THE MISSION.
THAT ALSO APPLIES TO MISS HEMLOCK, I AM AFRAID.
WHAT DO YOU MEAN ?
THE VAMPANEZE MIGHT TAUNT YOU WITH HER. IT WILL HURT...
...BUT YOU MUST PUT ALL THOUGHTS OF DEBBIE ASIDE UNTIL THE QUEST HAS BEEN SETTLED.

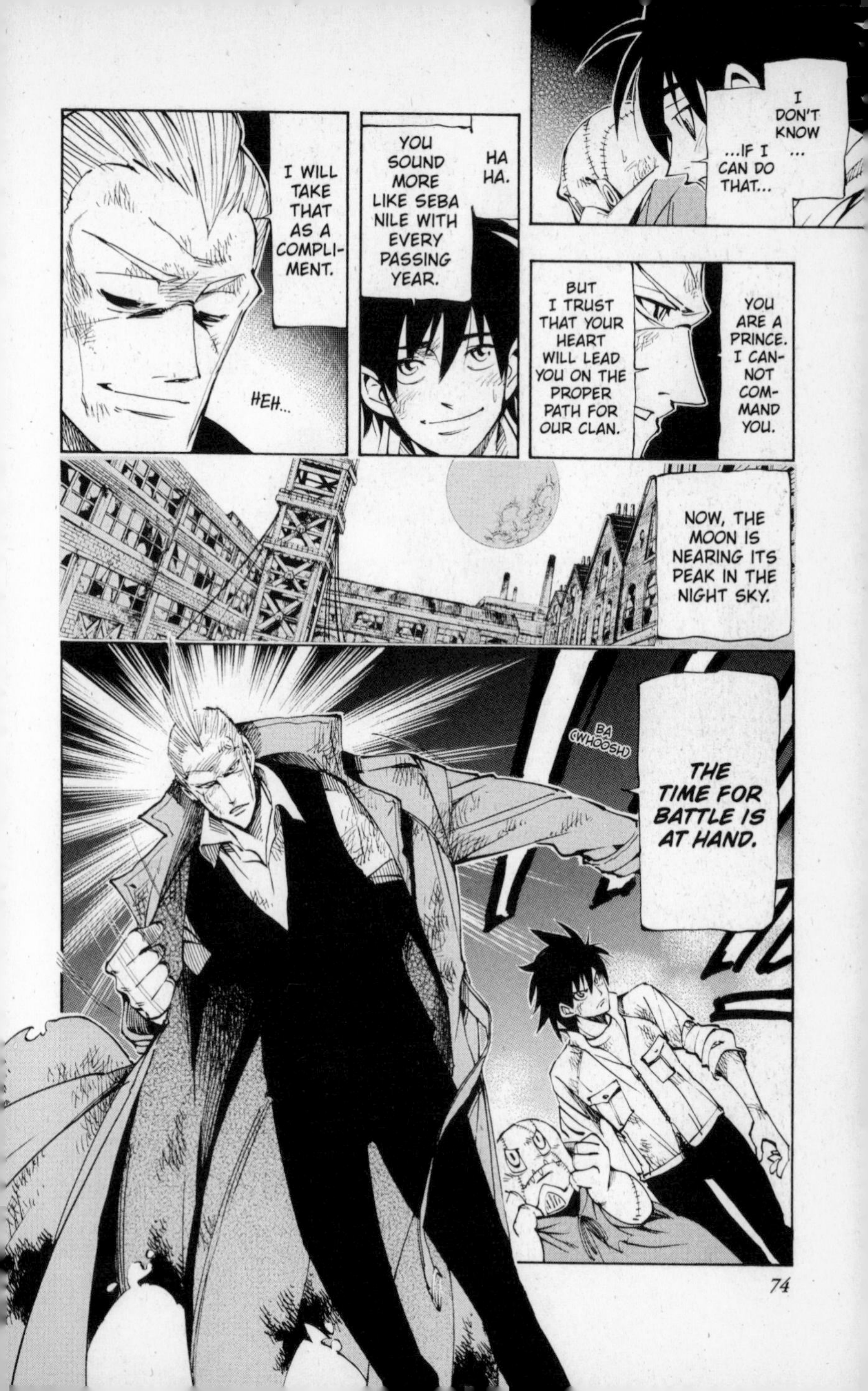
I DON'T KNOW ...
...IF I CAN DO THAT...
YOU ARE A PRINCE. I CANNOT COMMAND YOU.
BUT I TRUST THAT YOUR HEART WILL LEAD YOU ON THE PROPER PATH FOR OUR CLAN.
HA HA.
YOU SOUND MORE LIKE SEBA NILE WITH EVERY PASSING YEAR.
I WILL TAKE THAT AS A COMPLIMENT.
HEH...
NOW, THE MOON IS NEARING ITS PEAK IN THE NIGHT SKY.
THE TIME FOR BATTLE IS AT HAND.
BA (WHOOSH)

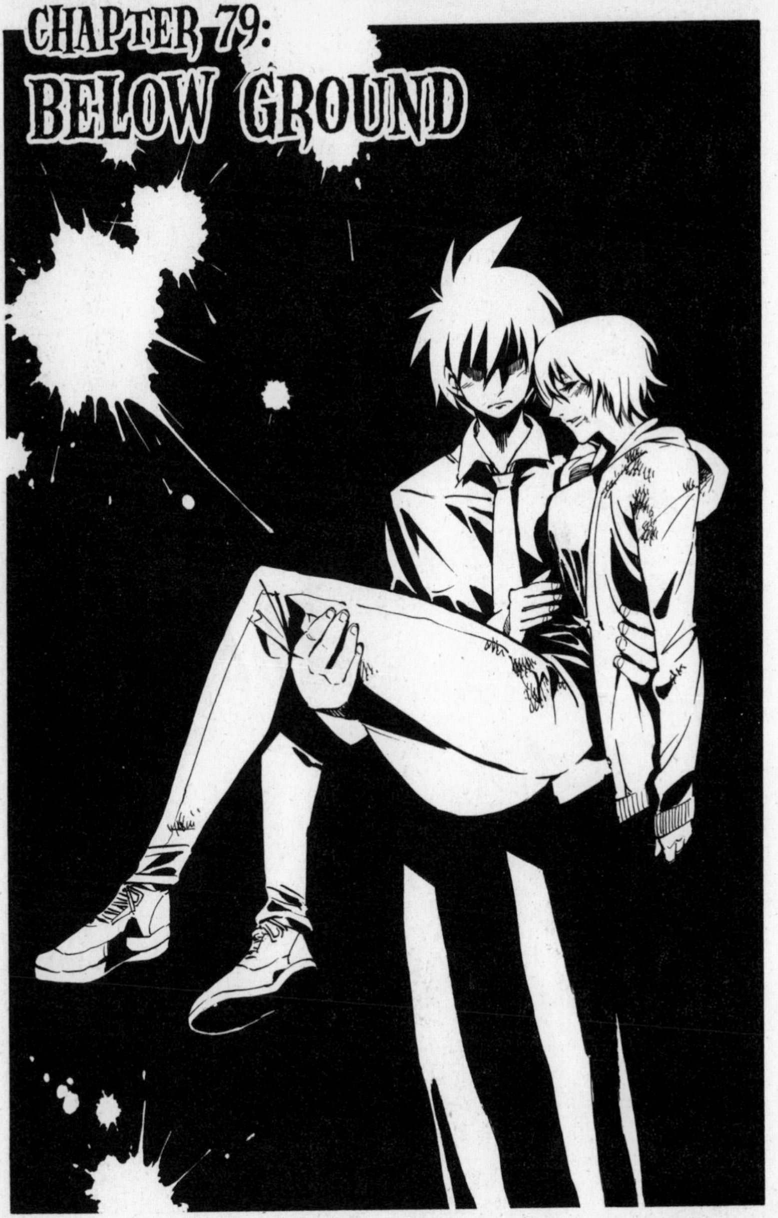
CHAPTER 79:
BELOW GROUND

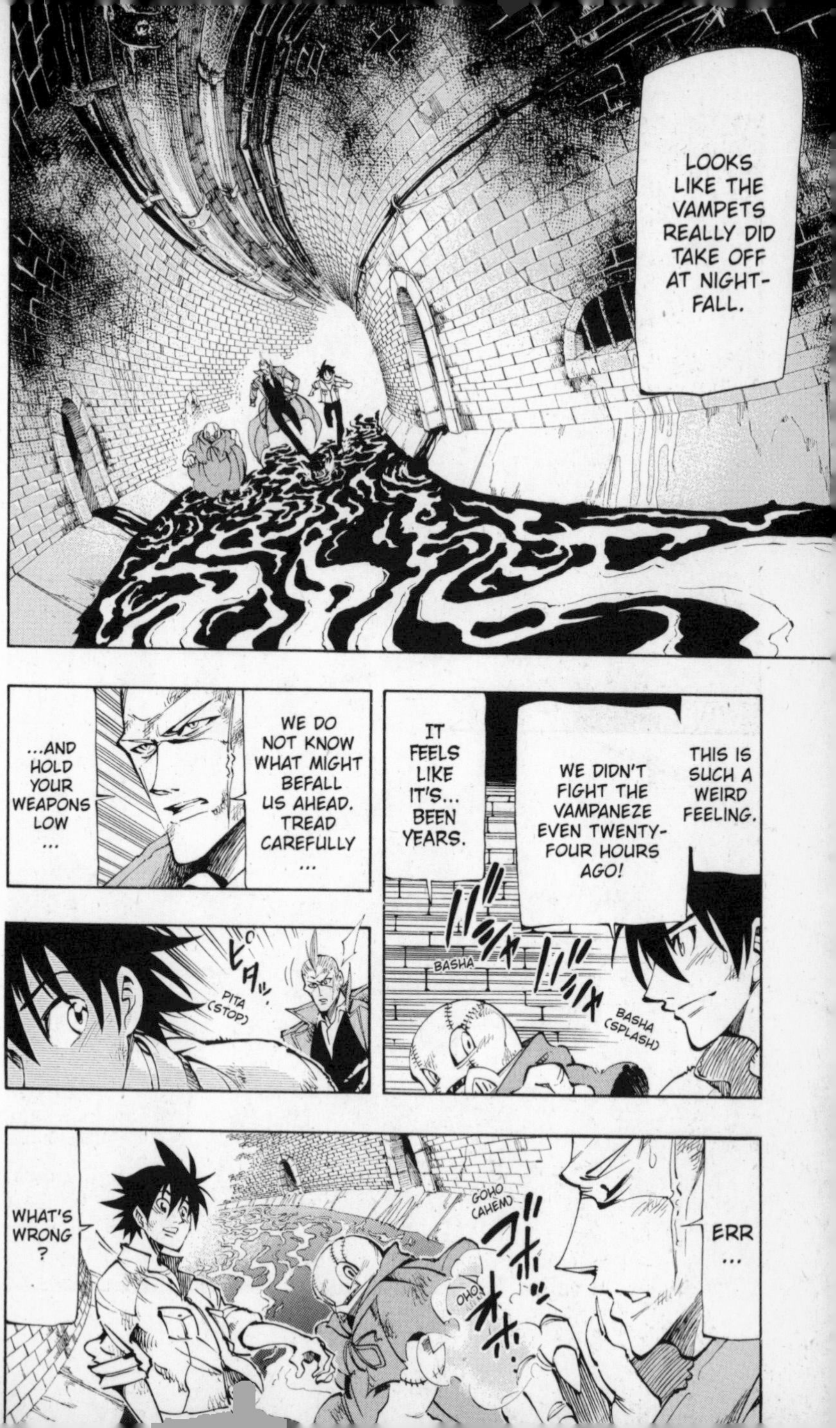

LOOKS LIKE THE VAMPETS REALLY DID TAKE OFF AT NIGHT-FALL.
THIS IS SUCH A WEIRD FEELING.
WE DIDN'T FIGHT THE VAMPANEZE EVEN TWENTY-FOUR HOURS AGO!
IT FEELS LIKE IT'S... BEEN YEARS.
WE DO NOT KNOW WHAT MIGHT BEFALL US AHEAD. TREAD CAREFULLY ...
...AND HOLD YOUR WEAPONS LOW ...
BASHA
BASHA (SPLASH)
PITA (STOP)
ERR ...
GOHO (AHEM)
OHO
WHAT'S WRONG ?

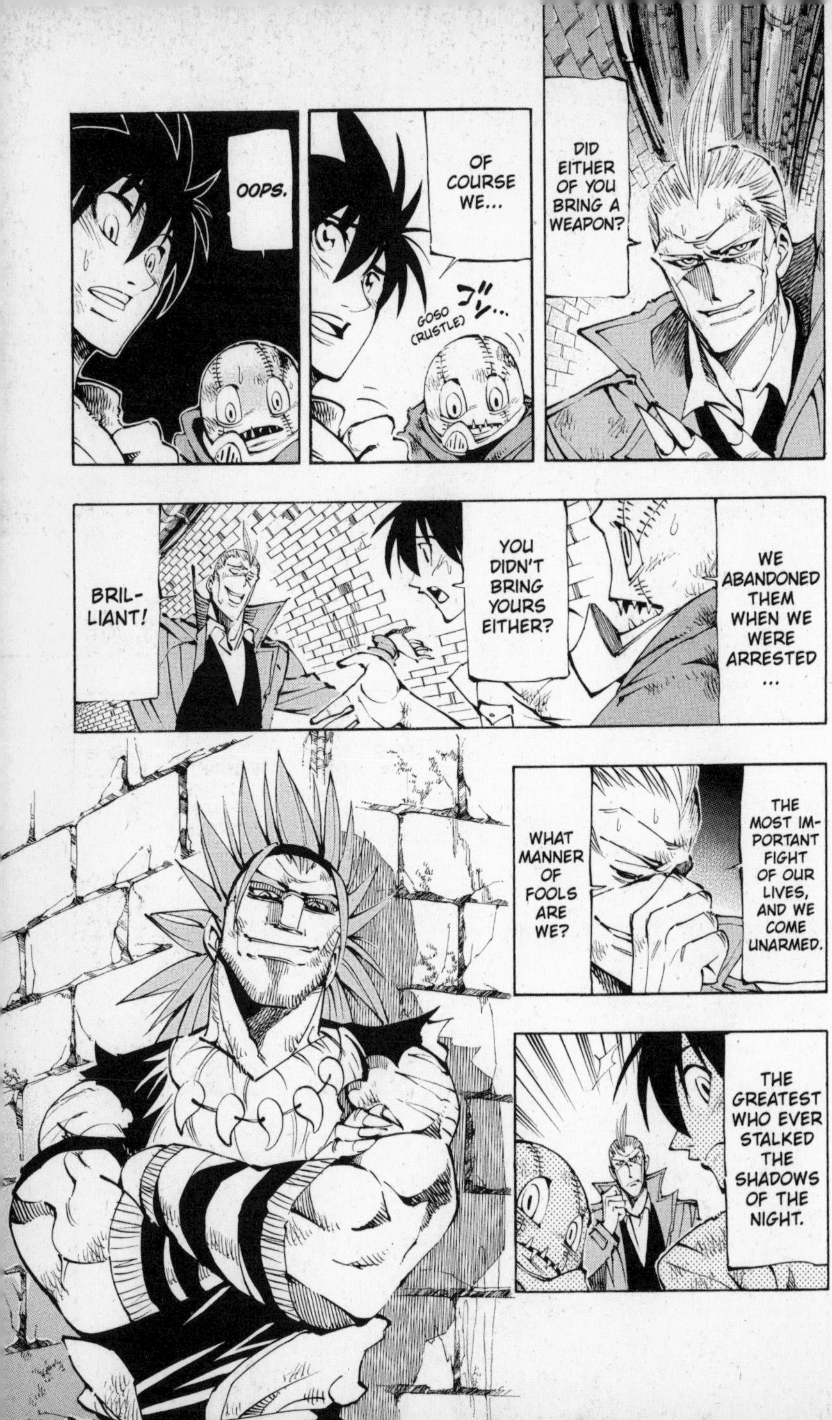
DID EITHER OF YOU BRING A WEAPON?
OF COURSE WE...
ゴソ…
GOSO (RUSTLE)
OOPS.
WE ABANDONED THEM WHEN WE WERE ARRESTED ...
YOU DIDN'T BRING YOURS EITHER?
BRIL-LIANT!
THE MOST IM-PORTANT FIGHT OF OUR LIVES, AND WE COME UNARMED.
WHAT MANNER OF FOOLS ARE WE?
THE GREATEST WHO EVER STALKED THE SHADOWS OF THE NIGHT.

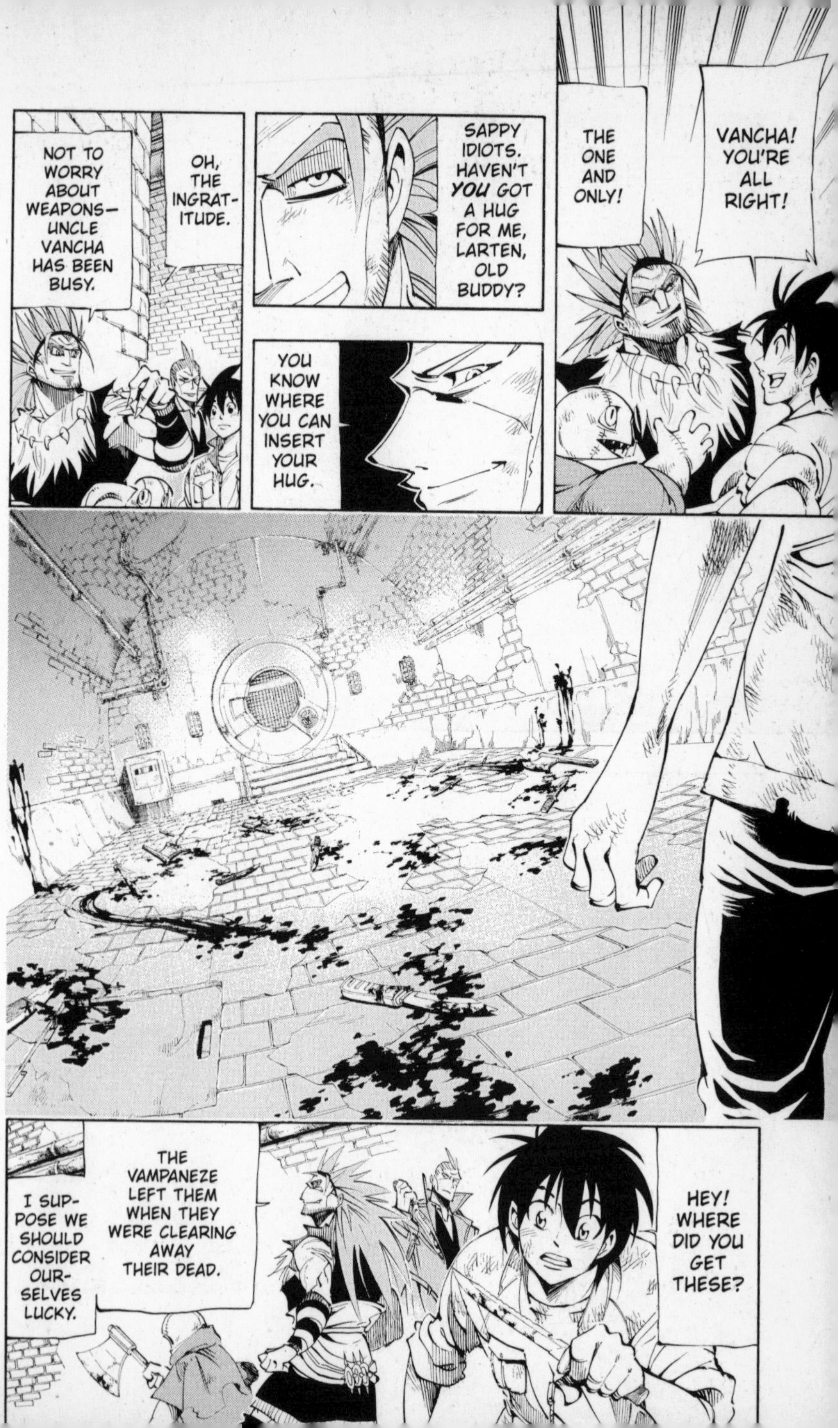
VANCHA! YOU'RE ALL RIGHT!
THE ONE AND ONLY!
SAPPY IDIOTS. HAVEN'T *YOU* GOT A HUG FOR ME, LARTEN, OLD BUDDY?
YOU KNOW WHERE YOU CAN INSERT YOUR HUG.
OH, THE INGRAT-ITUDE.
NOT TO WORRY ABOUT WEAPONS— UNCLE VANCHA HAS BEEN BUSY.
HEY! WHERE DID YOU GET THESE?
THE VAMPANEZE LEFT THEM WHEN THEY WERE CLEARING AWAY THEIR DEAD.
I SUP-POSE WE SHOULD CONSIDER OUR-SELVES LUCKY.

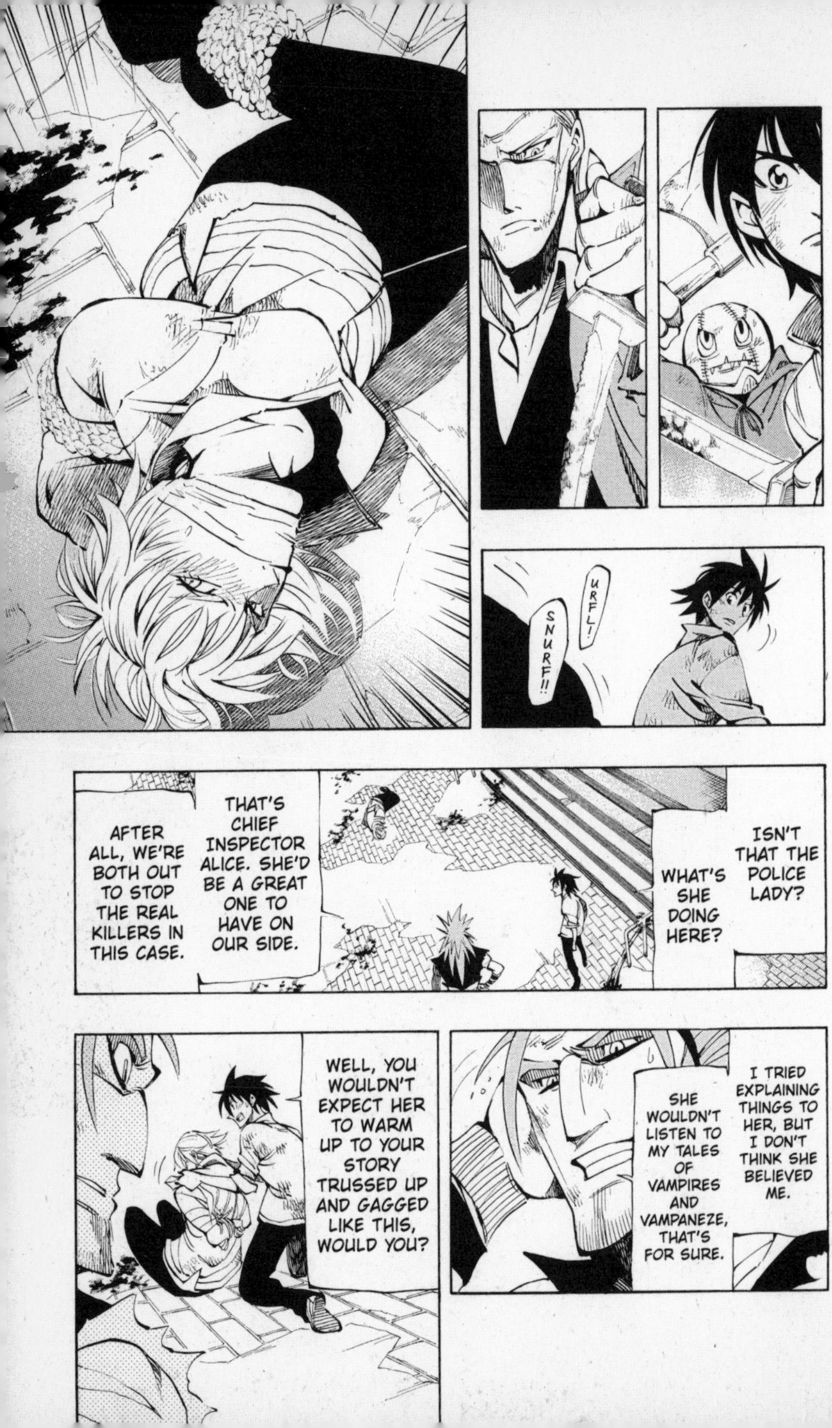
URFL!
SNURF!!
ISN'T THAT THE POLICE LADY?
WHAT'S SHE DOING HERE?
THAT'S CHIEF INSPECTOR ALICE. SHE'D BE A GREAT ONE TO HAVE ON OUR SIDE.
AFTER ALL, WE'RE BOTH OUT TO STOP THE REAL KILLERS IN THIS CASE.
I TRIED EXPLAINING THINGS TO HER, BUT I DON'T THINK SHE BELIEVED ME.
SHE WOULDN'T LISTEN TO MY TALES OF VAMPIRES AND VAMPANEZE, THAT'S FOR SURE.
WELL, YOU WOULDN'T EXPECT HER TO WARM UP TO YOUR STORY TRUSSED UP AND GAGGED LIKE THIS, WOULD YOU?

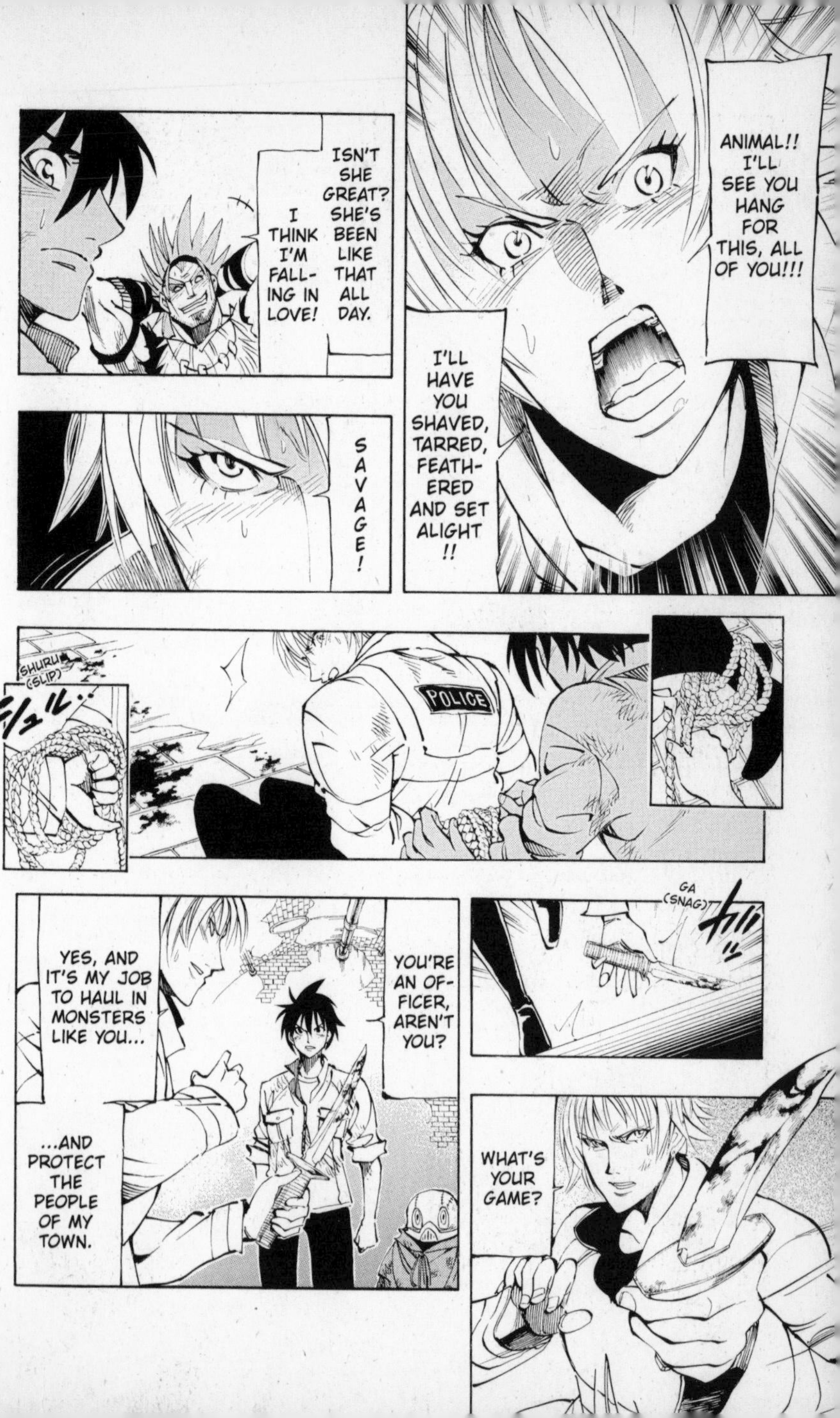
ANIMAL!! I'LL SEE YOU HANG FOR THIS, ALL OF YOU!!!
I'LL HAVE YOU SHAVED, TARRED, FEATH-ERED AND SET ALIGHT !!
ISN'T SHE GREAT? SHE'S BEEN LIKE THAT ALL DAY.
I THINK I'M FALL-ING IN LOVE!
SAVAGE!
POLICE
SHURU (SLIP)
GA (SNAG)
WHAT'S YOUR GAME?
YOU'RE AN OF-FICER, AREN'T YOU?
YES, AND IT'S MY JOB TO HAUL IN MONSTERS LIKE YOU...
...AND PROTECT THE PEOPLE OF MY TOWN.

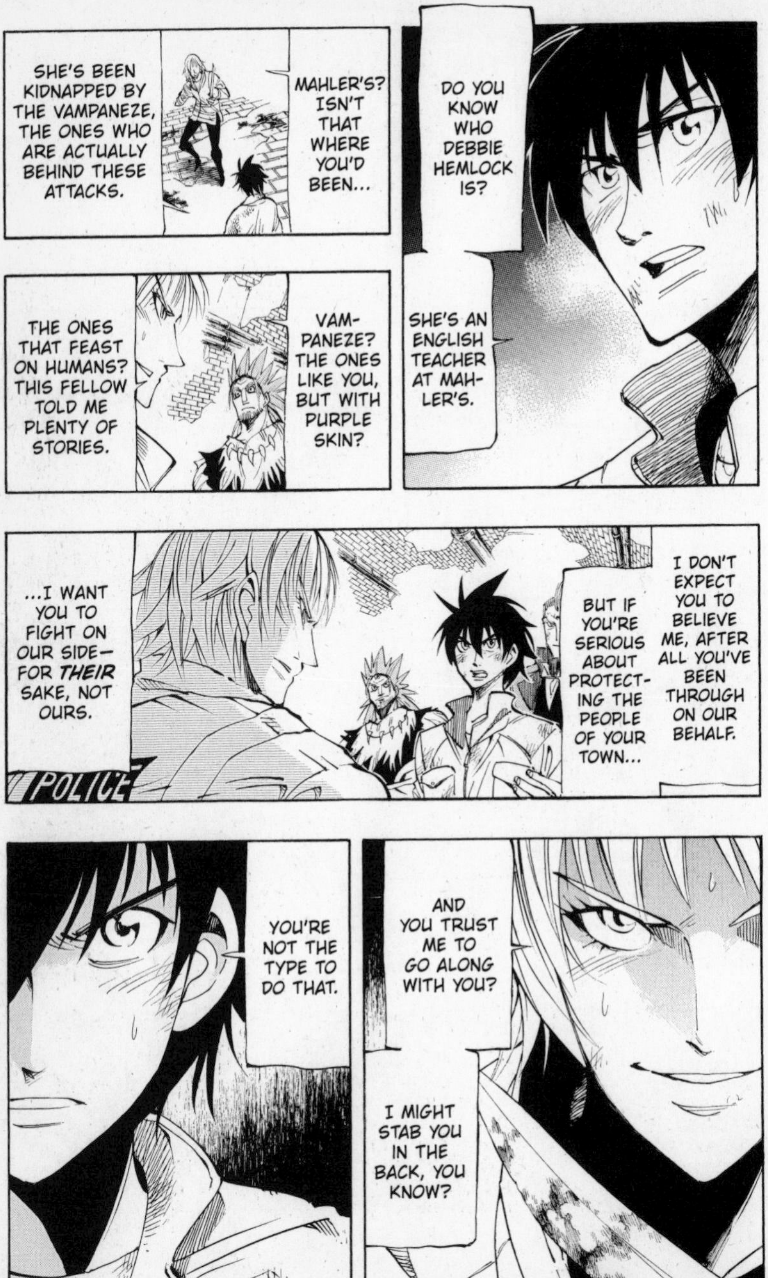
DO YOU KNOW WHO DEBBIE HEMLOCK IS?
SHE'S AN ENGLISH TEACHER AT MAHLER'S.
MAHLER'S? ISN'T THAT WHERE YOU'D BEEN...
SHE'S BEEN KIDNAPPED BY THE VAMPANEZE, THE ONES WHO ARE ACTUALLY BEHIND THESE ATTACKS.
VAMPANEZE? THE ONES LIKE YOU, BUT WITH PURPLE SKIN?
THE ONES THAT FEAST ON HUMANS? THIS FELLOW TOLD ME PLENTY OF STORIES.
I DON'T EXPECT YOU TO BELIEVE ME, AFTER ALL YOU'VE BEEN THROUGH ON OUR BEHALF.
BUT IF YOU'RE SERIOUS ABOUT PROTECTING THE PEOPLE OF YOUR TOWN...
...I WANT YOU TO FIGHT ON OUR SIDE—FOR *THEIR* SAKE, NOT OURS.
POLICE
AND YOU TRUST ME TO GO ALONG WITH YOU?
I MIGHT STAB YOU IN THE BACK, YOU KNOW?
YOU'RE NOT THE TYPE TO DO THAT.

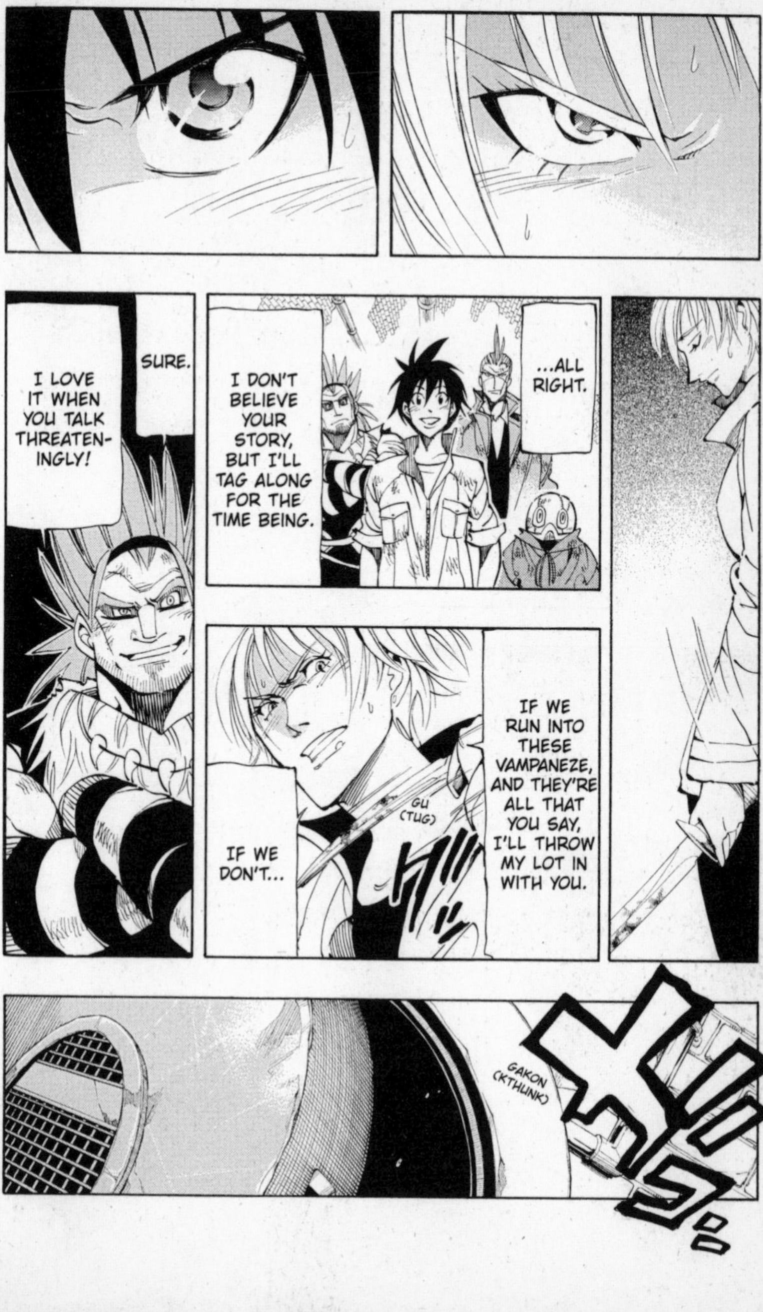
...ALL RIGHT.
I DON'T BELIEVE YOUR STORY, BUT I'LL TAG ALONG FOR THE TIME BEING.
IF WE RUN INTO THESE VAMPANEZE, AND THEY'RE ALL THAT YOU SAY, I'LL THROW MY LOT IN WITH YOU.
GU (TUG)
IF WE DON'T...
SURE.
I LOVE IT WHEN YOU TALK THREATEN-INGLY!
GAKON (KTHUNK)

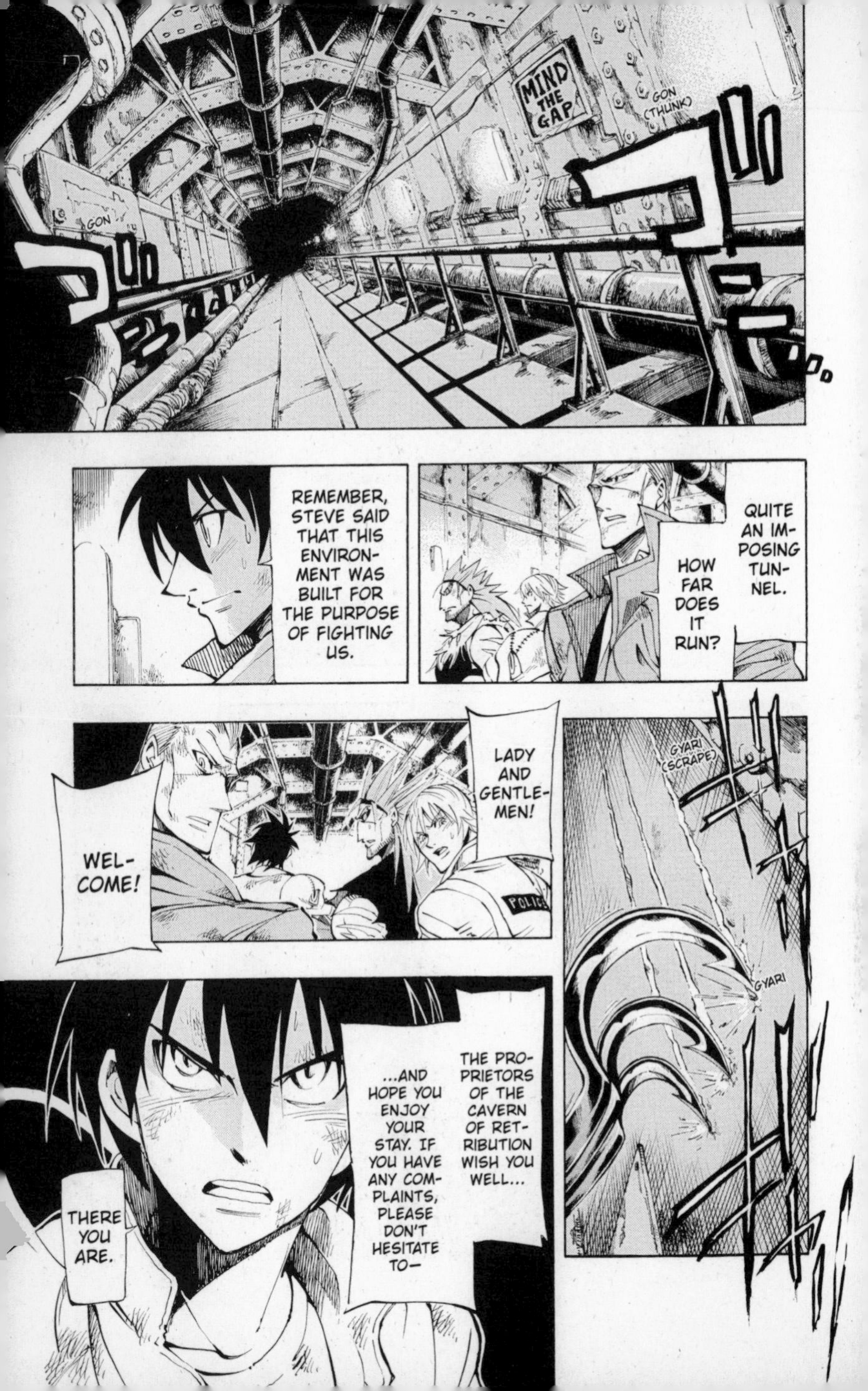
MIND THE GAP
GON (THUNK)
GON
QUITE AN IMPOSING TUNNEL.
HOW FAR DOES IT RUN?
REMEMBER, STEVE SAID THAT THIS ENVIRONMENT WAS BUILT FOR THE PURPOSE OF FIGHTING US.
GYARI (SCRAPE)
GYARI
LADY AND GENTLEMEN!
WELCOME!
THE PROPRIETORS OF THE CAVERN OF RETRIBUTION WISH YOU WELL...
...AND HOPE YOU ENJOY YOUR STAY. IF YOU HAVE ANY COMPLAINTS, PLEASE DON'T HESITATE TO—
THERE YOU ARE.

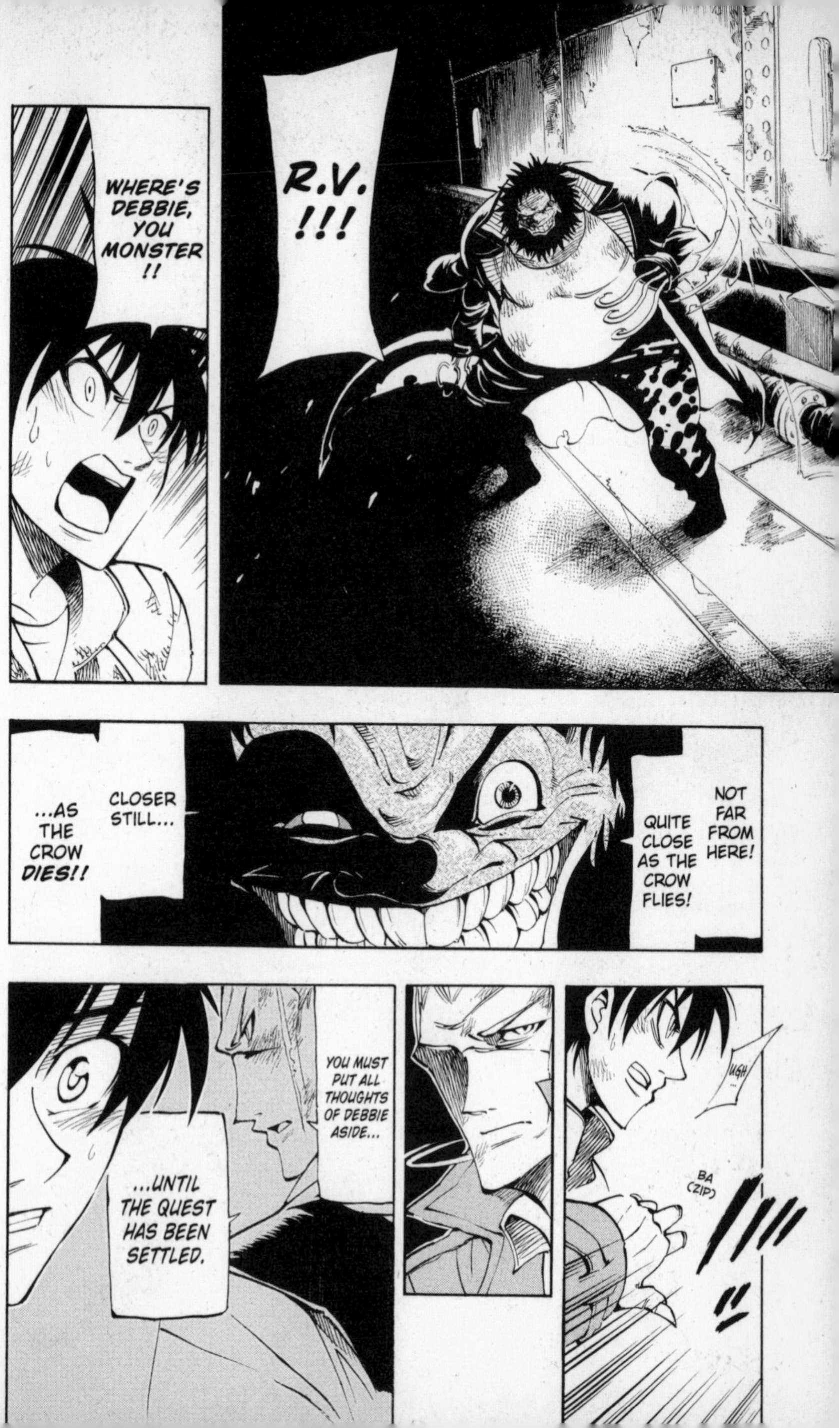
R.V. !!!
WHERE'S DEBBIE, YOU MONSTER !!
NOT FAR FROM HERE!
QUITE CLOSE AS THE CROW FLIES!
CLOSER STILL...
...AS THE CROW DIES!!
UGH
BA (ZIP)
YOU MUST PUT ALL THOUGHTS OF DEBBIE ASIDE...
...UNTIL THE QUEST HAS BEEN SETTLED.

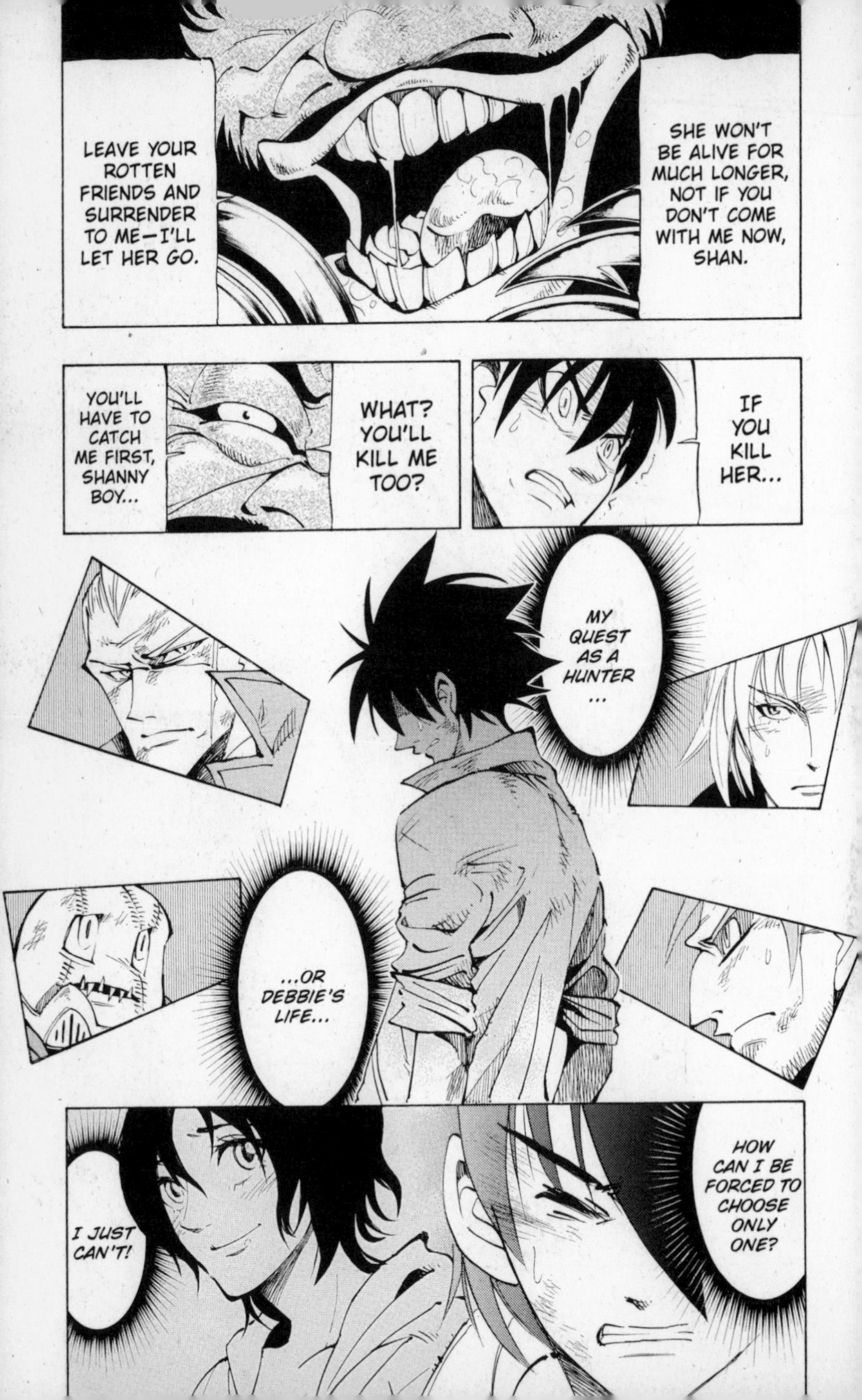
SHE WON'T BE ALIVE FOR MUCH LONGER, NOT IF YOU DON'T COME WITH ME NOW, SHAN.
LEAVE YOUR ROTTEN FRIENDS AND SURRENDER TO ME—I'LL LET HER GO.
IF YOU KILL HER...
WHAT? YOU'LL KILL ME TOO?
YOU'LL HAVE TO CATCH ME FIRST, SHANNY BOY...
MY QUEST AS A HUNTER...
...OR DEBBIE'S LIFE...
HOW CAN I BE FORCED TO CHOOSE ONLY ONE?
I JUST CAN'T!

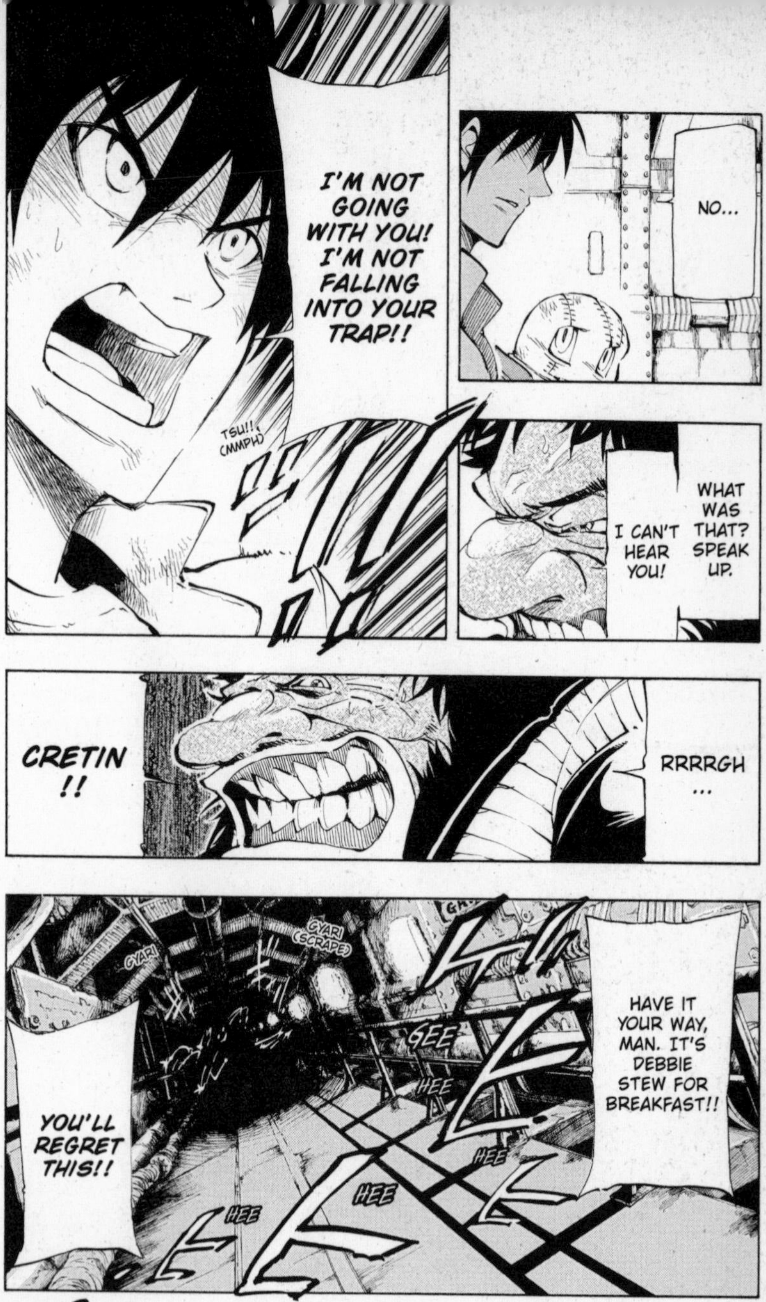
NO...
WHAT WAS THAT? SPEAK UP.
I CAN'T HEAR YOU!
I'M NOT GOING WITH YOU! I'M NOT FALLING INTO YOUR TRAP!!
TSU!! (MMPH)
RRRRGH ...
CRETIN !!
HAVE IT YOUR WAY, MAN. IT'S DEBBIE STEW FOR BREAKFAST!!
GYARI (SCRAPE)
GYARI
GEE
HEE
HEE
HEE
HEE
YOU'LL REGRET THIS!!

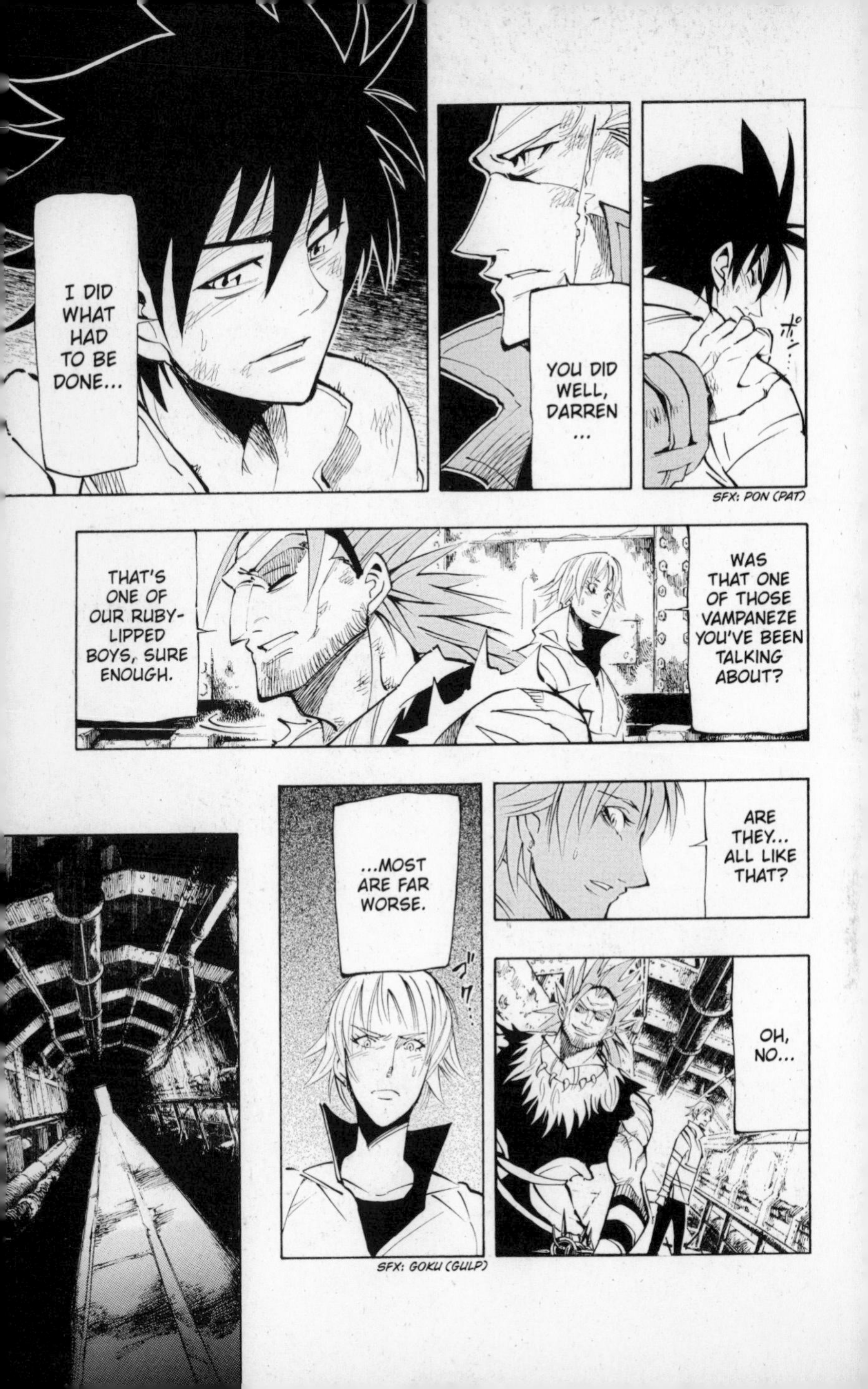
SFX: PON (PAT)
YOU DID WELL, DARREN ...
I DID WHAT HAD TO BE DONE...
WAS THAT ONE OF THOSE VAMPANEZE YOU'VE BEEN TALKING ABOUT?
THAT'S ONE OF OUR RUBY-LIPPED BOYS, SURE ENOUGH.
ARE THEY... ALL LIKE THAT?
OH, NO...
...MOST ARE FAR WORSE.
SFX: GOKU (GULP)

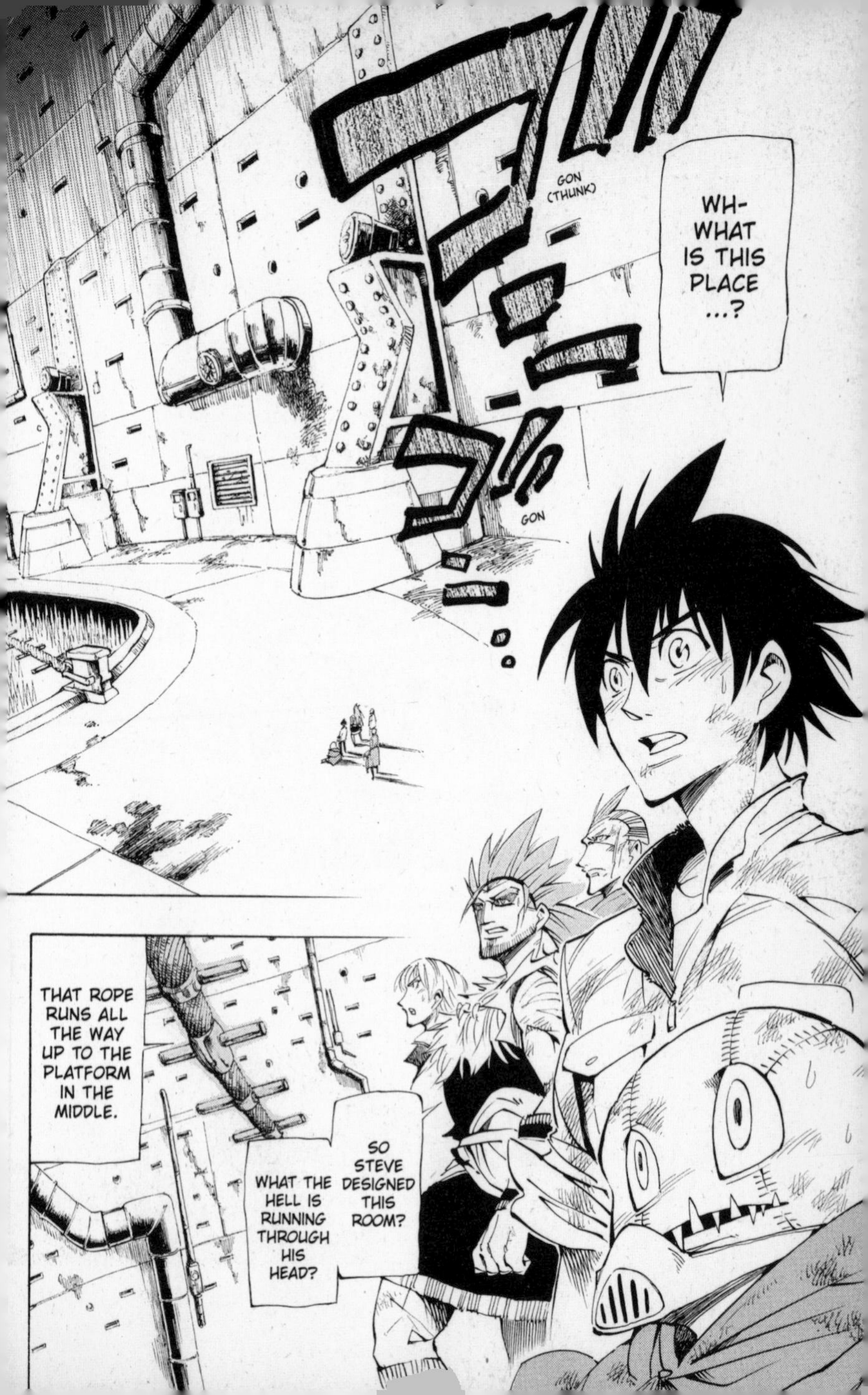
WH-WHAT IS THIS PLACE ...?
GON (THUNK)
GON
SO STEVE DESIGNED THIS ROOM?
WHAT THE HELL IS RUNNING THROUGH HIS HEAD?
THAT ROPE RUNS ALL THE WAY UP TO THE PLATFORM IN THE MIDDLE.

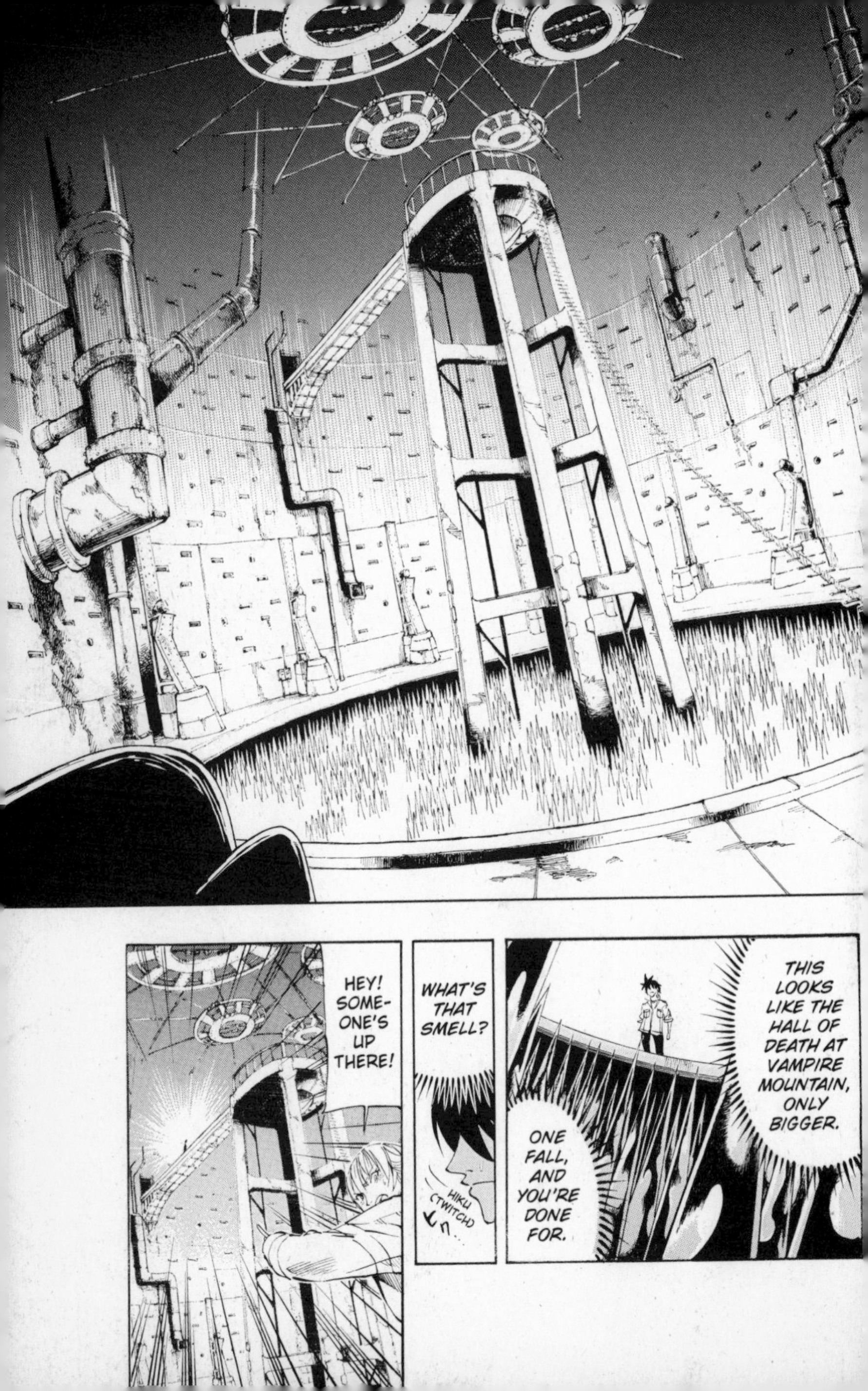
THIS LOOKS LIKE THE HALL OF DEATH AT VAMPIRE MOUNTAIN, ONLY BIGGER.
ONE FALL, AND YOU'RE DONE FOR.
WHAT'S THAT SMELL?
HIKU (TWITCH)
HEY! SOME-ONE'S UP THERE!

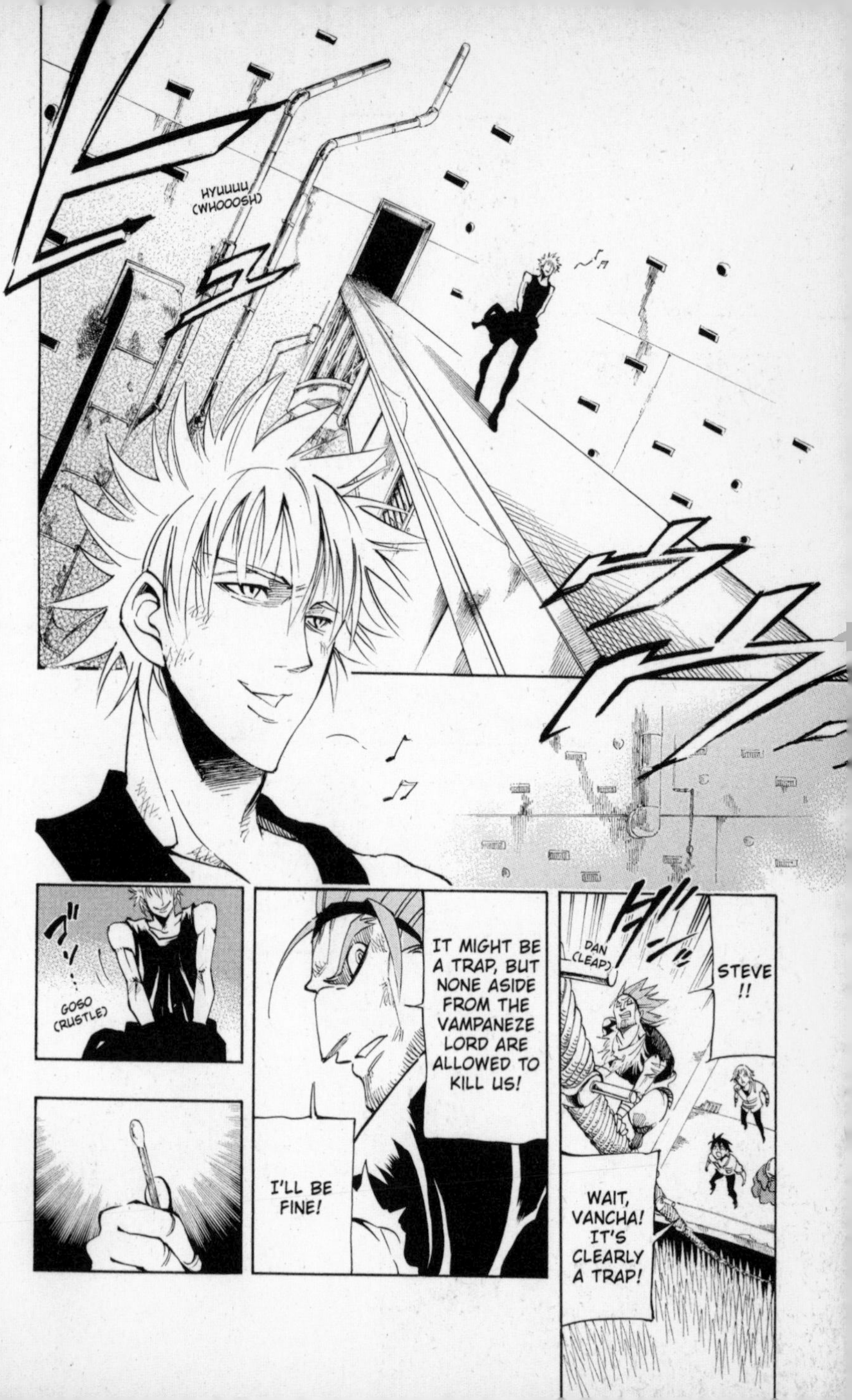
HYUUUU (WHOOOSH)
DAN (LEAP)
STEVE !!
WAIT, VANCHA! IT'S CLEARLY A TRAP!
IT MIGHT BE A TRAP, BUT NONE ASIDE FROM THE VAMPANEZE LORD ARE ALLOWED TO KILL US!
I'LL BE FINE!
GOSO (RUSTLE)

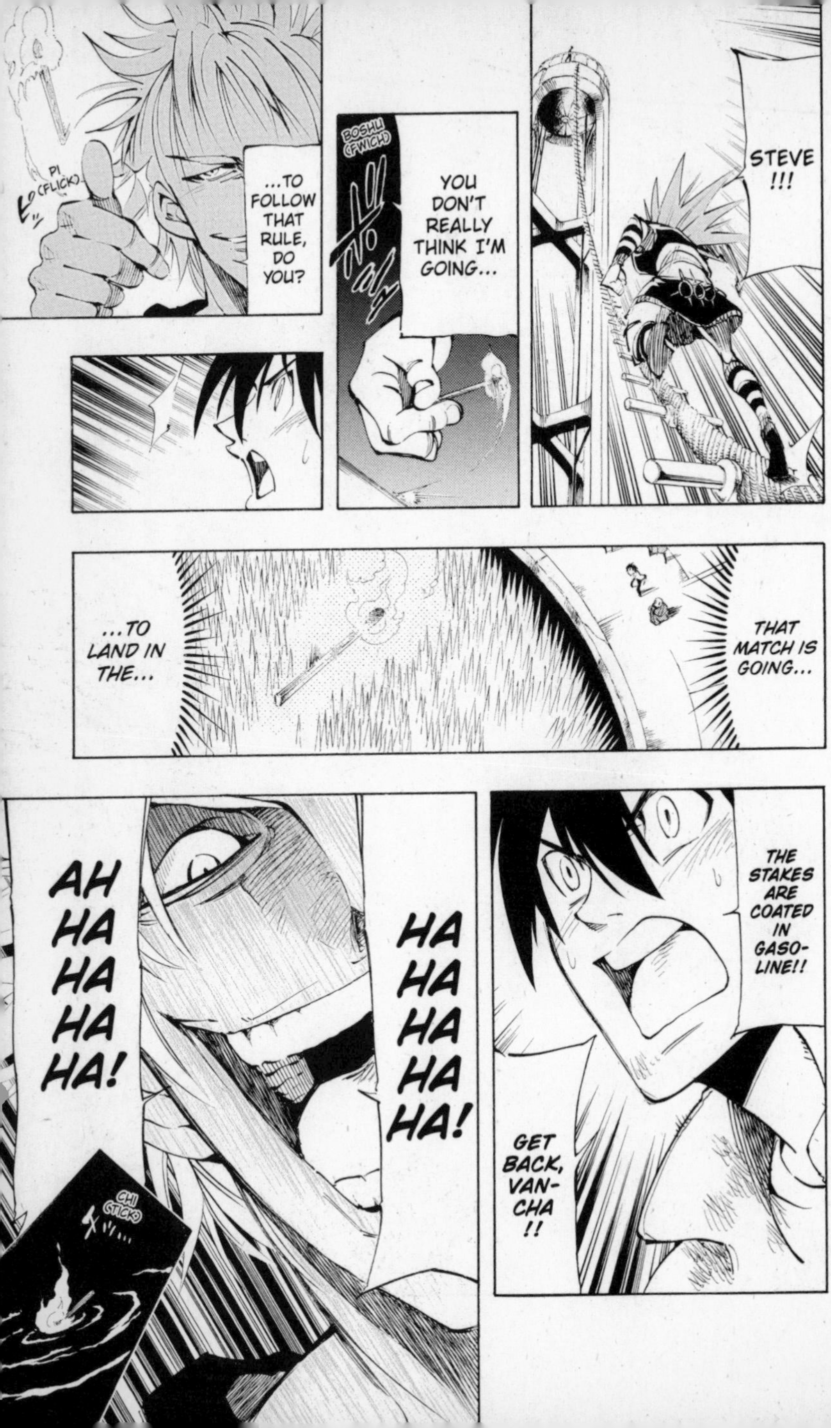
STEVE !!!
BOSHU (FWICH)
YOU DON'T REALLY THINK I'M GOING...
...TO FOLLOW THAT RULE, DO YOU?
PI (FLICK)
THAT MATCH IS GOING...
...TO LAND IN THE...
THE STAKES ARE COATED IN GASO-LINE!!
GET BACK, VAN-CHA!!
HA HA HA HA HA HA!
AH HA HA HA HA HA!
CHI (STICK)

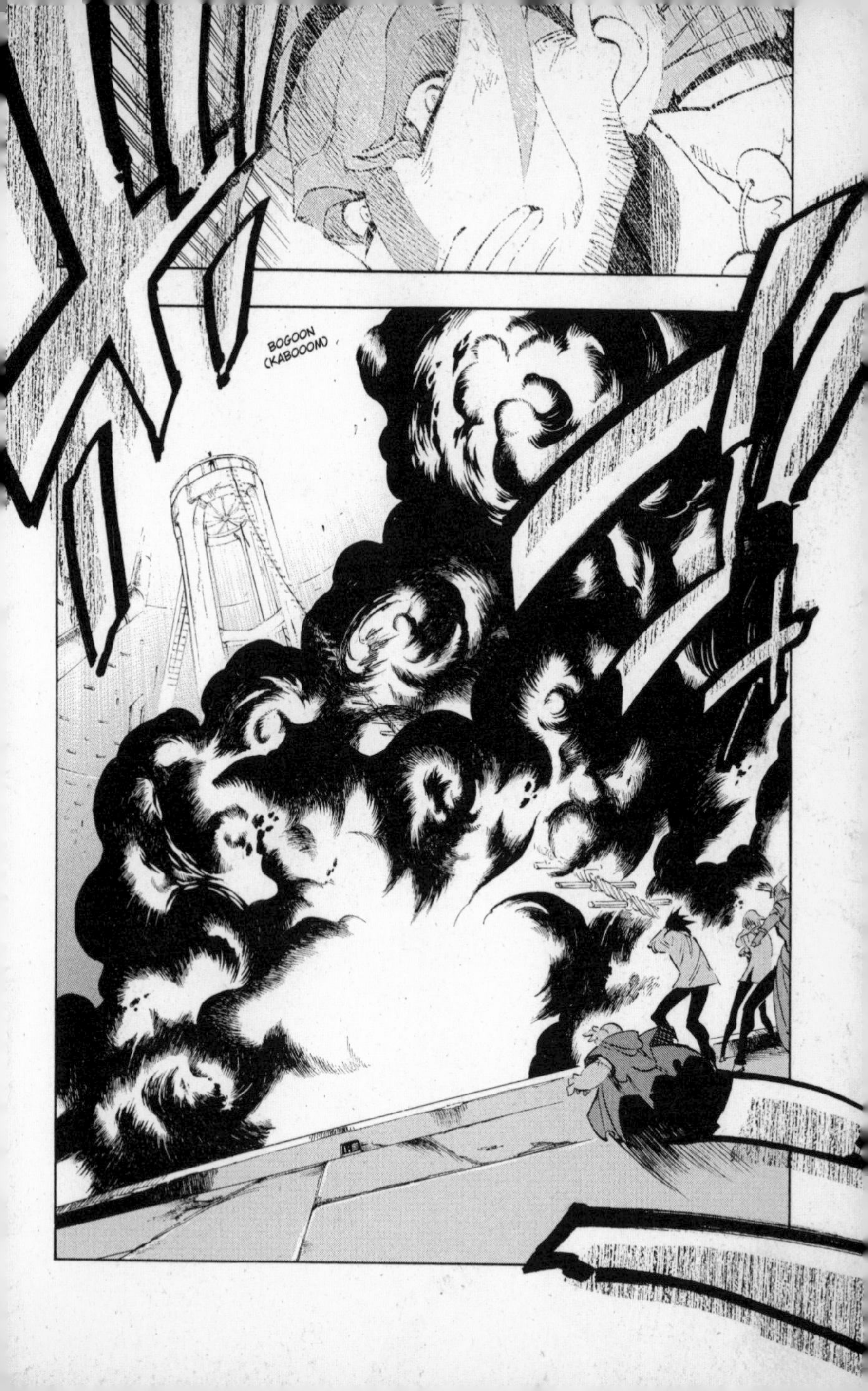
BOGOON
(KABOOOM)

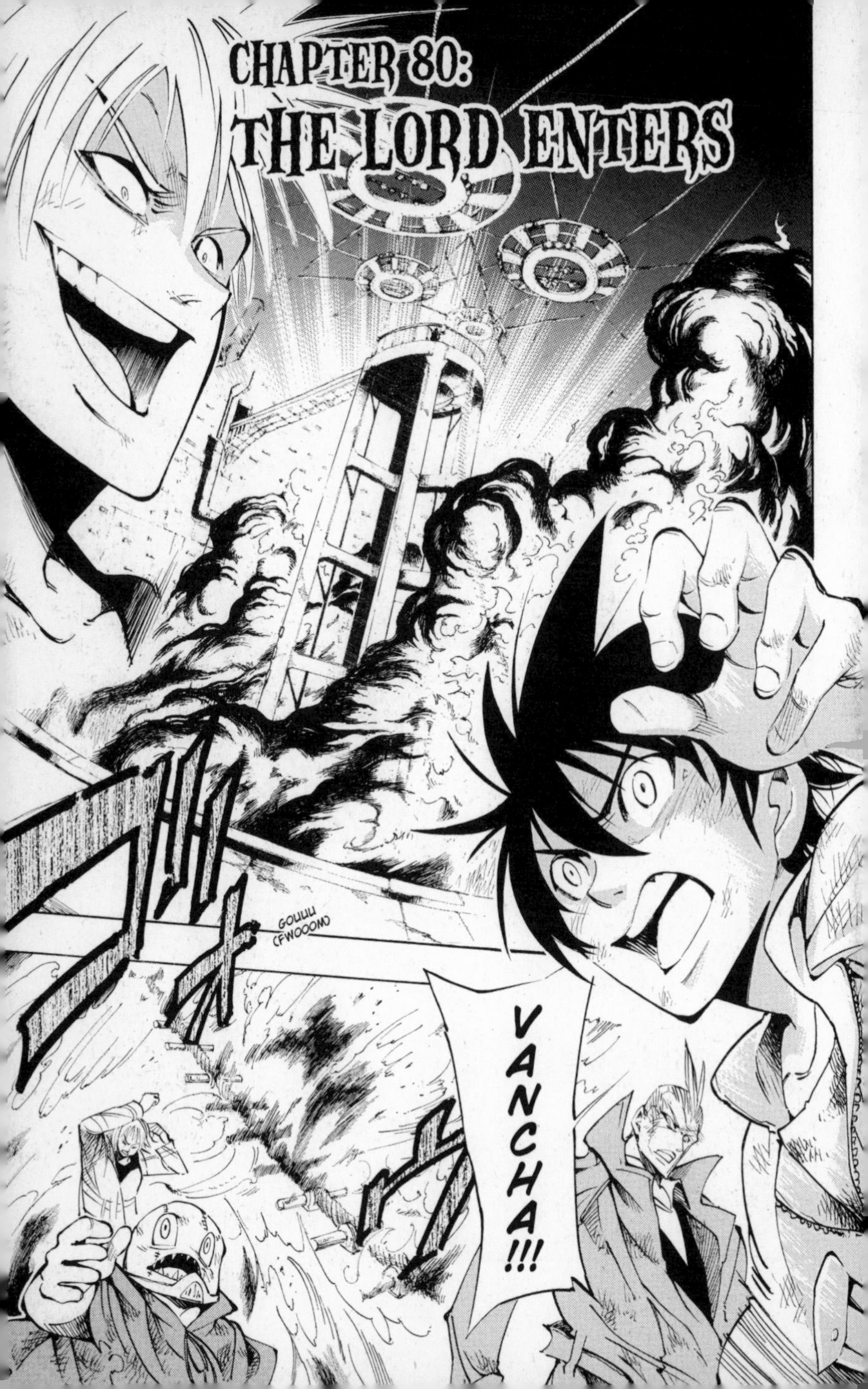
CHAPTER 80:
THE LORD ENTERS
GOUUU
(FWOOOM)
VANCHA!!!

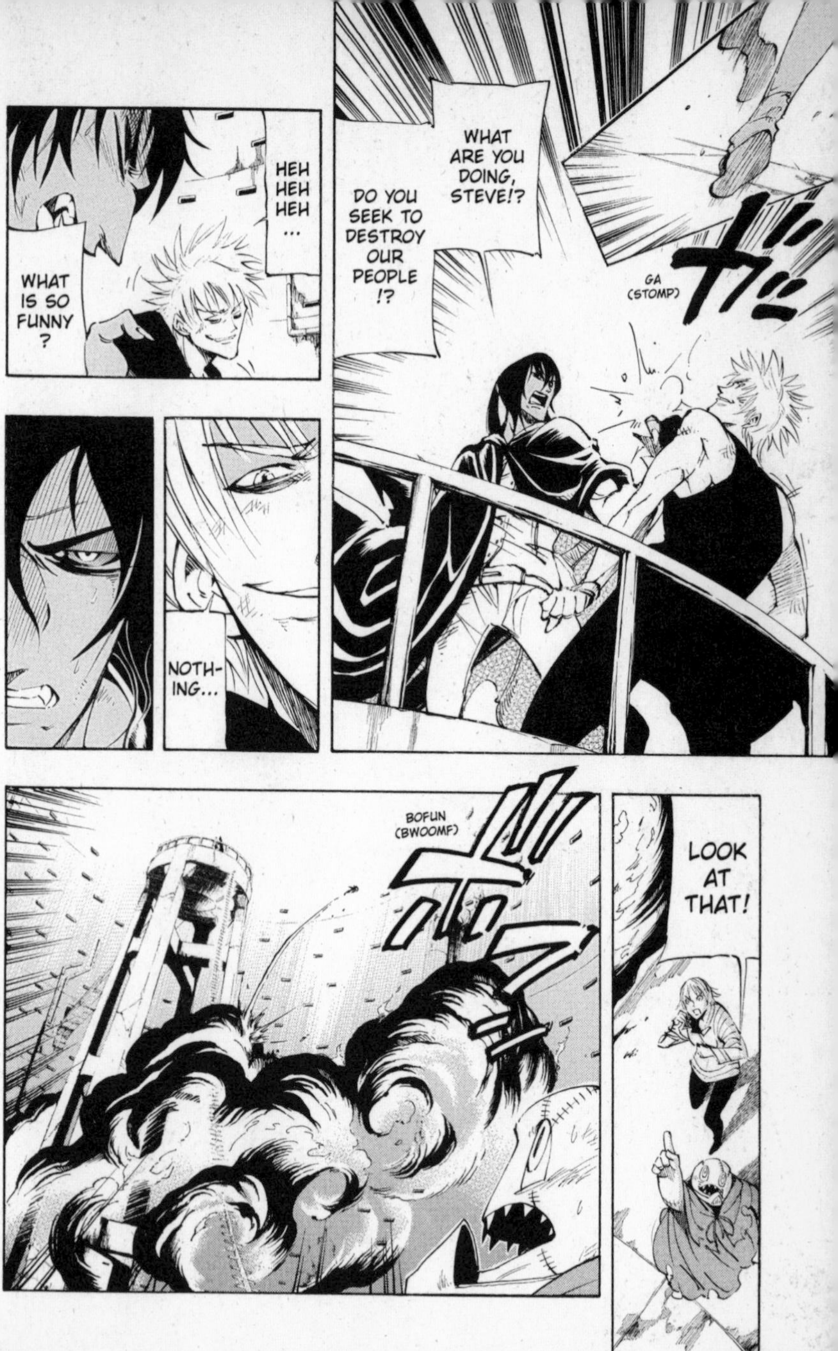

WHAT ARE YOU DOING, STEVE!?
DO YOU SEEK TO DESTROY OUR PEOPLE !?
GA (STOMP)
HEH HEH HEH ...
WHAT IS SO FUNNY ?
NOTH-ING...
LOOK AT THAT!
BOFUN (BWOOMF)

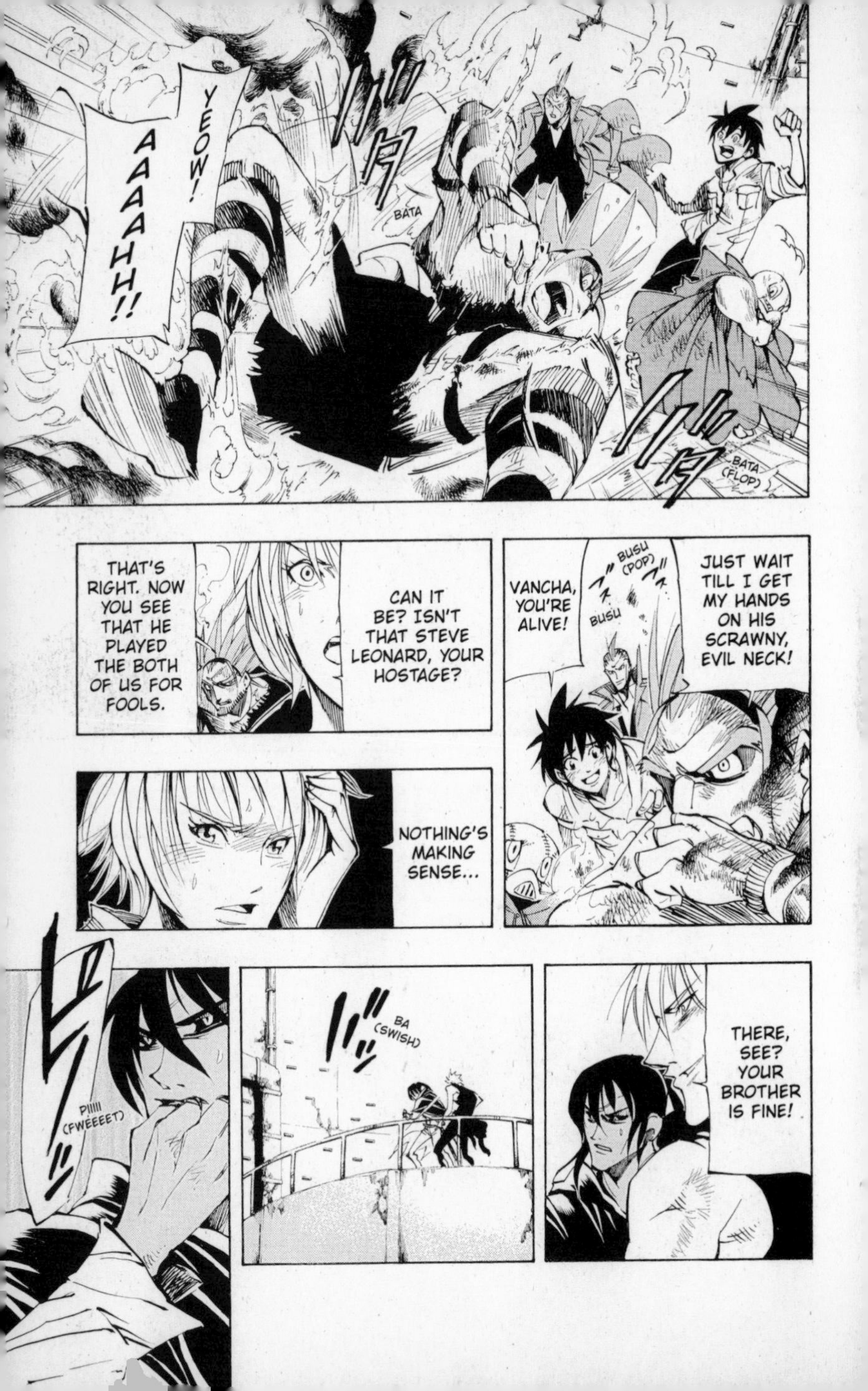
BATA
BATA (FLOP)
YEOW!
AAAAAHH!!
JUST WAIT TILL I GET MY HANDS ON HIS SCRAWNY, EVIL NECK!
BUSU (POP)
BUSU
VANCHA, YOU'RE ALIVE!
CAN IT BE? ISN'T THAT STEVE LEONARD, YOUR HOSTAGE?
THAT'S RIGHT. NOW YOU SEE THAT HE PLAYED THE BOTH OF US FOR FOOLS.
NOTHING'S MAKING SENSE...
THERE, SEE? YOUR BROTHER IS FINE!
BA (SWISH)
PIIII (FWEEEET)

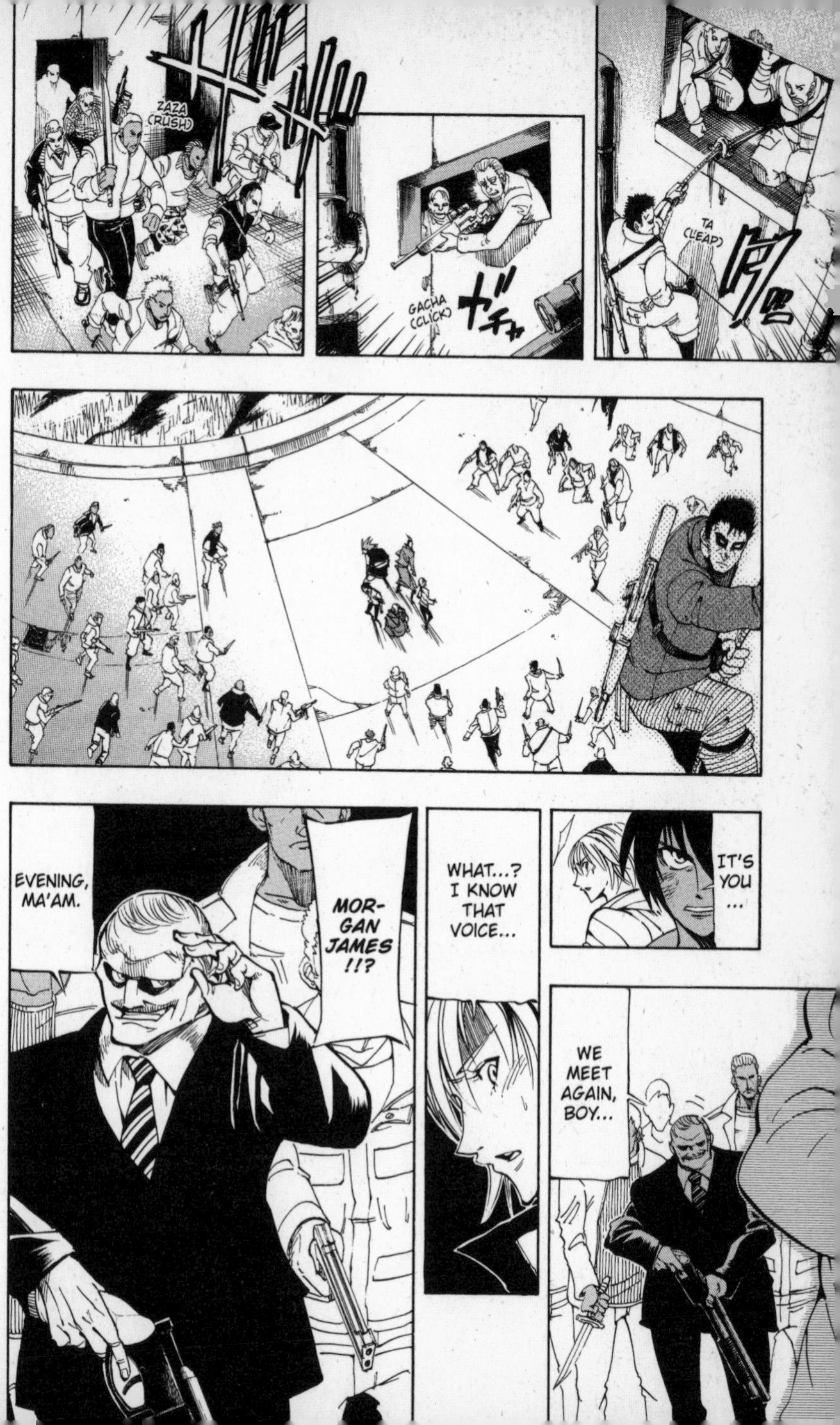
TA (LEAP)
GACHA (CLICK)
ZAZA (RUSH)
IT'S YOU...
WE MEET AGAIN, BOY...
WHAT...? I KNOW THAT VOICE...
MOR-GAN JAMES !!?
EVENING, MA'AM.

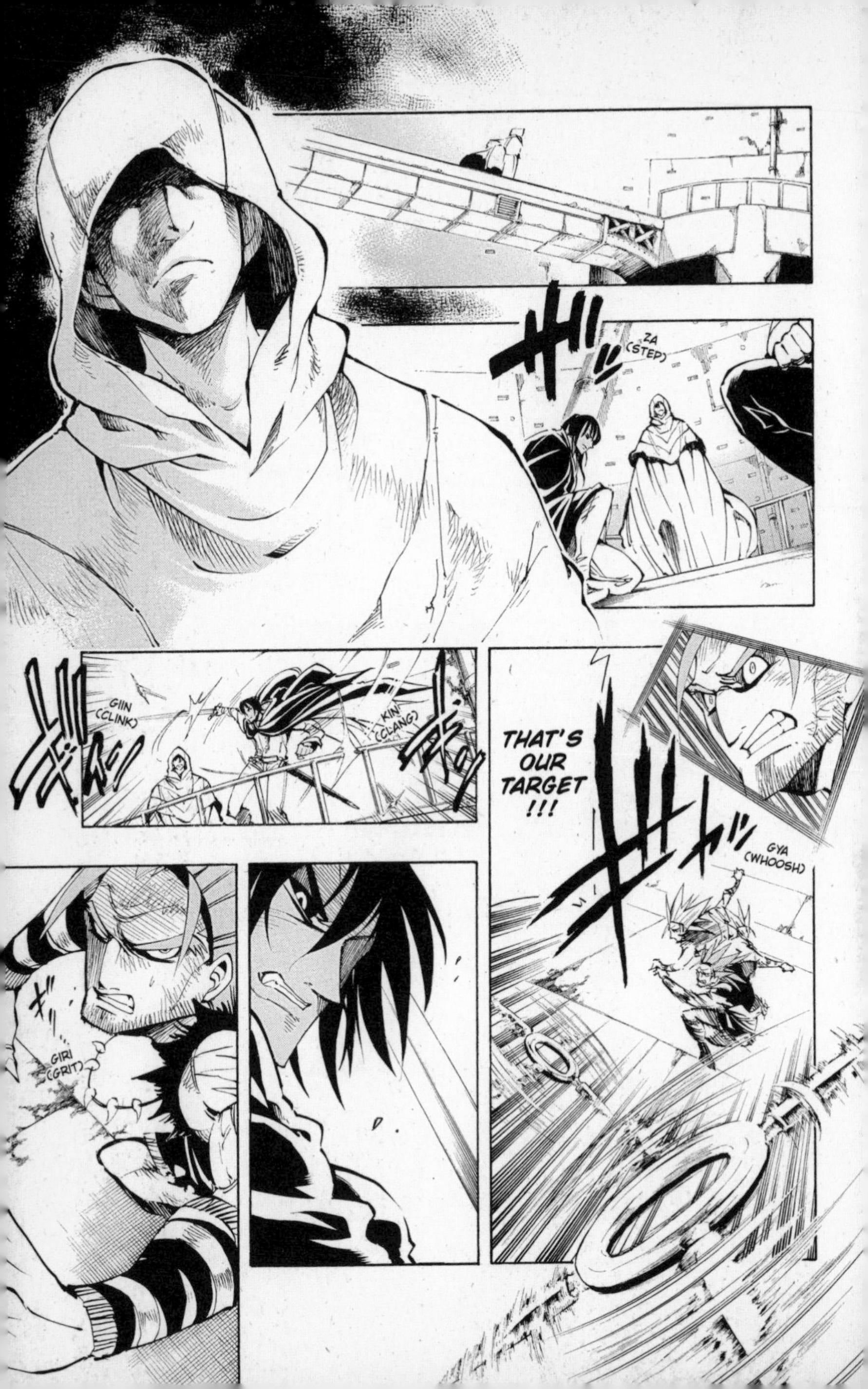
ZA
(STEP)
THAT'S OUR TARGET!!!
GYA
(WHOOSH)
KIN
(CLANG)
GIIN
(CLINK)
GIRI
(GRIT)

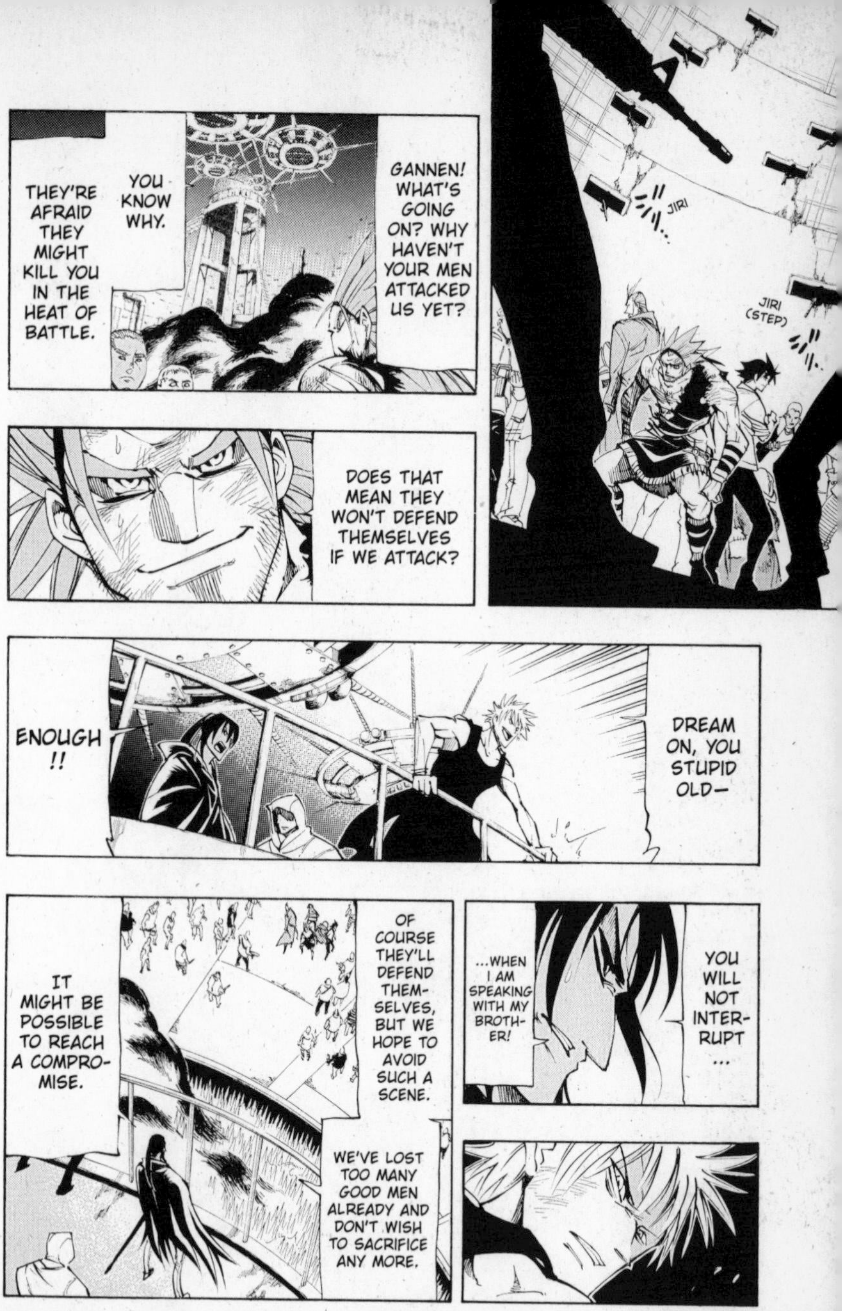

JIRI
JIRI (STEP)
GANNEN! WHAT'S GOING ON? WHY HAVEN'T YOUR MEN ATTACKED US YET?
YOU KNOW WHY.
THEY'RE AFRAID THEY MIGHT KILL YOU IN THE HEAT OF BATTLE.
DOES THAT MEAN THEY WON'T DEFEND THEMSELVES IF WE ATTACK?
DREAM ON, YOU STUPID OLD—
ENOUGH!!
YOU WILL NOT INTERRUPT...
...WHEN I AM SPEAKING WITH MY BROTHER!
OF COURSE THEY'LL DEFEND THEMSELVES, BUT WE HOPE TO AVOID SUCH A SCENE.
IT MIGHT BE POSSIBLE TO REACH A COMPROMISE.
WE'VE LOST TOO MANY GOOD MEN ALREADY AND DON'T WISH TO SACRIFICE ANY MORE.

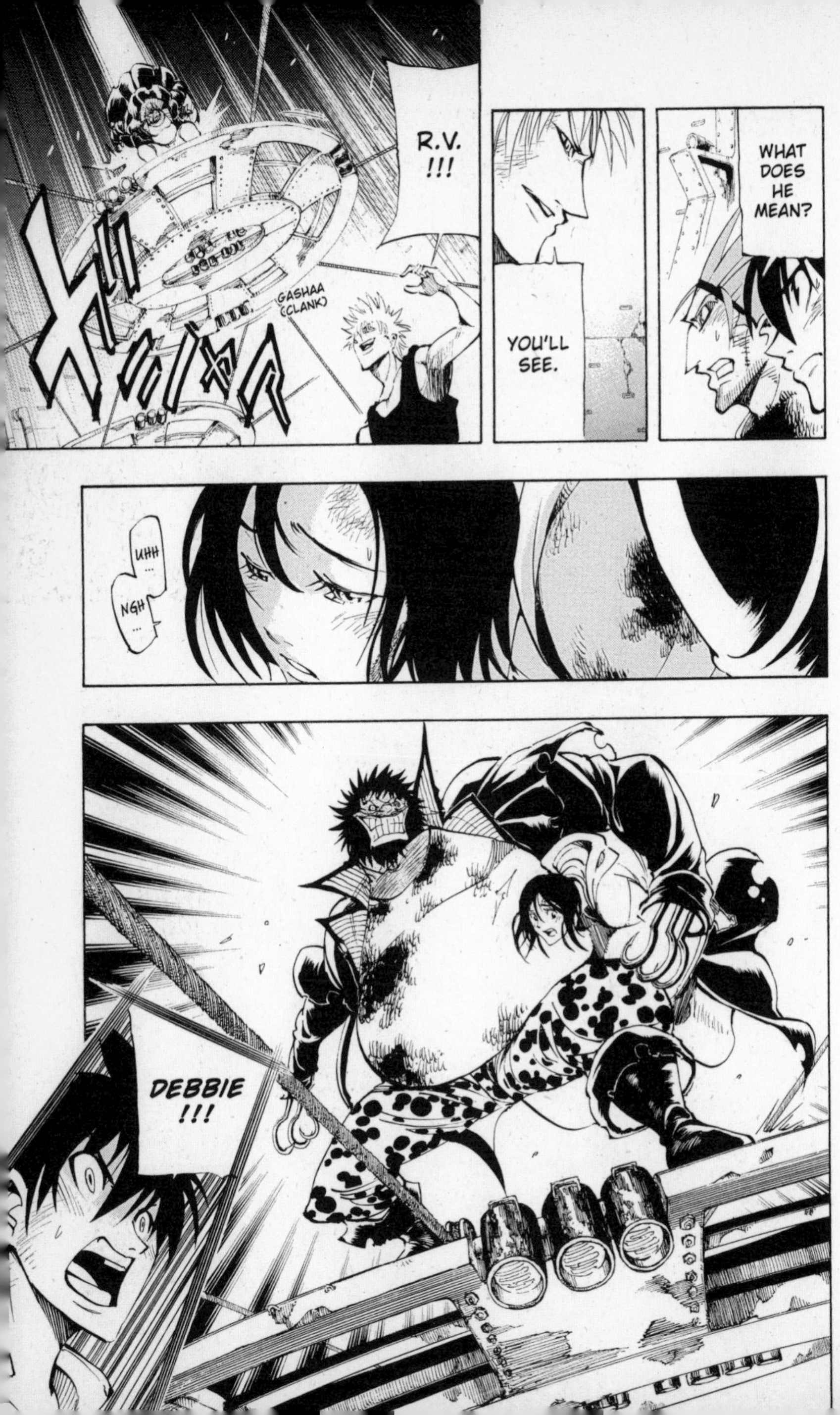
WHAT DOES HE MEAN?
YOU'LL SEE.
R.V. !!!
GASHAA (CLANK)
UHH ...
NGH ...
DEBBIE !!!

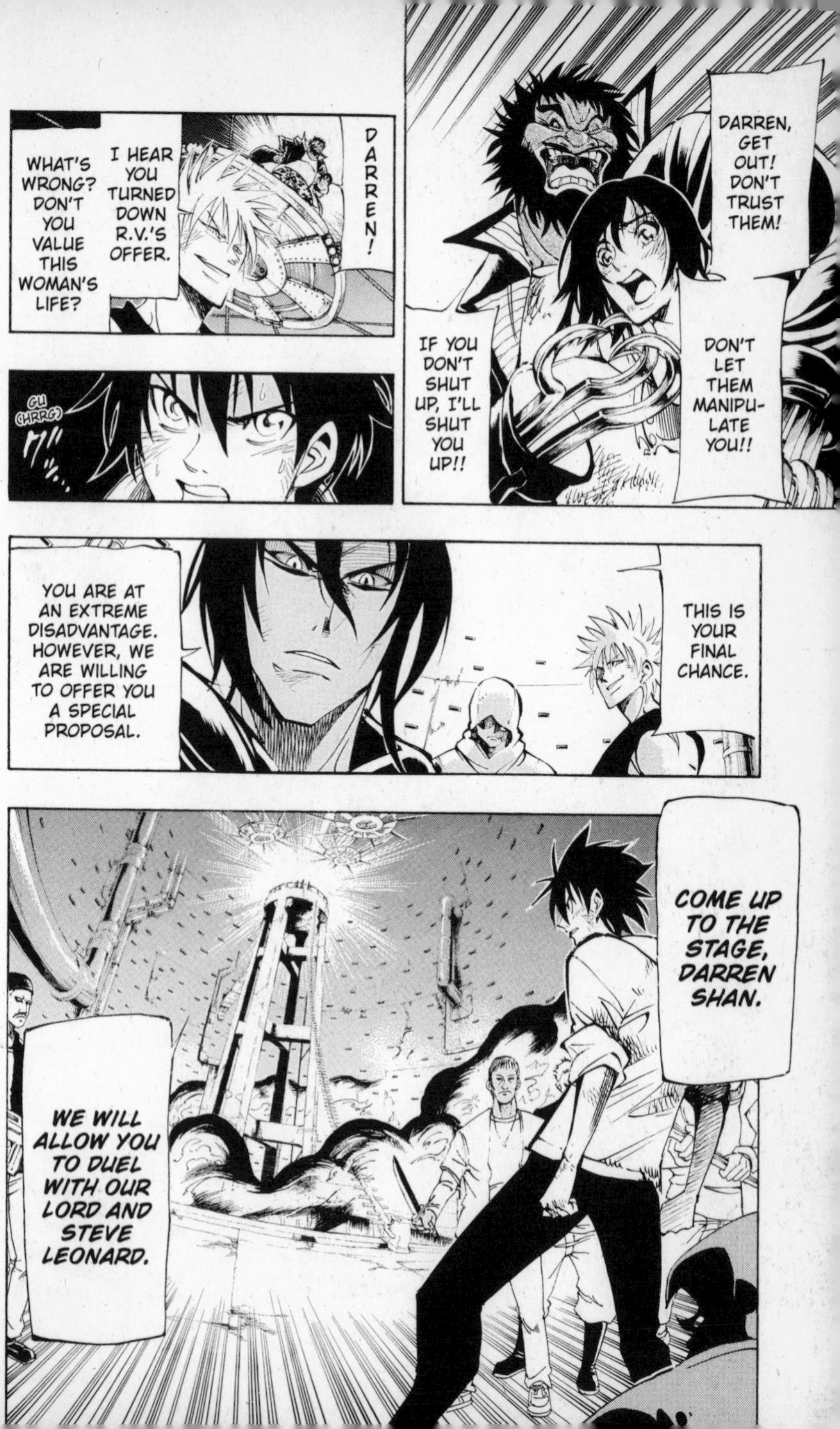
DARREN, GET OUT! DON'T TRUST THEM!
DON'T LET THEM MANIPULATE YOU!!
IF YOU DON'T SHUT UP, I'LL SHUT YOU UP!!
DARREN!
I HEAR YOU TURNED DOWN R.V.'S OFFER.
WHAT'S WRONG? DON'T YOU VALUE THIS WOMAN'S LIFE?
GU (HRRG)
THIS IS YOUR FINAL CHANCE.
YOU ARE AT AN EXTREME DISADVANTAGE. HOWEVER, WE ARE WILLING TO OFFER YOU A SPECIAL PROPOSAL.
COME UP TO THE STAGE, DARREN SHAN.
WE WILL ALLOW YOU TO DUEL WITH OUR LORD AND STEVE LEONARD.

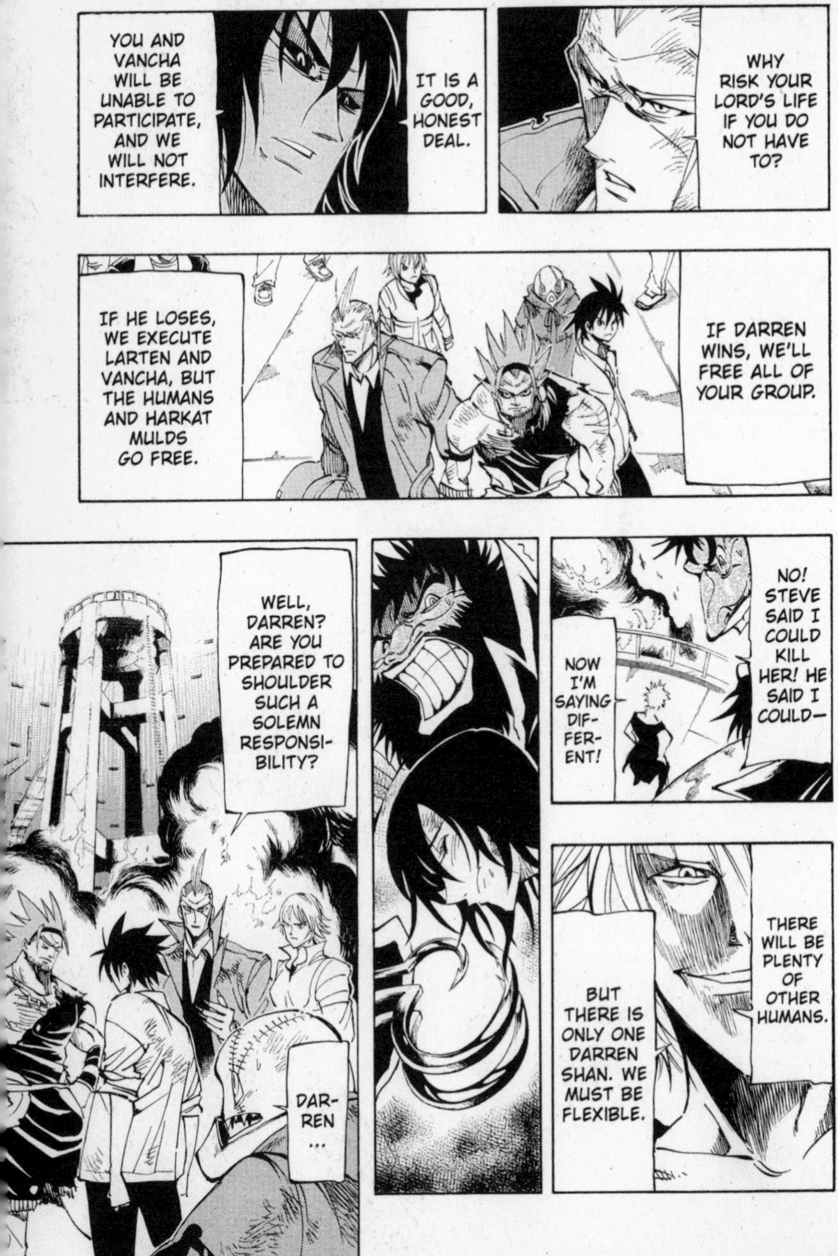
WHY RISK YOUR LORD'S LIFE IF YOU DO NOT HAVE TO?
YOU AND VANCHA WILL BE UNABLE TO PARTICIPATE, AND WE WILL NOT INTERFERE.
IT IS A GOOD, HONEST DEAL.
IF DARREN WINS, WE'LL FREE ALL OF YOUR GROUP.
IF HE LOSES, WE EXECUTE LARTEN AND VANCHA, BUT THE HUMANS AND HARKAT MULDS GO FREE.
NO! STEVE SAID I COULD KILL HER! HE SAID I COULD—
NOW I'M SAYING DIF-FER-ENT!
THERE WILL BE PLENTY OF OTHER HUMANS.
BUT THERE IS ONLY ONE DARREN SHAN. WE MUST BE FLEXIBLE.
WELL, DARREN? ARE YOU PREPARED TO SHOULDER SUCH A SOLEMN RESPONSI-BILITY?
DAR-REN...

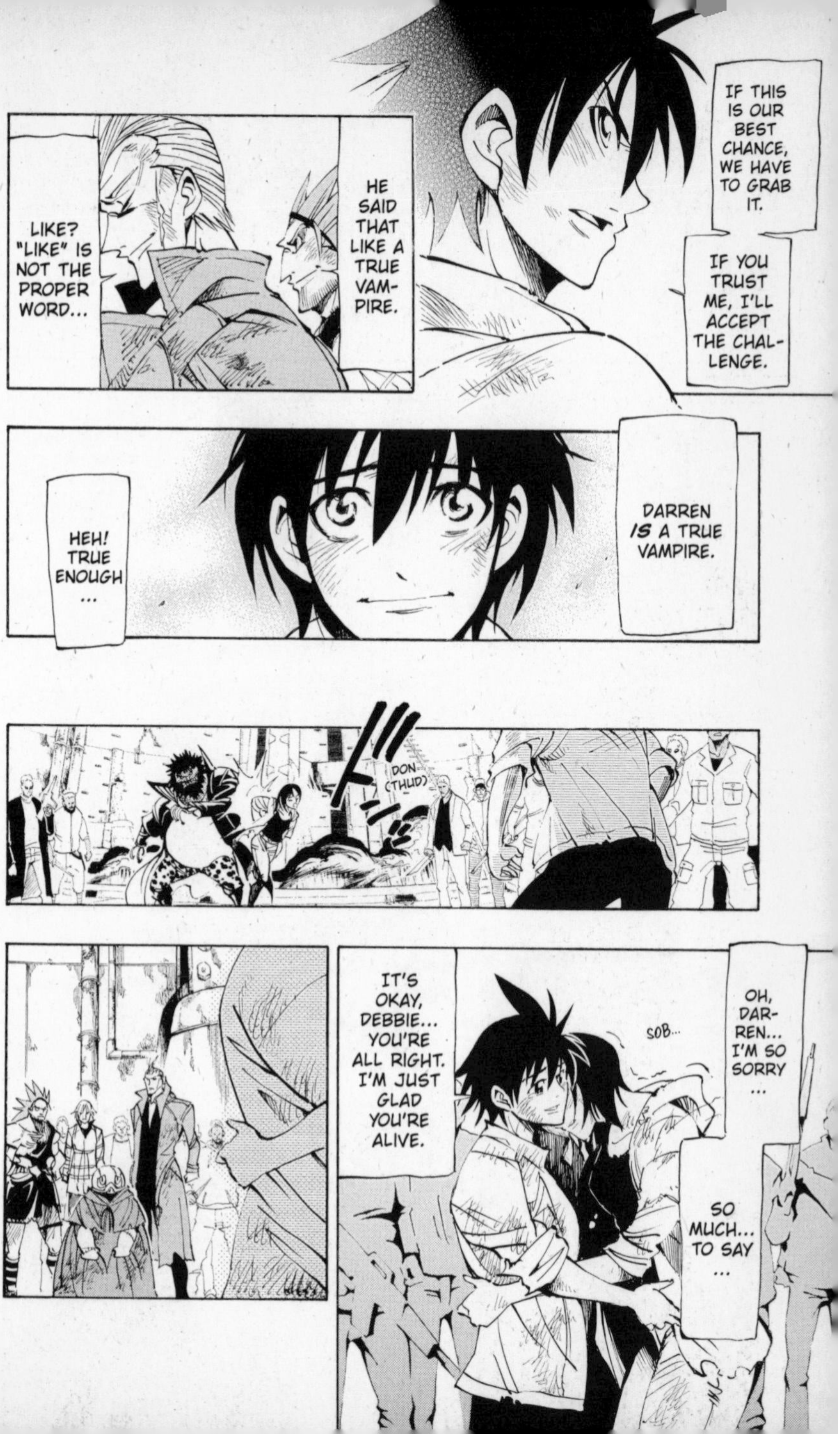
IF THIS IS OUR BEST CHANCE, WE HAVE TO GRAB IT.
IF YOU TRUST ME, I'LL ACCEPT THE CHALLENGE.
HE SAID THAT LIKE A TRUE VAMPIRE.
LIKE? "LIKE" IS NOT THE PROPER WORD...
DARREN *IS* A TRUE VAMPIRE.
HEH! TRUE ENOUGH...
DON (THUD)
OH, DARREN... I'M SO SORRY...
SOB...
IT'S OKAY, DEBBIE... YOU'RE ALL RIGHT. I'M JUST GLAD YOU'RE ALIVE.
SO MUCH... TO SAY...

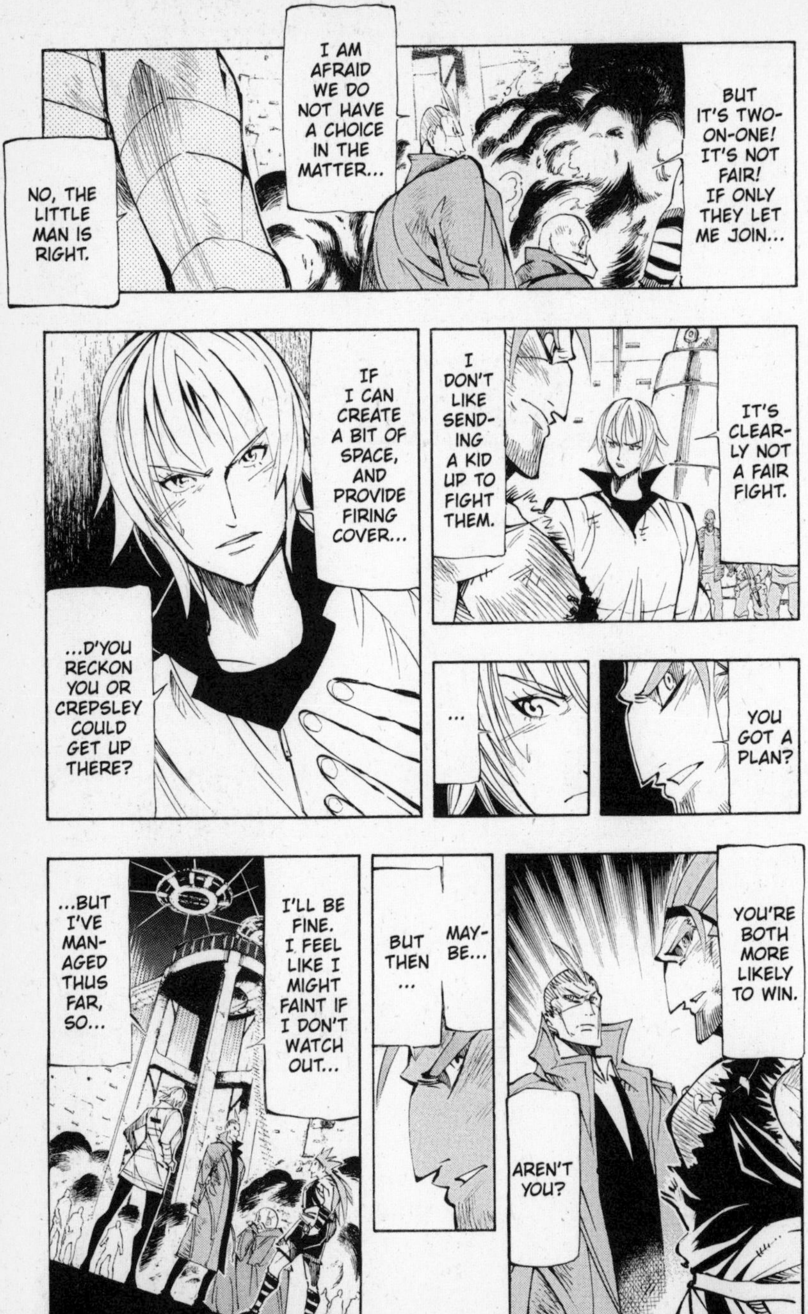
BUT IT'S TWO-ON-ONE! IT'S NOT FAIR! IF ONLY THEY LET ME JOIN...
I AM AFRAID WE DO NOT HAVE A CHOICE IN THE MATTER...
NO, THE LITTLE MAN IS RIGHT.
IT'S CLEAR-LY NOT A FAIR FIGHT.
I DON'T LIKE SEND-ING A KID UP TO FIGHT THEM.
YOU GOT A PLAN?
...
IF I CAN CREATE A BIT OF SPACE, AND PROVIDE FIRING COVER...
...D'YOU RECKON YOU OR CREPSLEY COULD GET UP THERE?
YOU'RE BOTH MORE LIKELY TO WIN.
AREN'T YOU?
MAY-BE...
BUT THEN ...
I'LL BE FINE. I FEEL LIKE I MIGHT FAINT IF I DON'T WATCH OUT...
...BUT I'VE MAN-AGED THUS FAR, SO...

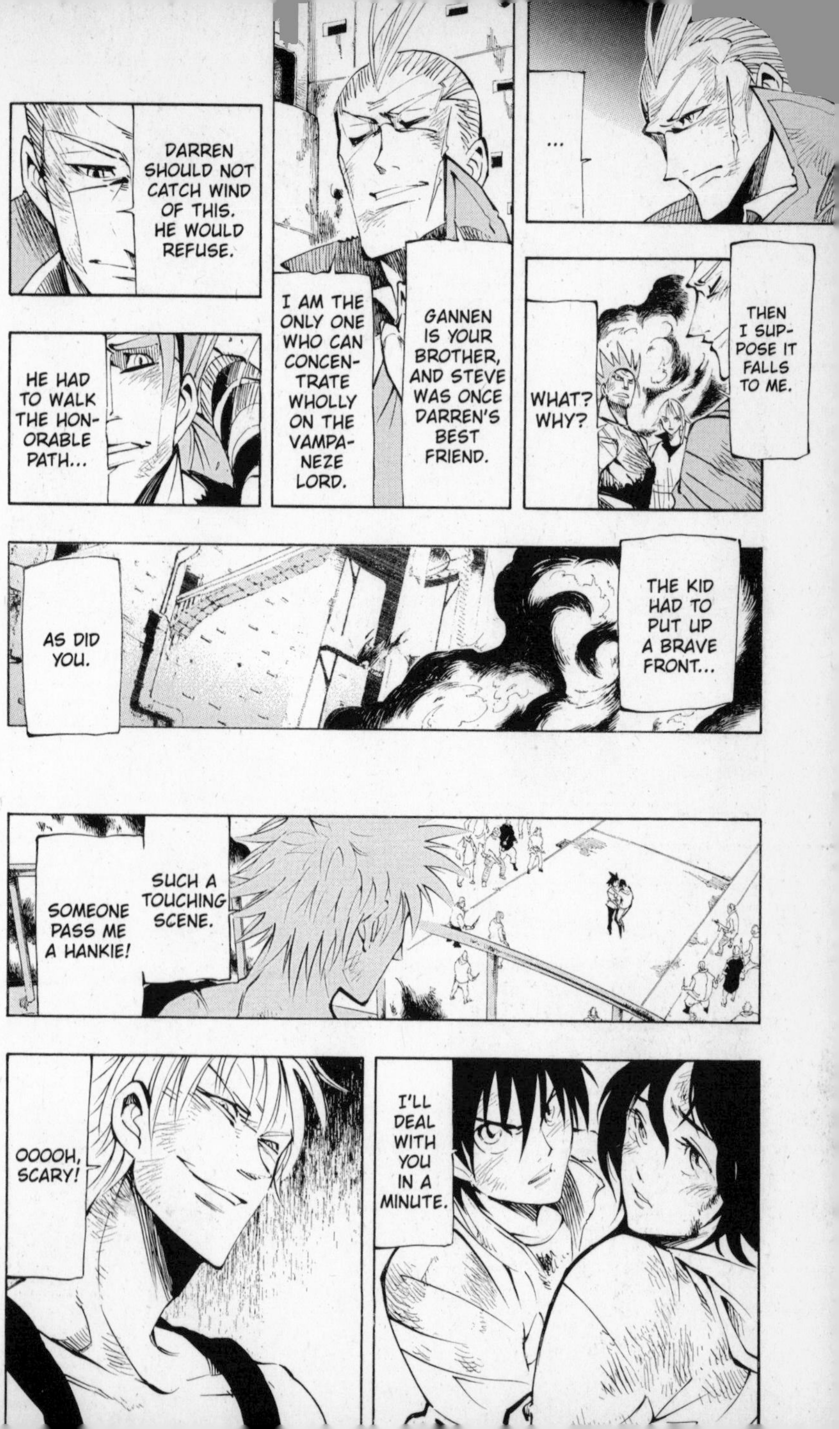
...
THEN I SUPPOSE IT FALLS TO ME.
WHAT? WHY?
GANNEN IS YOUR BROTHER, AND STEVE WAS ONCE DARREN'S BEST FRIEND.
I AM THE ONLY ONE WHO CAN CONCENTRATE WHOLLY ON THE VAMPANEZE LORD.
DARREN SHOULD NOT CATCH WIND OF THIS. HE WOULD REFUSE.
HE HAD TO WALK THE HONORABLE PATH...
THE KID HAD TO PUT UP A BRAVE FRONT...
AS DID YOU.
SUCH A TOUCHING SCENE.
SOMEONE PASS ME A HANKIE!
I'LL DEAL WITH YOU IN A MINUTE.
OOOOH, SCARY!

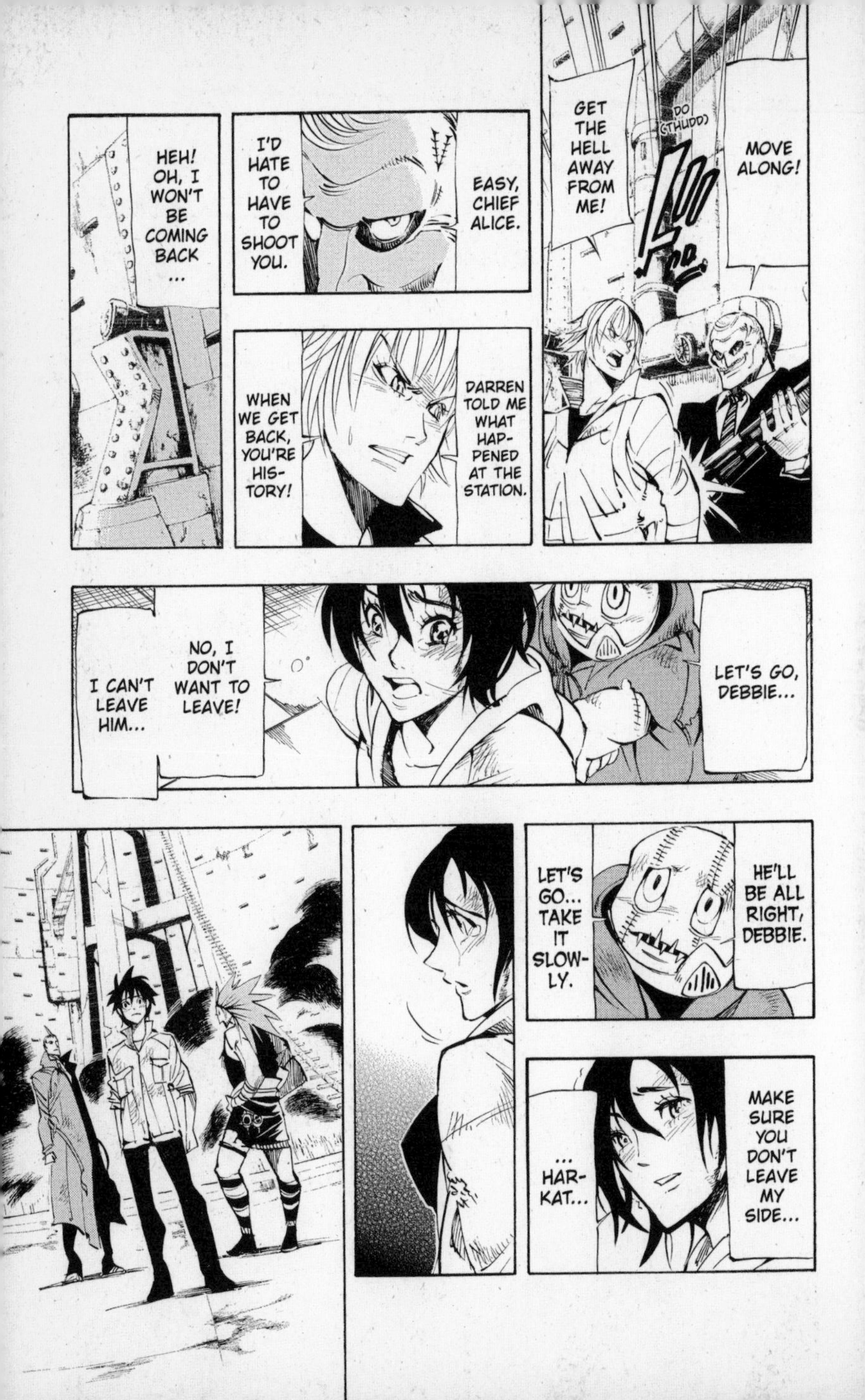
MOVE ALONG!
DO (THUDD)
GET THE HELL AWAY FROM ME!
EASY, CHIEF ALICE.
I'D HATE TO HAVE TO SHOOT YOU.
DARREN TOLD ME WHAT HAPPENED AT THE STATION.
WHEN WE GET BACK, YOU'RE HISTORY!
HEH! OH, I WON'T BE COMING BACK ...
LET'S GO, DEBBIE...
NO, I DON'T WANT TO LEAVE!
I CAN'T LEAVE HIM...
HE'LL BE ALL RIGHT, DEBBIE.
LET'S GO... TAKE IT SLOWLY.
MAKE SURE YOU DON'T LEAVE MY SIDE...
... HARKAT...

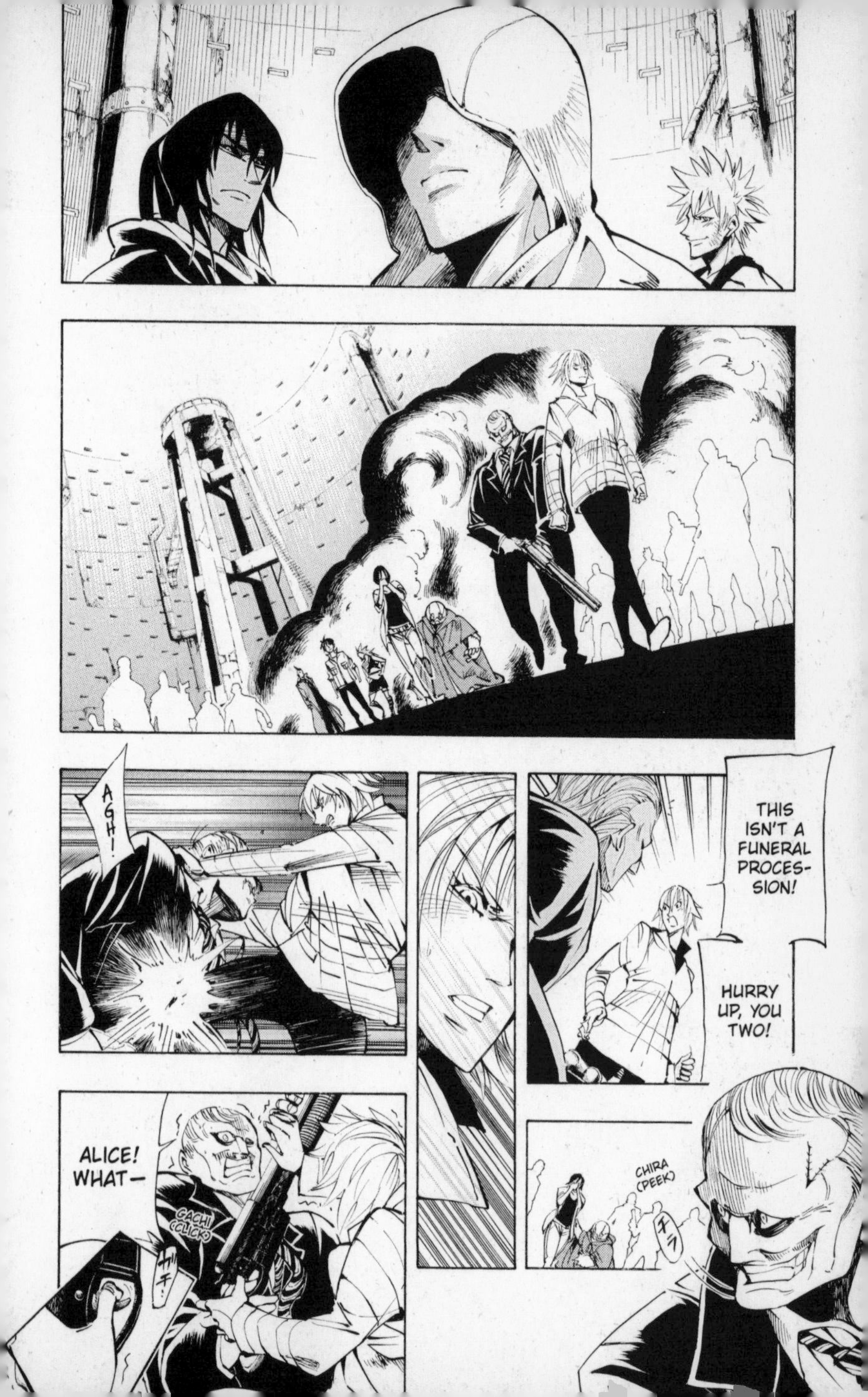
THIS ISN'T A FUNERAL PROCES-SION!
HURRY UP, YOU TWO!
CHIRA (PEEK)
チラ
AGH!
ALICE! WHAT—
GACHI (CLICK)
ガチ

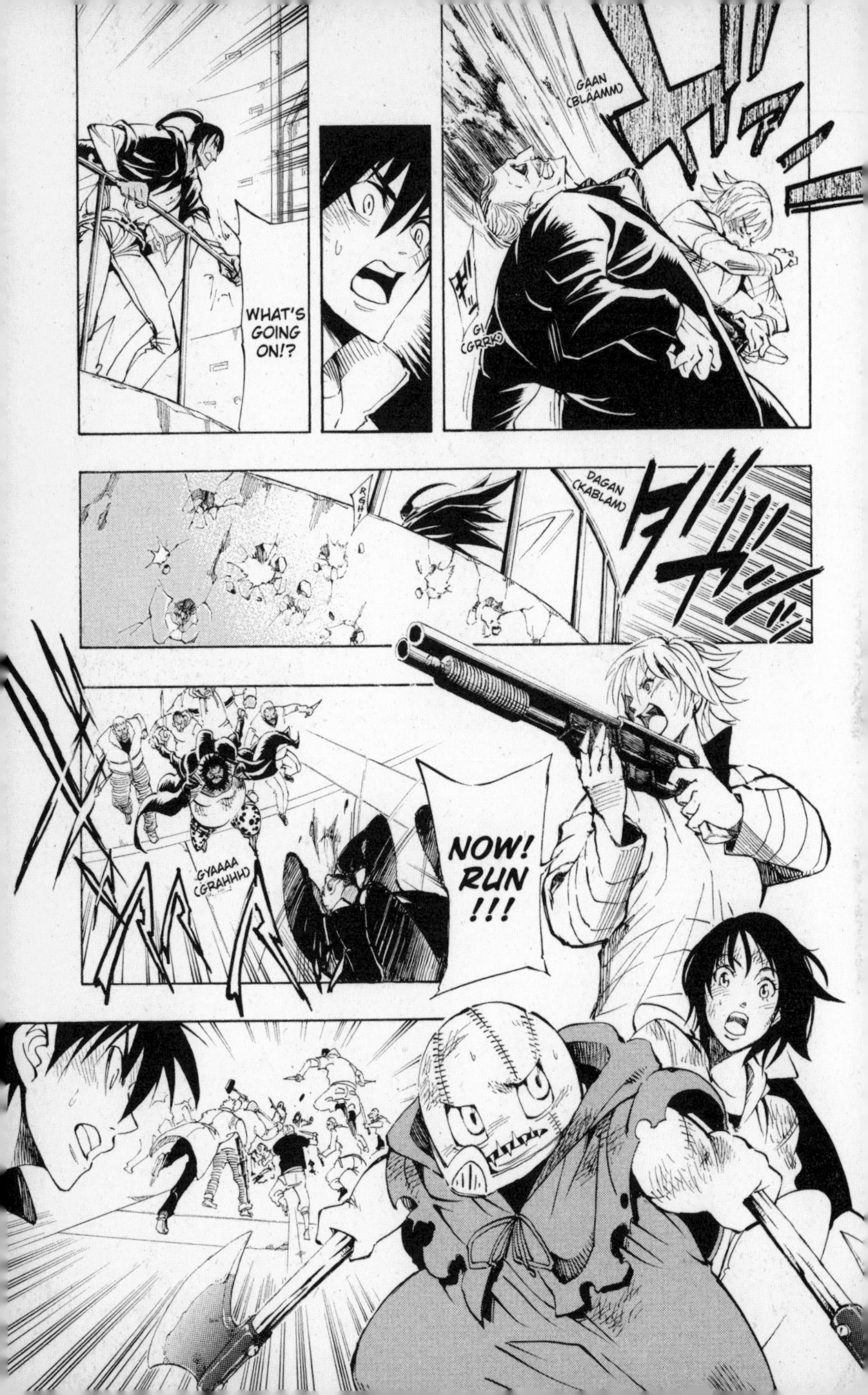
GAAN (BLAAMM)
GI (GRRK)
WHAT'S GOING ON!?
DAGAN (KABLAM)
RGH!
NOW! RUN!!!
GYAAAA (GRAHHH)

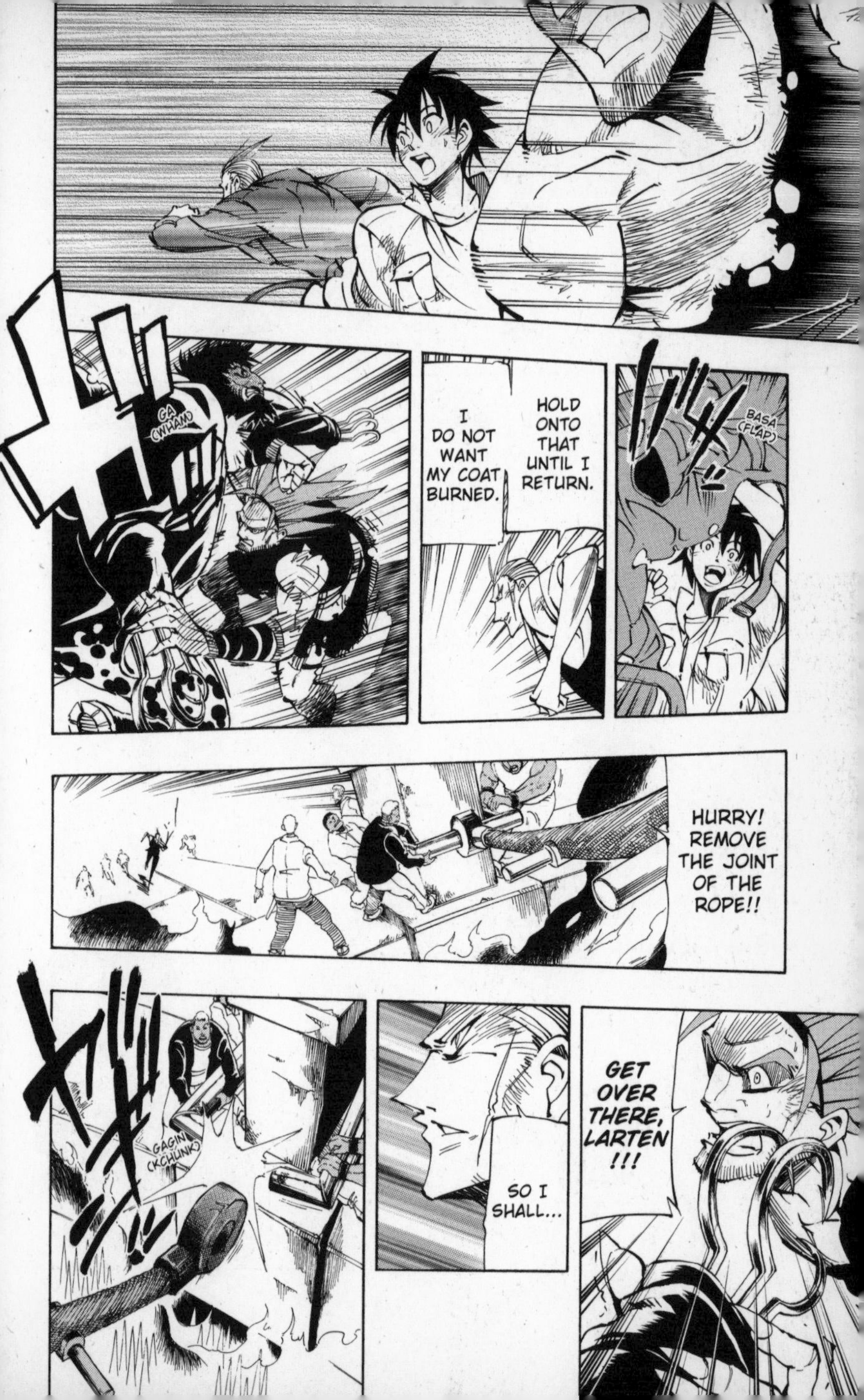
BASA (FLAP)
HOLD ONTO THAT UNTIL I RETURN.
I DO NOT WANT MY COAT BURNED.
GA (WHAM)
HURRY! REMOVE THE JOINT OF THE ROPE!!
GET OVER THERE, LARTEN!!!
SO I SHALL...
GAGIN (KCHUNK)

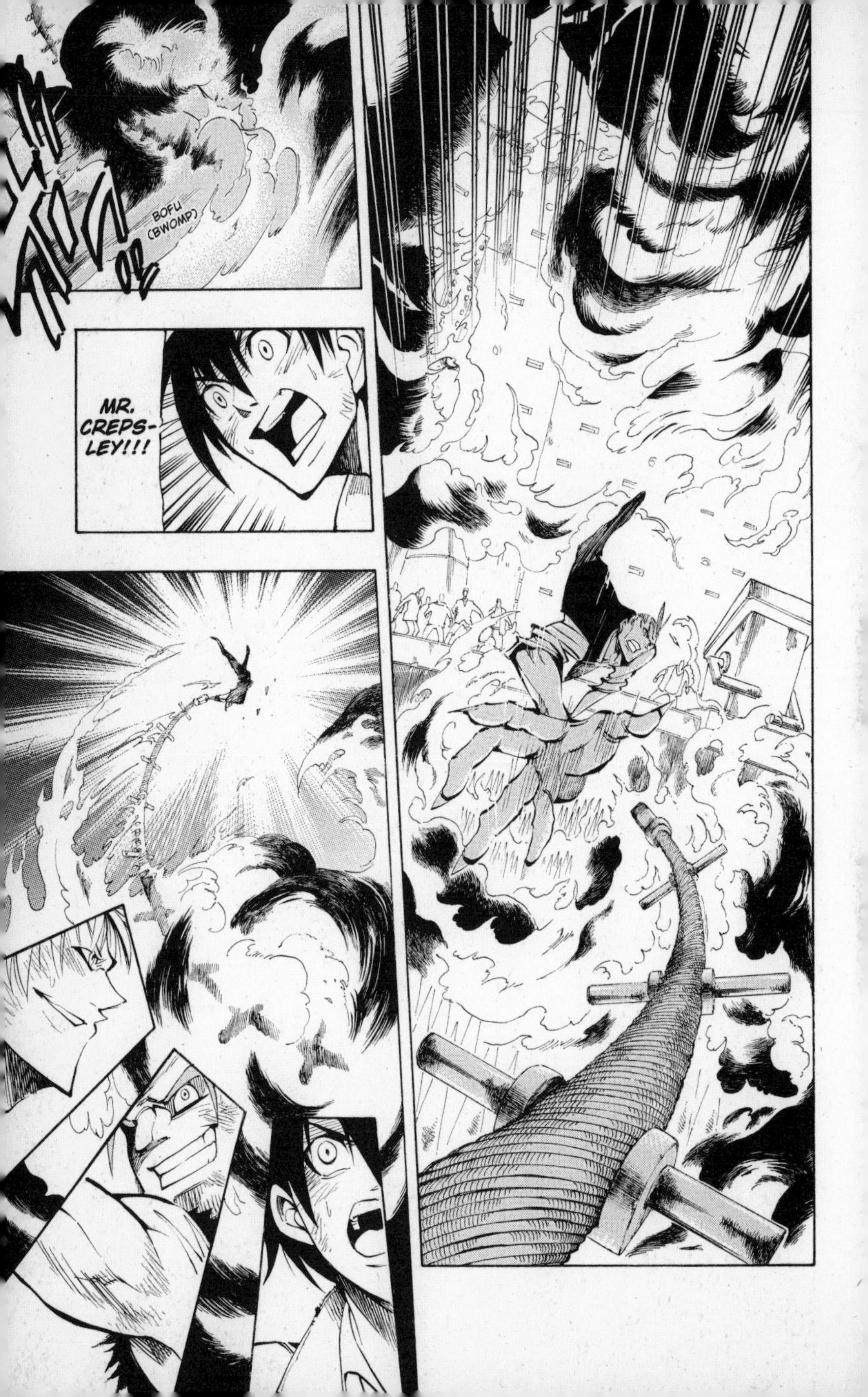
BOFU
(BWOMP)
MR. CREPS-LEY!!!

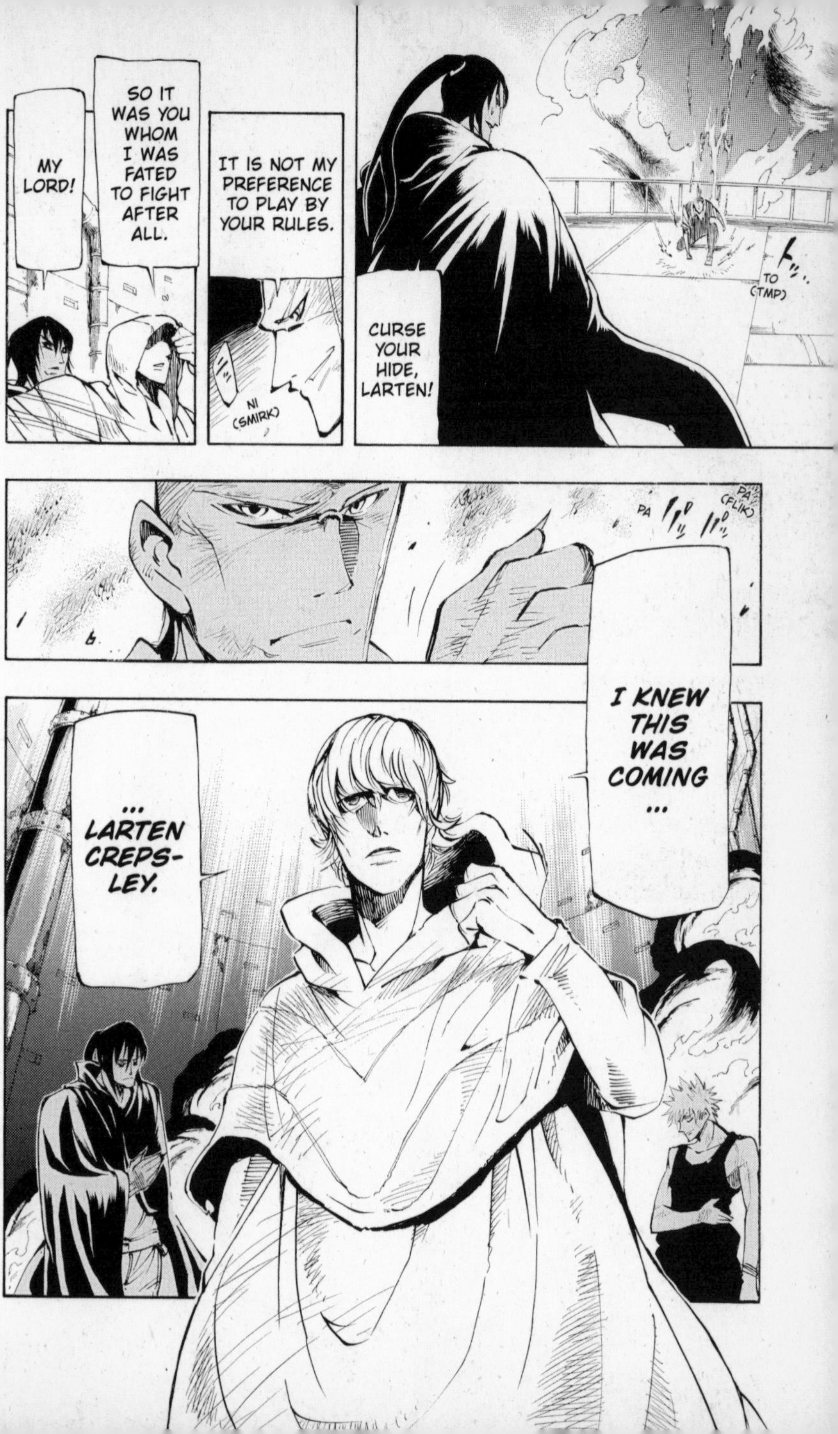
TO (TMP)
CURSE YOUR HIDE, LARTEN!
IT IS NOT MY PREFERENCE TO PLAY BY YOUR RULES.
NI (SMIRK)
SO IT WAS YOU WHOM I WAS FATED TO FIGHT AFTER ALL.
MY LORD!
PA PA (FLIK)
I KNEW THIS WAS COMING ...
... LARTEN CREPS-LEY.

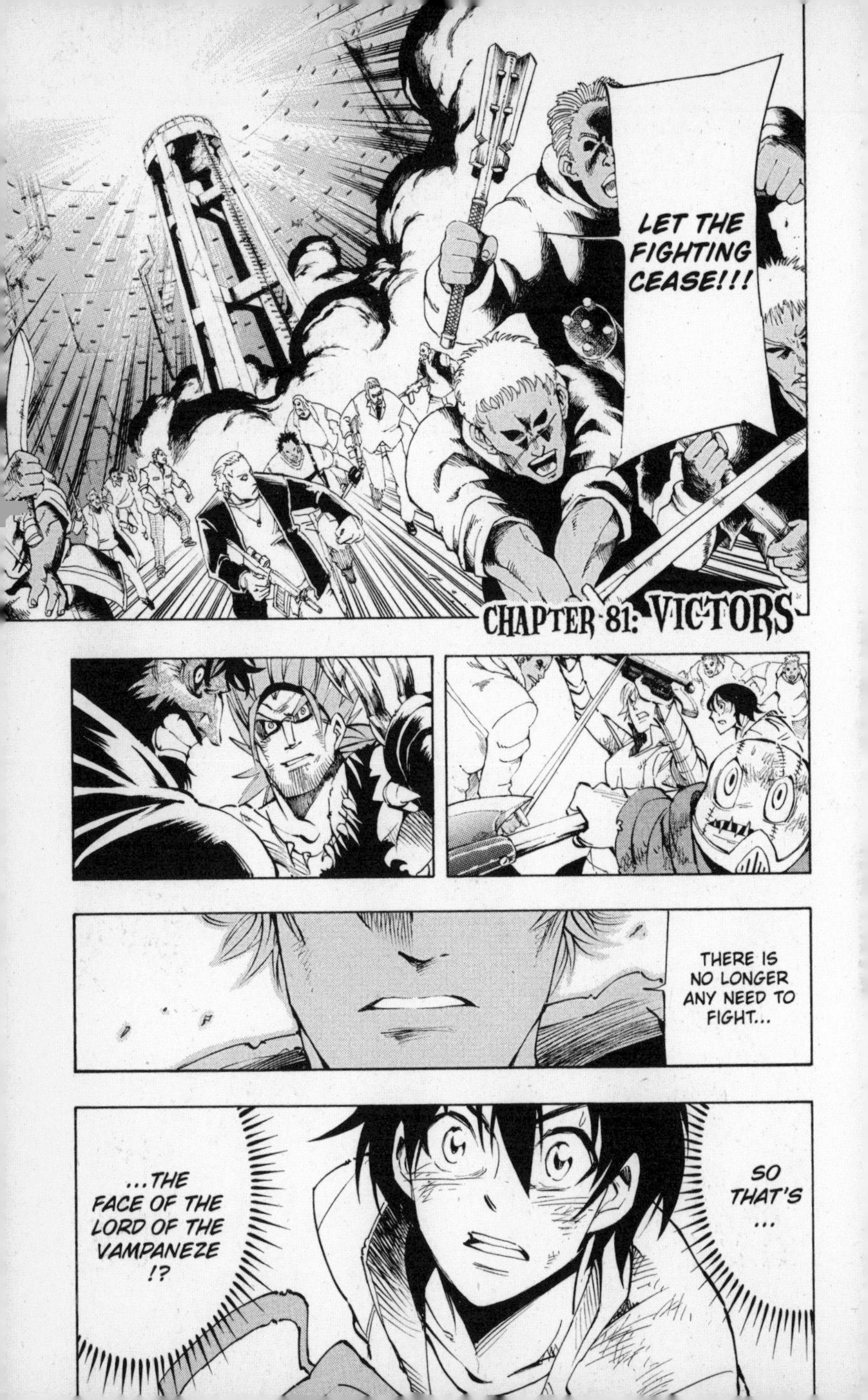
LET THE FIGHTING CEASE!!!
CHAPTER 81: VICTORS
THERE IS NO LONGER ANY NEED TO FIGHT...
SO THAT'S ...
...THE FACE OF THE LORD OF THE VAMPANEZE !?

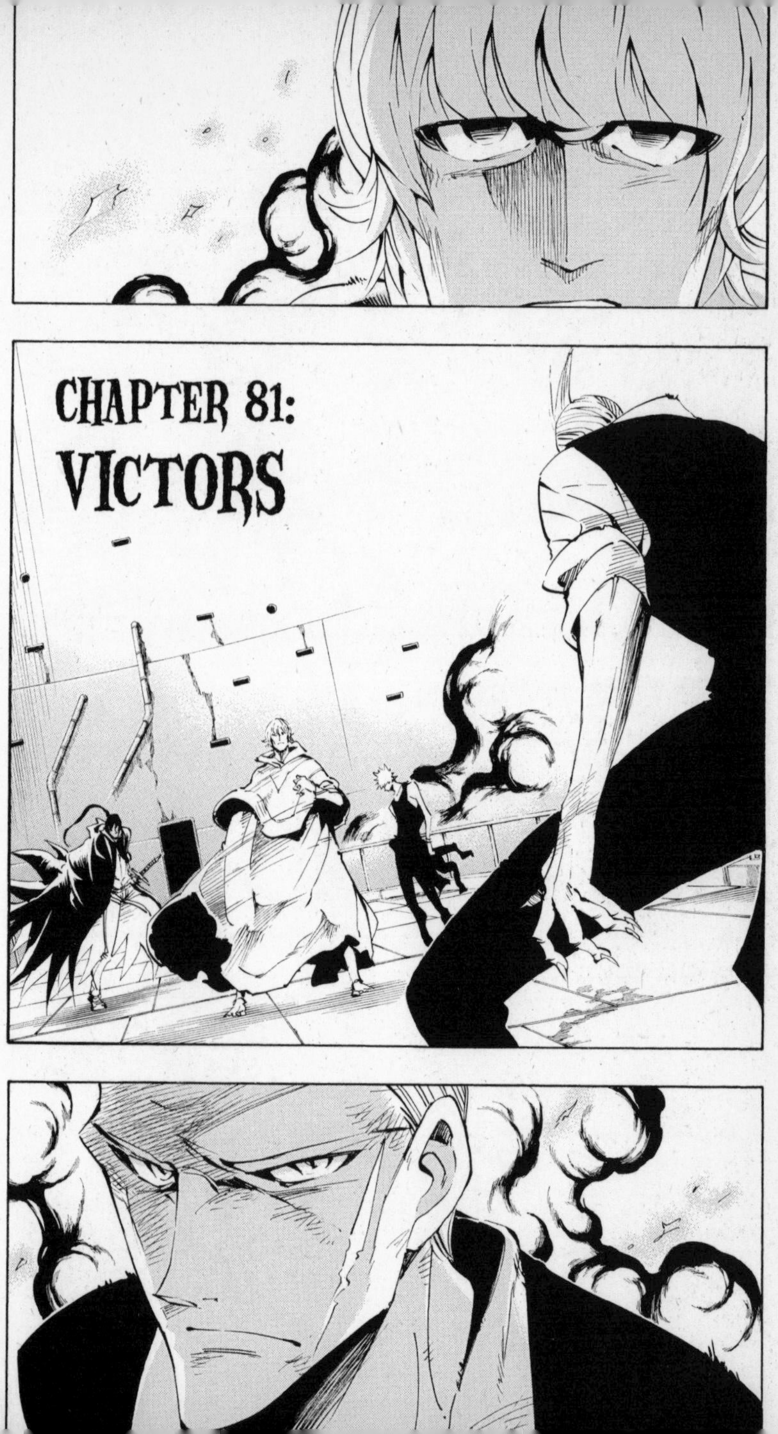
CHAPTER 81:
VICTORS

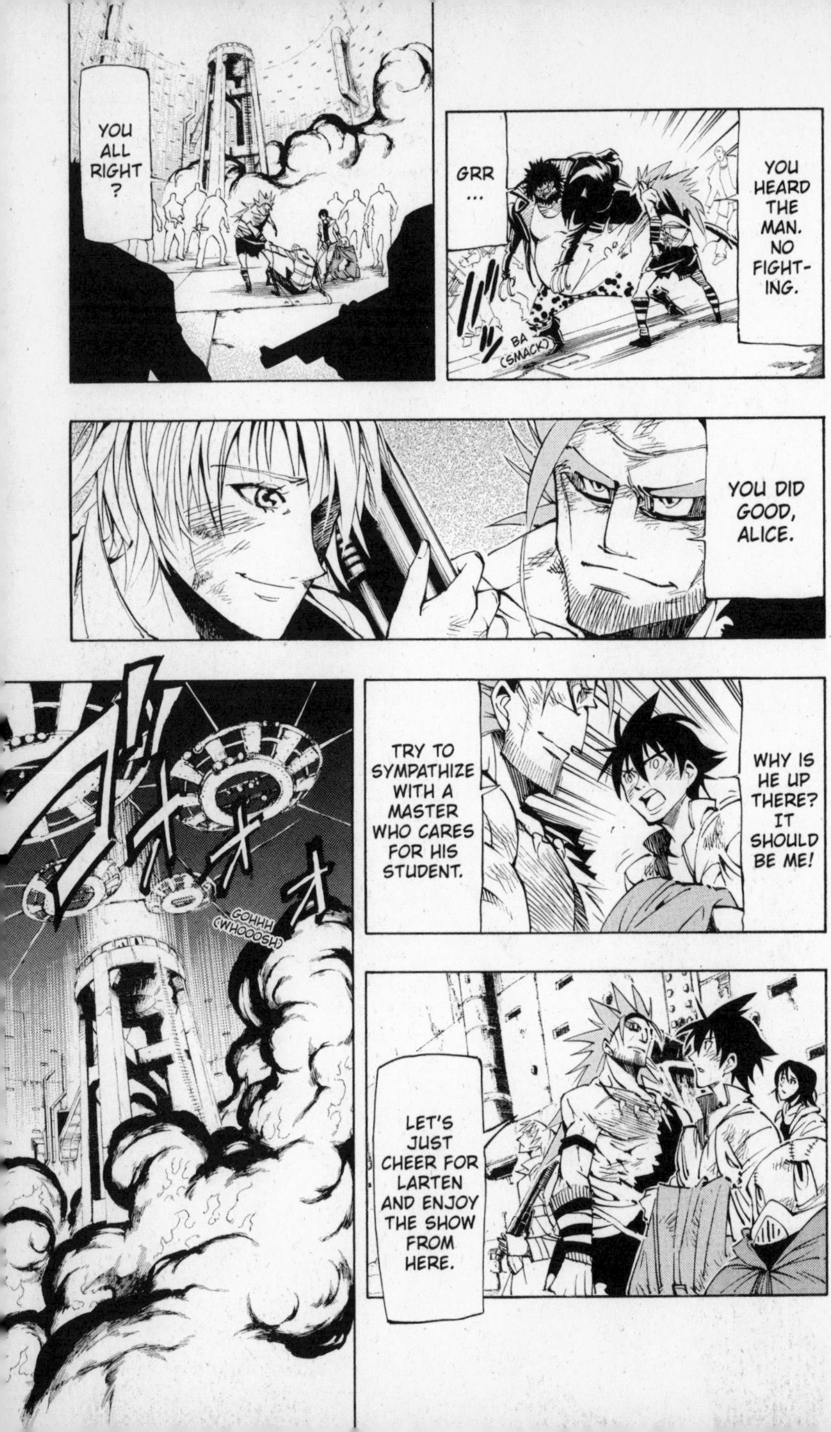
YOU HEARD THE MAN. NO FIGHT-ING.
GRR ...
BA (SMACK)
YOU ALL RIGHT?
YOU DID GOOD, ALICE.
WHY IS HE UP THERE? IT SHOULD BE ME!
TRY TO SYMPATHIZE WITH A MASTER WHO CARES FOR HIS STUDENT.
LET'S JUST CHEER FOR LARTEN AND ENJOY THE SHOW FROM HERE.
GOHHH (WHOOOSH)

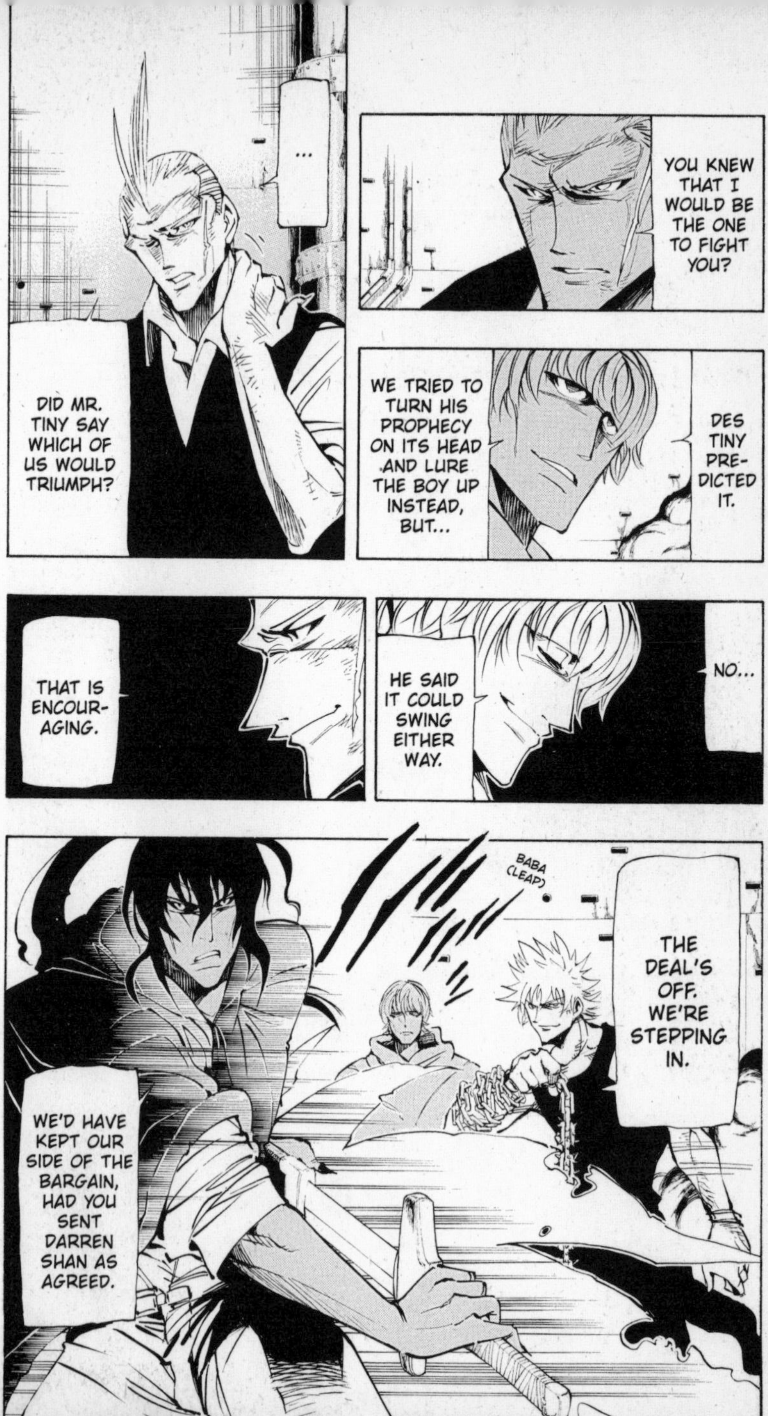
YOU KNEW THAT I WOULD BE THE ONE TO FIGHT YOU?
DES TINY PRE-DICTED IT.
WE TRIED TO TURN HIS PROPHECY ON ITS HEAD AND LURE THE BOY UP INSTEAD, BUT...
...
DID MR. TINY SAY WHICH OF US WOULD TRIUMPH?
NO...
HE SAID IT COULD SWING EITHER WAY.
THAT IS ENCOUR-AGING.
BABA (LEAP)
THE DEAL'S OFF. WE'RE STEPPING IN.
WE'D HAVE KEPT OUR SIDE OF THE BARGAIN, HAD YOU SENT DARREN SHAN AS AGREED.

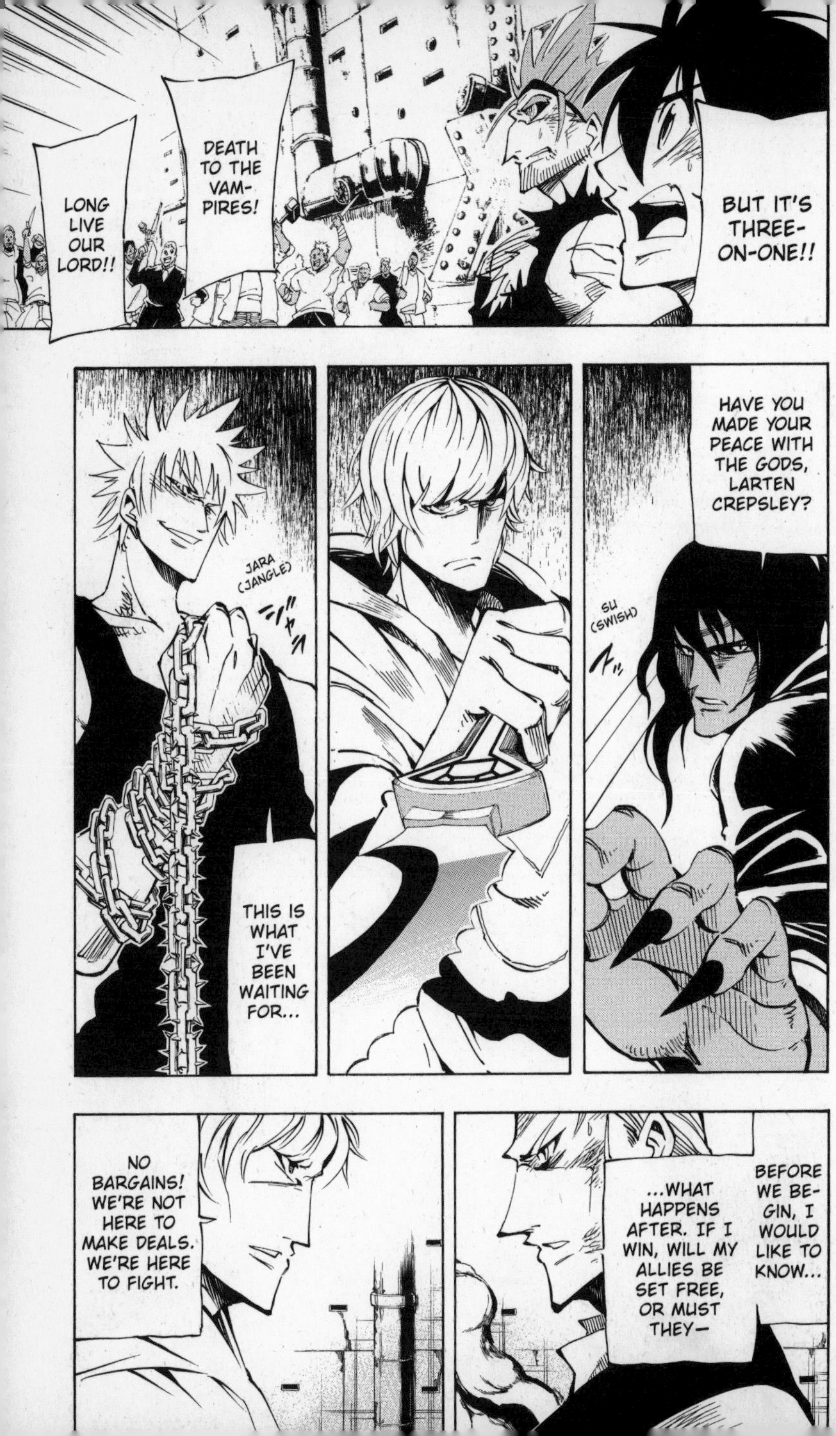

BUT IT'S THREE-ON-ONE!!
DEATH TO THE VAMPIRES!
LONG LIVE OUR LORD!!
HAVE YOU MADE YOUR PEACE WITH THE GODS, LARTEN CREPSLEY?
SU (SWISH)
JARA (JANGLE)
THIS IS WHAT I'VE BEEN WAITING FOR...
BEFORE WE BEGIN, I WOULD LIKE TO KNOW...
...WHAT HAPPENS AFTER. IF I WIN, WILL MY ALLIES BE SET FREE, OR MUST THEY—
NO BARGAINS! WE'RE NOT HERE TO MAKE DEALS. WE'RE HERE TO FIGHT.

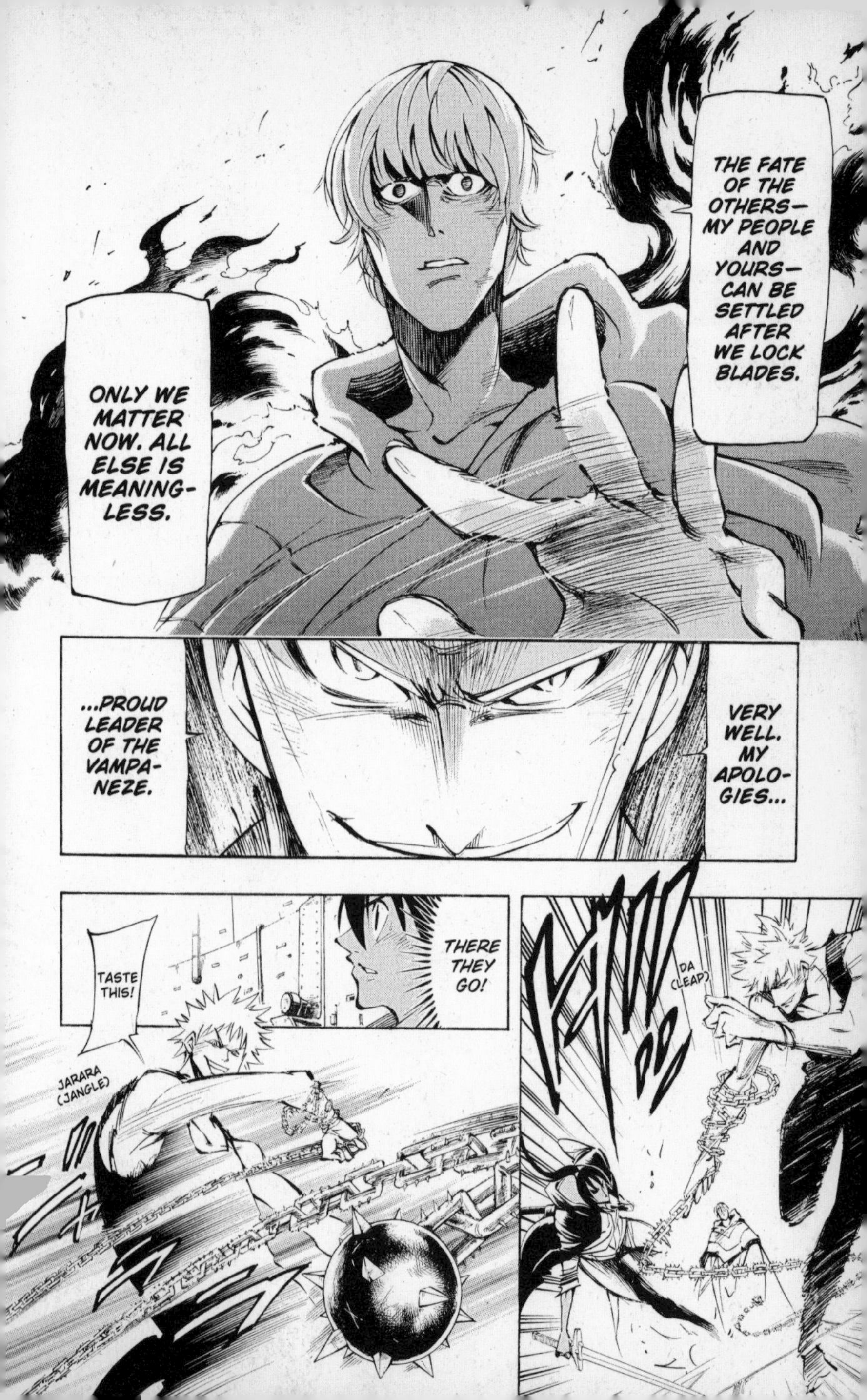
THE FATE OF THE OTHERS— MY PEOPLE AND YOURS— CAN BE SETTLED AFTER WE LOCK BLADES.
ONLY WE MATTER NOW. ALL ELSE IS MEANING-LESS.
VERY WELL. MY APOLO-GIES...
...PROUD LEADER OF THE VAMPA-NEZE.
DA (LEAP)
THERE THEY GO!
TASTE THIS!
JARARA (JANGLE)

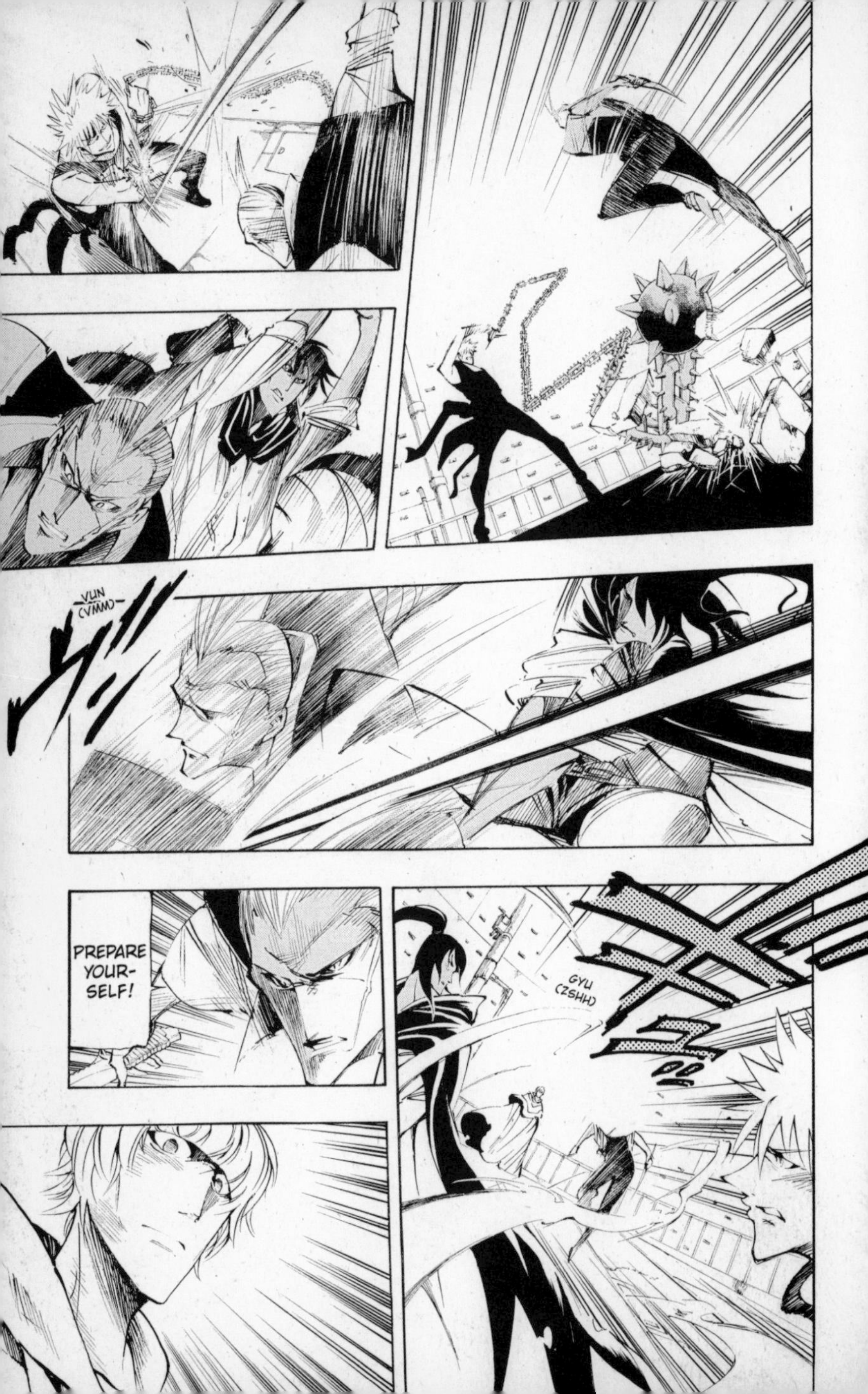
VUN (VIMM)
GYU (ZSHH)
PREPARE YOUR-SELF!

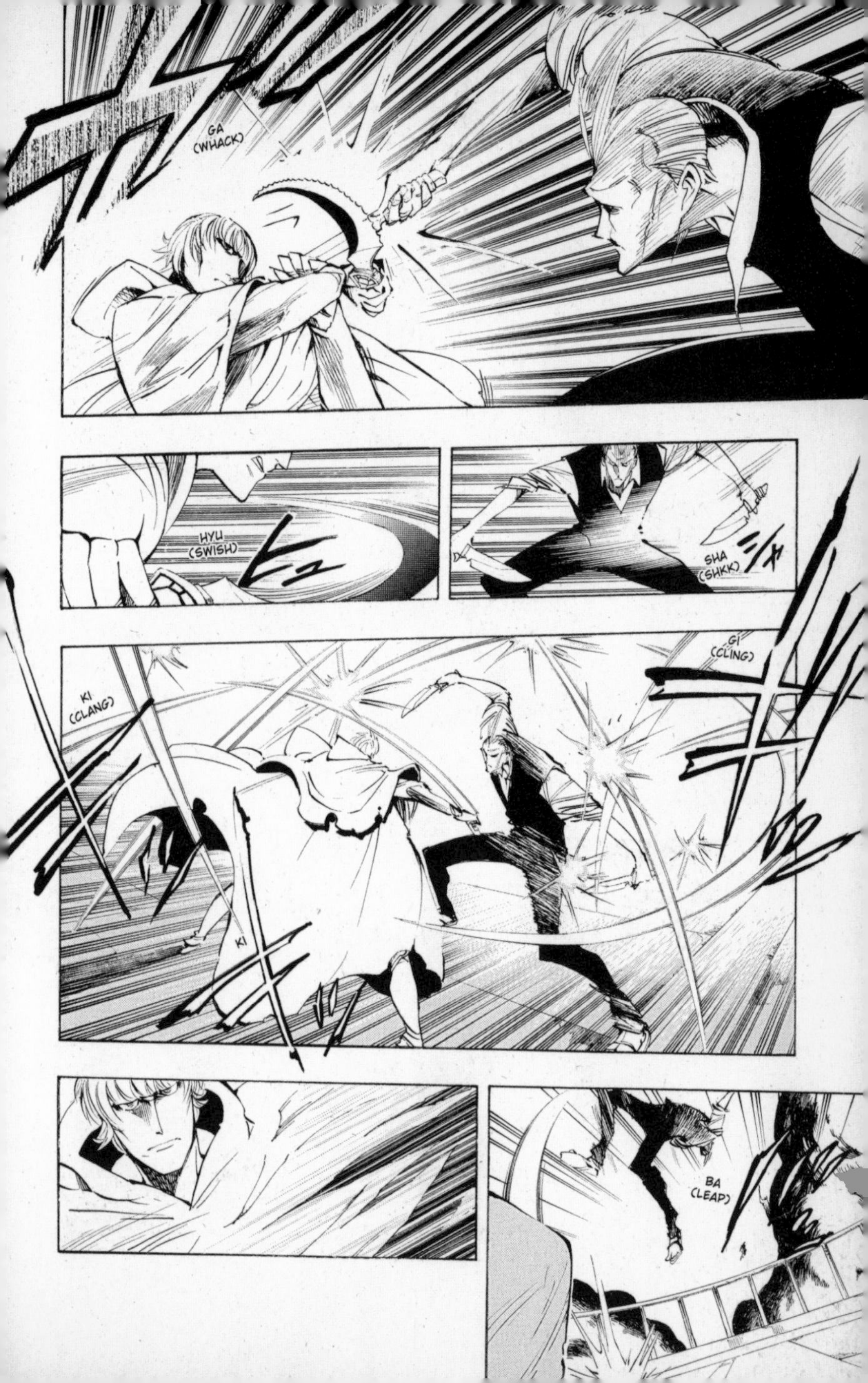
GA (WHACK)
SHA (SHKK)
HYU (SWISH)
GI (CLING)
KI (CLANG)
KI
BA (LEAP)

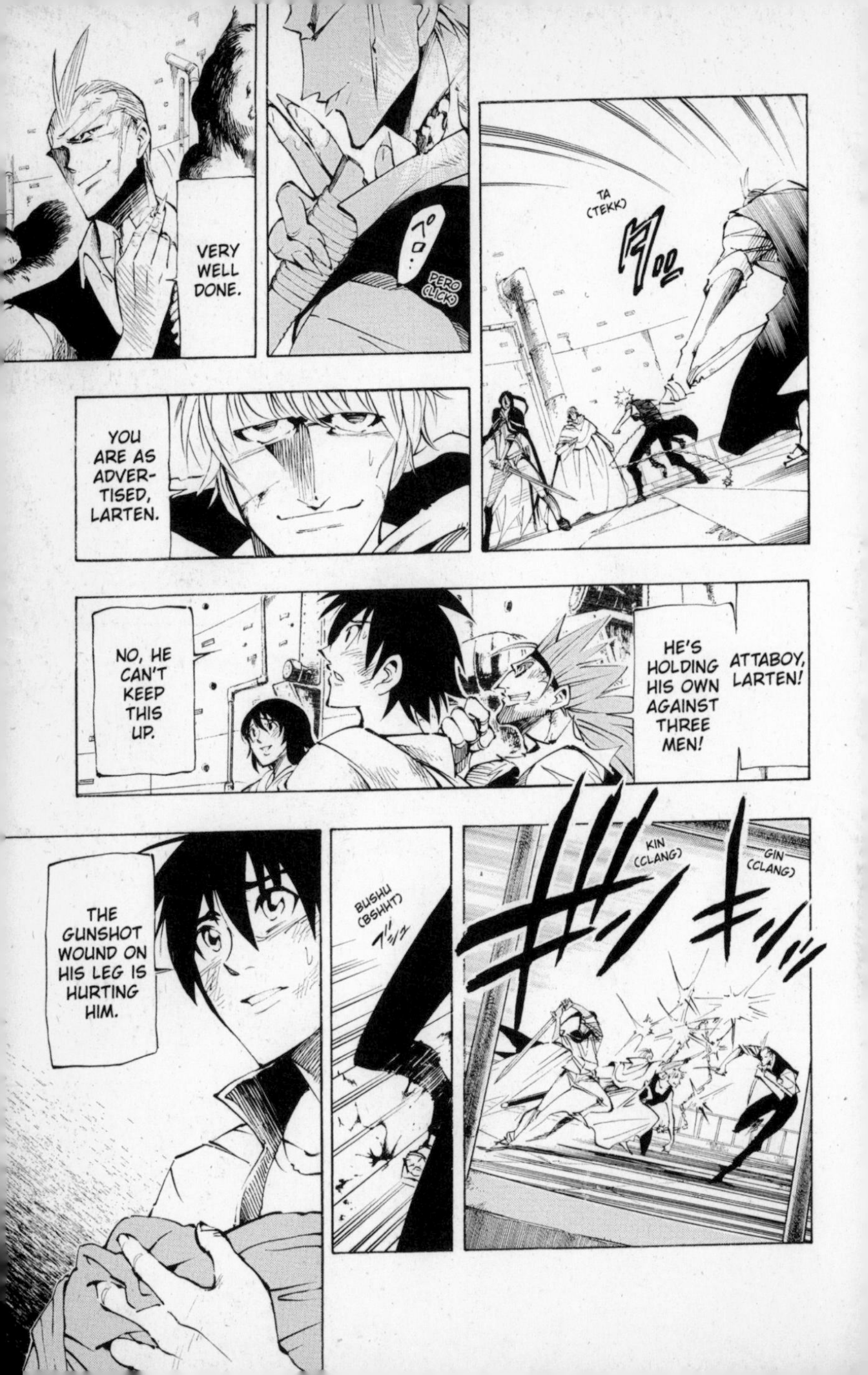
TA
(TEKK)
ペロ…
PERO
(LICK)
VERY WELL DONE.
YOU ARE AS ADVERTISED, LARTEN.
ATTABOY, LARTEN!
HE'S HOLDING HIS OWN AGAINST THREE MEN!
NO, HE CAN'T KEEP THIS UP.
GIN
(CLANG)
KIN
(CLANG)
BUSHU
(BSHHT)
ブシュ
THE GUNSHOT WOUND ON HIS LEG IS HURTING HIM.

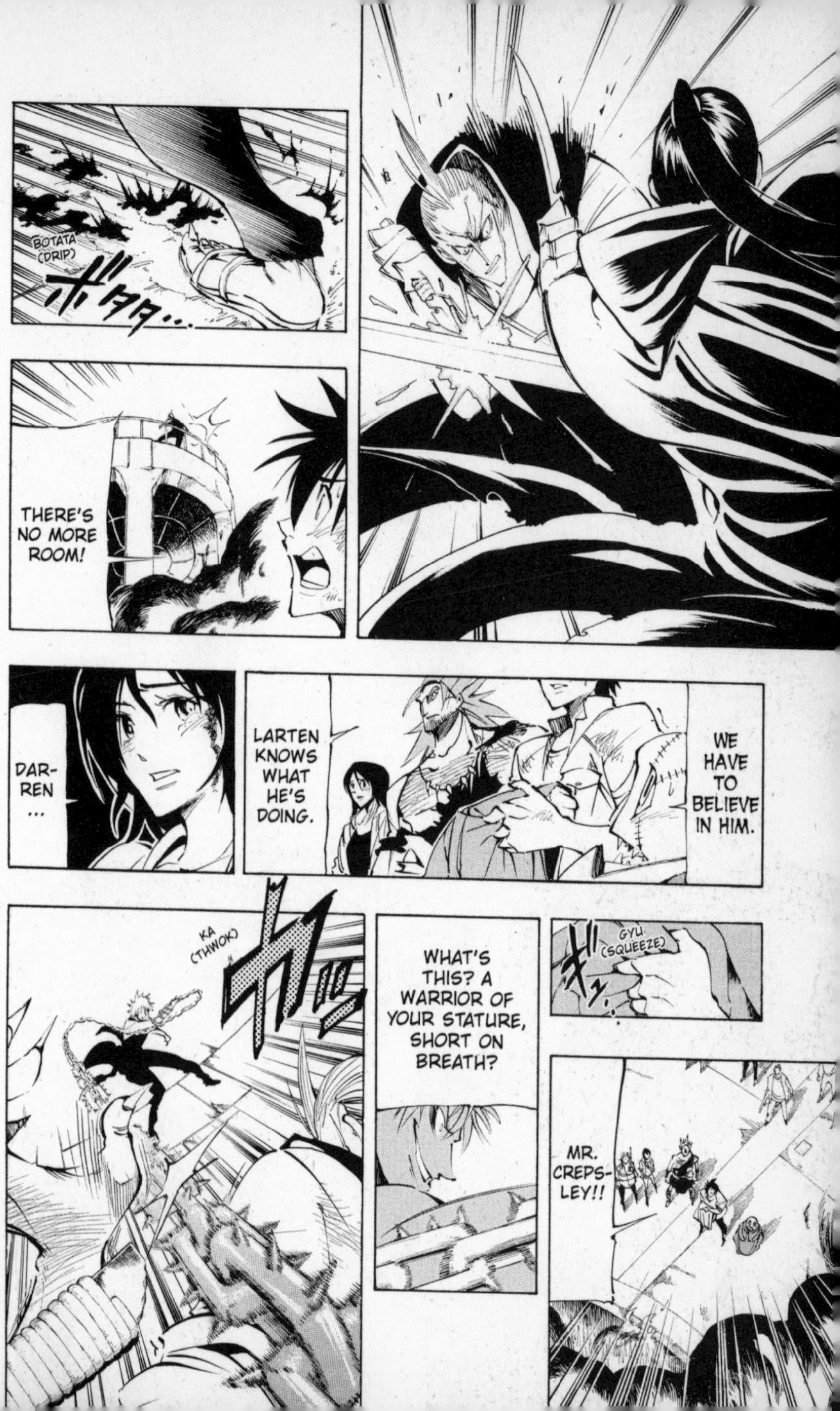
BOTATA (DRIP)
THERE'S NO MORE ROOM!
WE HAVE TO BELIEVE IN HIM.
LARTEN KNOWS WHAT HE'S DOING.
DAR-REN ...
GYU (SQUEEZE)
MR. CREPS-LEY!!
WHAT'S THIS? A WARRIOR OF YOUR STATURE, SHORT ON BREATH?
KA (THWOK)

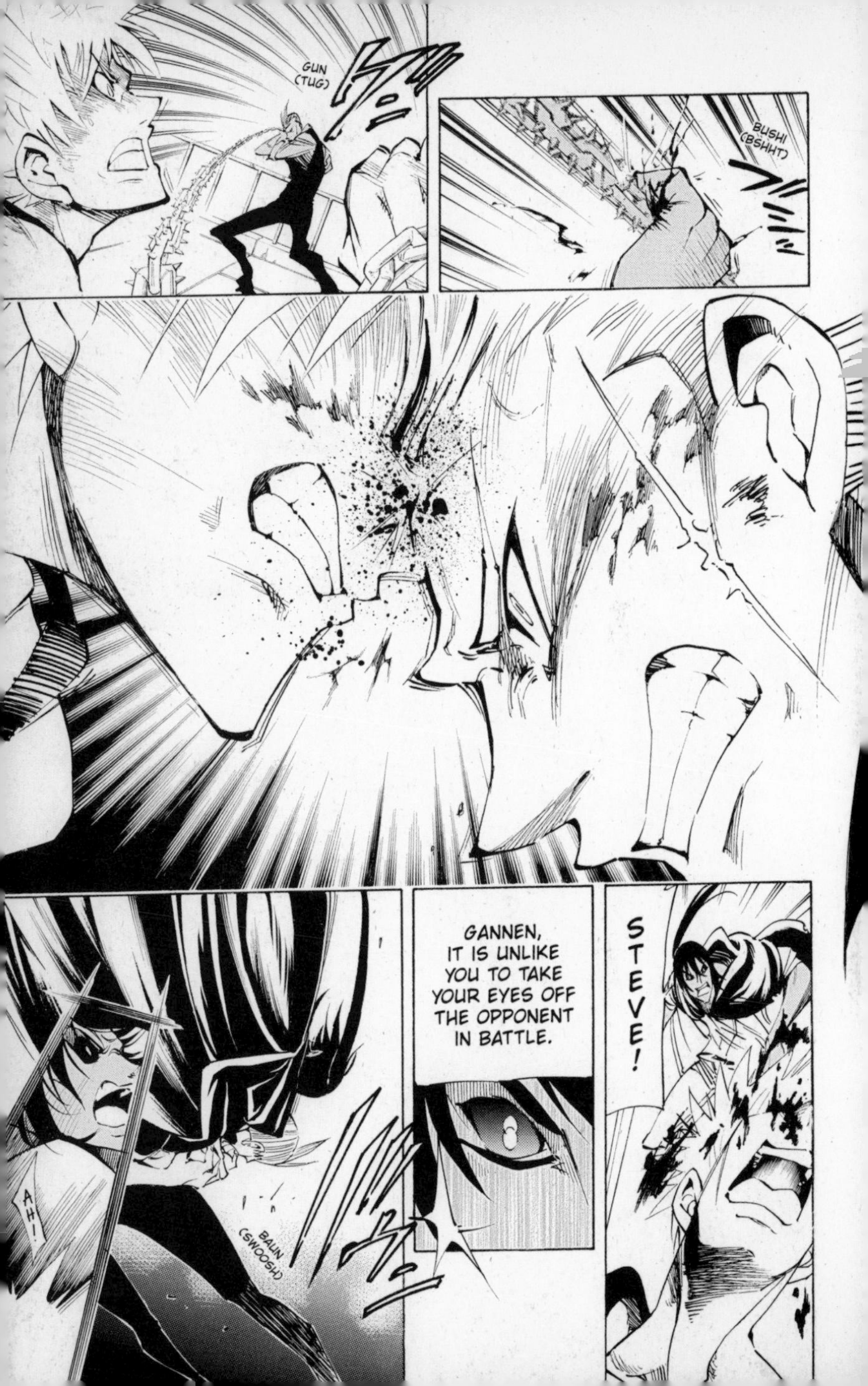
BUSHI
(BSHHT)
GUN
(TUG)
STEVE!
GANNEN, IT IS UNLIKE YOU TO TAKE YOUR EYES OFF THE OPPONENT IN BATTLE.
AH!
BAUN
(SWOOSH)

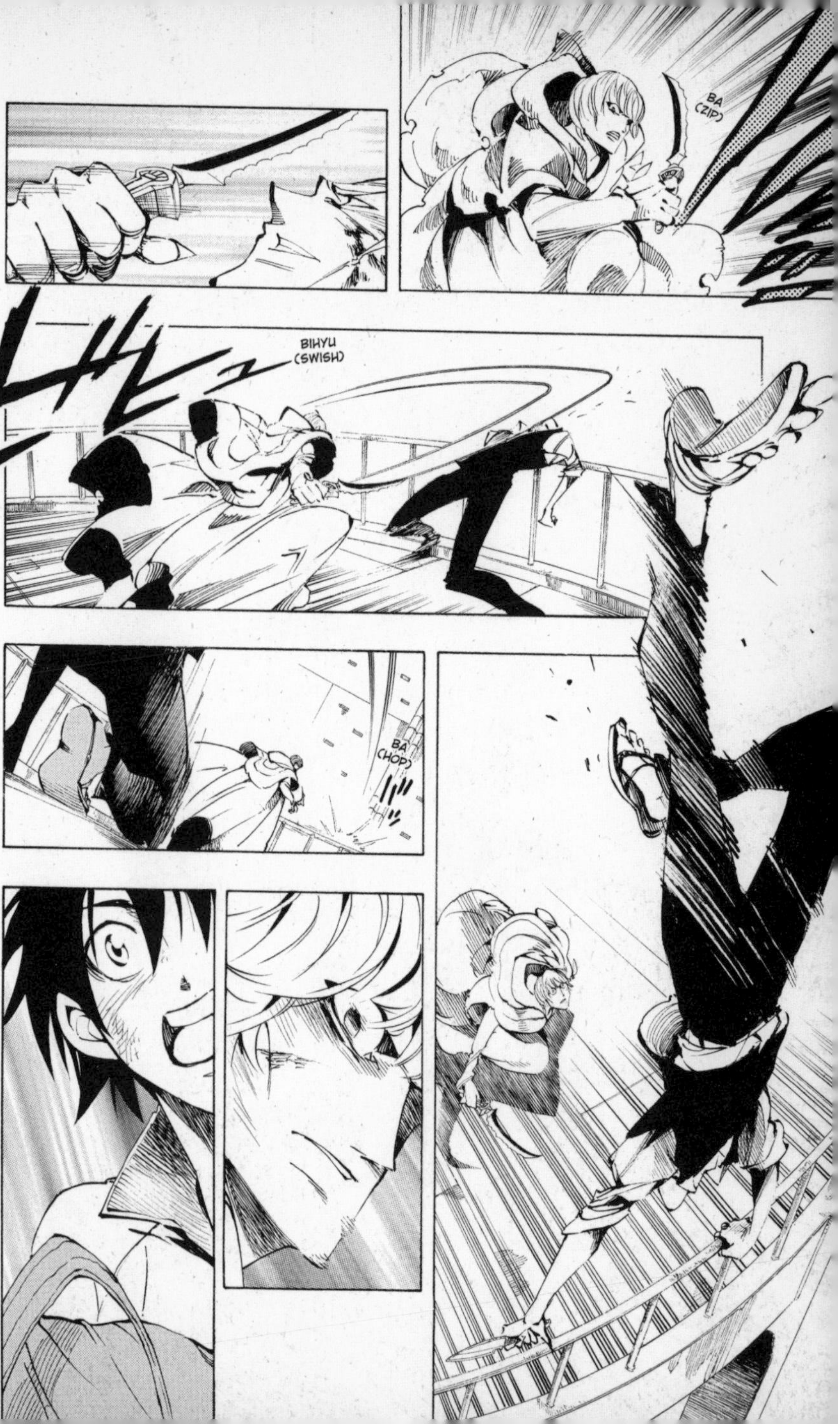
BA
(ZIP)
BIHYU
(SWISH)
BA
(HOP)

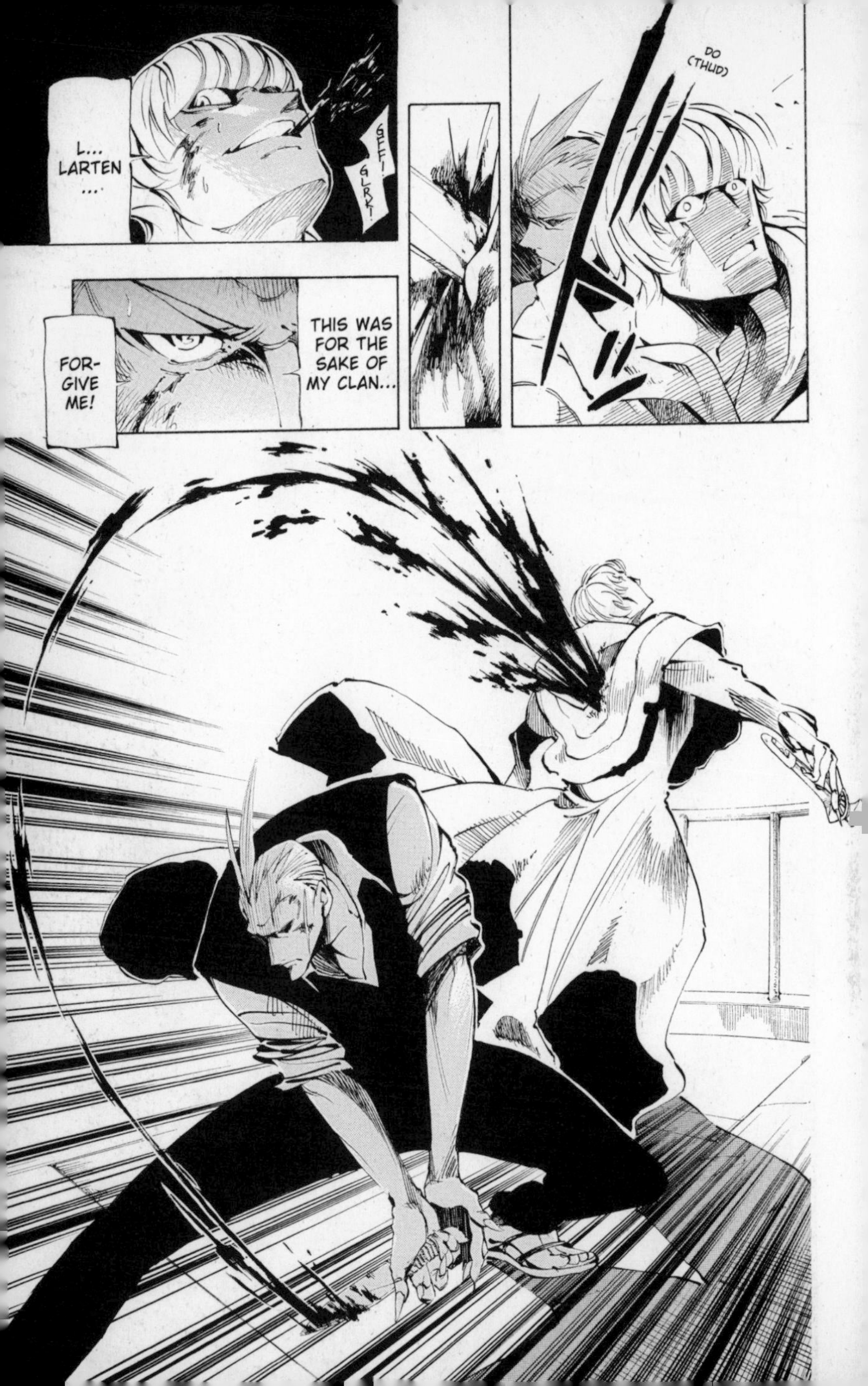
DO (THUD)
GFF! GLRK!
L... LARTEN ...
THIS WAS FOR THE SAKE OF MY CLAN...
FOR-GIVE ME!

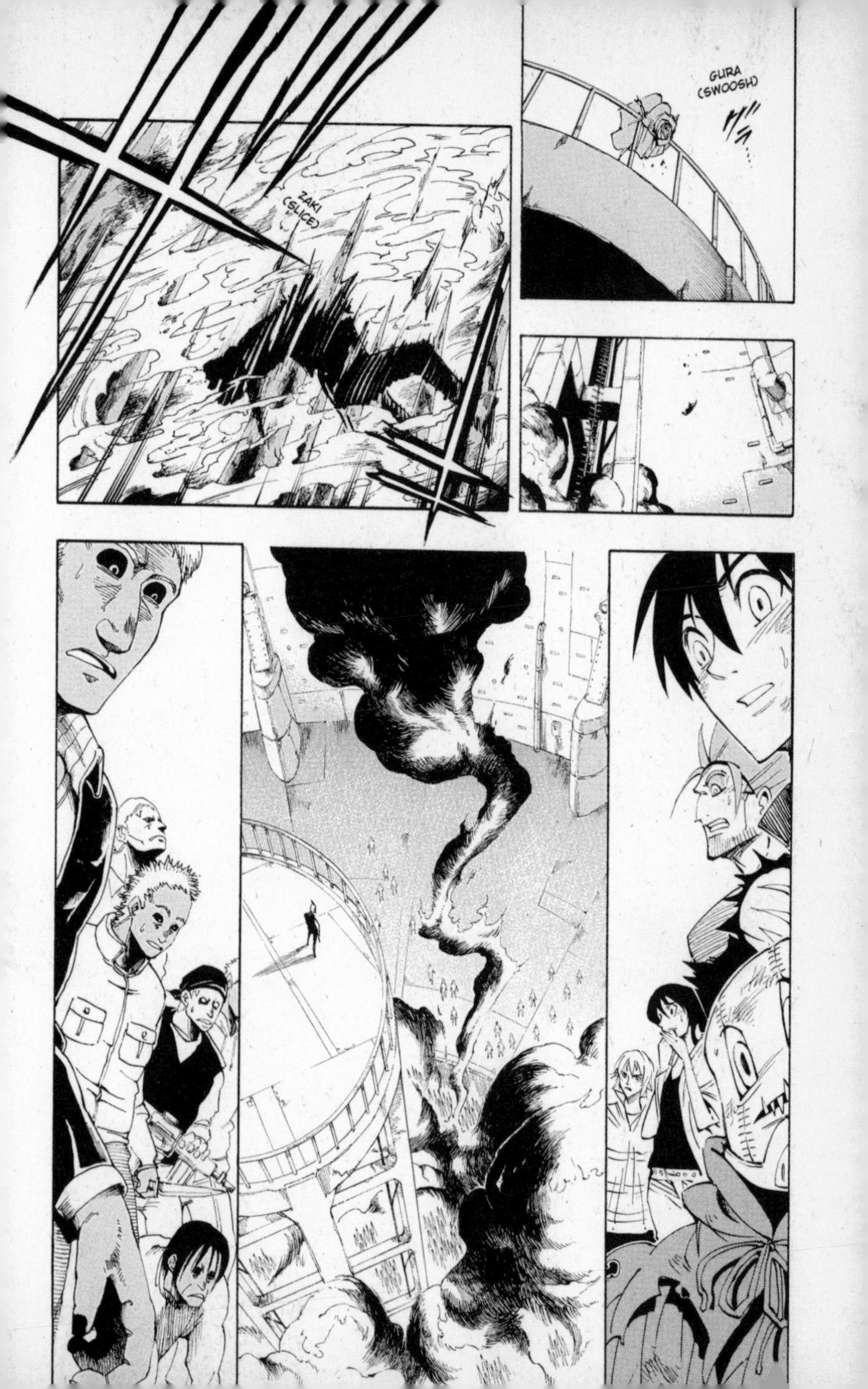
GURA (SWOOSH)
ZAKI (SLICE)

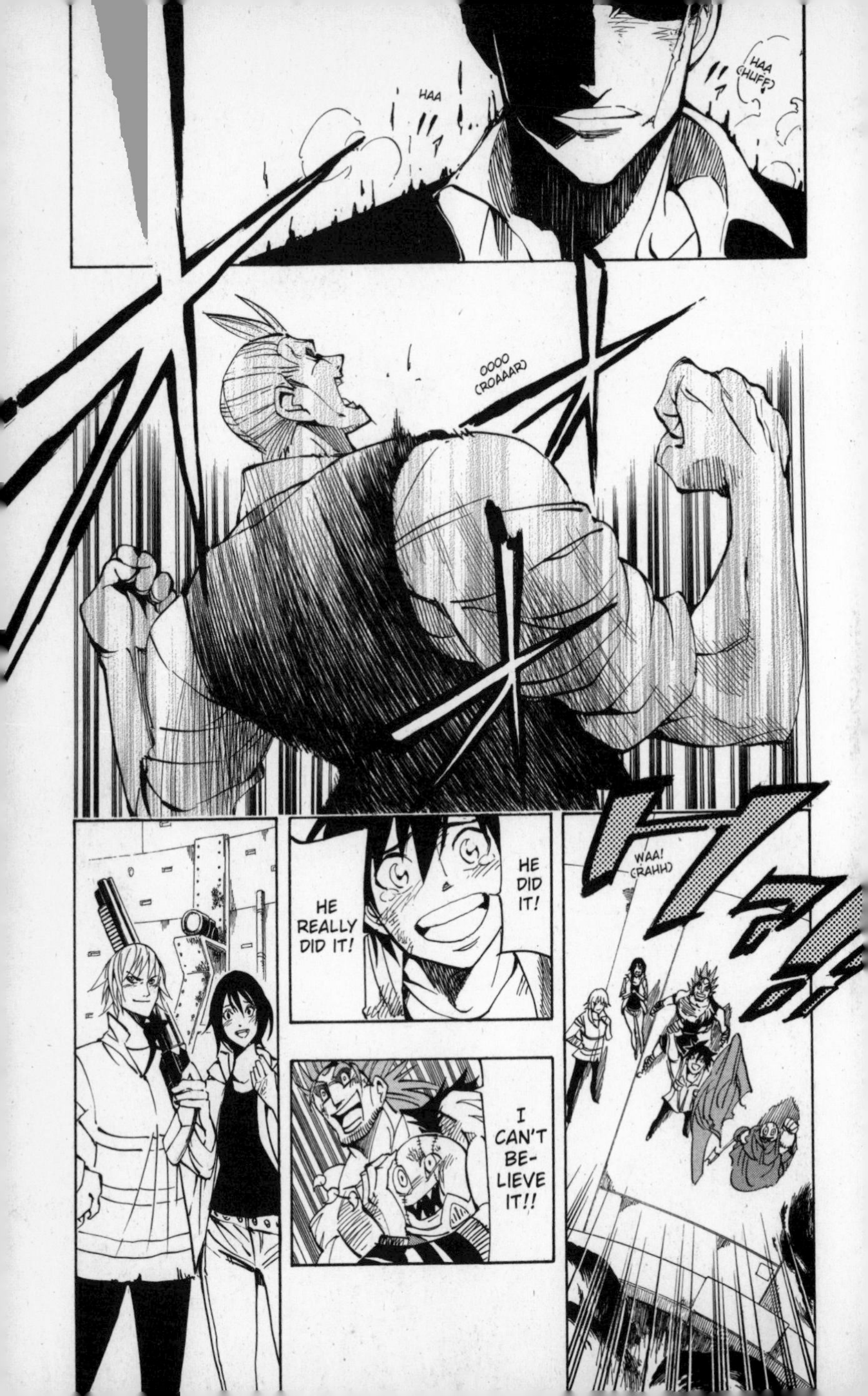
HAA (HUFF)
HAA
OOOO (ROAAAR)
WAA! (RAHH)
HE DID IT!
HE REALLY DID IT!
I CAN'T BE-LIEVE IT!!

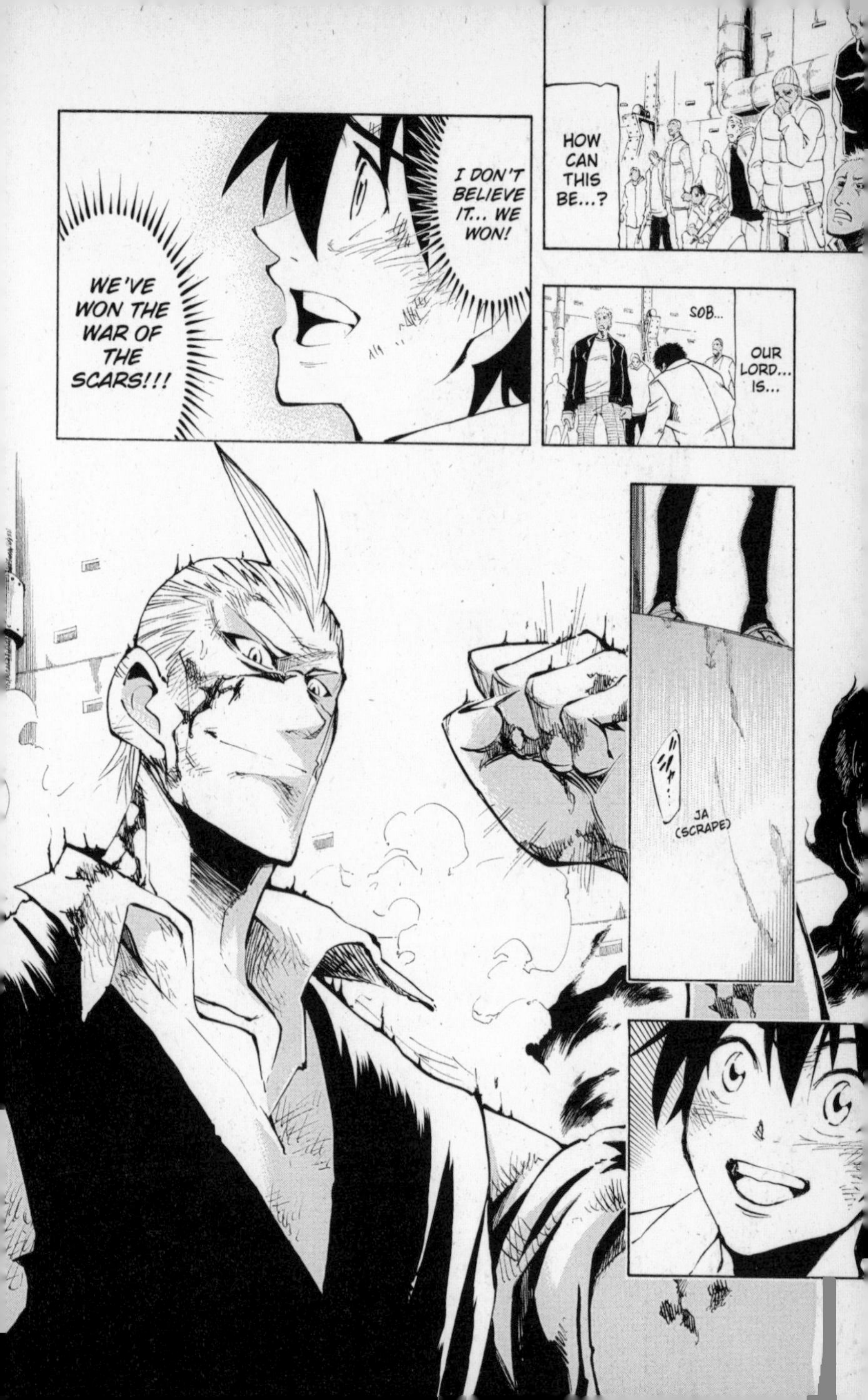
HOW CAN THIS BE...?
SOB...
OUR LORD... IS...
I DON'T BELIEVE IT... WE WON!
WE'VE WON THE WAR OF THE SCARS!!!
JA (SCRAPE)

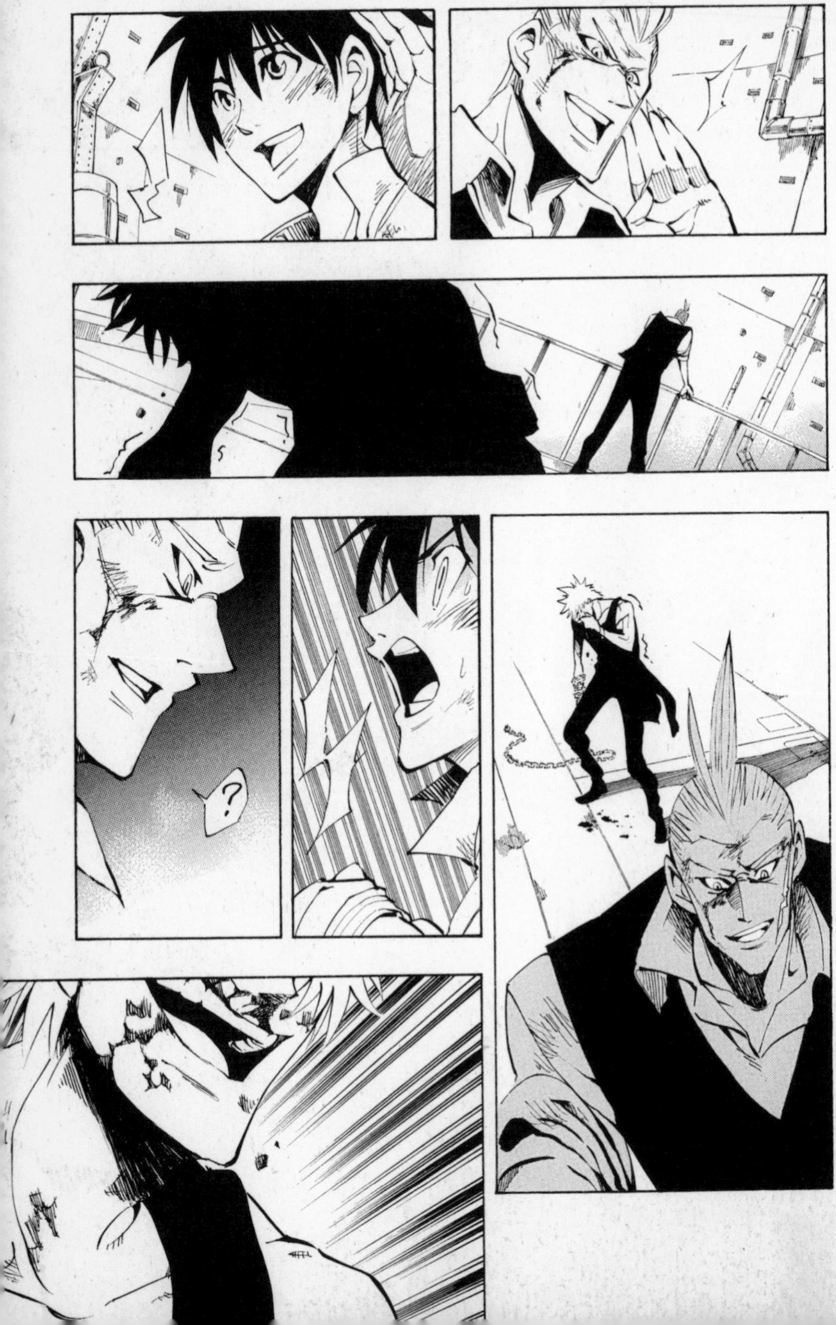
?

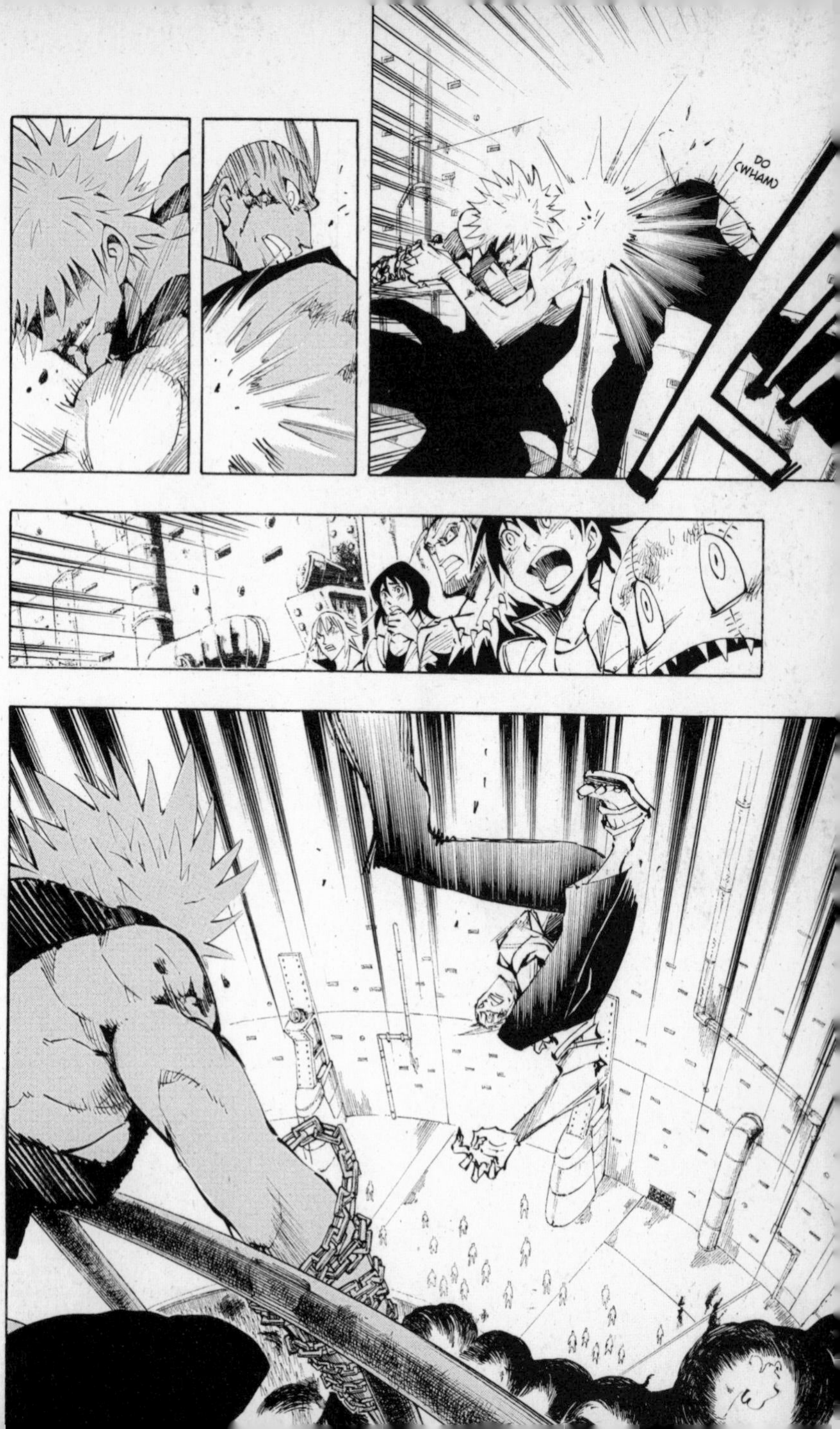
DO (WHAM)

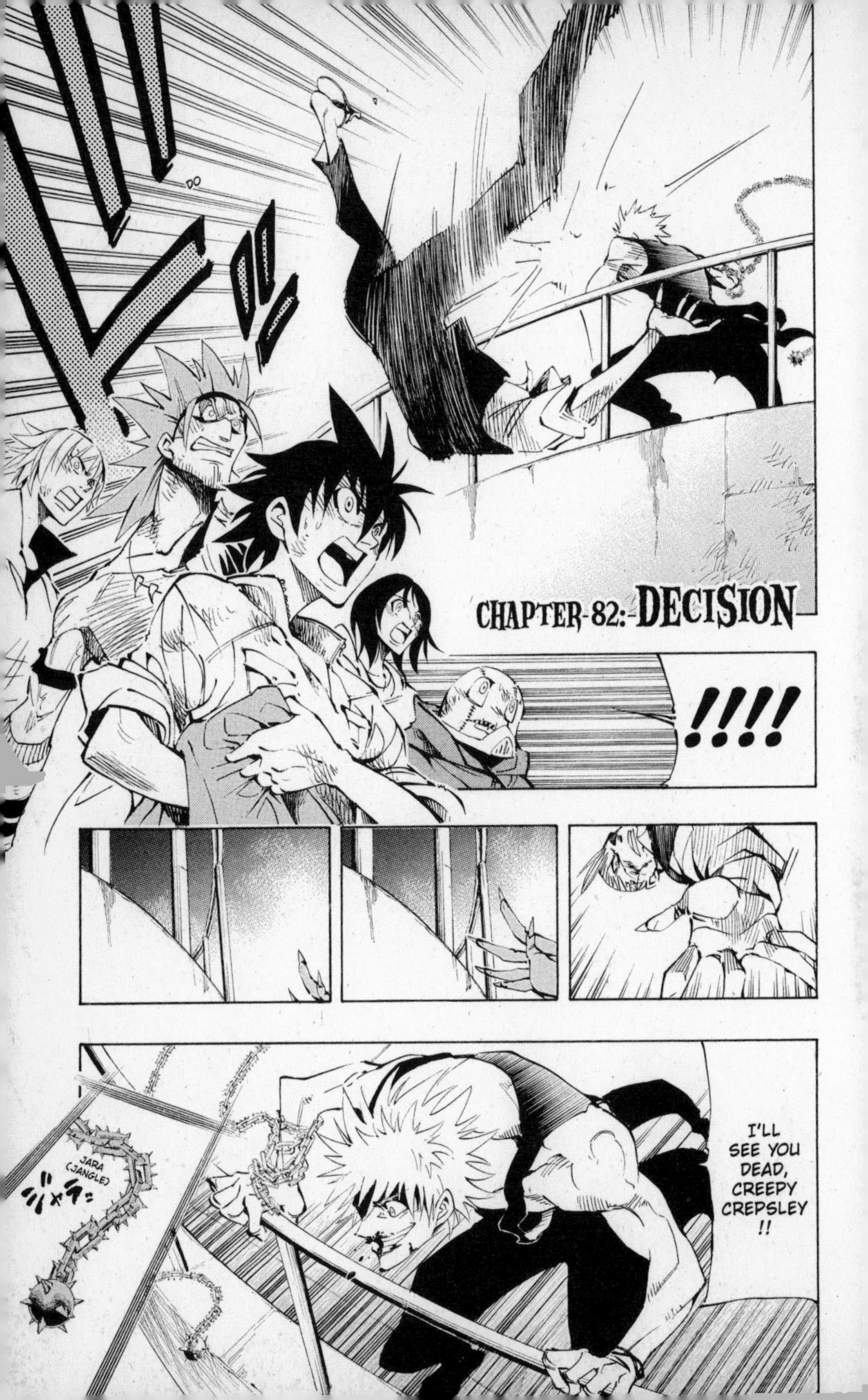
DO
CHAPTER-82:-DECISION
!!!!
I'LL SEE YOU DEAD, CREEPY CREPSLEY !!
JARA (JANGLE)

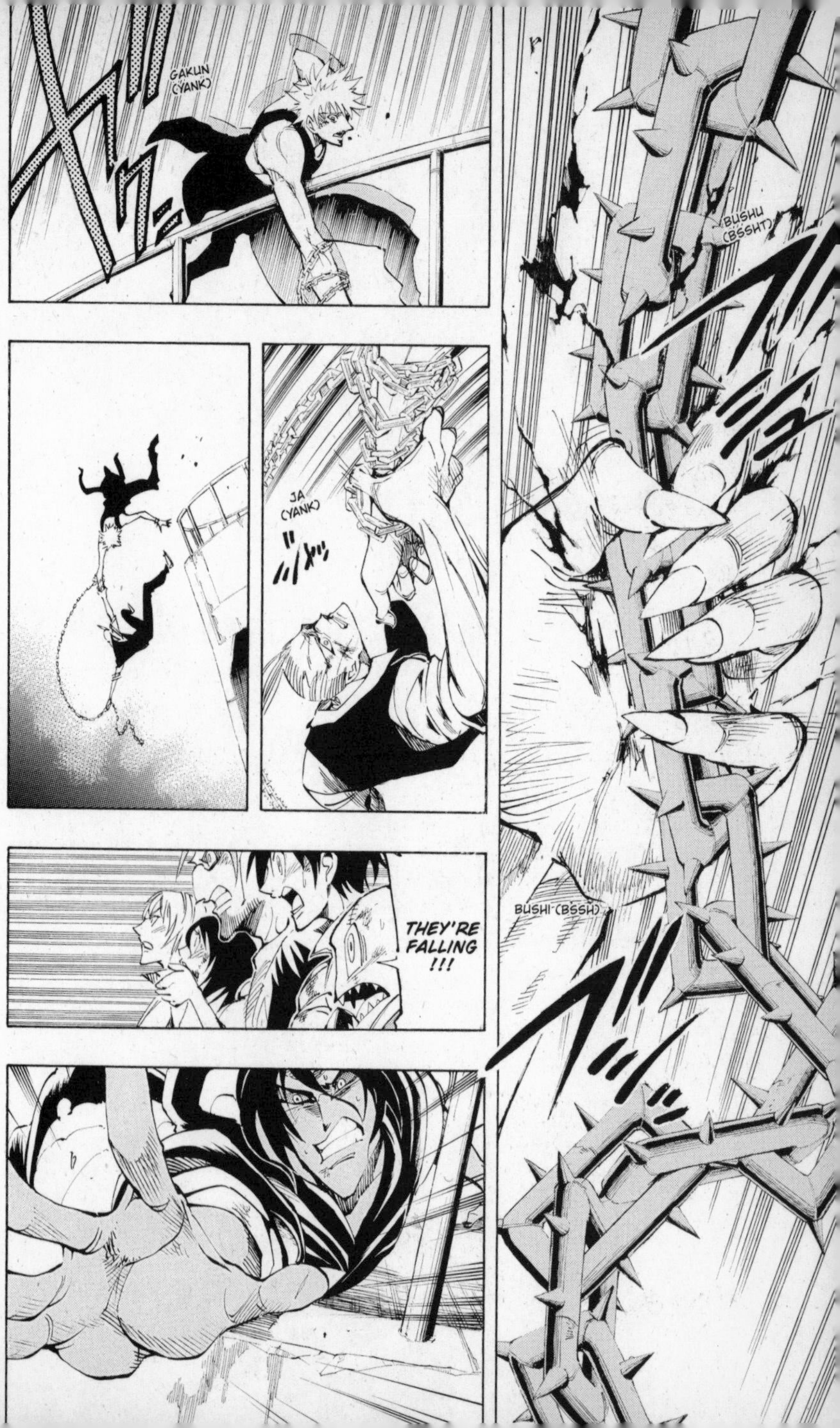
BUSHU (BSSHT)
BUSHI (BSSH)
GAKUN (YANK)
JA (YANK)
THEY'RE FALLING !!!

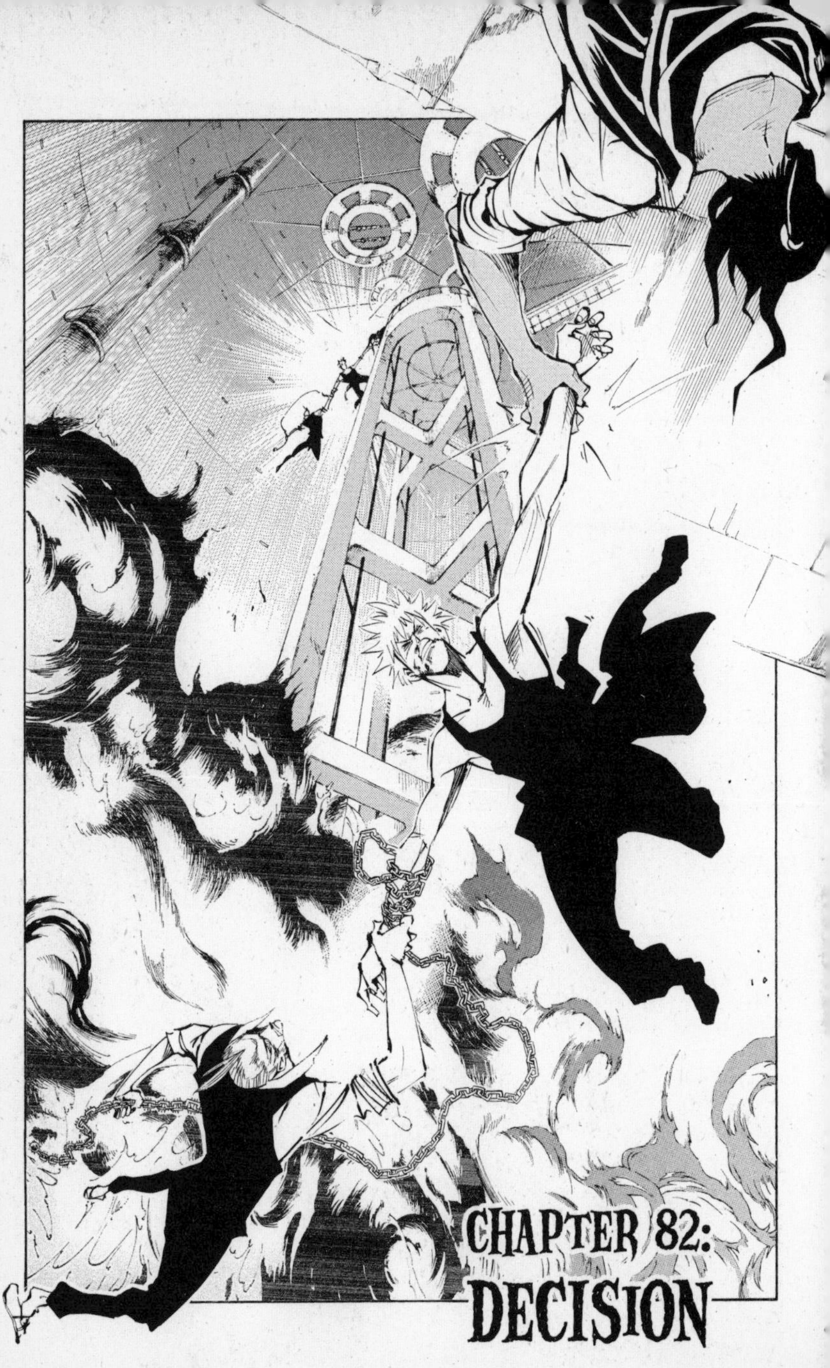
CHAPTER 82:
DECISION

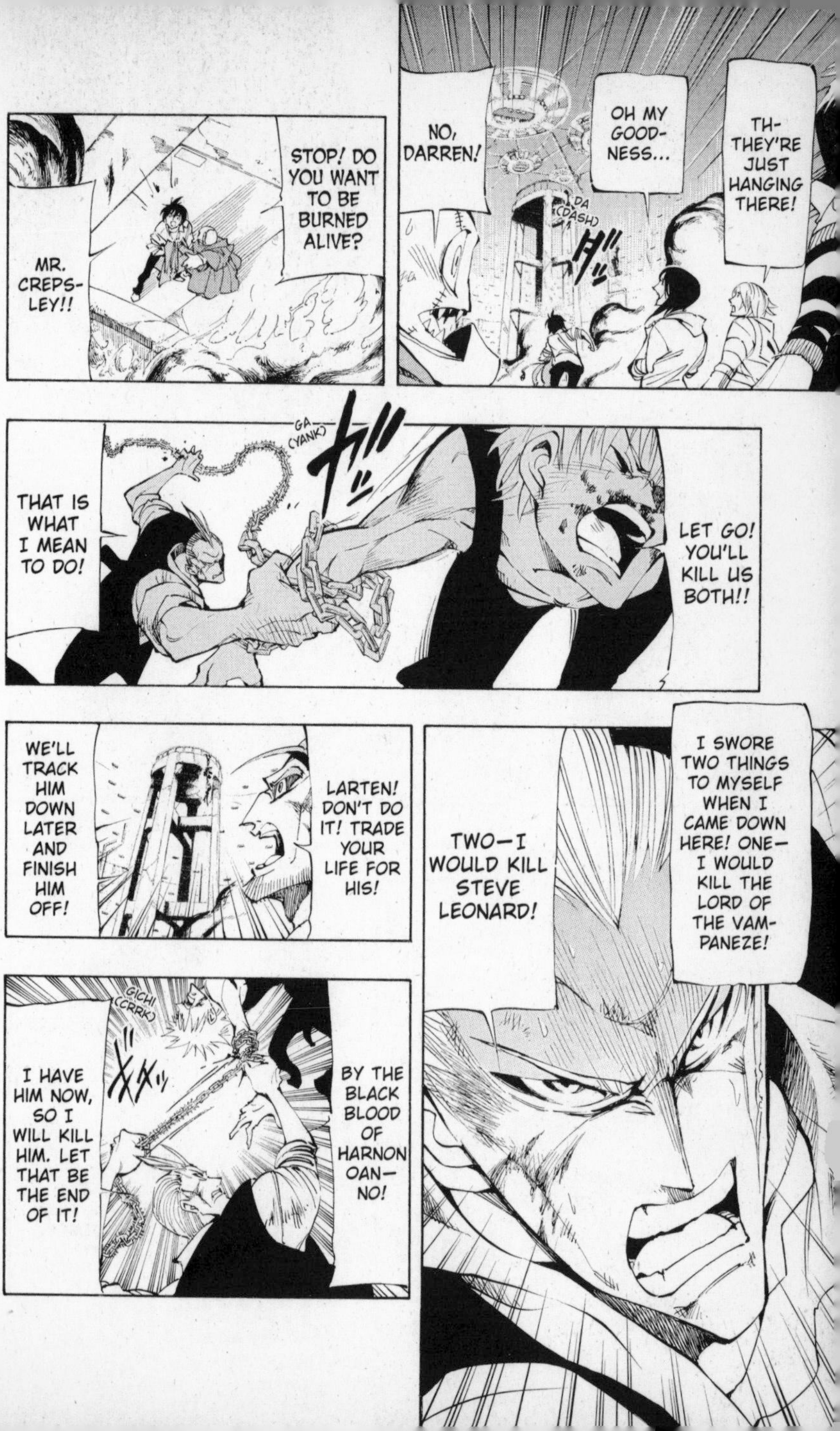
TH-THEY'RE JUST HANGING THERE!
OH MY GOODNESS...
NO, DARREN!
DA (DASH)
STOP! DO YOU WANT TO BE BURNED ALIVE?
MR. CREPS-LEY!!
GA (YANK)
LET GO! YOU'LL KILL US BOTH!!
THAT IS WHAT I MEAN TO DO!
I SWORE TWO THINGS TO MYSELF WHEN I CAME DOWN HERE! ONE—I WOULD KILL THE LORD OF THE VAM-PANEZE!
TWO—I WOULD KILL STEVE LEONARD!
LARTEN! DON'T DO IT! TRADE YOUR LIFE FOR HIS!
WE'LL TRACK HIM DOWN LATER AND FINISH HIM OFF!
GICHI (CRRK)
BY THE BLACK BLOOD OF HARNON OAN—NO!
I HAVE HIM NOW, SO I WILL KILL HIM. LET THAT BE THE END OF IT!

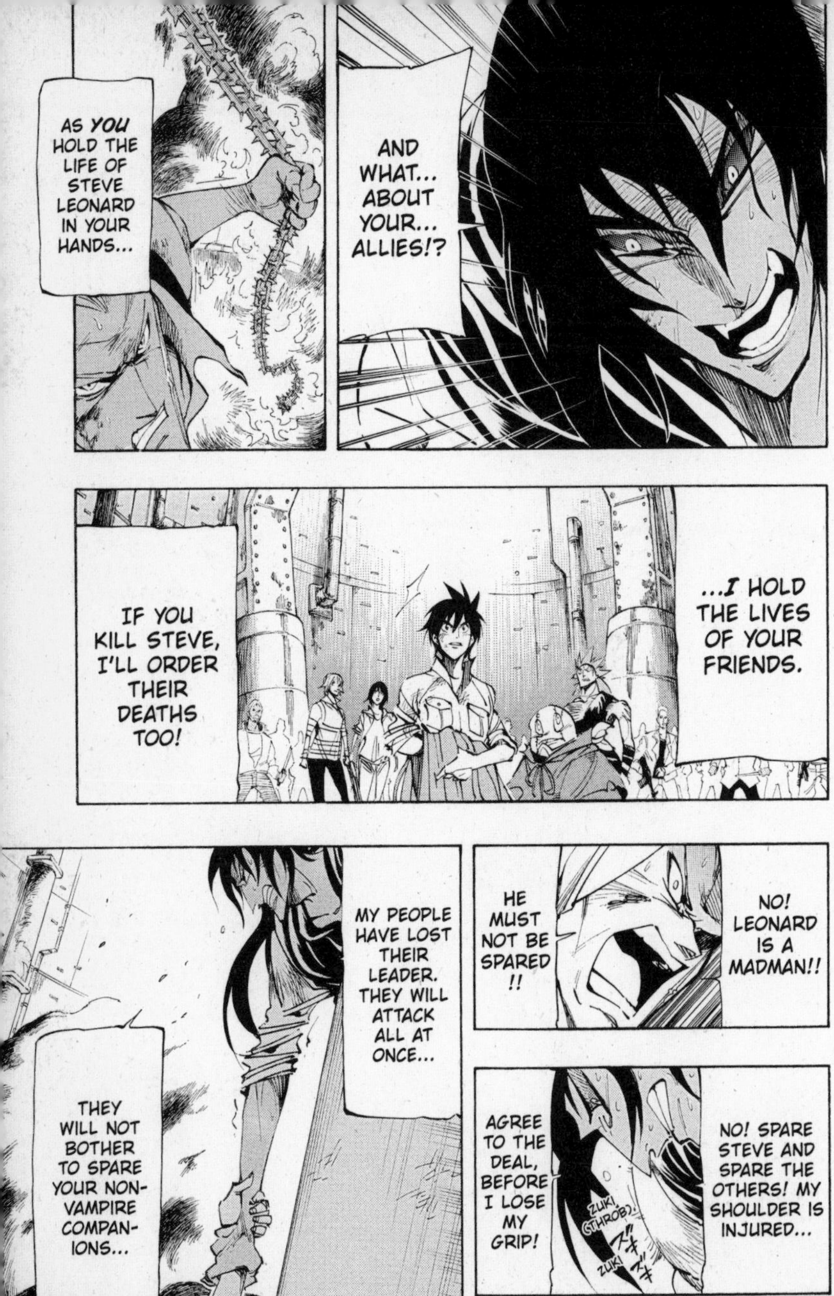
AND WHAT... ABOUT YOUR... ALLIES!?
AS YOU HOLD THE LIFE OF STEVE LEONARD IN YOUR HANDS...
...I HOLD THE LIVES OF YOUR FRIENDS.
IF YOU KILL STEVE, I'LL ORDER THEIR DEATHS TOO!
NO! LEONARD IS A MADMAN!!
HE MUST NOT BE SPARED!!
NO! SPARE STEVE AND SPARE THE OTHERS! MY SHOULDER IS INJURED...
AGREE TO THE DEAL, BEFORE I LOSE MY GRIP!
ZUKI (THROB)
ZUKI
MY PEOPLE HAVE LOST THEIR LEADER. THEY WILL ATTACK ALL AT ONCE...
THEY WILL NOT BOTHER TO SPARE YOUR NON-VAMPIRE COMPANIONS...

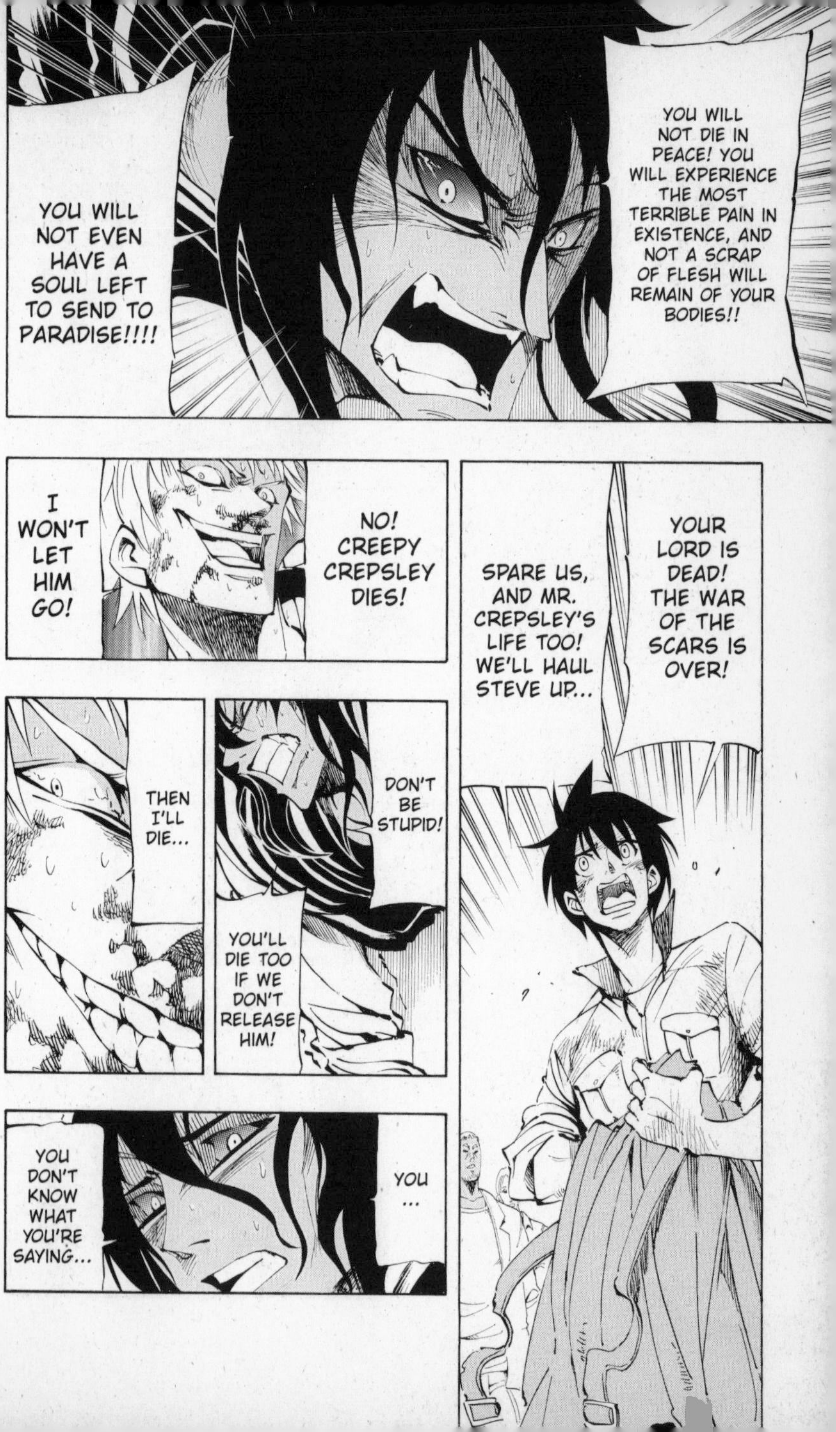
YOU WILL NOT DIE IN PEACE! YOU WILL EXPERIENCE THE MOST TERRIBLE PAIN IN EXISTENCE, AND NOT A SCRAP OF FLESH WILL REMAIN OF YOUR BODIES!!
YOU WILL NOT EVEN HAVE A SOUL LEFT TO SEND TO PARADISE!!!!
YOUR LORD IS DEAD! THE WAR OF THE SCARS IS OVER!
SPARE US, AND MR. CREPSLEY'S LIFE TOO! WE'LL HAUL STEVE UP...
NO! CREEPY CREPSLEY DIES!
I WON'T LET HIM GO!
DON'T BE STUPID!
YOU'LL DIE TOO IF WE DON'T RELEASE HIM!
THEN I'LL DIE...
YOU ...
YOU DON'T KNOW WHAT YOU'RE SAYING...

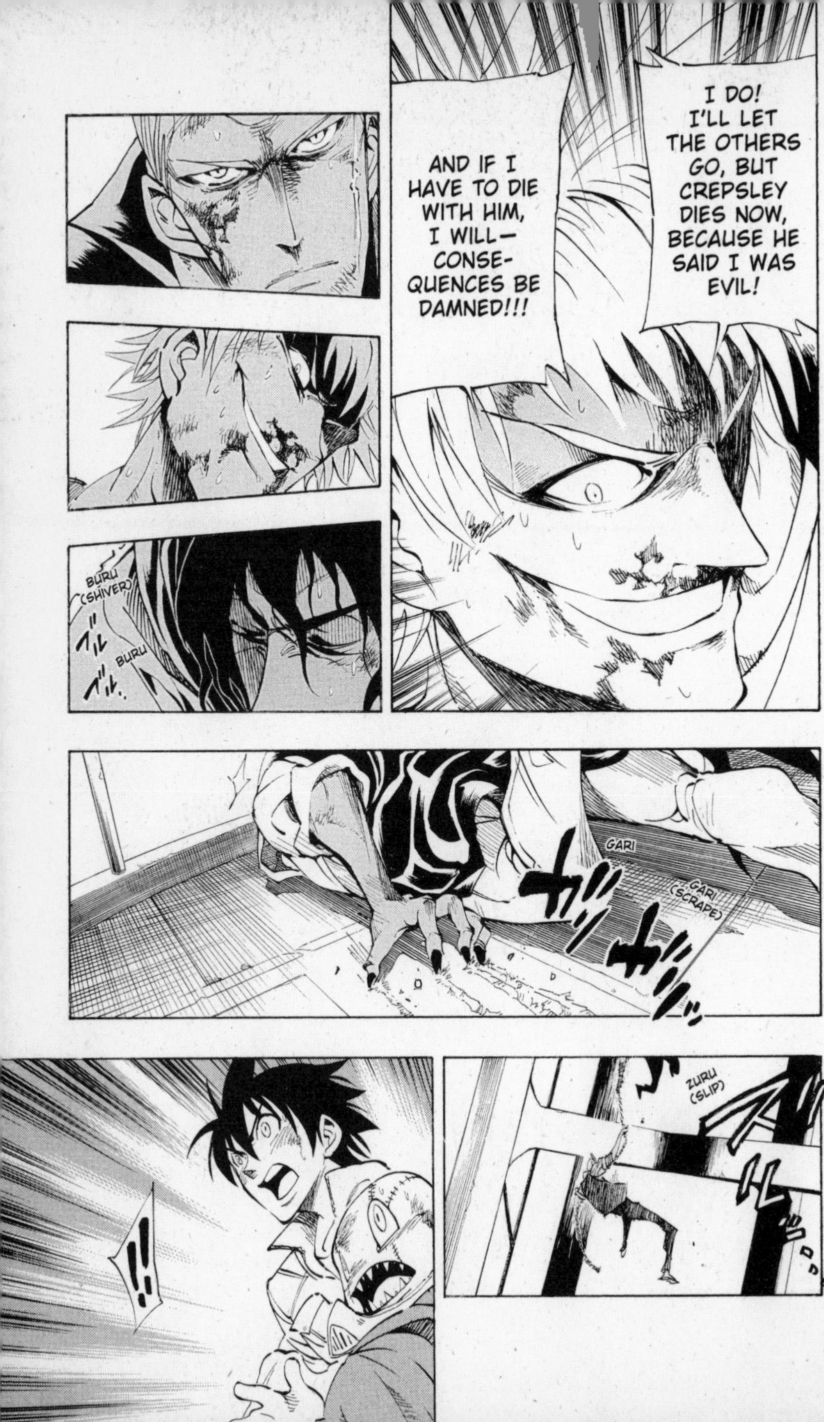
I DO! I'LL LET THE OTHERS GO, BUT CREPSLEY DIES NOW, BECAUSE HE SAID I WAS EVIL!
AND IF I HAVE TO DIE WITH HIM, I WILL— CONSE-QUENCES BE DAMNED!!!
BURU (SHIVER)
BURU
GARI
GARI (SCRAPE)
ZURU (SLIP)
!!

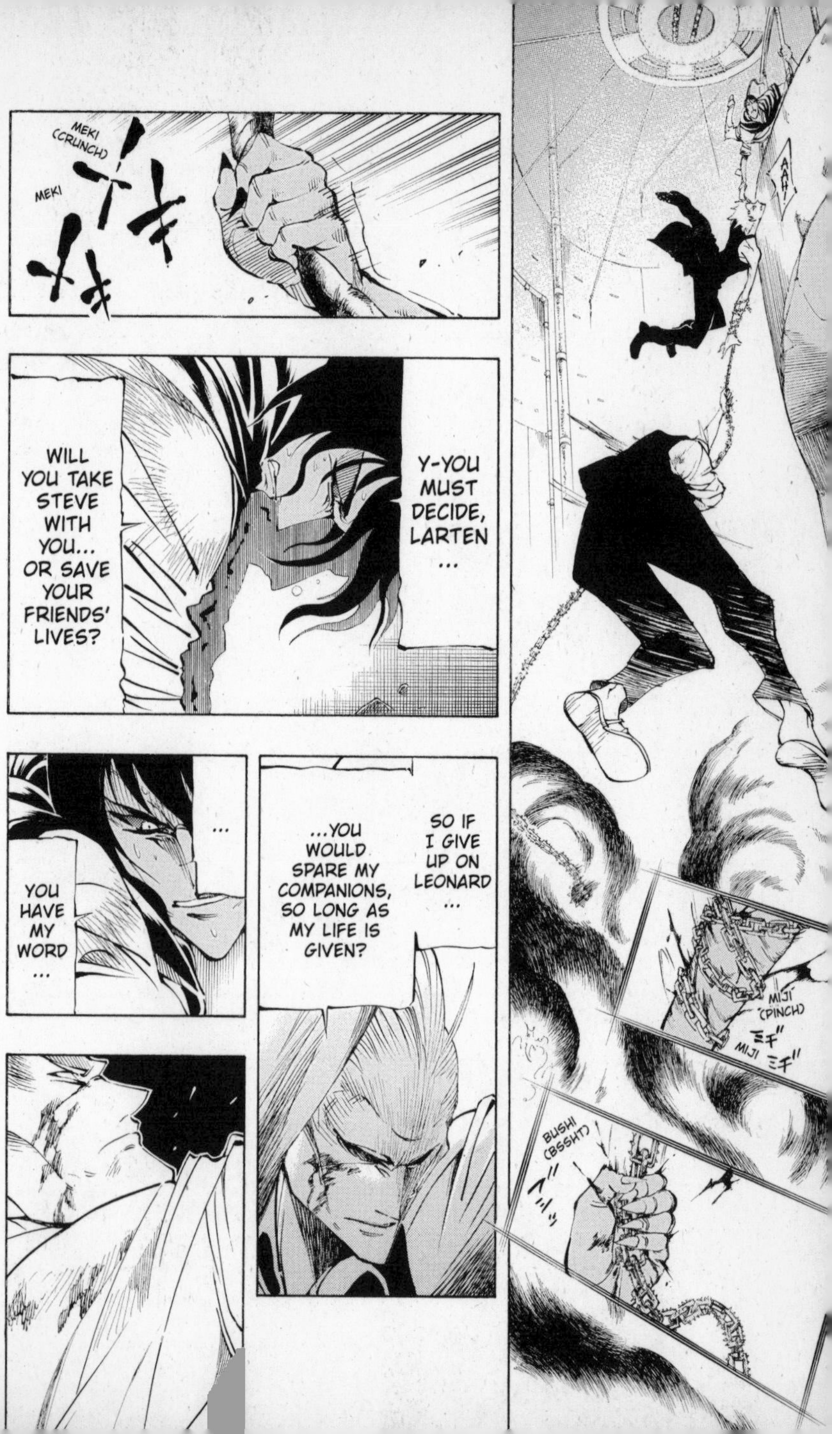
AAH!
MIJI (PINCH)
ミヂ
MIJI
ミヂ
BUSHI (BSSHT)
ブッ
MEKI (CRUNCH)
メキ
MEKI
メキ
Y-YOU MUST DECIDE, LARTEN ...
WILL YOU TAKE STEVE WITH YOU... OR SAVE YOUR FRIENDS' LIVES?
SO IF I GIVE UP ON LEONARD ...
...YOU WOULD SPARE MY COMPANIONS, SO LONG AS MY LIFE IS GIVEN?
...
YOU HAVE MY WORD ...

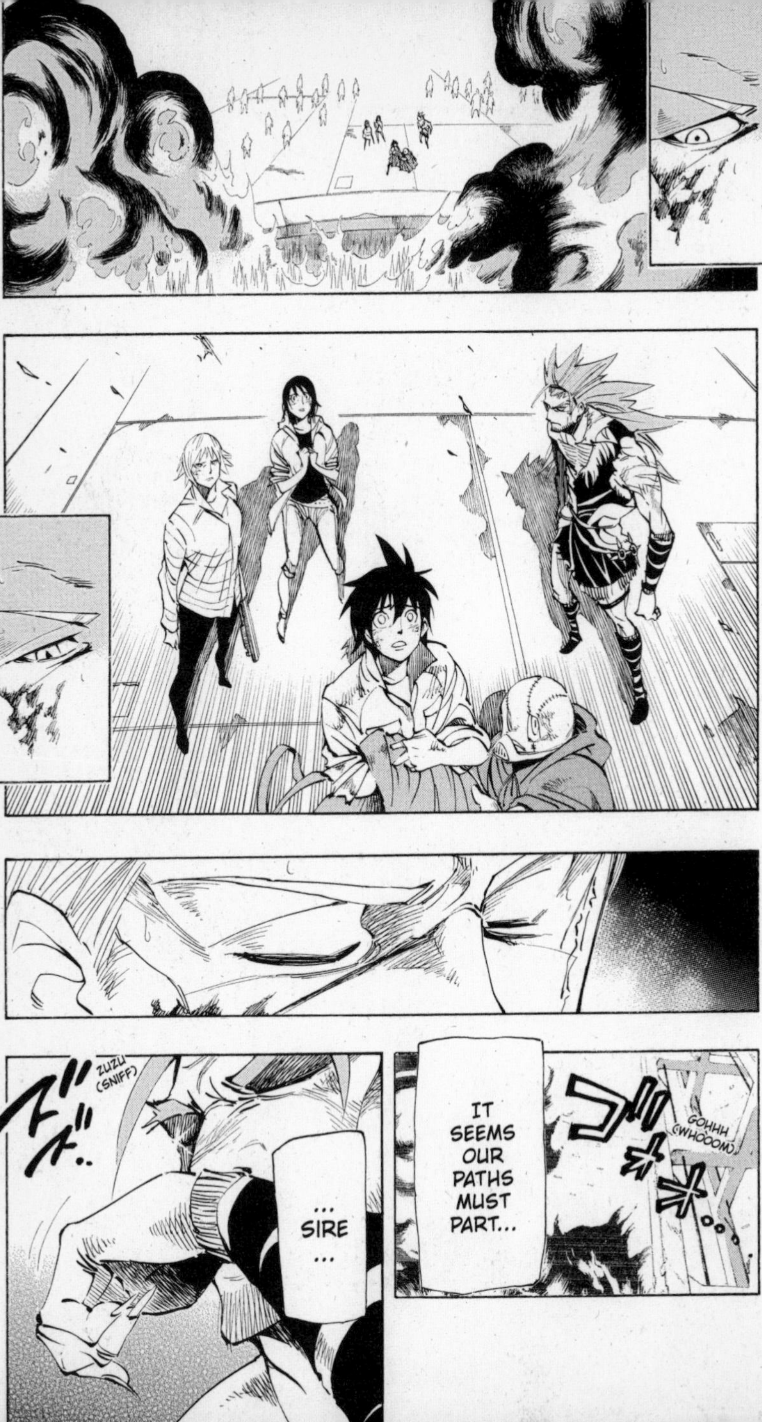
GOHHH (WHOOOM)
IT SEEMS OUR PATHS MUST PART...
ZUZU (SNIFF)
... SIRE ...

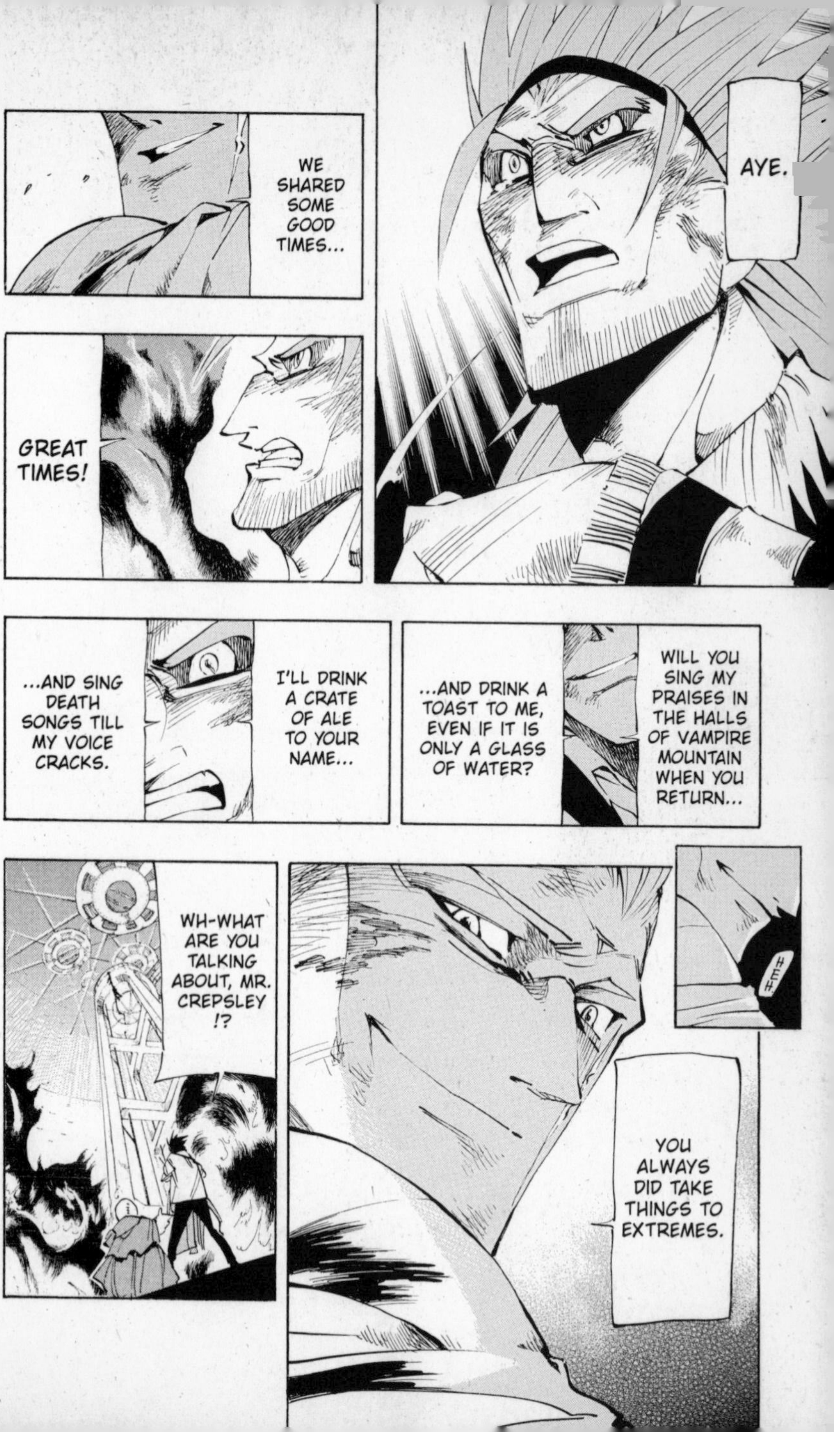
AYE.
WE SHARED SOME GOOD TIMES...
GREAT TIMES!
WILL YOU SING MY PRAISES IN THE HALLS OF VAMPIRE MOUNTAIN WHEN YOU RETURN...
...AND DRINK A TOAST TO ME, EVEN IF IT IS ONLY A GLASS OF WATER?
I'LL DRINK A CRATE OF ALE TO YOUR NAME...
...AND SING DEATH SONGS TILL MY VOICE CRACKS.
HEH
YOU ALWAYS DID TAKE THINGS TO EXTREMES.
WH-WHAT ARE YOU TALKING ABOUT, MR. CREPSLEY !?

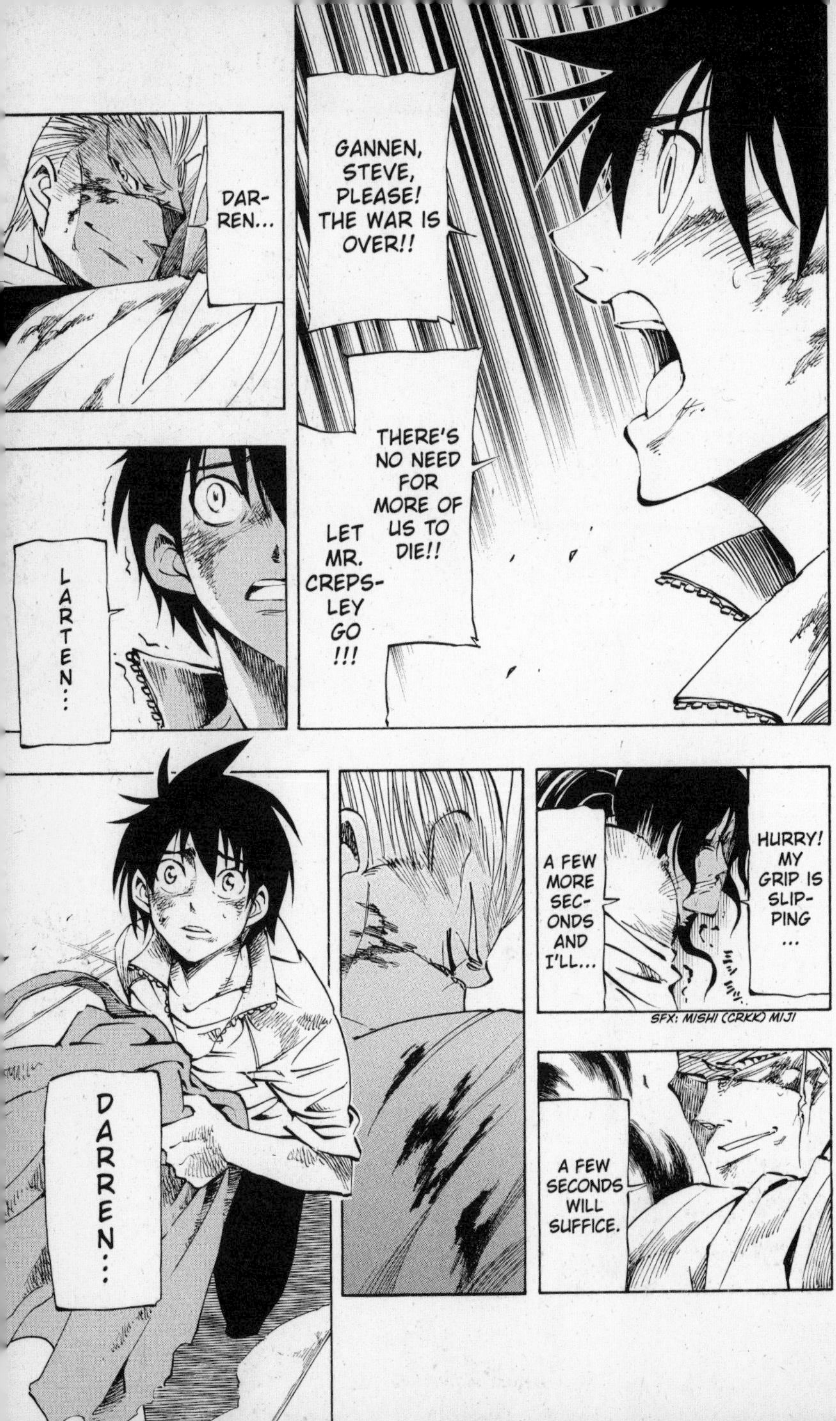
GANNEN, STEVE, PLEASE! THE WAR IS OVER!!
THERE'S NO NEED FOR MORE OF US TO DIE!!
LET MR. CREPS-LEY GO!!!
DAR-REN...
LARTEN...
HURRY! MY GRIP IS SLIP-PING...
A FEW MORE SEC-ONDS AND I'LL...
SFX: MISHI (CRKK) MIJI
A FEW SECONDS WILL SUFFICE.
DARREN...

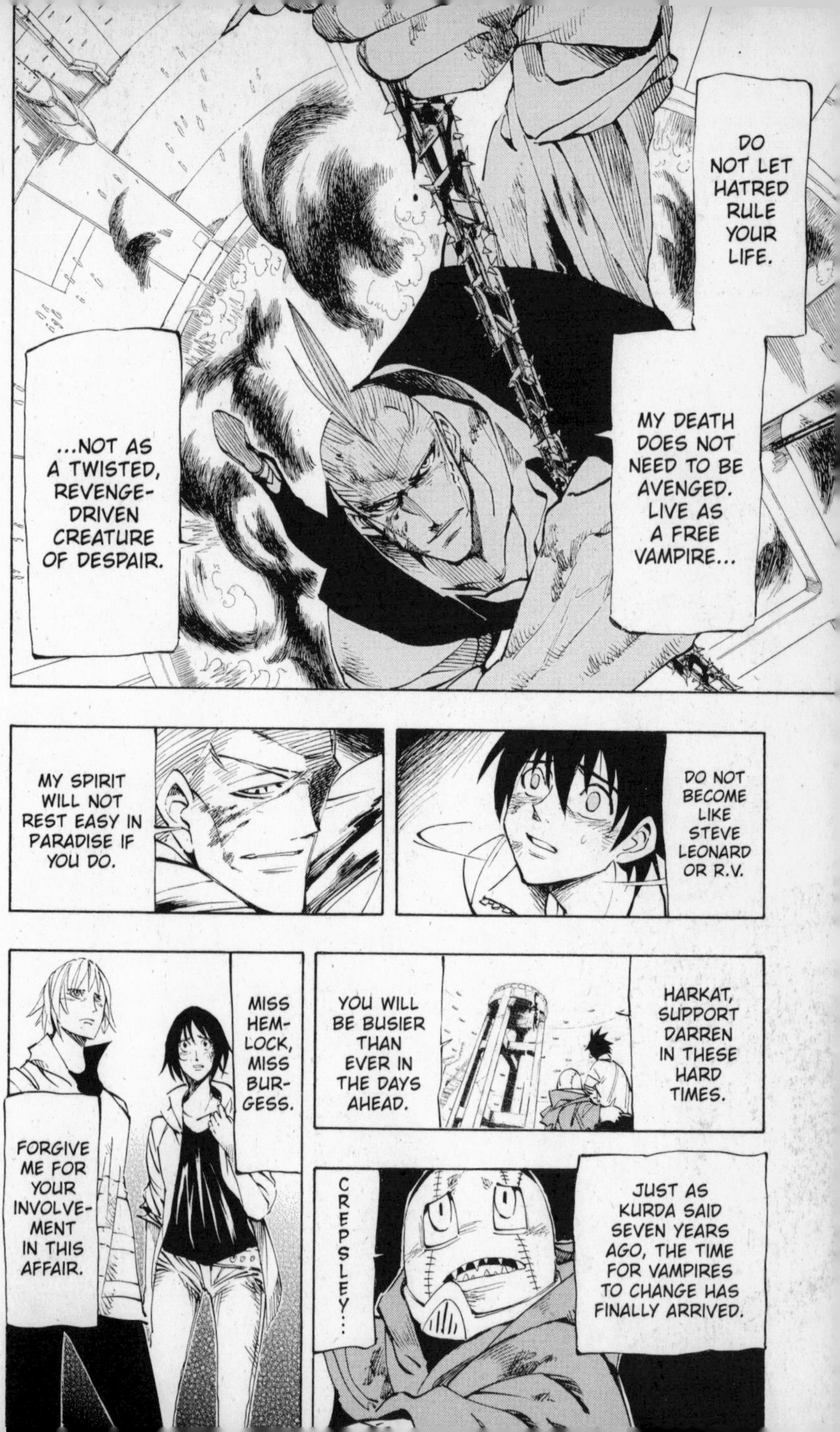
DO NOT LET HATRED RULE YOUR LIFE.
MY DEATH DOES NOT NEED TO BE AVENGED. LIVE AS A FREE VAMPIRE...
...NOT AS A TWISTED, REVENGE-DRIVEN CREATURE OF DESPAIR.
DO NOT BECOME LIKE STEVE LEONARD OR R.V.
MY SPIRIT WILL NOT REST EASY IN PARADISE IF YOU DO.
HARKAT, SUPPORT DARREN IN THESE HARD TIMES.
YOU WILL BE BUSIER THAN EVER IN THE DAYS AHEAD.
JUST AS KURDA SAID SEVEN YEARS AGO, THE TIME FOR VAMPIRES TO CHANGE HAS FINALLY ARRIVED.
CREPSLEY...
MISS HEMLOCK, MISS BURGESS.
FORGIVE ME FOR YOUR INVOLVEMENT IN THIS AFFAIR.

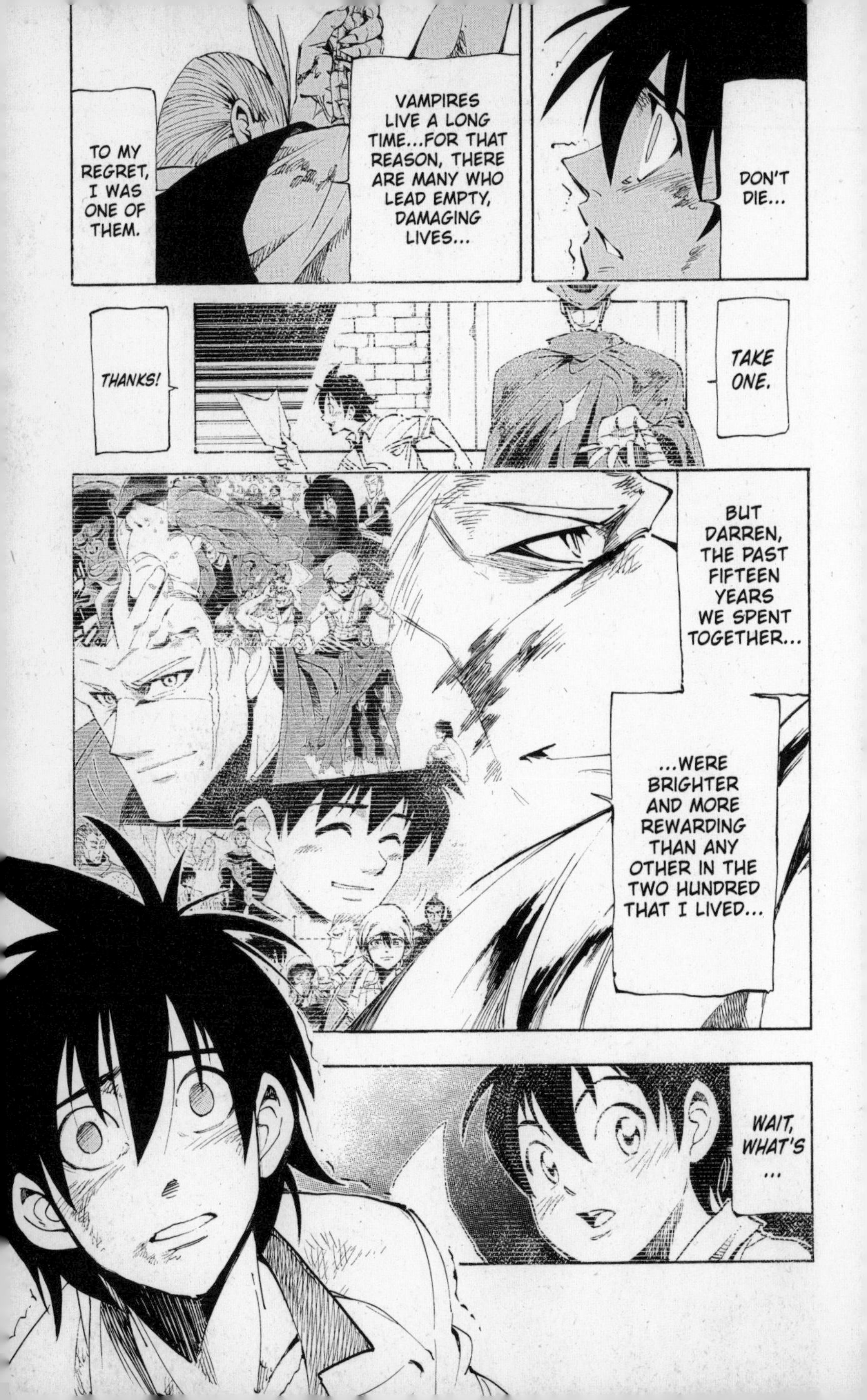
DON'T DIE...
VAMPIRES LIVE A LONG TIME...FOR THAT REASON, THERE ARE MANY WHO LEAD EMPTY, DAMAGING LIVES...
TO MY REGRET, I WAS ONE OF THEM.
TAKE ONE.
THANKS!
BUT DARREN, THE PAST FIFTEEN YEARS WE SPENT TOGETHER...
...WERE BRIGHTER AND MORE REWARDING THAN ANY OTHER IN THE TWO HUNDRED THAT I LIVED...
WAIT, WHAT'S ...

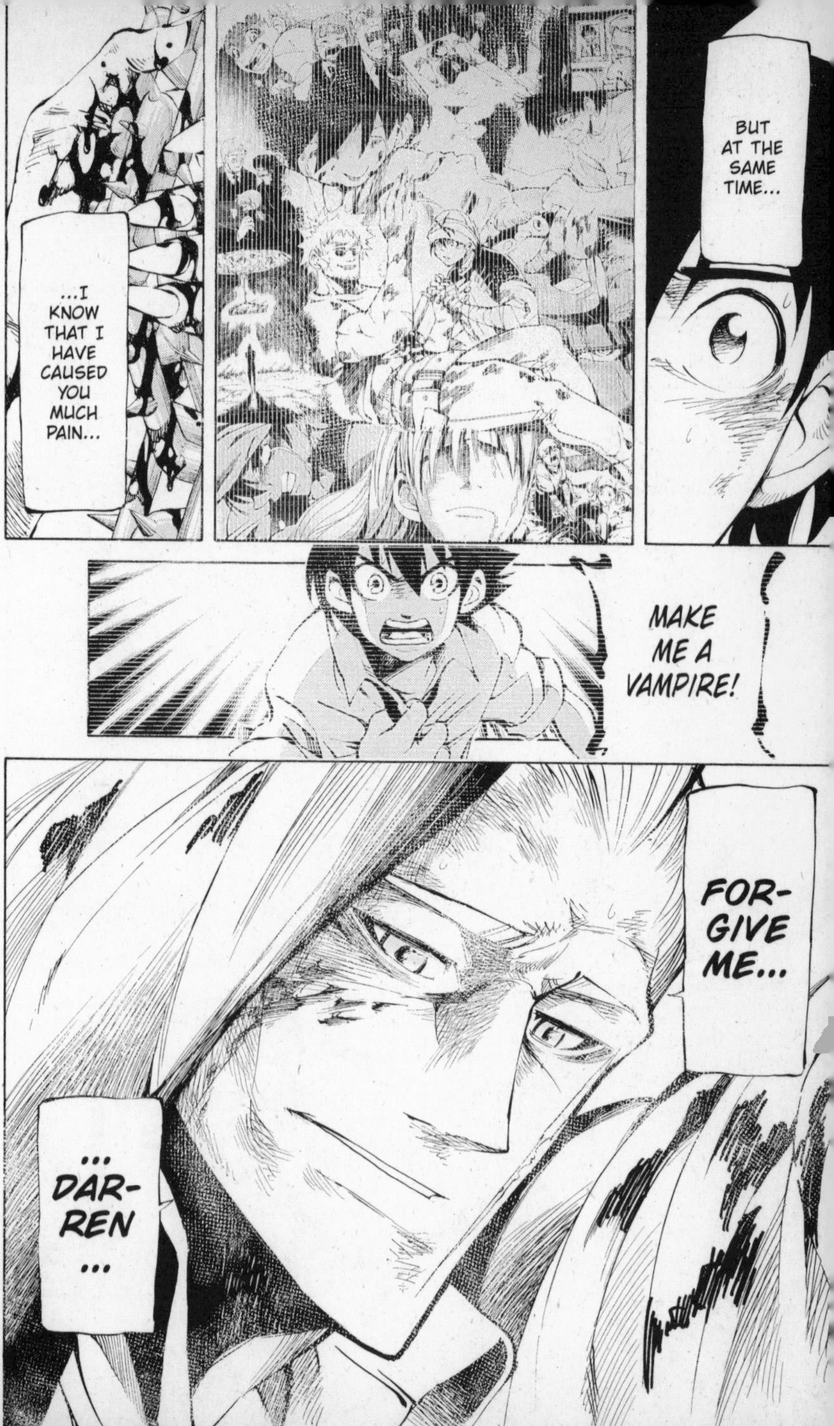
BUT AT THE SAME TIME...
...I KNOW THAT I HAVE CAUSED YOU MUCH PAIN...
MAKE ME A VAMPIRE!
FOR-GIVE ME...
...DAR-REN...

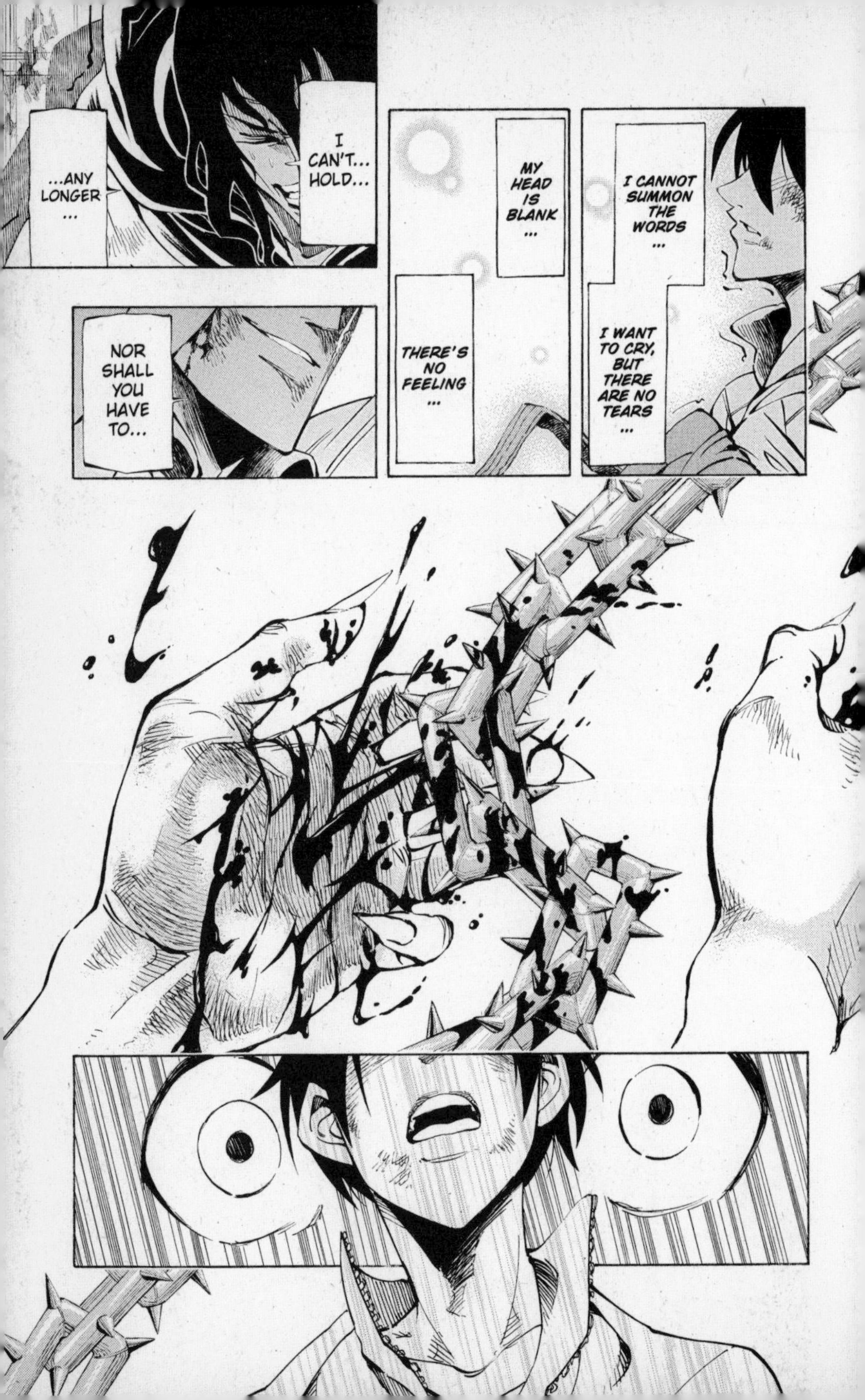
I CANNOT SUMMON THE WORDS...
I WANT TO CRY, BUT THERE ARE NO TEARS...
MY HEAD IS BLANK...
THERE'S NO FEELING...
I CAN'T... HOLD...
...ANY LONGER...
NOR SHALL YOU HAVE TO...

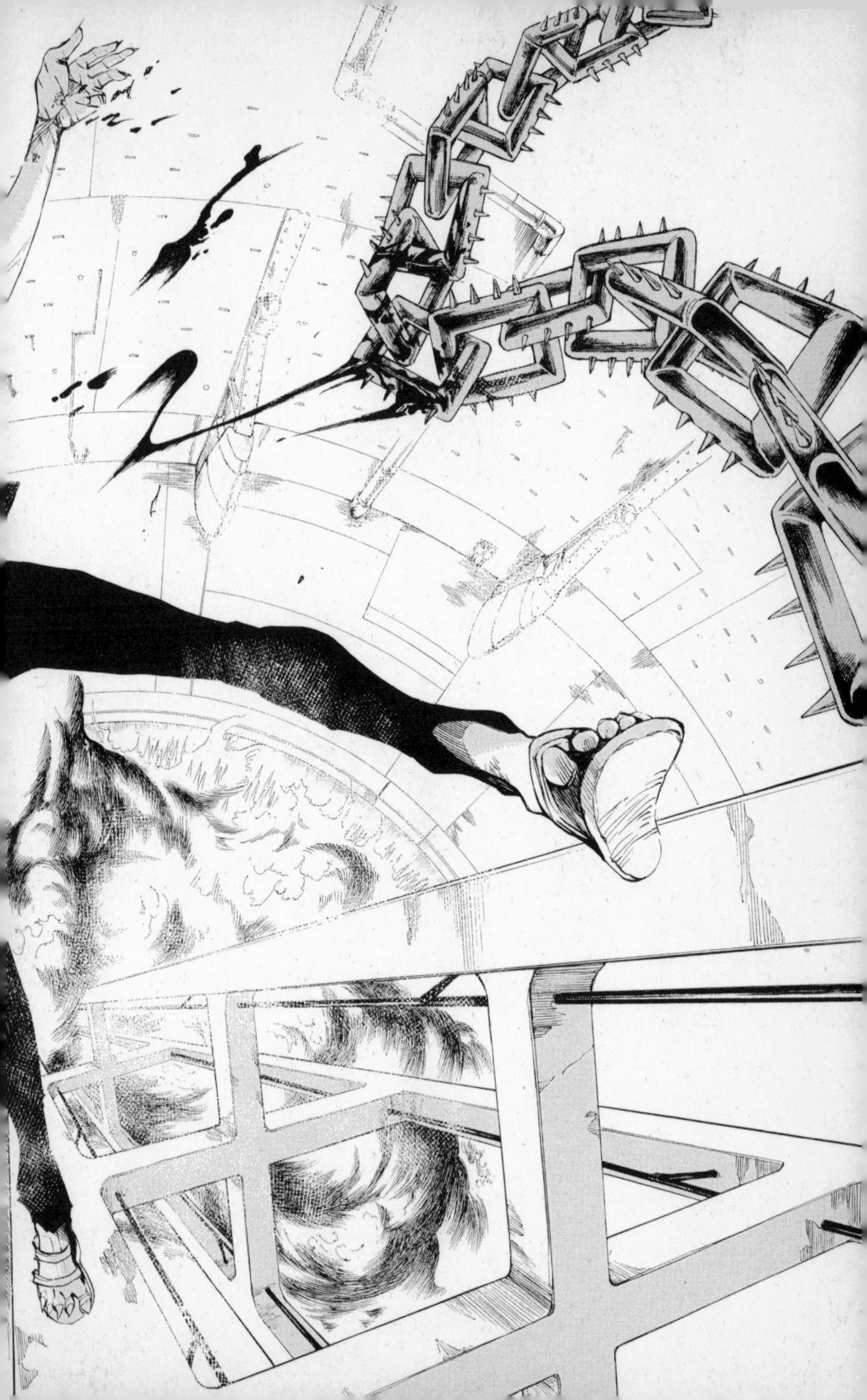

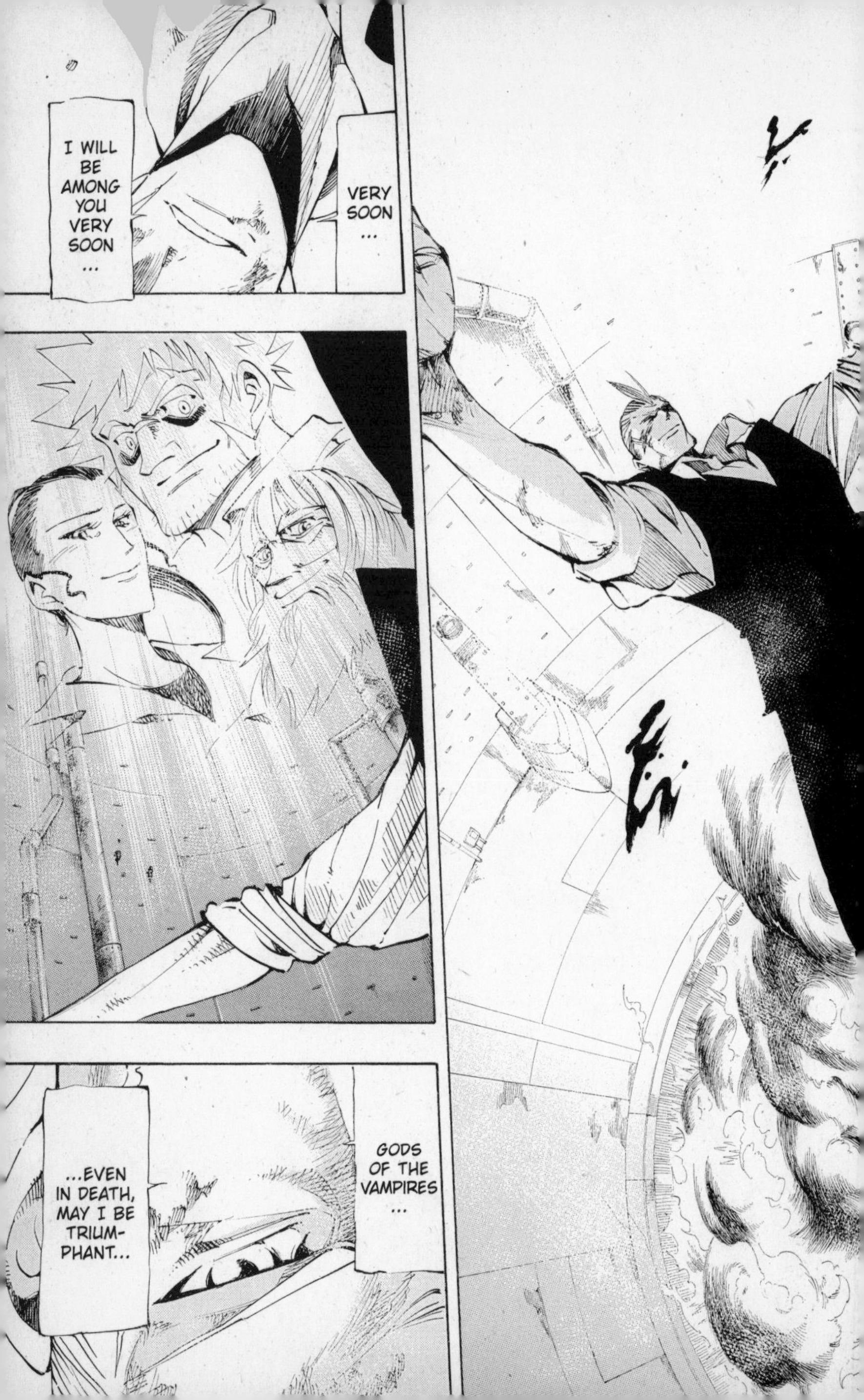
VERY SOON ...
I WILL BE AMONG YOU VERY SOON ...
GODS OF THE VAMPIRES ...
...EVEN IN DEATH, MAY I BE TRIUM-PHANT...

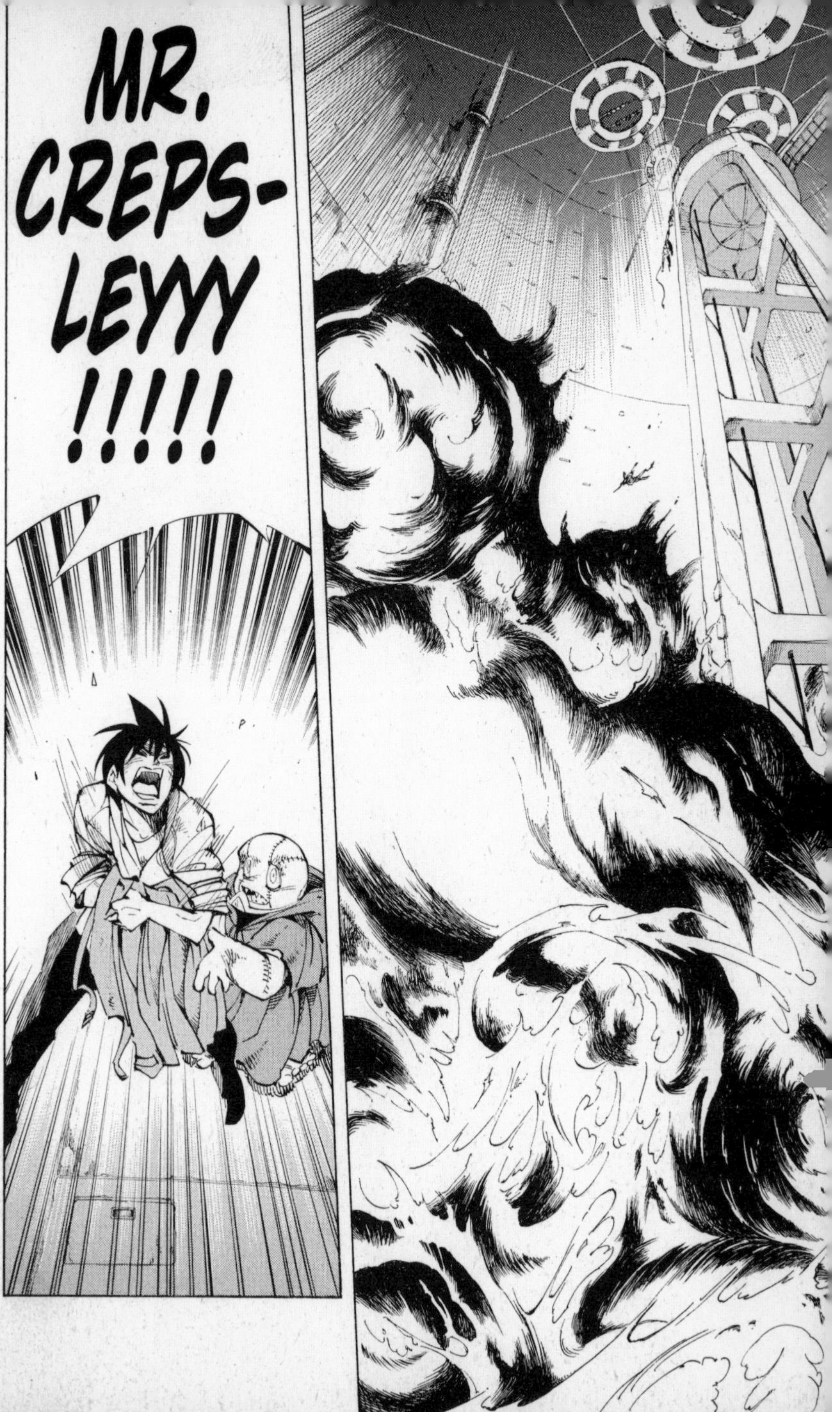
MR. CREPS-LEYYY !!!!!

CHAPTER 83: THE CAVALRY

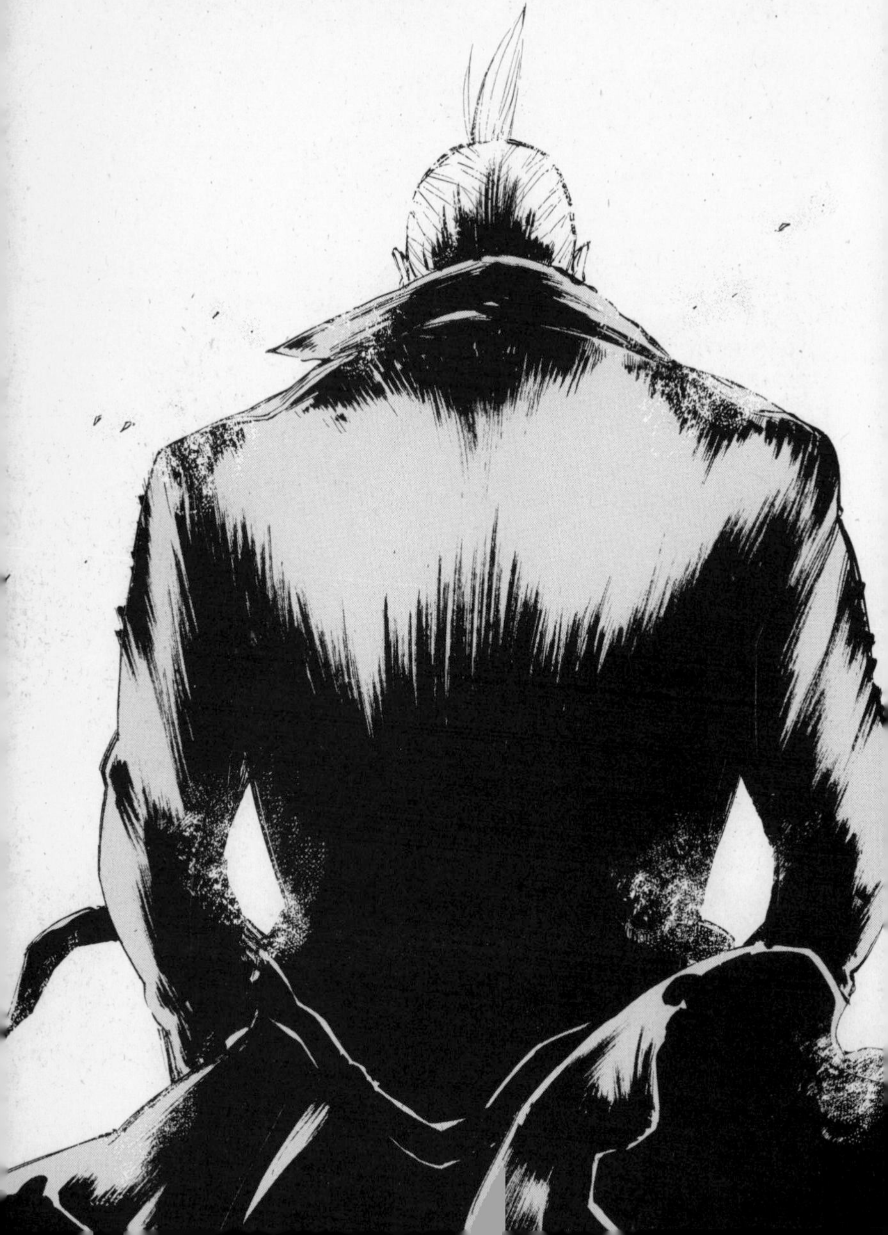

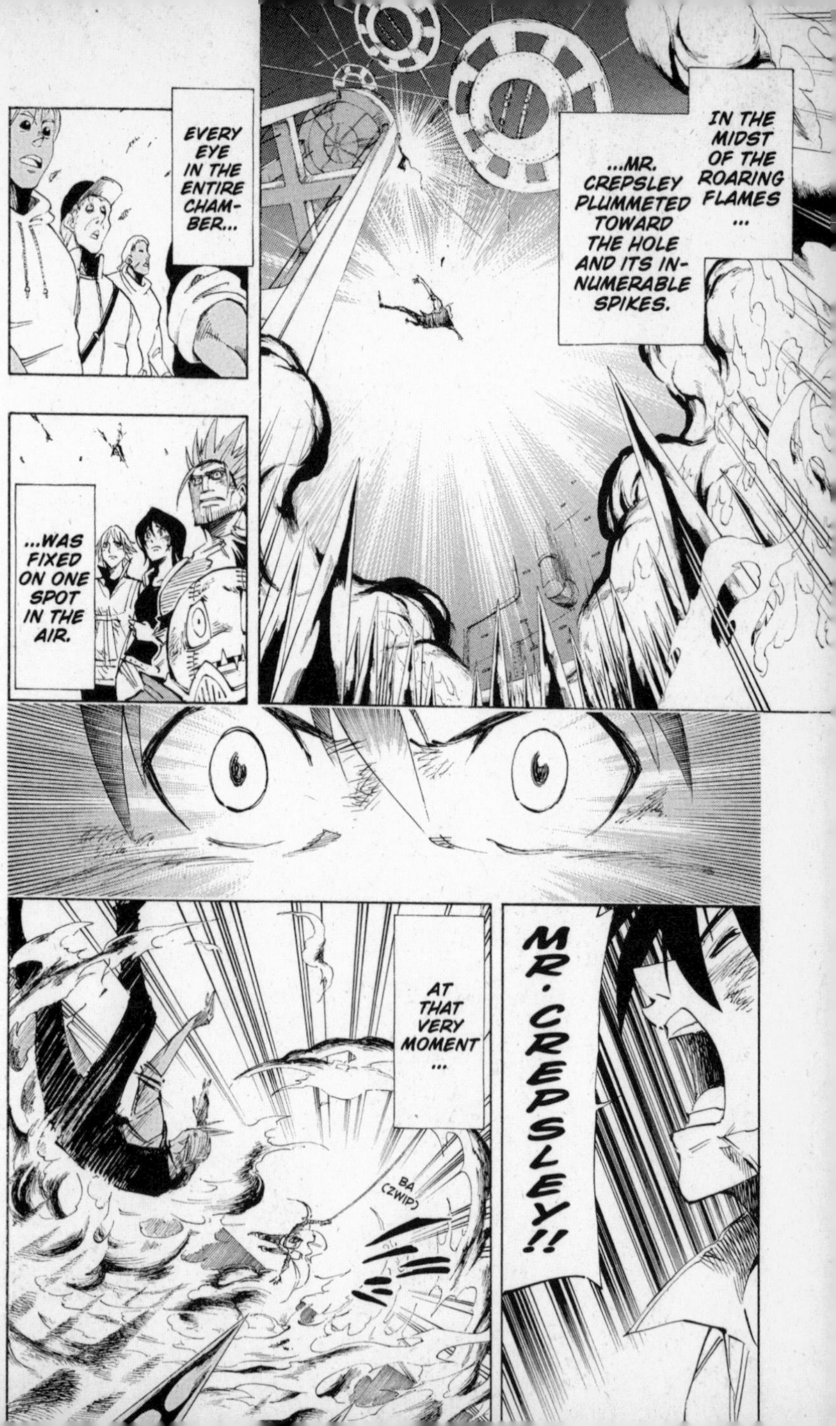
IN THE MIDST OF THE ROARING FLAMES...
...MR. CREPSLEY PLUMMETED TOWARD THE HOLE AND ITS INNUMERABLE SPIKES.
EVERY EYE IN THE ENTIRE CHAMBER...
...WAS FIXED ON ONE SPOT IN THE AIR.
MR. CREPSLEY!!
AT THAT VERY MOMENT...
BA (ZWIP)

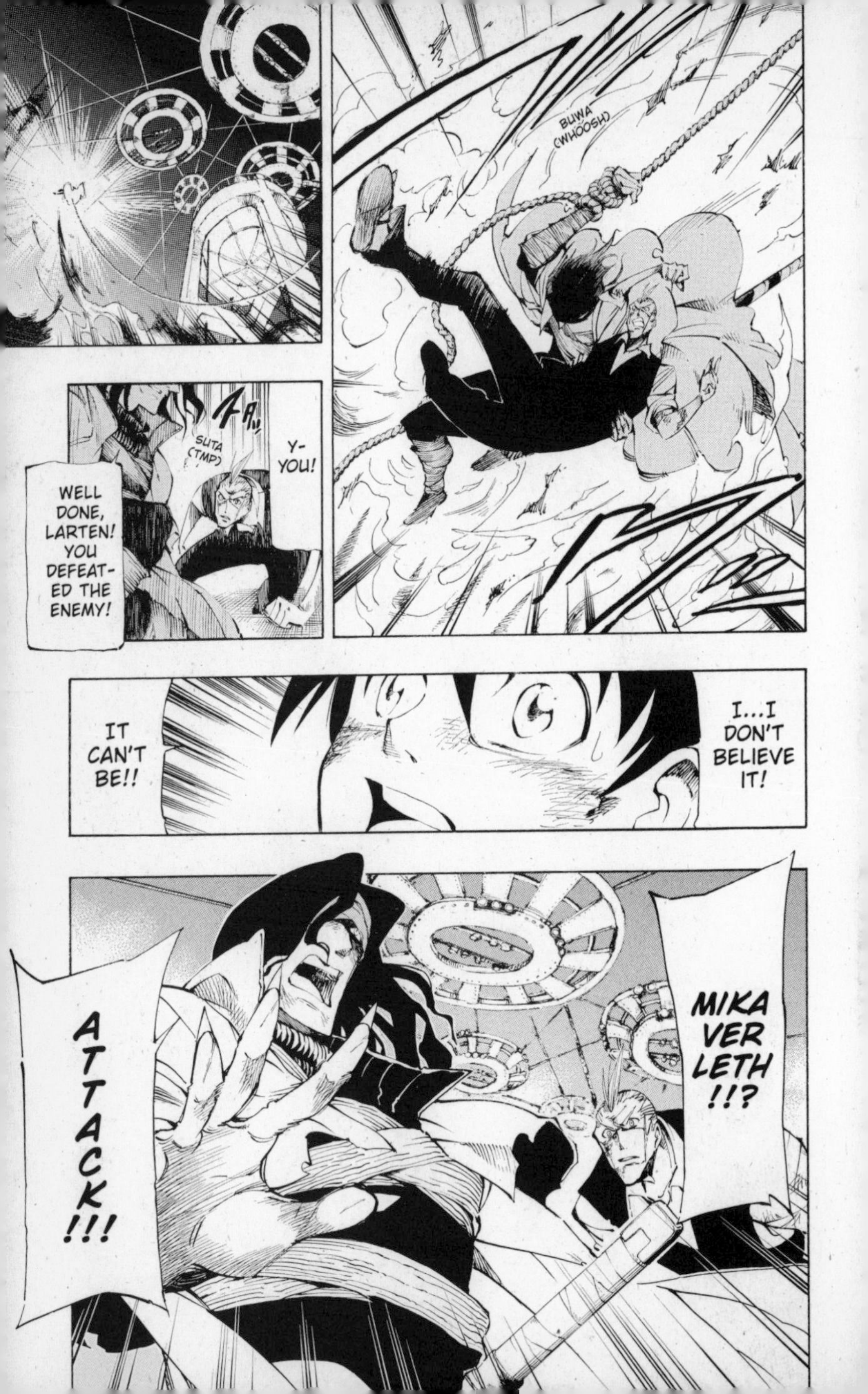
BUWA (WHOOSH)
Y-YOU!
SUTA (TMP)
WELL DONE, LARTEN! YOU DEFEATED THE ENEMY!
I...I DON'T BELIEVE IT!
IT CAN'T BE!!
MIKA VER LETH!!?
ATTACK!!!

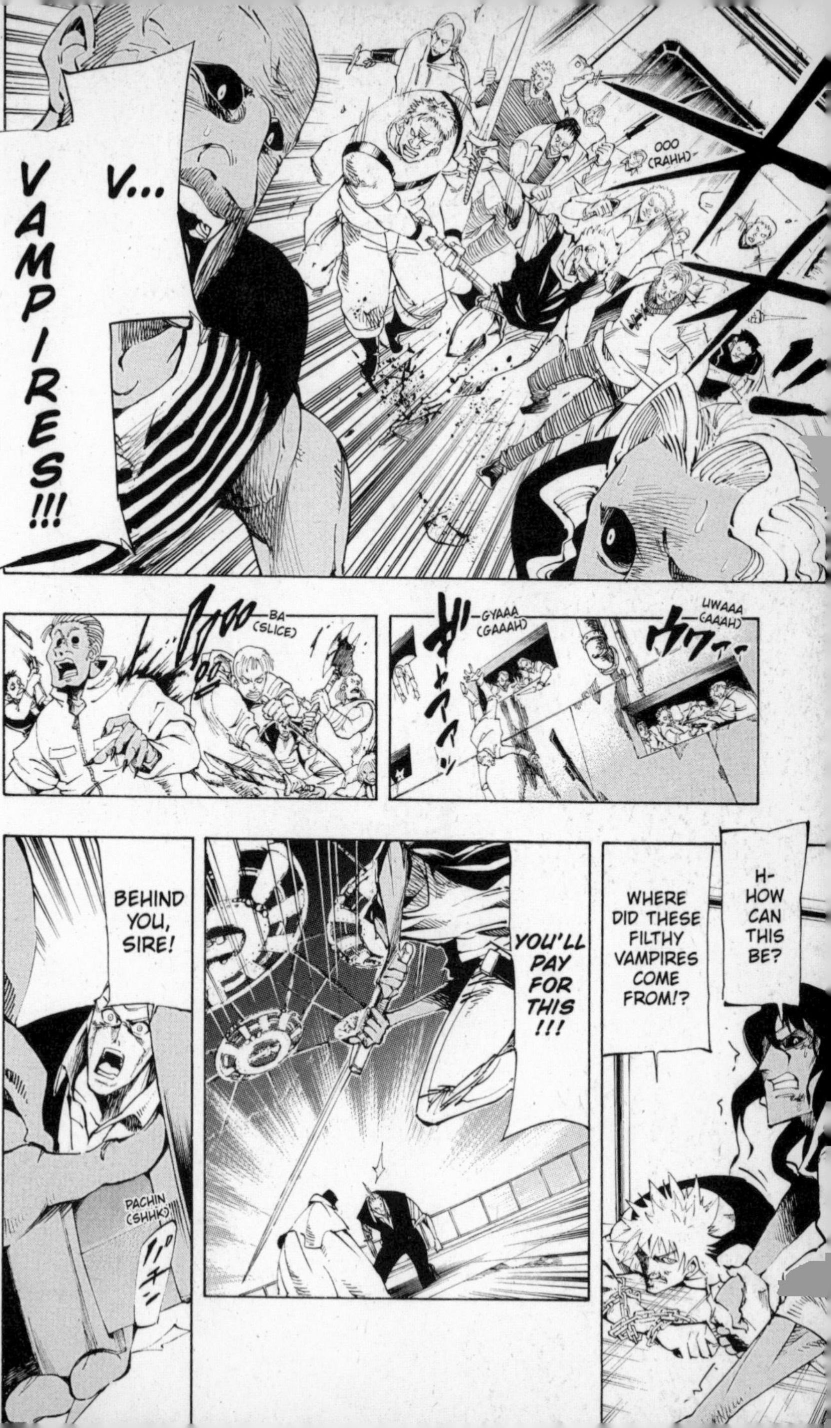
OOO (RAHH)
V... VAMPIRES!!!
UWAAA (AAAH)
GYAAA (GAAAH)
BA (SLICE)
H- HOW CAN THIS BE?
WHERE DID THESE FILTHY VAMPIRES COME FROM!?
YOU'LL PAY FOR THIS!!!
BEHIND YOU, SIRE!
PACHIN (SHHK)

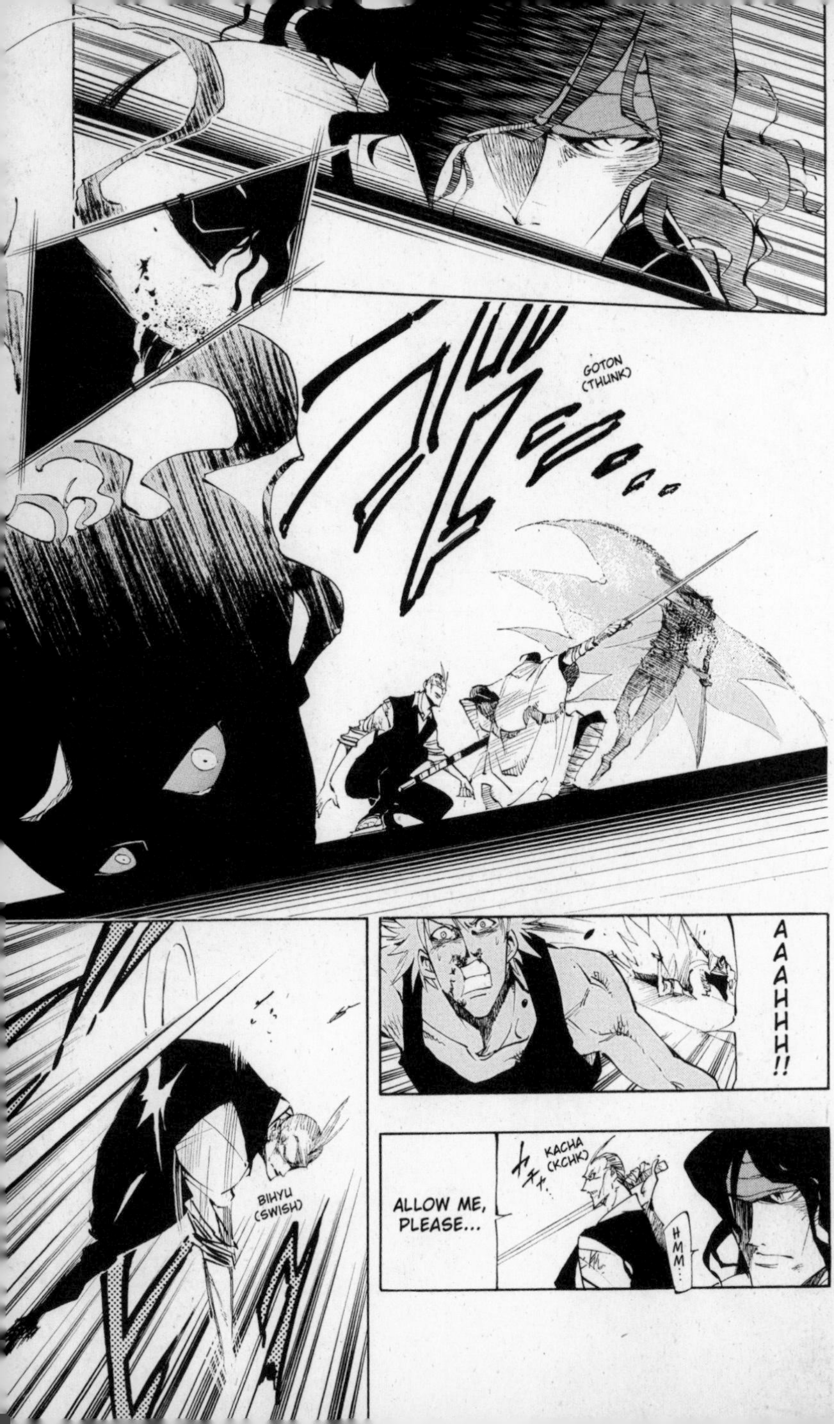
GOTON (THUNK)
AAAHHH!!
KACHA (KCHK)
ALLOW ME, PLEASE...
HMM...
BIHYU (SWISH)

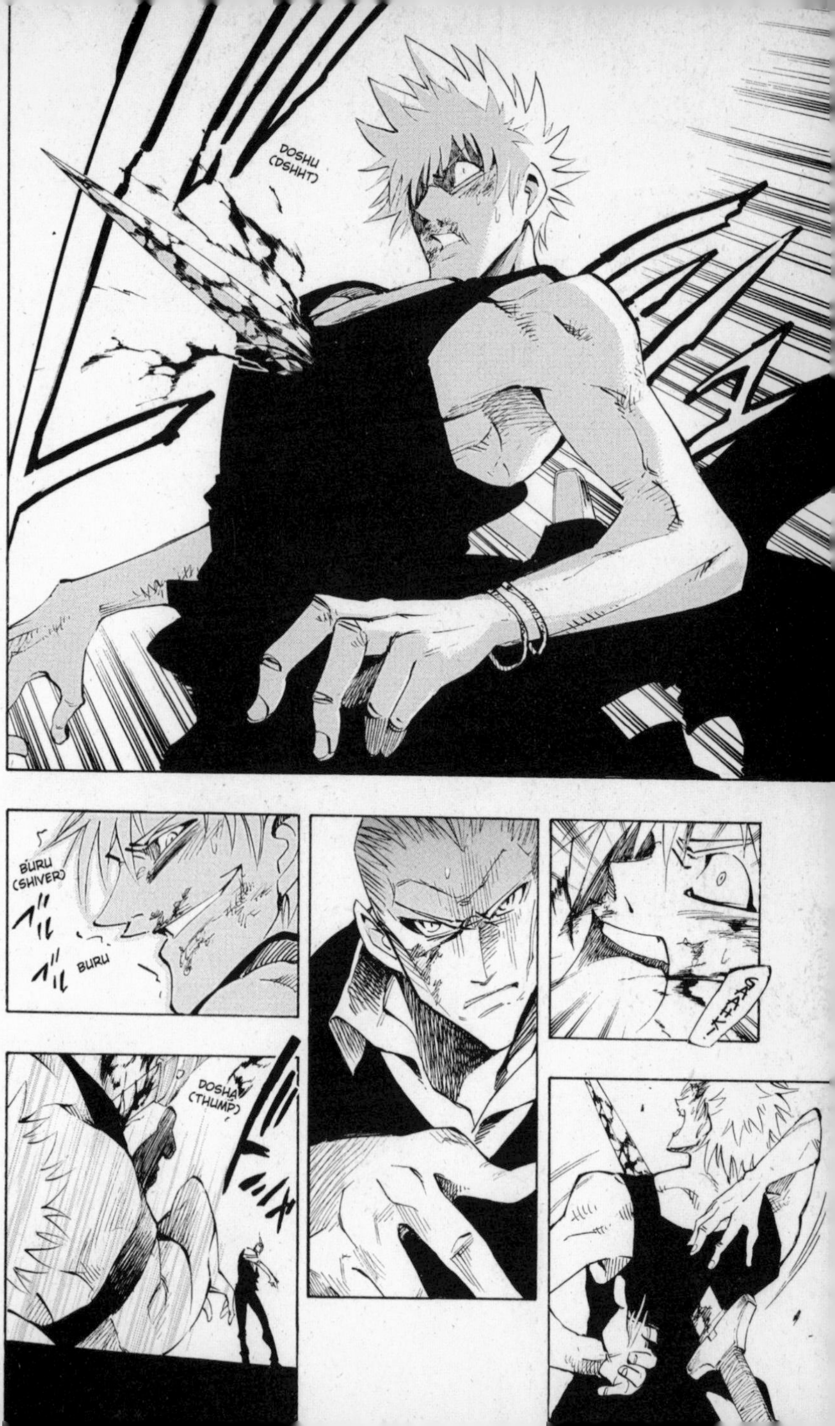
DOSHU (DSHHT)
BURU (SHIVER)
ブル
ブル BURU
DOSHA (THUMP)
ドシャ

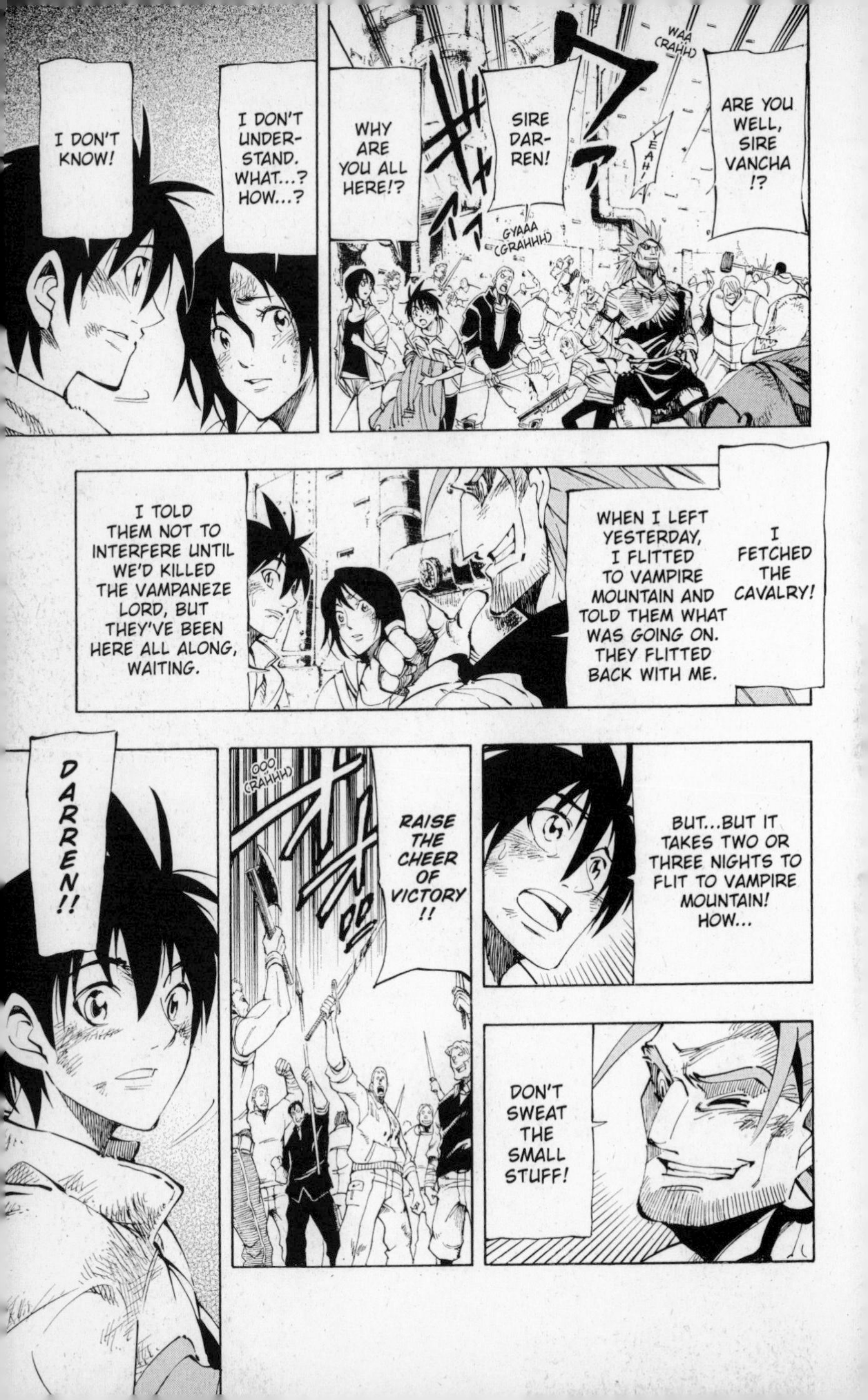
ARE YOU WELL, SIRE VANCHA!?
WAA (RAHH)
YEAH!
SIRE DARREN!
GYAAA (GRAHHH)
WHY ARE YOU ALL HERE!?
I DON'T UNDER-STAND. WHAT...? HOW...?
I DON'T KNOW!
I FETCHED THE CAVALRY!
WHEN I LEFT YESTERDAY, I FLITTED TO VAMPIRE MOUNTAIN AND TOLD THEM WHAT WAS GOING ON. THEY FLITTED BACK WITH ME.
I TOLD THEM NOT TO INTERFERE UNTIL WE'D KILLED THE VAMPANEZE LORD, BUT THEY'VE BEEN HERE ALL ALONG, WAITING.
BUT...BUT IT TAKES TWO OR THREE NIGHTS TO FLIT TO VAMPIRE MOUNTAIN! HOW...
DON'T SWEAT THE SMALL STUFF!
OOO (RAHHH)
RAISE THE CHEER OF VICTORY!!
DARREN!!

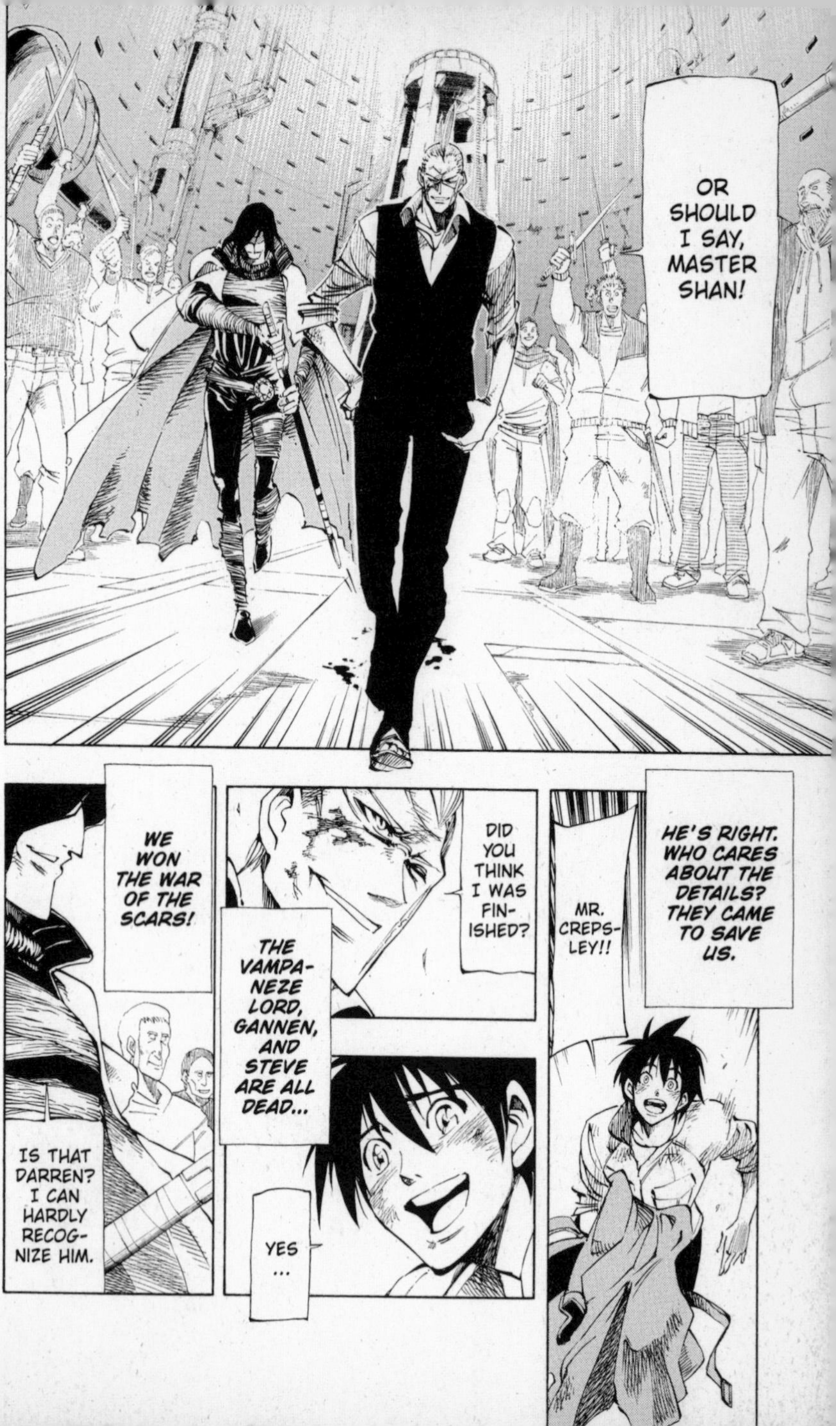
OR SHOULD I SAY, MASTER SHAN!
HE'S RIGHT. WHO CARES ABOUT THE DETAILS? THEY CAME TO SAVE US.
MR. CREPS-LEY!!
DID YOU THINK I WAS FIN-ISHED?
THE VAMPA-NEZE LORD, GANNEN, AND STEVE ARE ALL DEAD...
YES ...
WE WON THE WAR OF THE SCARS!
IS THAT DARREN? I CAN HARDLY RECOG-NIZE HIM.

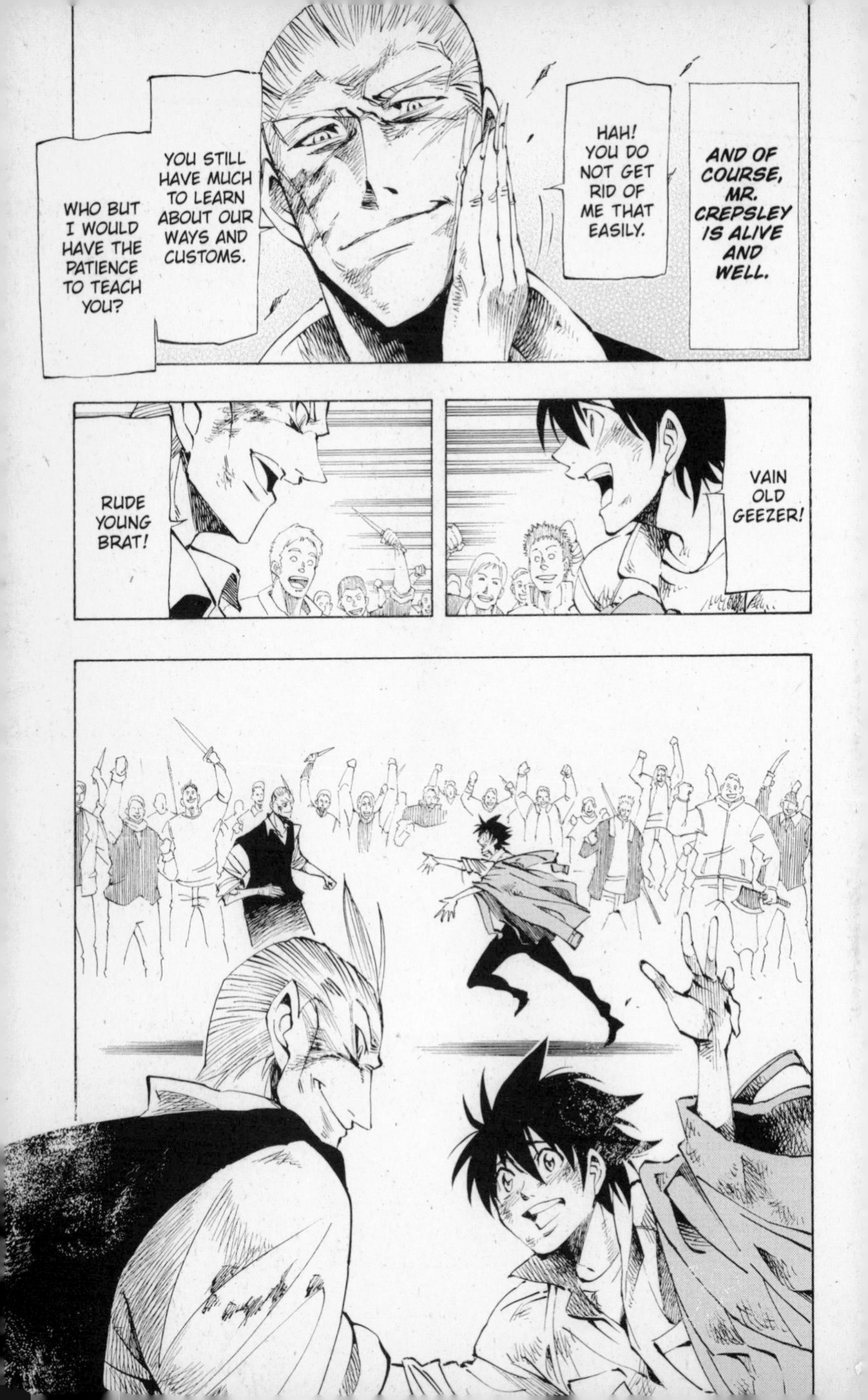
AND OF COURSE, MR. CREPSLEY IS ALIVE AND WELL.
HAH! YOU DO NOT GET RID OF ME THAT EASILY.
YOU STILL HAVE MUCH TO LEARN ABOUT OUR WAYS AND CUSTOMS.
WHO BUT I WOULD HAVE THE PATIENCE TO TEACH YOU?
VAIN OLD GEEZER!
RUDE YOUNG BRAT!

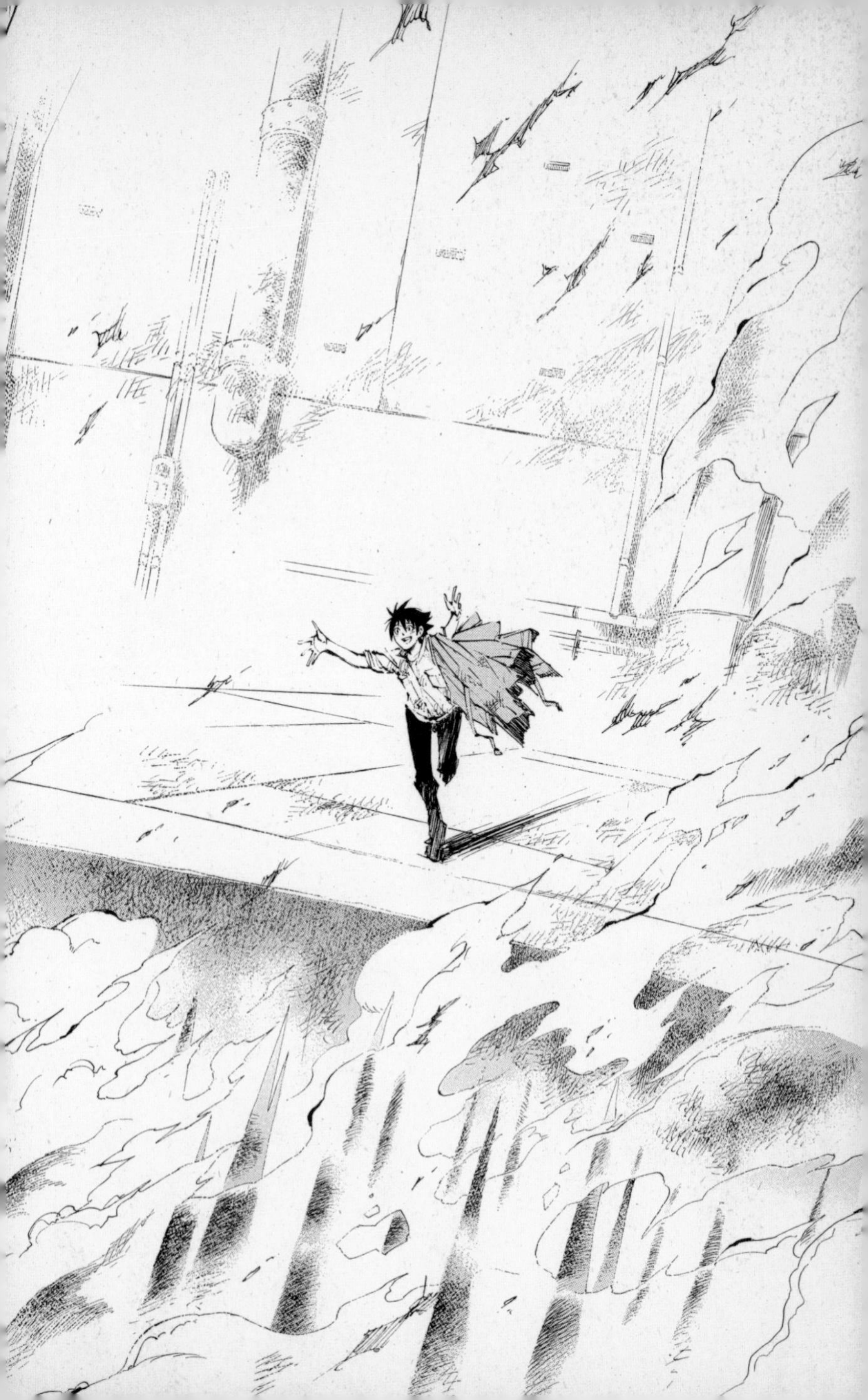

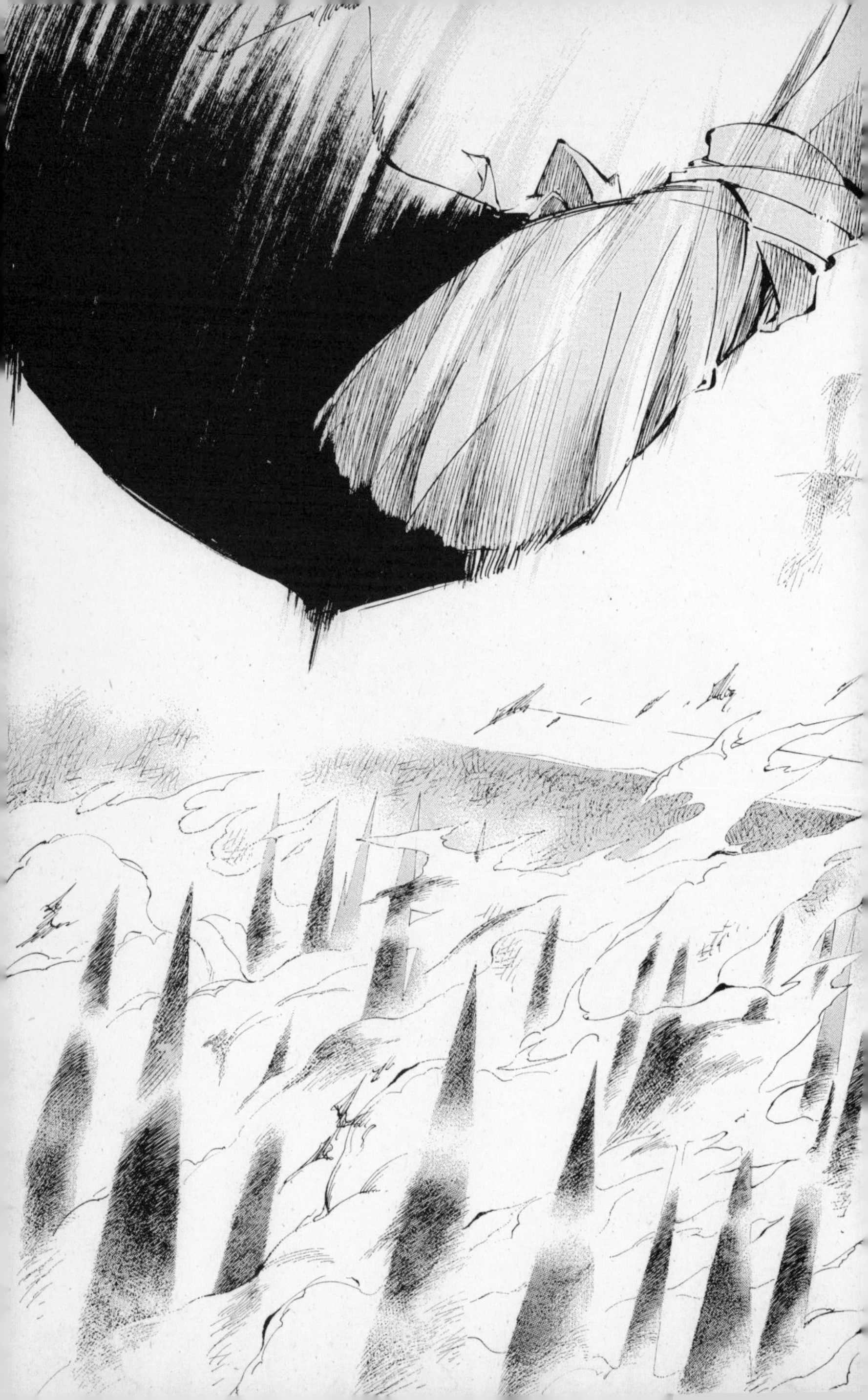

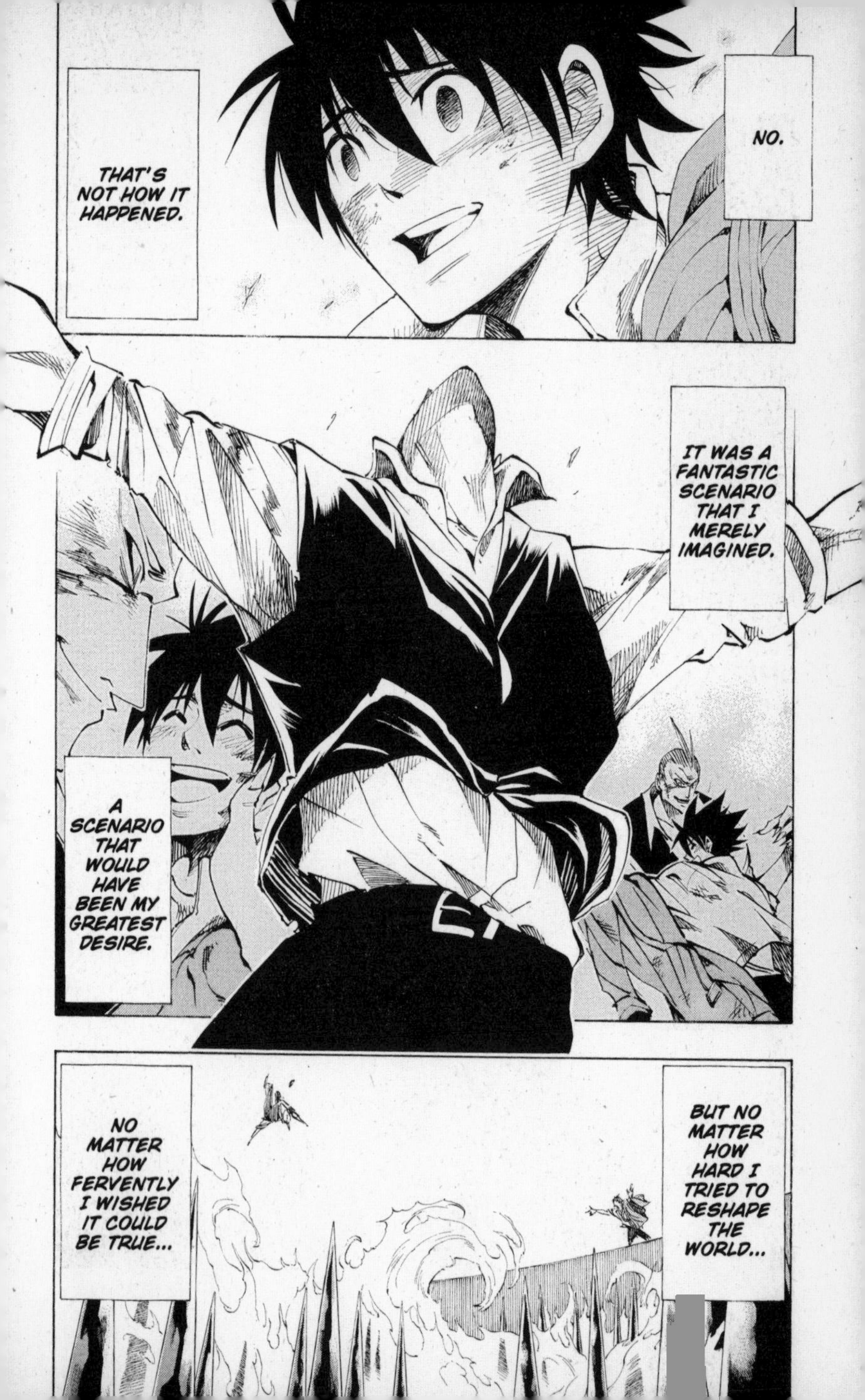
NO.
THAT'S NOT HOW IT HAPPENED.
IT WAS A FANTASTIC SCENARIO THAT I MERELY IMAGINED.
A SCENARIO THAT WOULD HAVE BEEN MY GREATEST DESIRE.
BUT NO MATTER HOW HARD I TRIED TO RESHAPE THE WORLD...
NO MATTER HOW FERVENTLY I WISHED IT COULD BE TRUE...

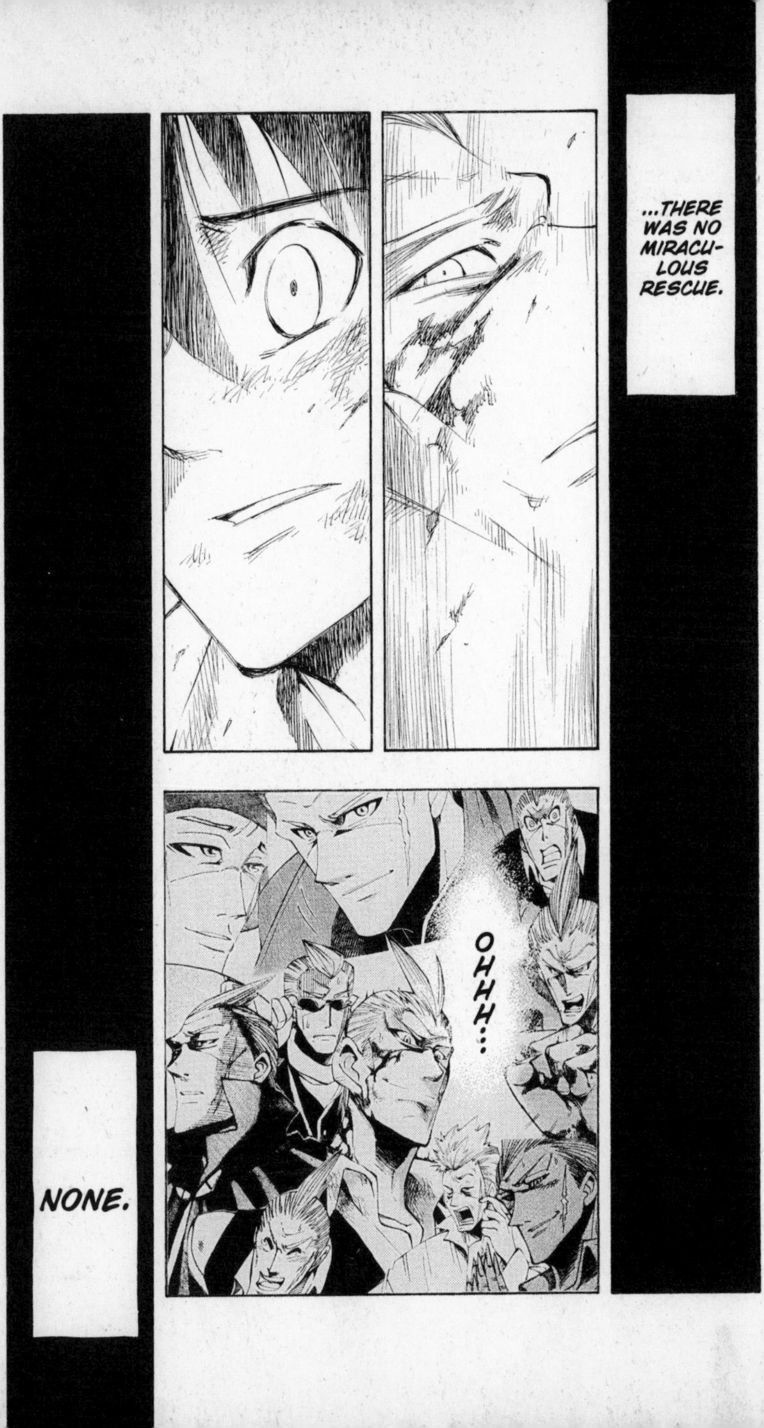
...THERE WAS NO MIRACULOUS RESCUE.
OHHH...
NONE.

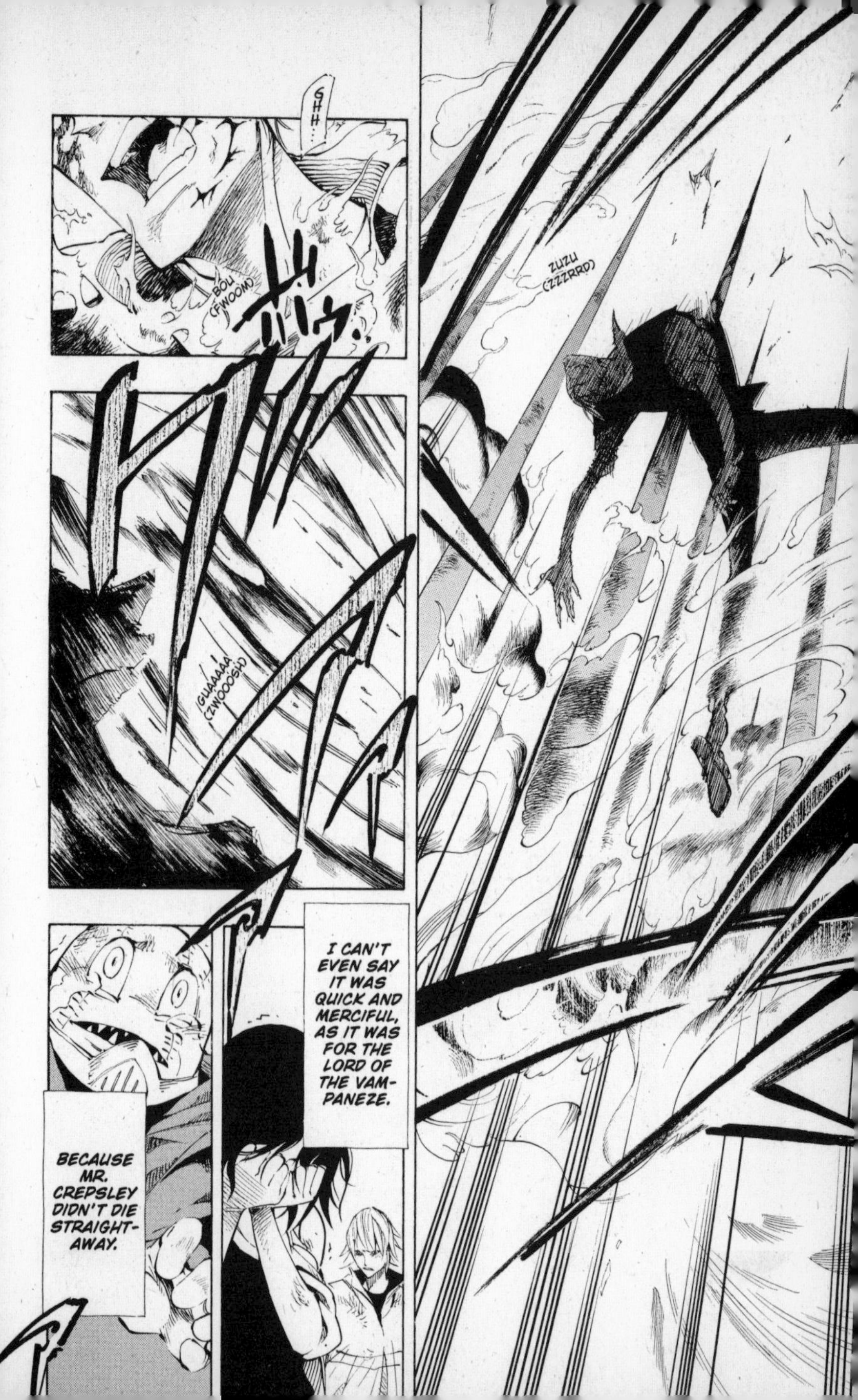
ZUZU (ZZZRRD)
GHH...
BOU (FWOOM)
GUAAAAA (ZWOOOSH)
I CAN'T EVEN SAY IT WAS QUICK AND MERCIFUL, AS IT WAS FOR THE LORD OF THE VAM-PANEZE.
BECAUSE MR. CREPSLEY DIDN'T DIE STRAIGHT-AWAY.

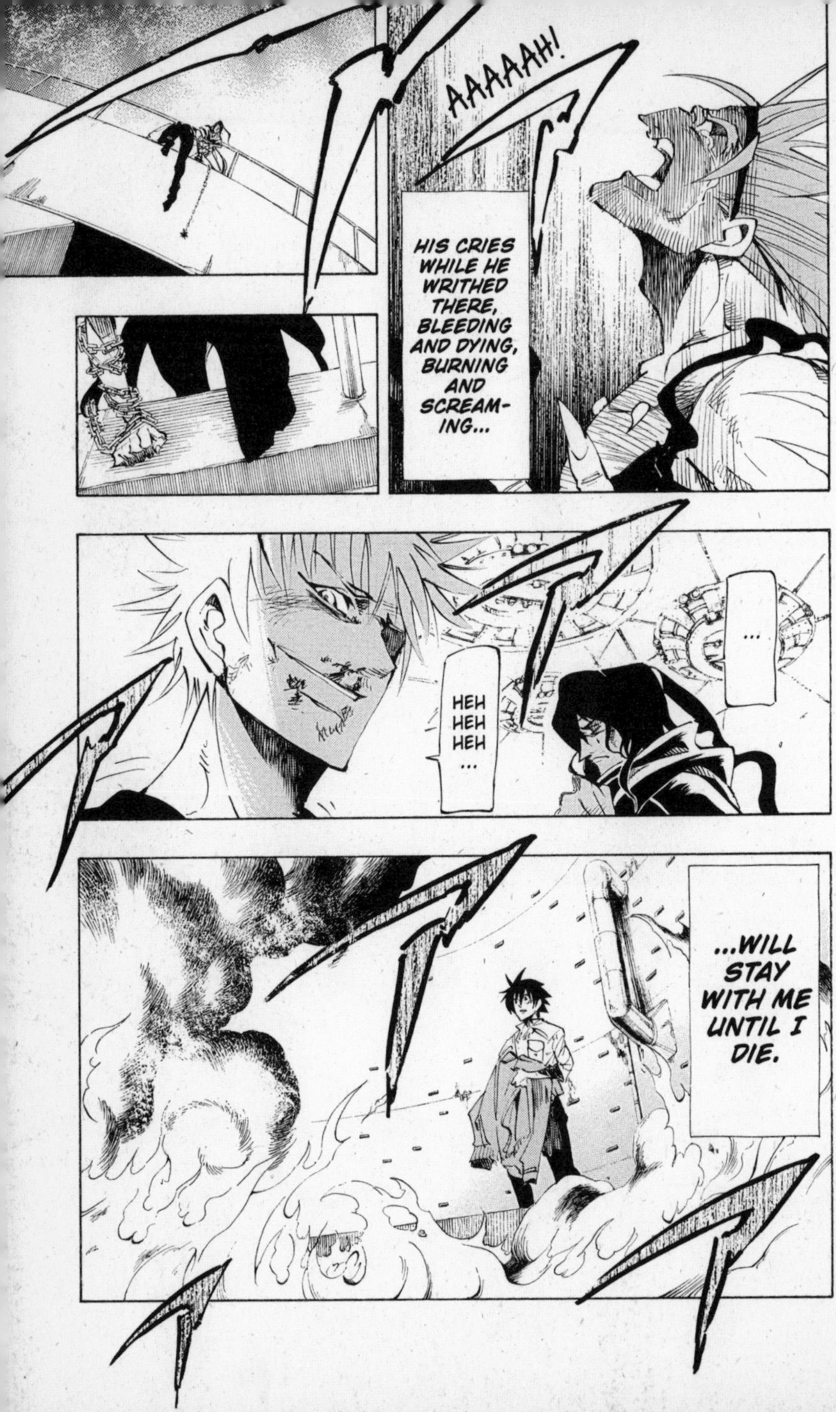
AAAAAH!
HIS CRIES WHILE HE WRITHED THERE, BLEEDING AND DYING, BURNING AND SCREAM-ING...
...
HEH HEH HEH ...
...WILL STAY WITH ME UNTIL I DIE.

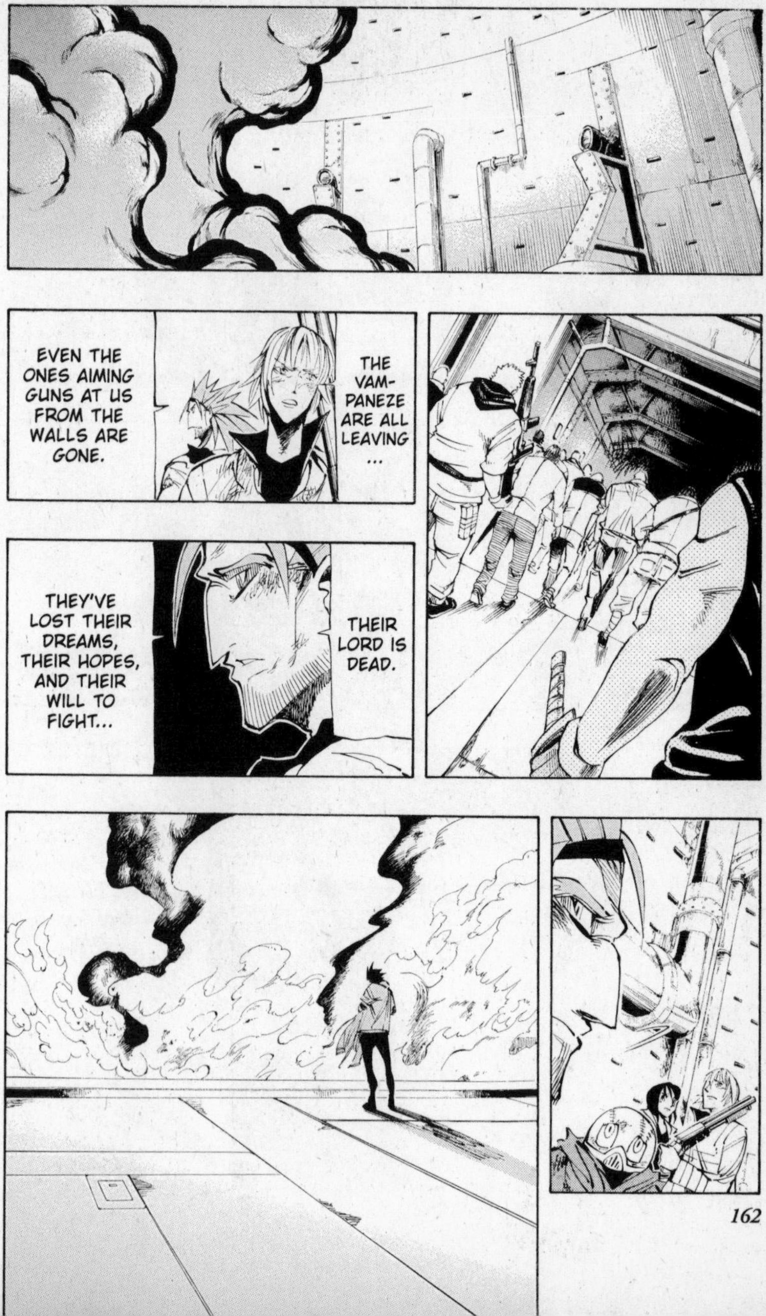
THE VAM-PANEZE ARE ALL LEAVING ...
EVEN THE ONES AIMING GUNS AT US FROM THE WALLS ARE GONE.
THEIR LORD IS DEAD.
THEY'VE LOST THEIR DREAMS, THEIR HOPES, AND THEIR WILL TO FIGHT...

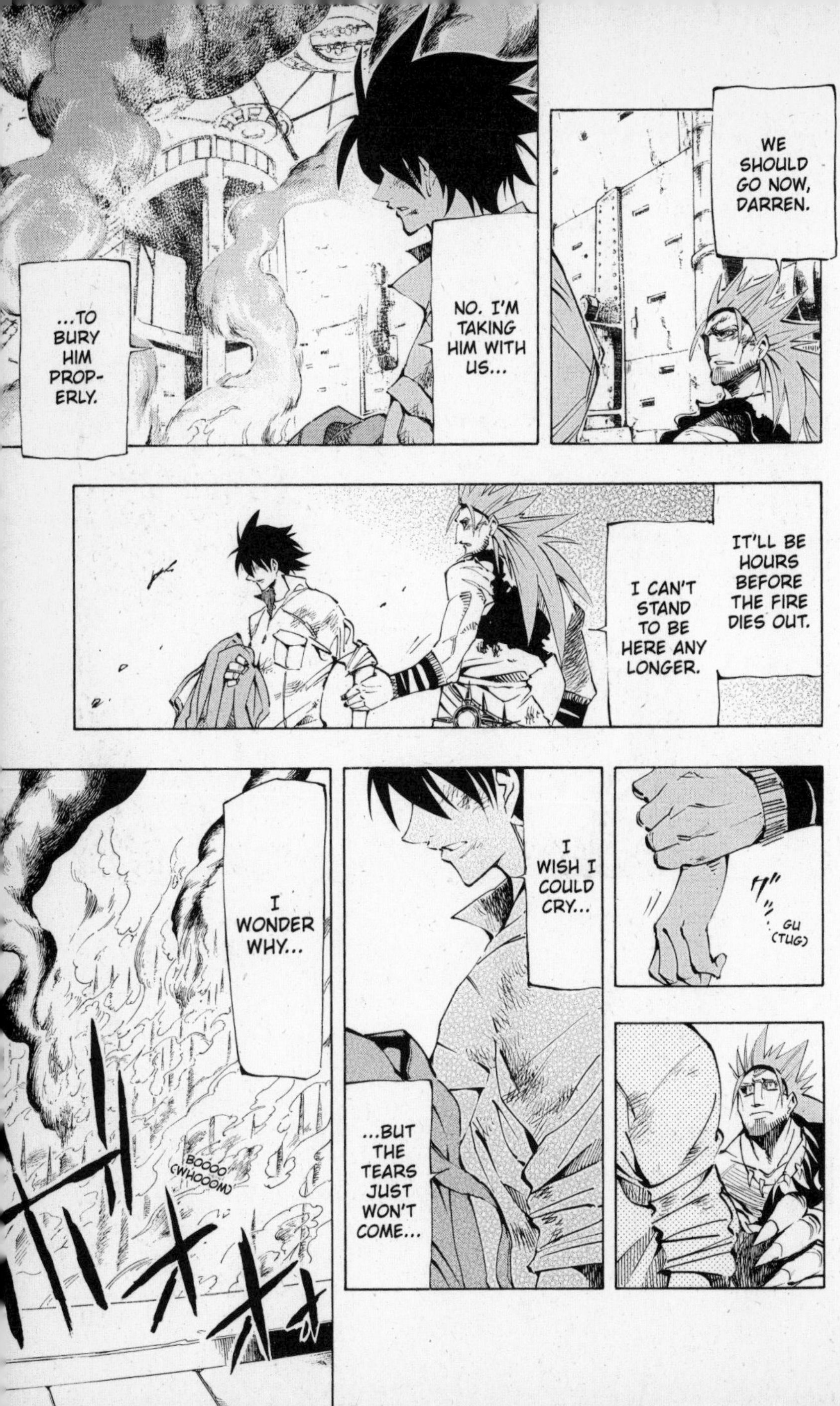
WE SHOULD GO NOW, DARREN.
NO. I'M TAKING HIM WITH US...
...TO BURY HIM PROPERLY.
IT'LL BE HOURS BEFORE THE FIRE DIES OUT.
I CAN'T STAND TO BE HERE ANY LONGER.
GU (TUG)
I WISH I COULD CRY...
...BUT THE TEARS JUST WON'T COME...
I WONDER WHY...
BOOOO (WHOOOM)

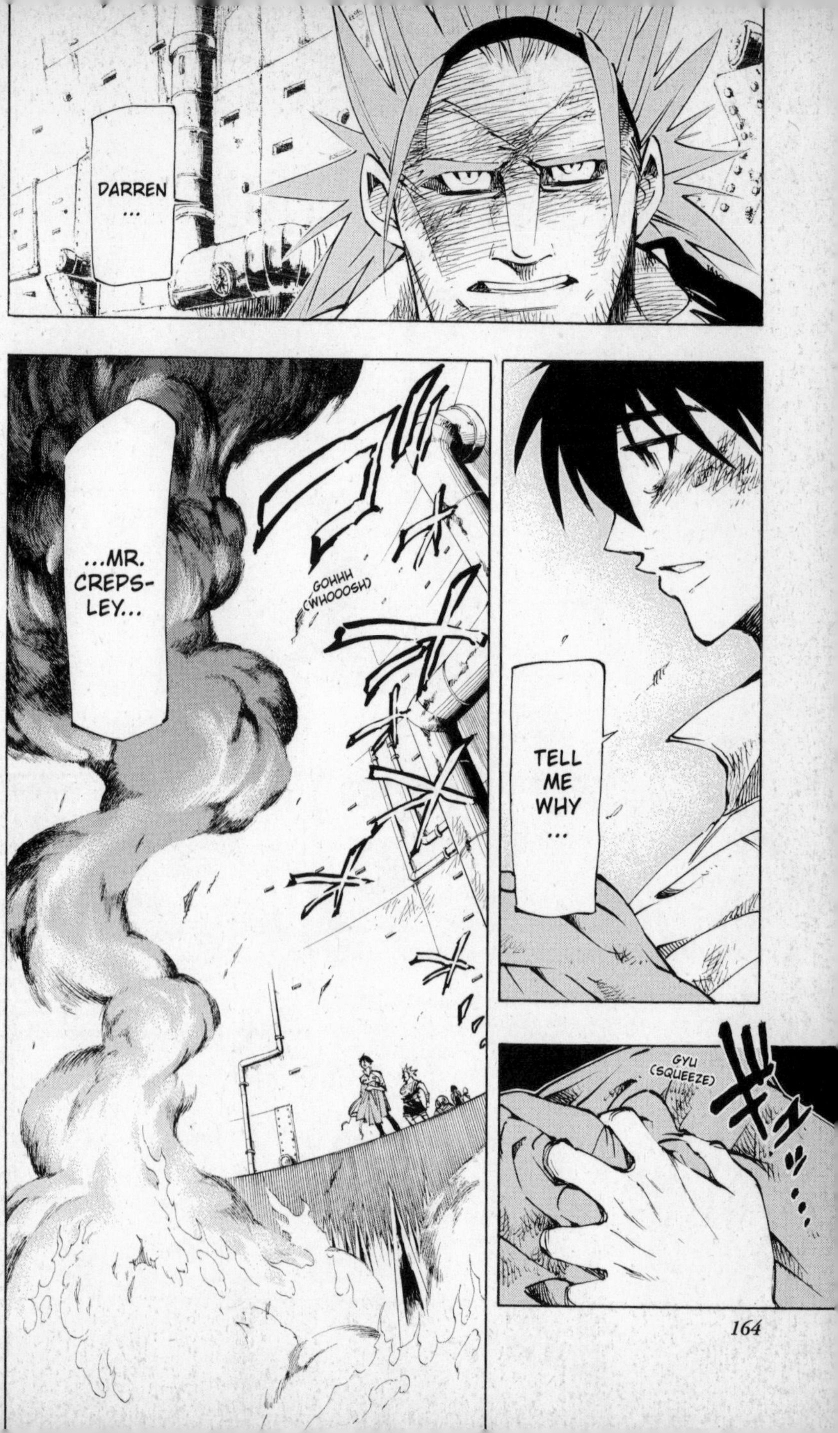
DARREN ...
TELL ME WHY ...
GYU (SQUEEZE)
...MR. CREPS-LEY...
GOHHH (WHOOOSH)

CHAPTER [illegible]: THE DEVIL'S WHISPER

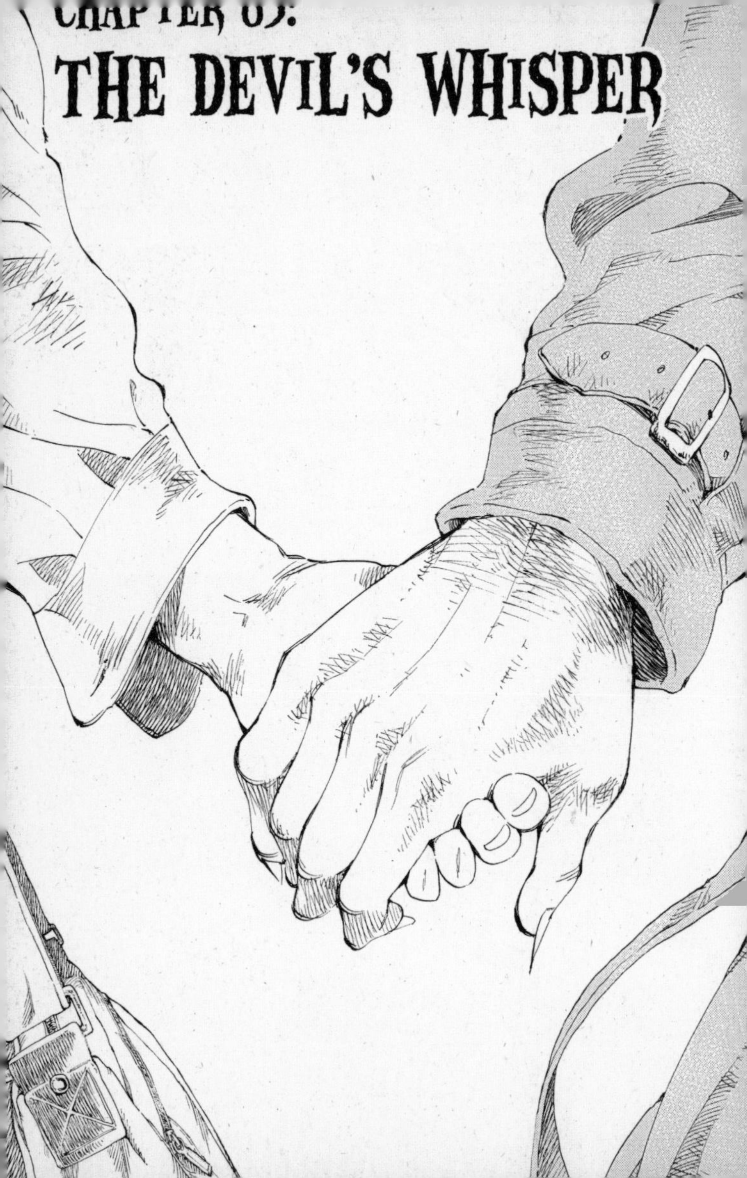

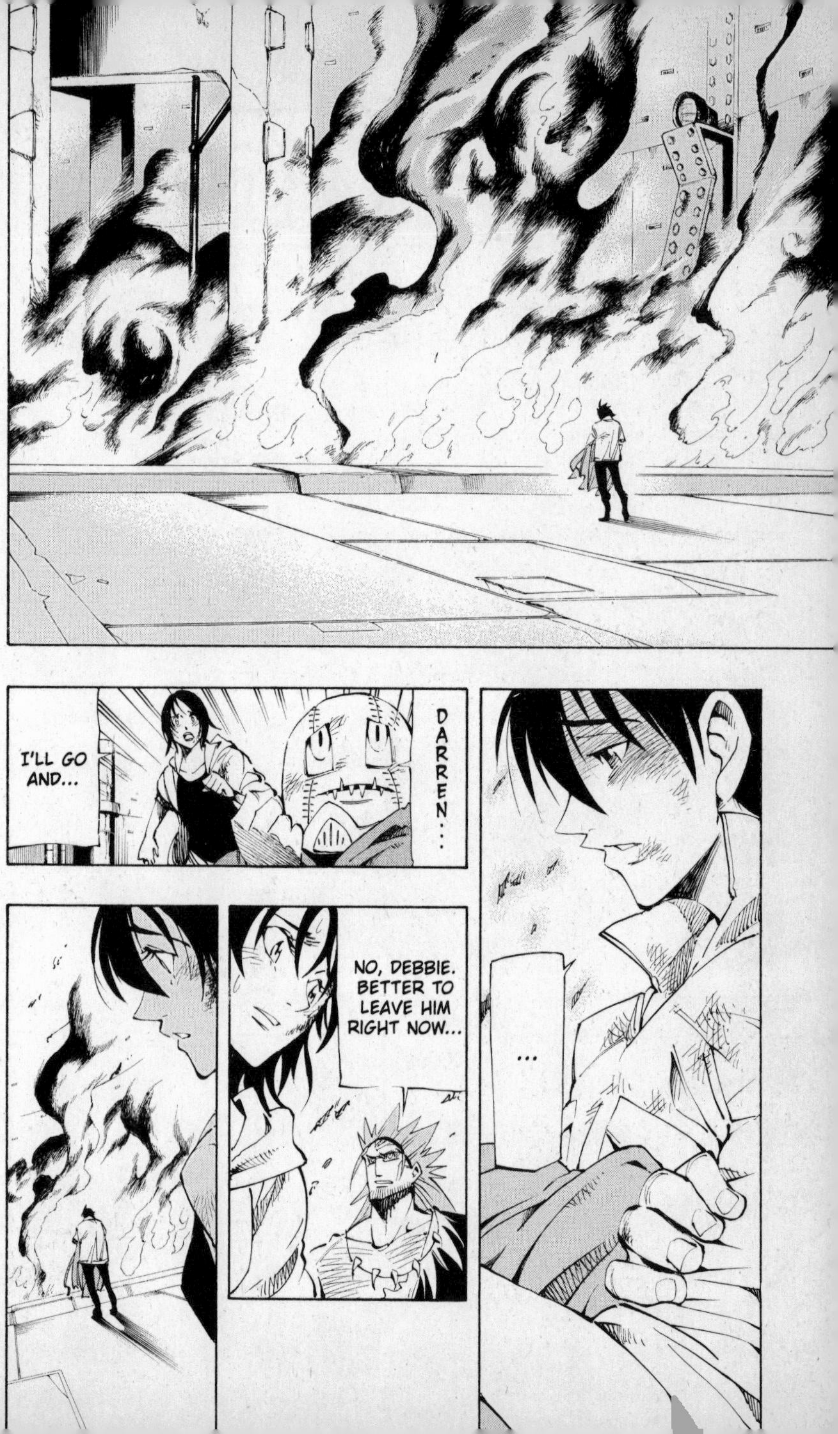
...
DARREN...
I'LL GO AND...
NO, DEBBIE. BETTER TO LEAVE HIM RIGHT NOW...

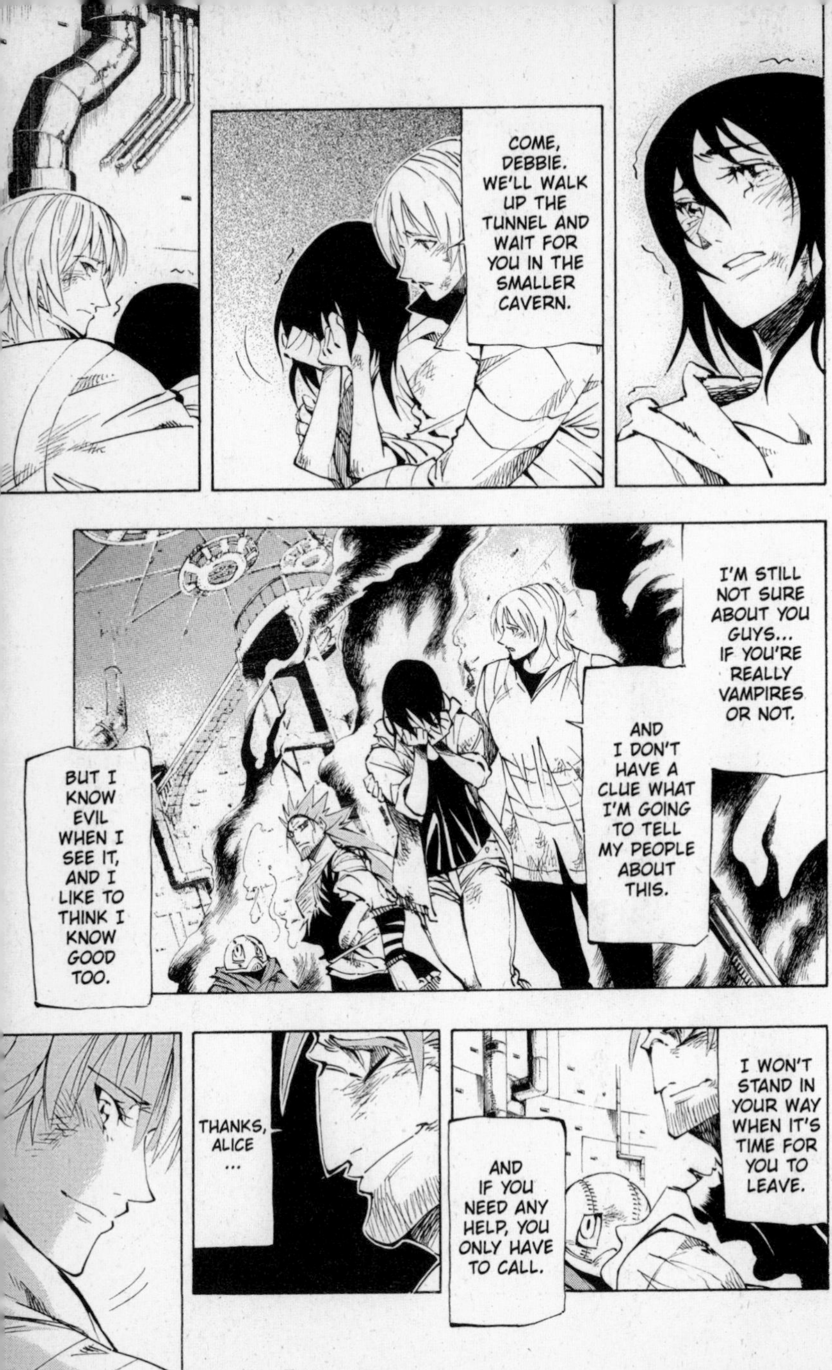

COME, DEBBIE. WE'LL WALK UP THE TUNNEL AND WAIT FOR YOU IN THE SMALLER CAVERN.
I'M STILL NOT SURE ABOUT YOU GUYS... IF YOU'RE REALLY VAMPIRES OR NOT.
AND I DON'T HAVE A CLUE WHAT I'M GOING TO TELL MY PEOPLE ABOUT THIS.
BUT I KNOW EVIL WHEN I SEE IT, AND I LIKE TO THINK I KNOW GOOD TOO.
I WON'T STAND IN YOUR WAY WHEN IT'S TIME FOR YOU TO LEAVE.
AND IF YOU NEED ANY HELP, YOU ONLY HAVE TO CALL.
THANKS, ALICE ...

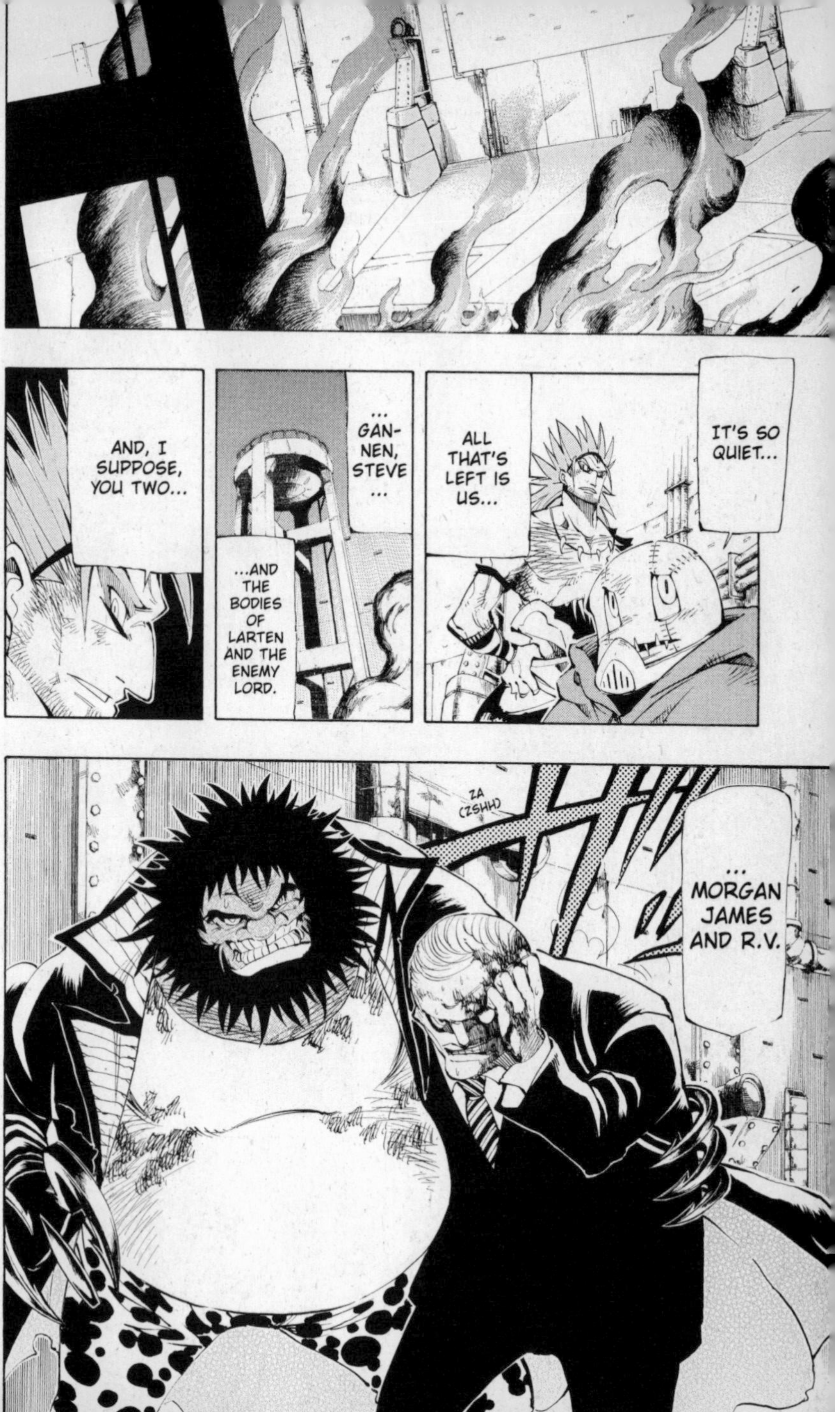
IT'S SO QUIET...
ALL THAT'S LEFT IS US...
...GAN-NEN, STEVE...
...AND THE BODIES OF LARTEN AND THE ENEMY LORD.
AND, I SUPPOSE, YOU TWO...
ZA (ZSHH)
...MORGAN JAMES AND R.V.

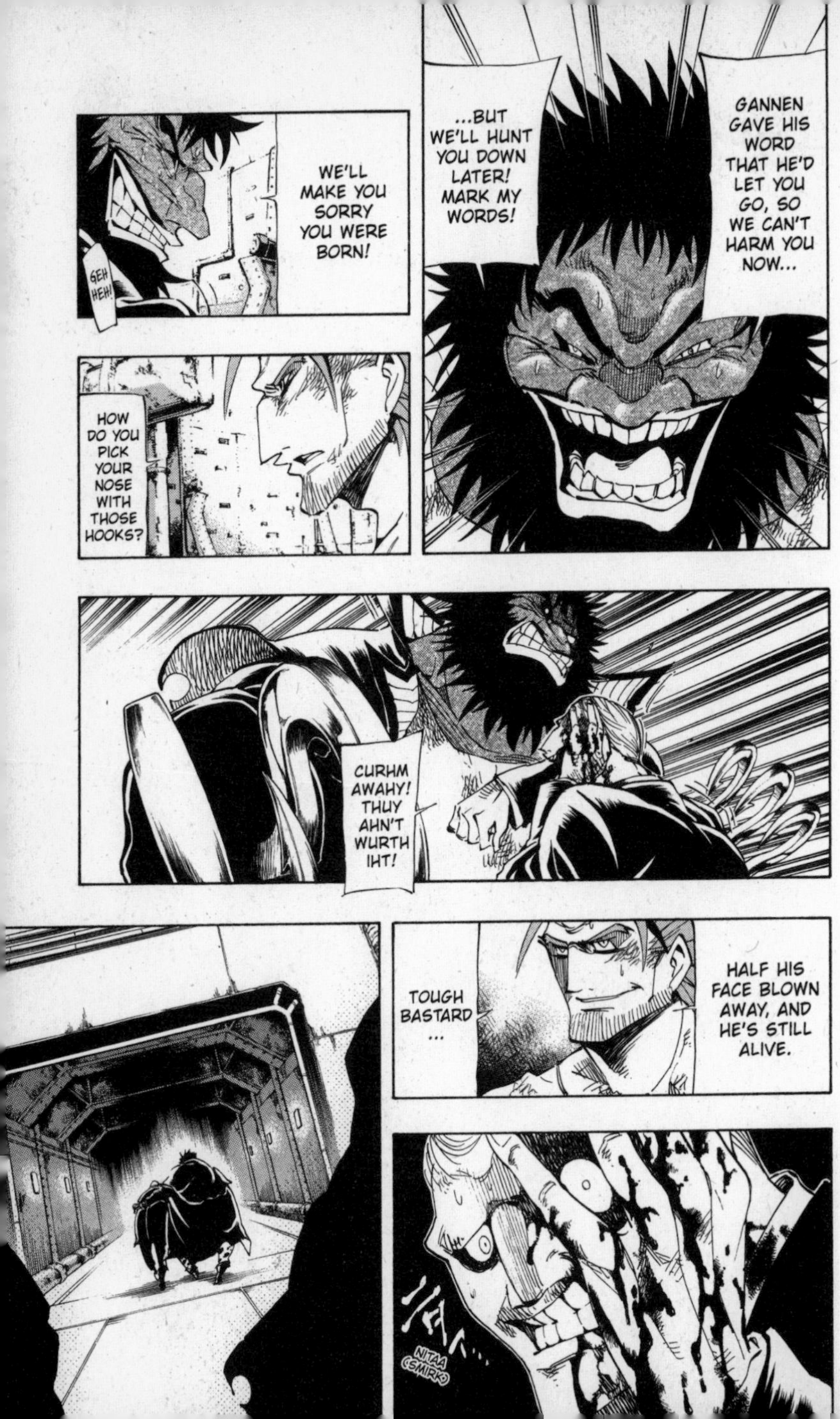
GANNEN GAVE HIS WORD THAT HE'D LET YOU GO, SO WE CAN'T HARM YOU NOW...
...BUT WE'LL HUNT YOU DOWN LATER! MARK MY WORDS!
WE'LL MAKE YOU SORRY YOU WERE BORN!
GEH HEH!
HOW DO YOU PICK YOUR NOSE WITH THOSE HOOKS?
CURHM AWAHY! THUY AHN'T WURTH IHT!
HALF HIS FACE BLOWN AWAY, AND HE'S STILL ALIVE.
TOUGH BASTARD ...
NITAA (SMIRK)

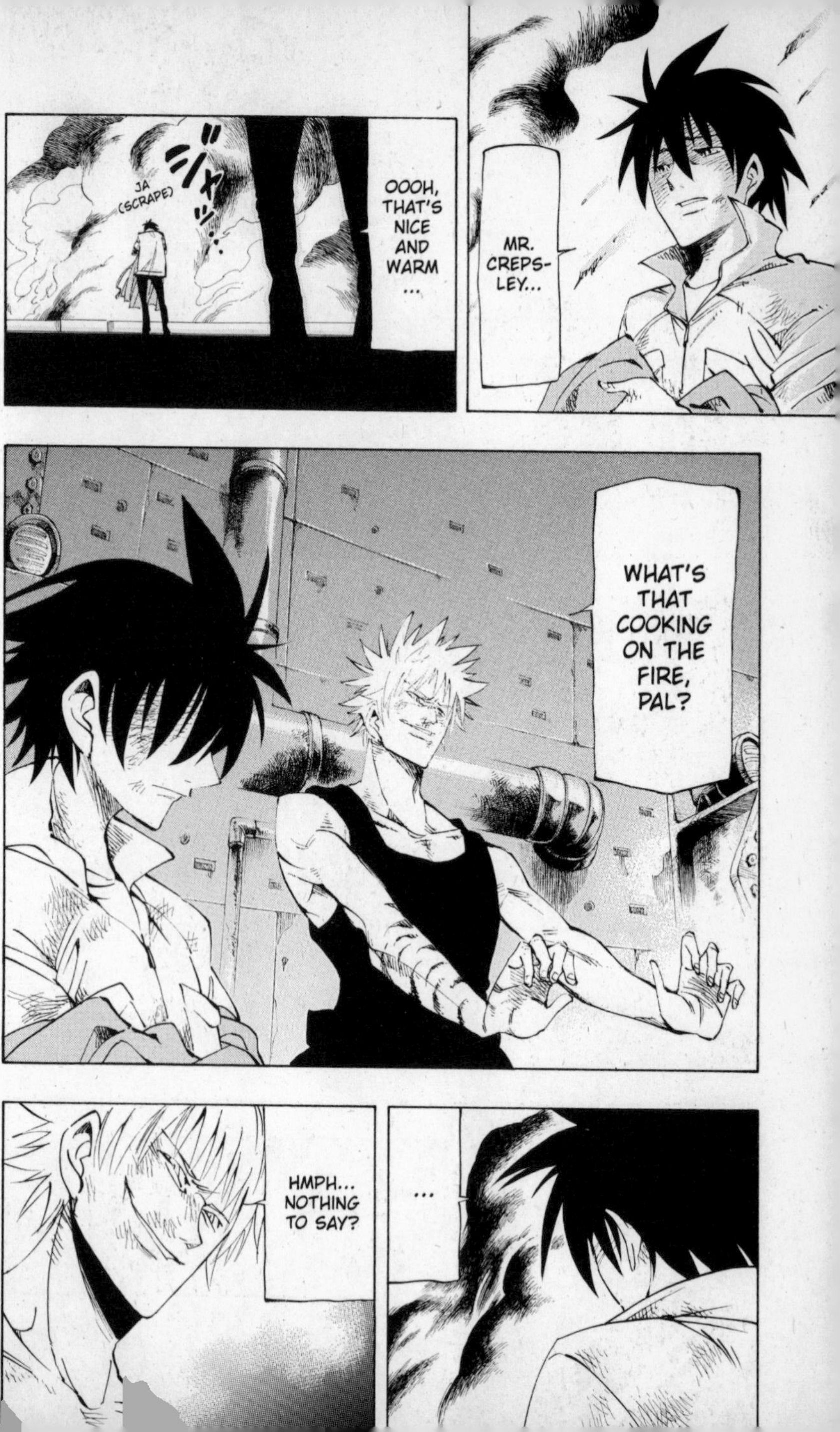
MR. CREPS-LEY...
ジャッ
JA (SCRAPE)
OOOH, THAT'S NICE AND WARM ...
WHAT'S THAT COOKING ON THE FIRE, PAL?
...
HMPH... NOTHING TO SAY?

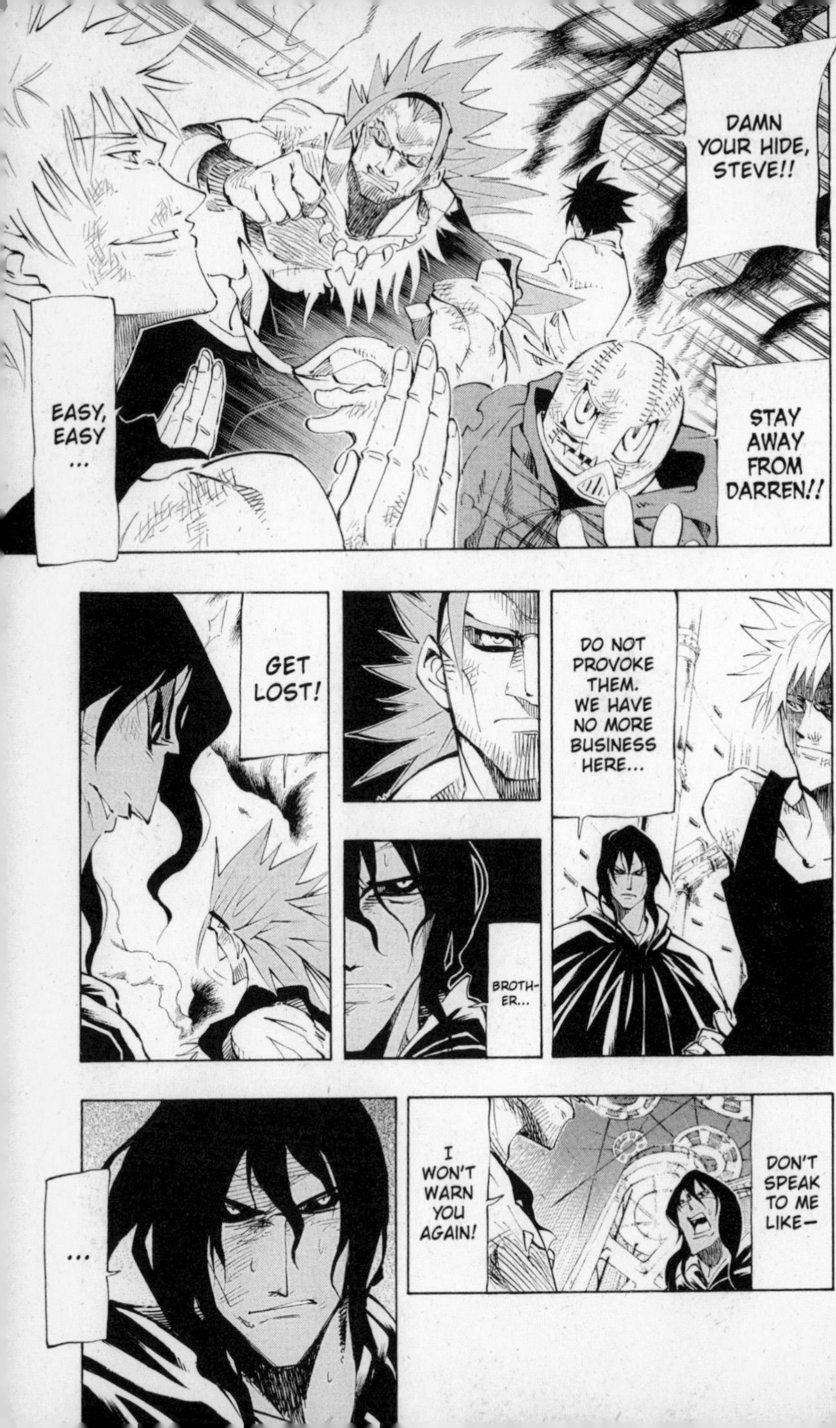
DAMN YOUR HIDE, STEVE!!
STAY AWAY FROM DARREN!!
EASY, EASY ...
DO NOT PROVOKE THEM. WE HAVE NO MORE BUSINESS HERE...
BROTH-ER...
GET LOST!
DON'T SPEAK TO ME LIKE—
I WON'T WARN YOU AGAIN!
...

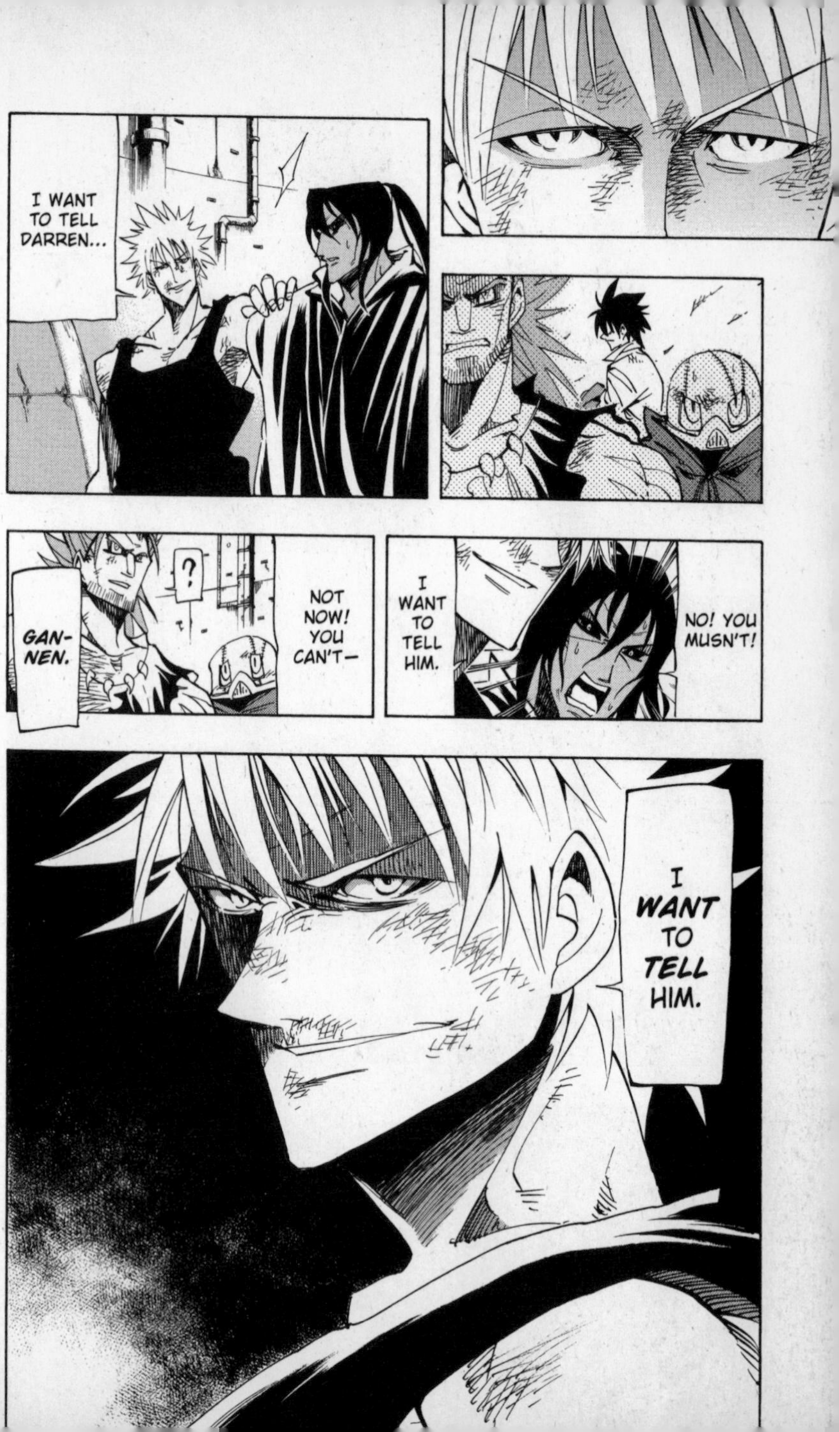
I WANT TO TELL DARREN...
NO! YOU MUSN'T!
I WANT TO TELL HIM.
NOT NOW! YOU CAN'T—
?
GAN-NEN.
I WANT TO TELL HIM.

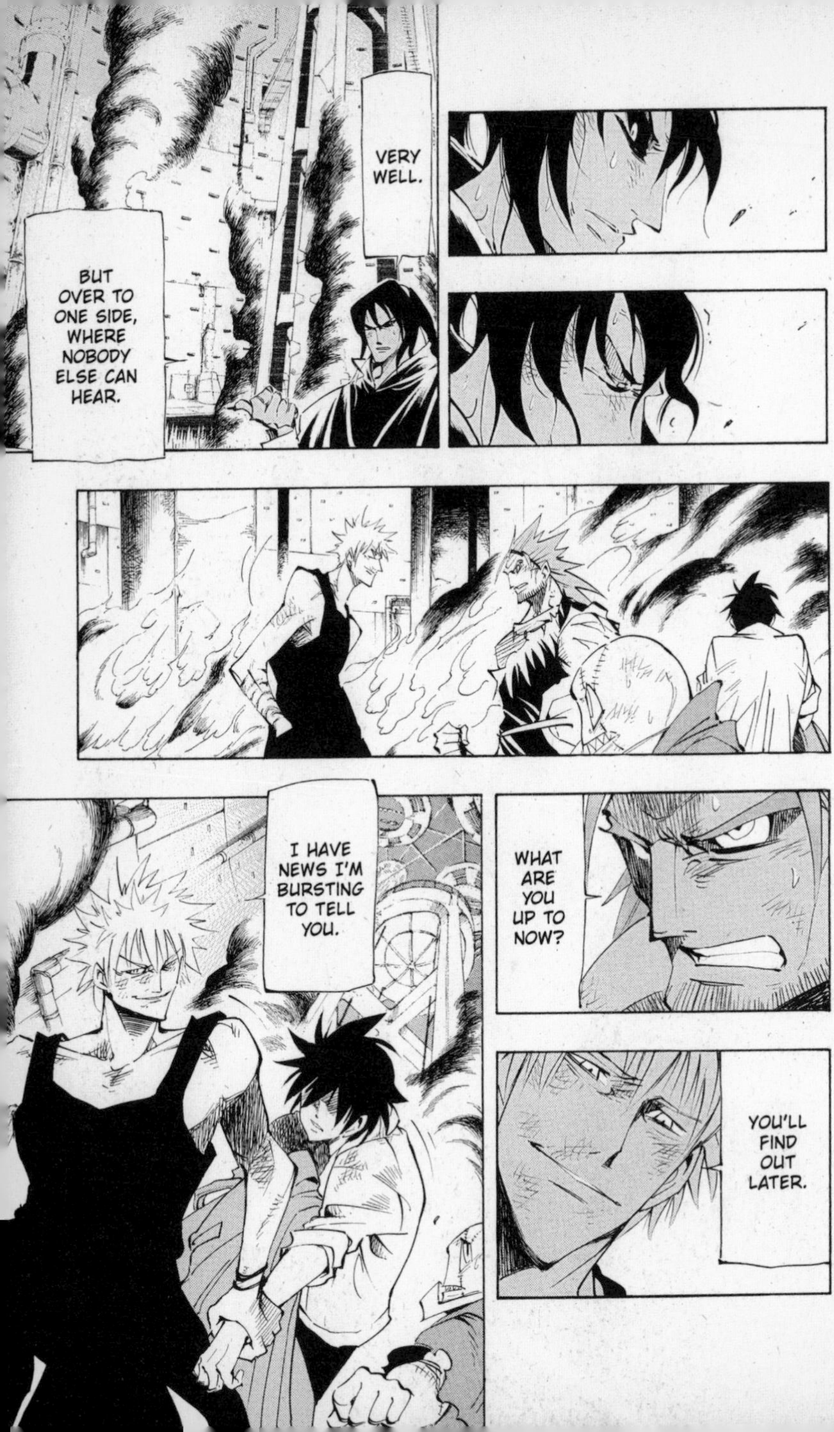
VERY WELL.
BUT OVER TO ONE SIDE, WHERE NOBODY ELSE CAN HEAR.
WHAT ARE YOU UP TO NOW?
YOU'LL FIND OUT LATER.
I HAVE NEWS I'M BURSTING TO TELL YOU.

...

WE
WON'T.

IF YOU
HURT
HIM—!

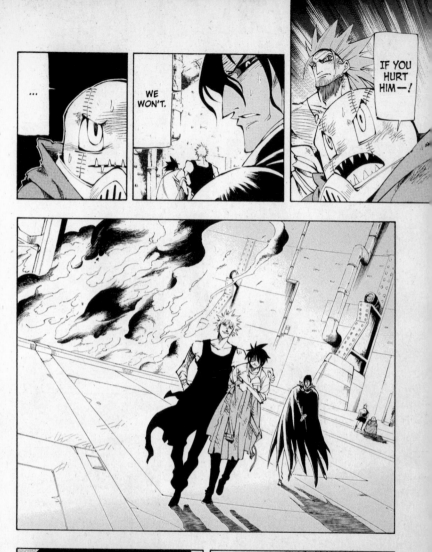

WE'VE COME
A LONG WAY,
HAVEN'T WE,
DARREN?

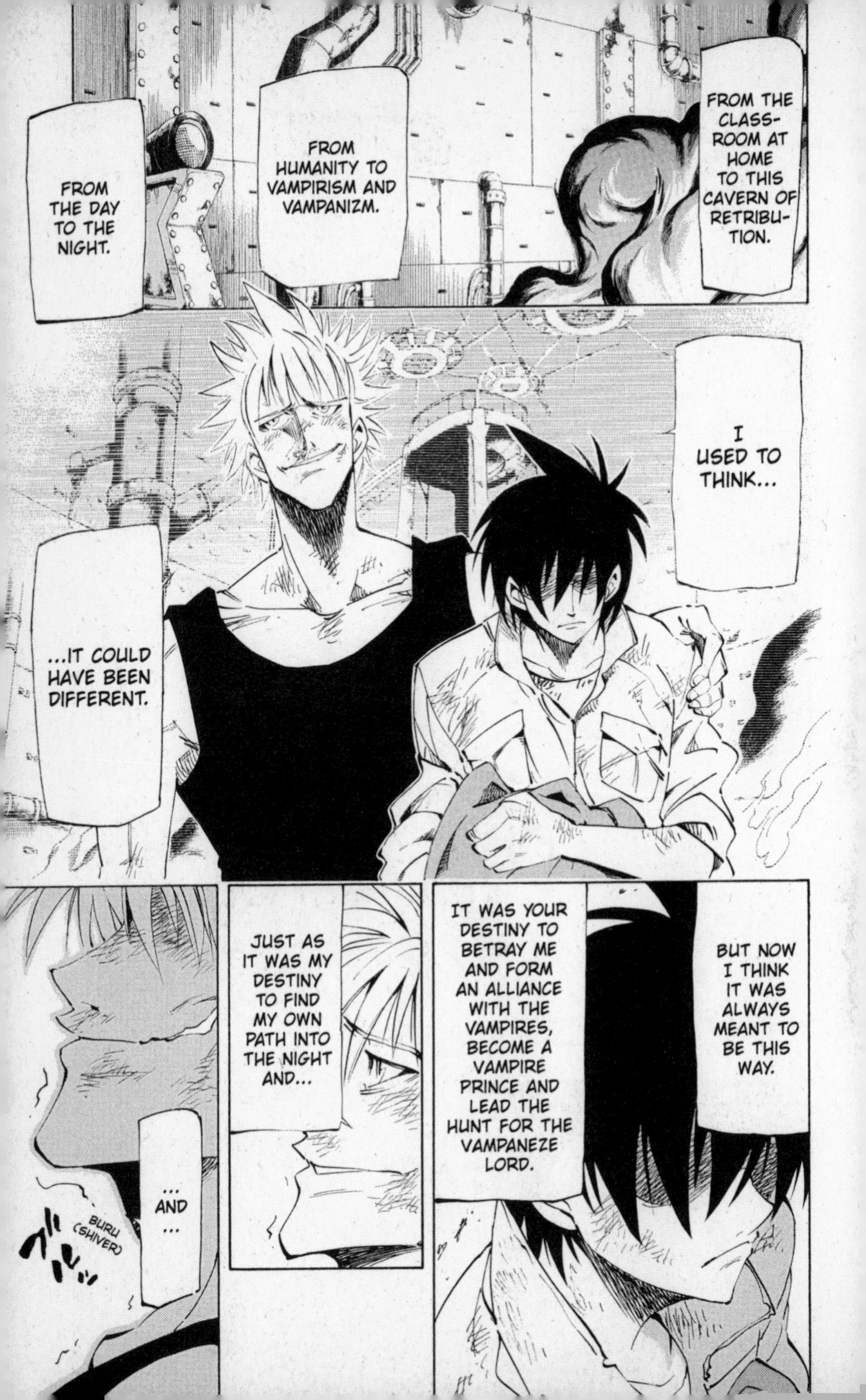
FROM THE CLASS-ROOM AT HOME TO THIS CAVERN OF RETRIBU-TION.
FROM HUMANITY TO VAMPIRISM AND VAMPANIZM.
FROM THE DAY TO THE NIGHT.
I USED TO THINK...
...IT COULD HAVE BEEN DIFFERENT.
BUT NOW I THINK IT WAS ALWAYS MEANT TO BE THIS WAY.
IT WAS YOUR DESTINY TO BETRAY ME AND FORM AN ALLIANCE WITH THE VAMPIRES, BECOME A VAMPIRE PRINCE AND LEAD THE HUNT FOR THE VAMPANEZE LORD.
JUST AS IT WAS MY DESTINY TO FIND MY OWN PATH INTO THE NIGHT AND...
...AND...
BURU (SHIVER)

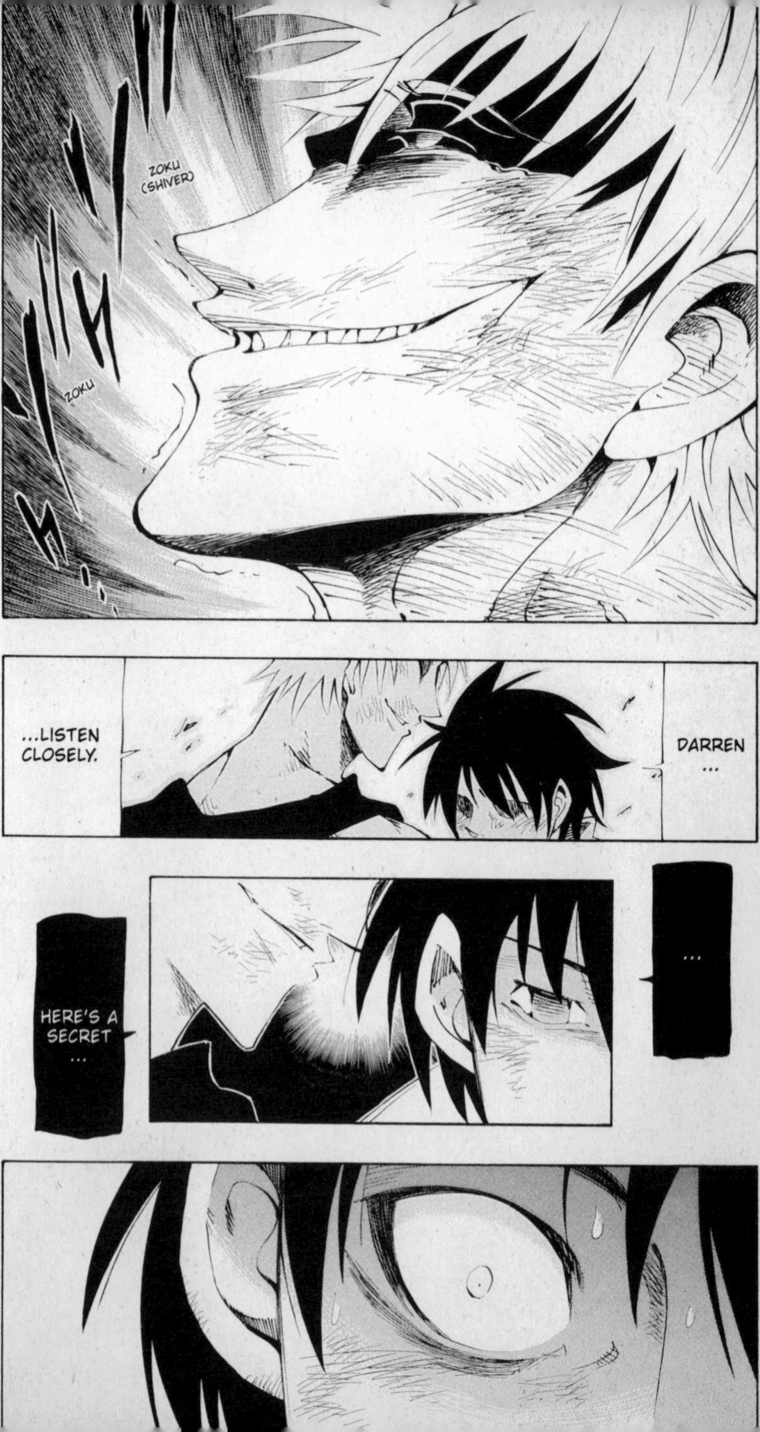
ZOKU (SHIVER)
ZOKU
DARREN ...
...LISTEN CLOSELY.
...
HERE'S A SECRET ...

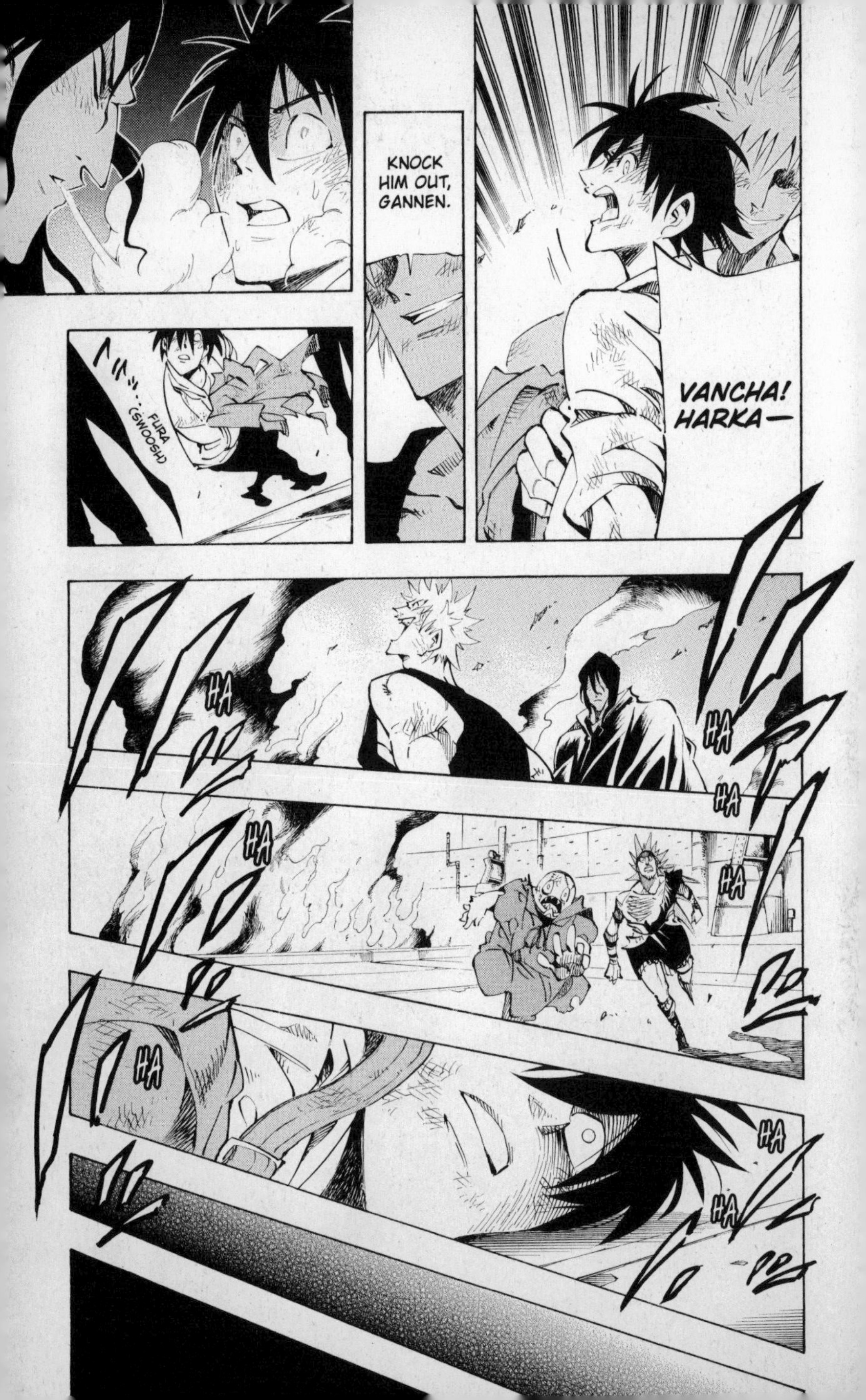
VANCHA! HARKA—
KNOCK HIM OUT, GANNEN.
FURA (SWOOSH)
HA
HA
HA
HA
HA
HA
HA
HA

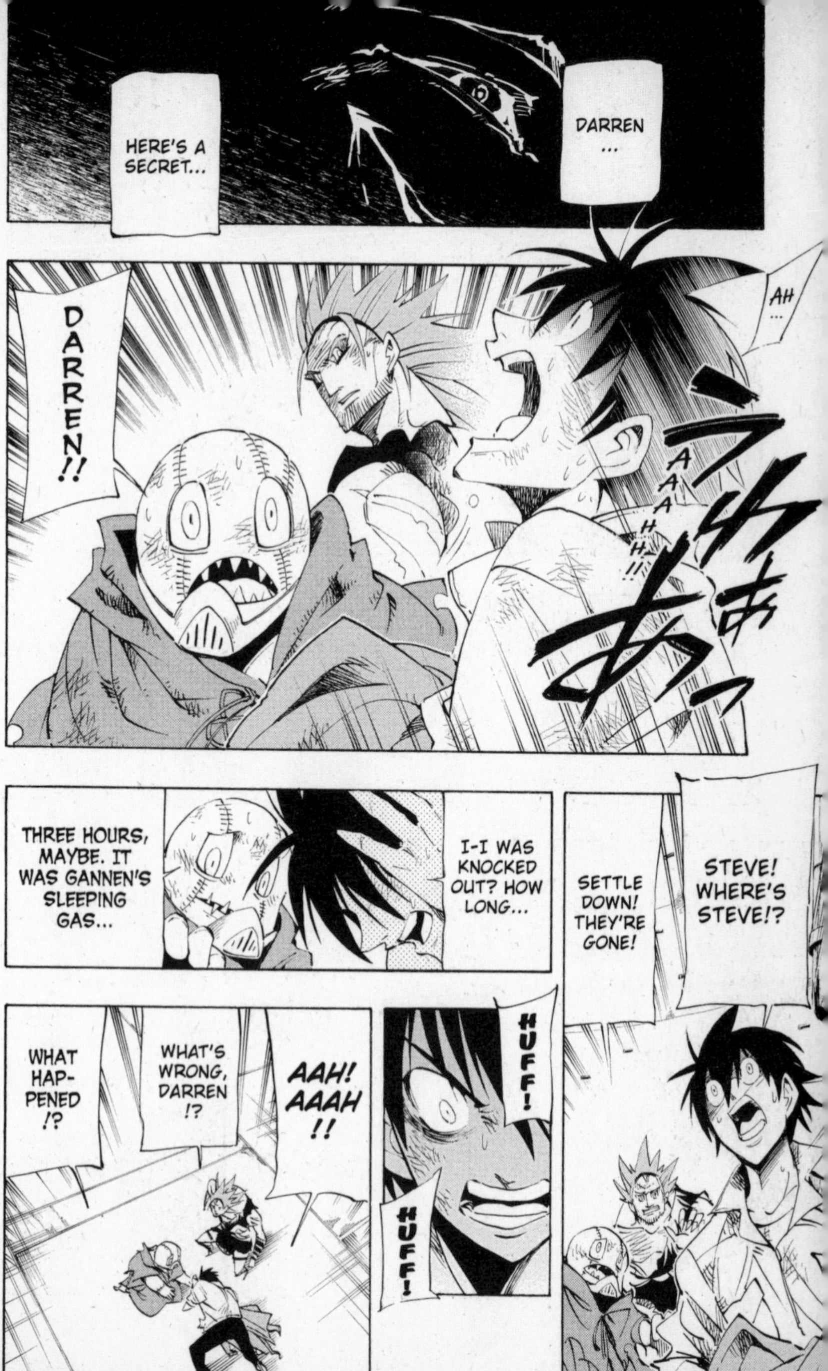

DARREN ...
HERE'S A SECRET...
AH ...
AAAAHH!!
DARREN!!
STEVE! WHERE'S STEVE!?
SETTLE DOWN! THEY'RE GONE!
I-I WAS KNOCKED OUT? HOW LONG...
THREE HOURS, MAYBE. IT WAS GANNEN'S SLEEPING GAS...
HUFF!
HUFF!
AAH! AAAH!!
WHAT'S WRONG, DARREN!?
WHAT HAP-PENED!?

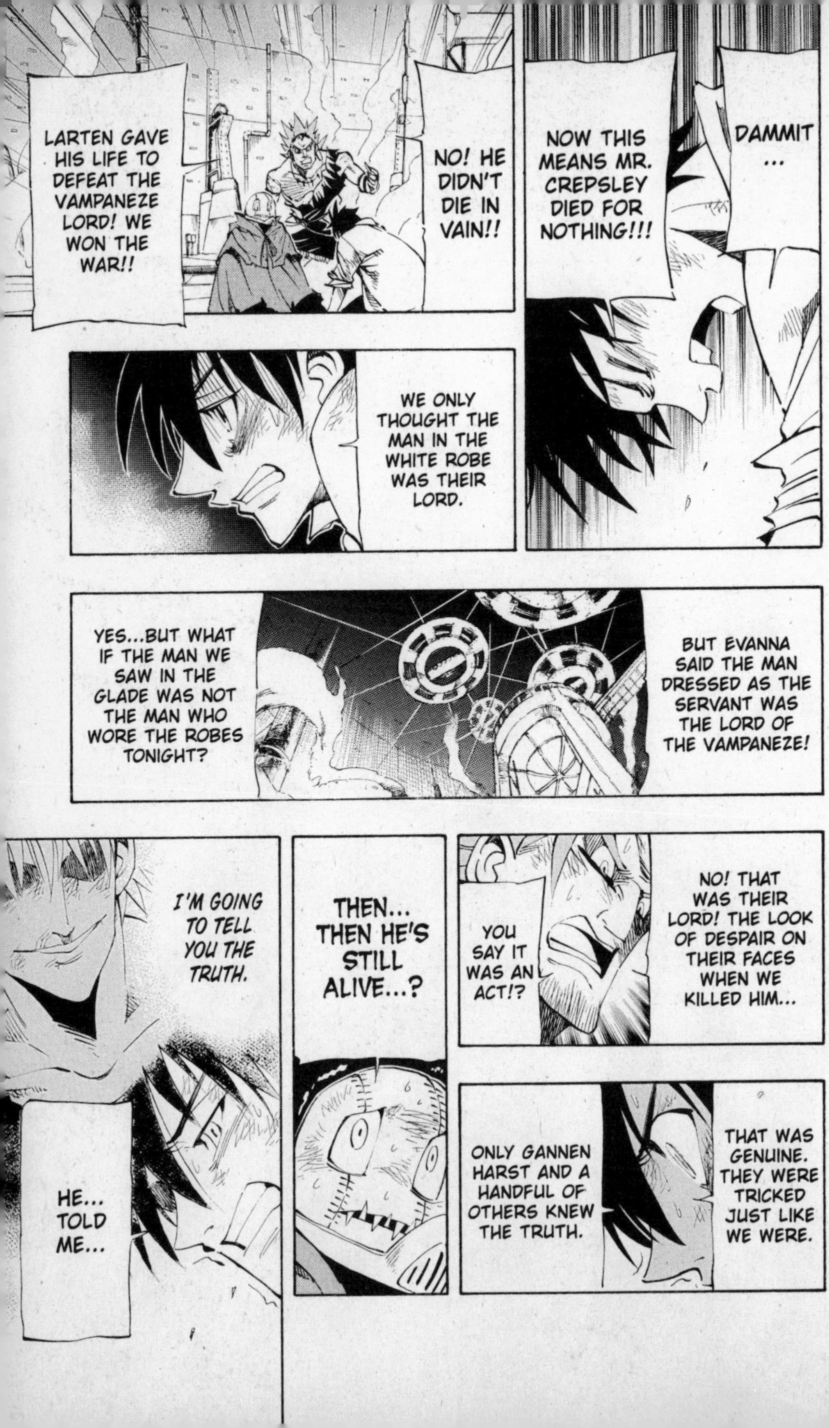
DAMMIT ...
NOW THIS MEANS MR. CREPSLEY DIED FOR NOTHING!!!
NO! HE DIDN'T DIE IN VAIN!!
LARTEN GAVE HIS LIFE TO DEFEAT THE VAMPANEZE LORD! WE WON THE WAR!!
WE ONLY THOUGHT THE MAN IN THE WHITE ROBE WAS THEIR LORD.
BUT EVANNA SAID THE MAN DRESSED AS THE SERVANT WAS THE LORD OF THE VAMPANEZE!
YES...BUT WHAT IF THE MAN WE SAW IN THE GLADE WAS NOT THE MAN WHO WORE THE ROBES TONIGHT?
NO! THAT WAS THEIR LORD! THE LOOK OF DESPAIR ON THEIR FACES WHEN WE KILLED HIM...
YOU SAY IT WAS AN ACT!?
THAT WAS GENUINE. THEY WERE TRICKED JUST LIKE WE WERE.
ONLY GANNEN HARST AND A HANDFUL OF OTHERS KNEW THE TRUTH.
THEN... THEN HE'S STILL ALIVE...?
I'M GOING TO TELL YOU THE TRUTH.
HE... TOLD ME...

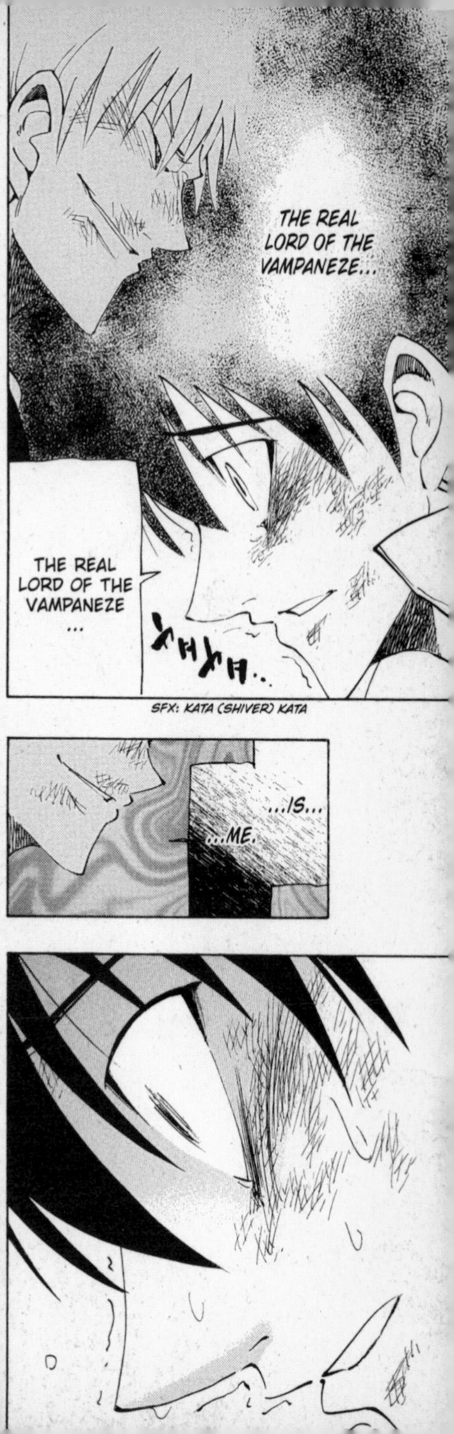
THE REAL LORD OF THE VAMPANEZE...
THE REAL LORD OF THE VAMPANEZE ...
SFX: KATA (SHIVER) KATA
...IS...
...ME.

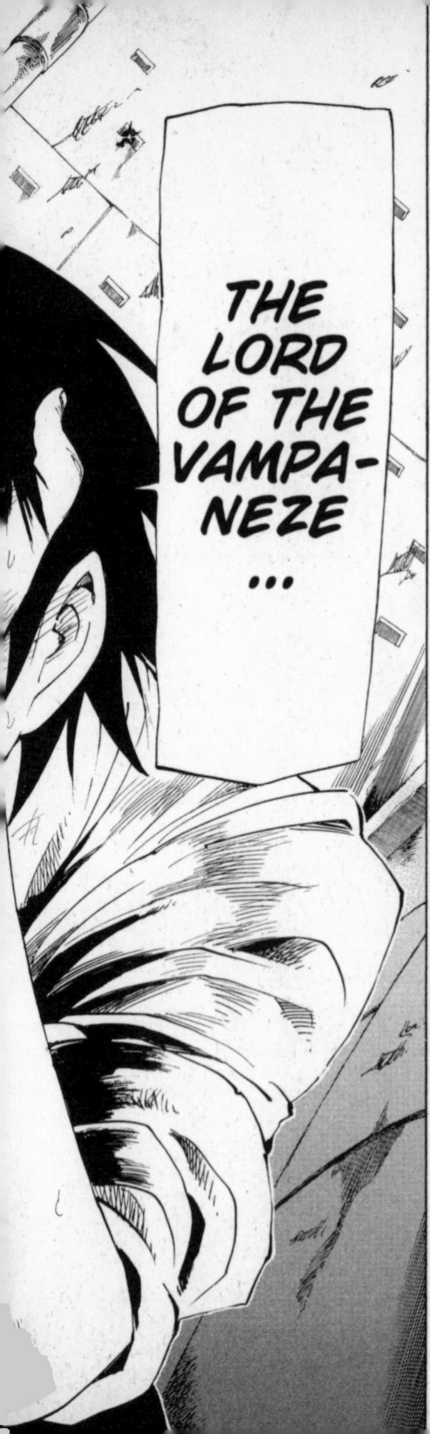
THE LORD OF THE VAMPA-NEZE ...

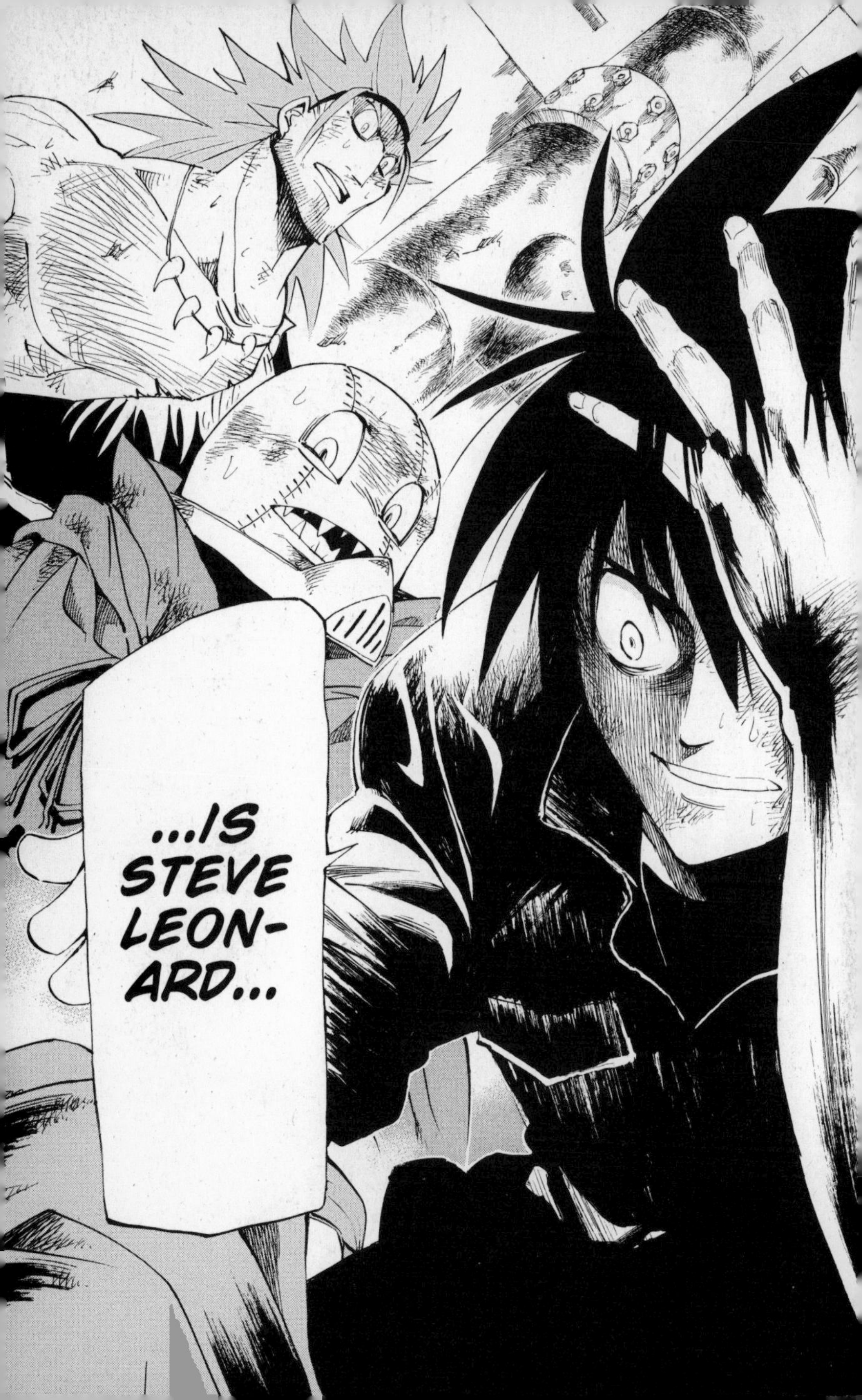
...IS STEVE LEON-ARD...

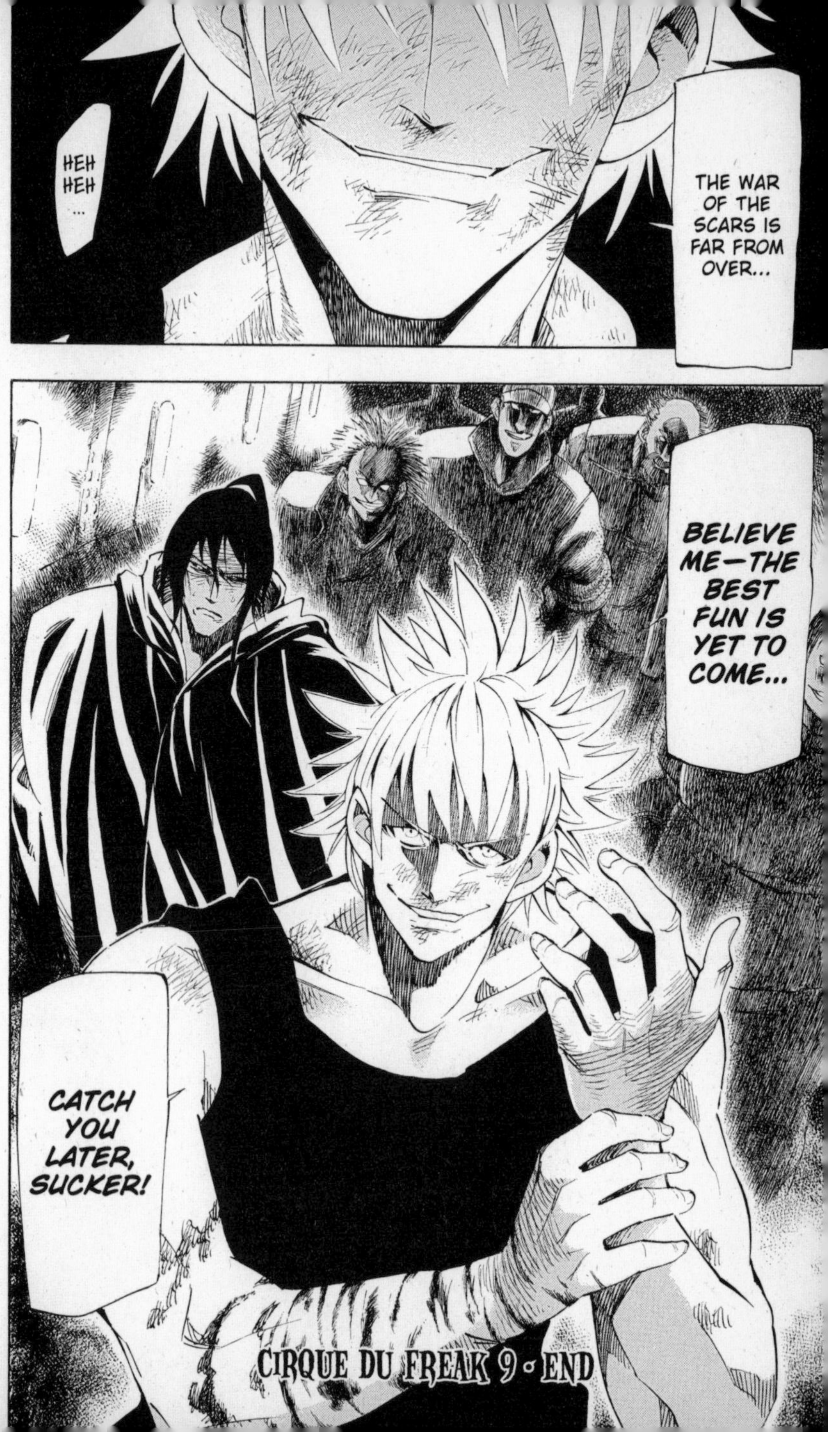
THE WAR OF THE SCARS IS FAR FROM OVER...
HEH HEH ...
BELIEVE ME—THE BEST FUN IS YET TO COME...
CATCH YOU LATER, SUCKER!
CIRQUE DU FREAK 9 • END

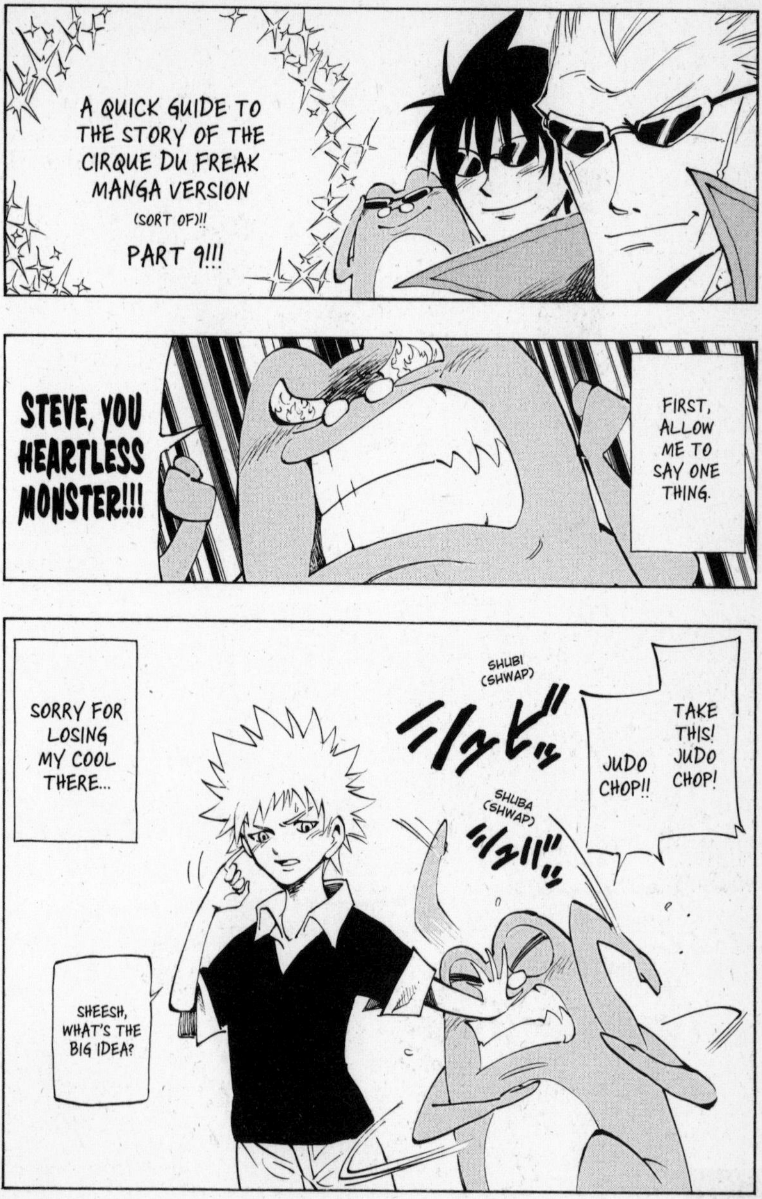
A QUICK GUIDE TO THE STORY OF THE CIRQUE DU FREAK MANGA VERSION
(SORT OF)!!
PART 9!!!
FIRST, ALLOW ME TO SAY ONE THING.
STEVE, YOU HEARTLESS MONSTER!!!
TAKE THIS! JUDO CHOP!
JUDO CHOP!!
SHUBI (SHWAP)
SHUBA (SHWAP)
SORRY FOR LOSING MY COOL THERE...
SHEESH, WHAT'S THE BIG IDEA?

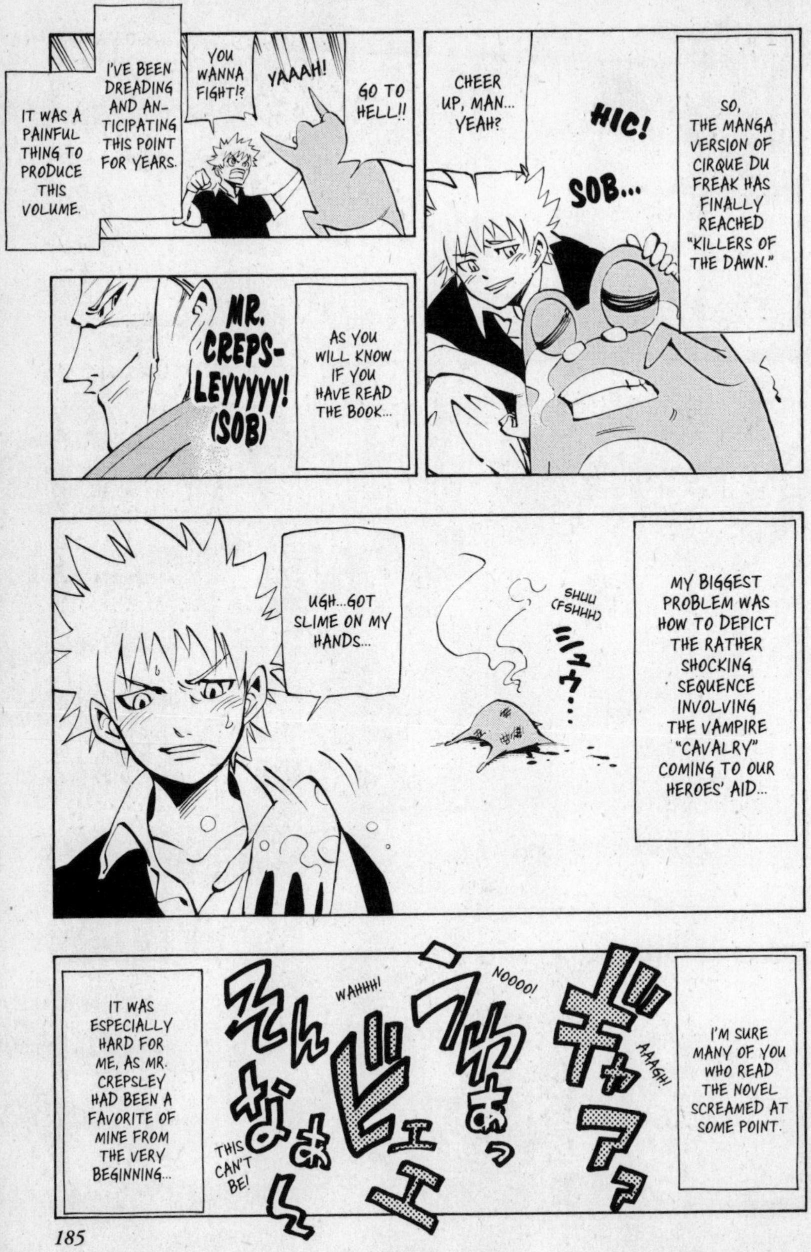
SO, THE MANGA VERSION OF CIRQUE DU FREAK HAS FINALLY REACHED "KILLERS OF THE DAWN."
HIC!
SOB...
CHEER UP, MAN... YEAH?
GO TO HELL!!
YAAAH!
YOU WANNA FIGHT!?
I'VE BEEN DREADING AND ANTICIPATING THIS POINT FOR YEARS.
IT WAS A PAINFUL THING TO PRODUCE THIS VOLUME.
AS YOU WILL KNOW IF YOU HAVE READ THE BOOK...
MR. CREPSLEYYYYY! (SOB)
MY BIGGEST PROBLEM WAS HOW TO DEPICT THE RATHER SHOCKING SEQUENCE INVOLVING THE VAMPIRE "CAVALRY" COMING TO OUR HEROES' AID...
シュウ…
SHUU (FSHHH)
UGH...GOT SLIME ON MY HANDS...
I'M SURE MANY OF YOU WHO READ THE NOVEL SCREAMED AT SOME POINT.
ギャァァ
AAAGH!
うわぁっ
NOOOO!
ビェエ
WAHHH!
そんなぁ〜
THIS CAN'T BE!
IT WAS ESPECIALLY HARD FOR ME, AS MR. CREPSLEY HAD BEEN A FAVORITE OF MINE FROM THE VERY BEGINNING...

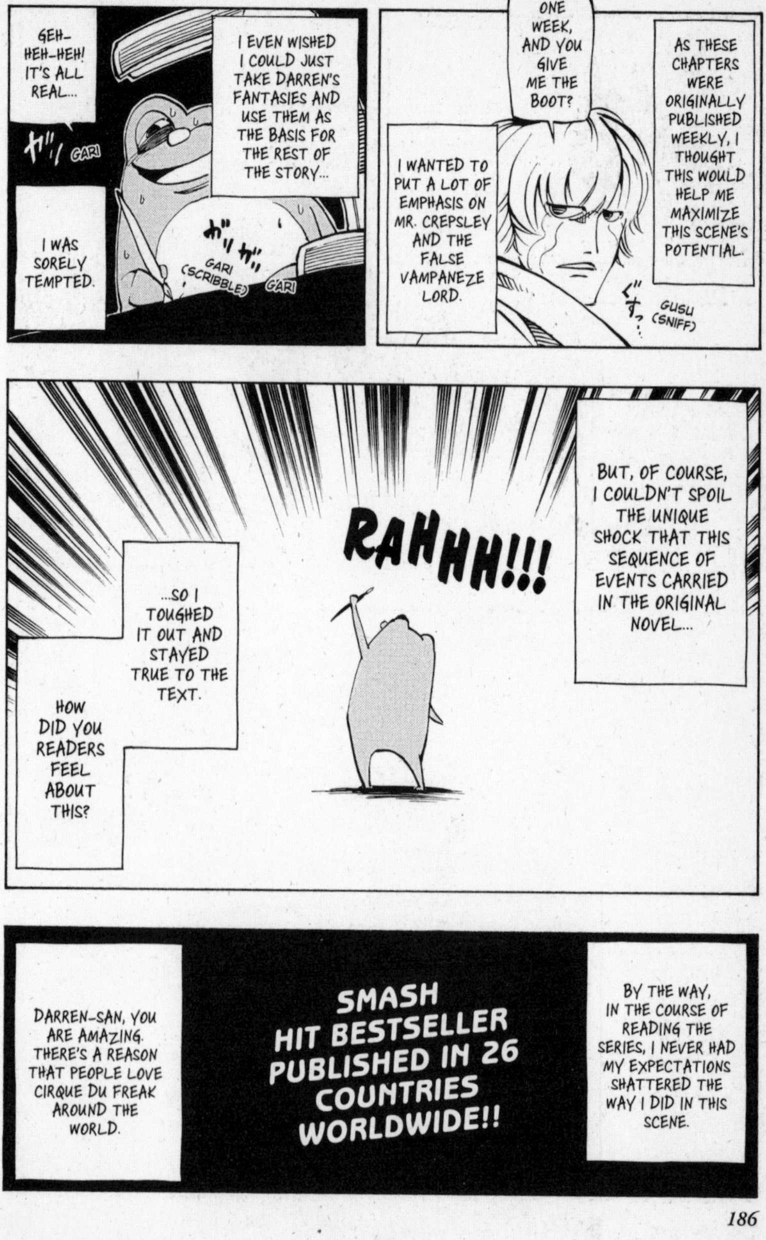
AS THESE CHAPTERS WERE ORIGINALLY PUBLISHED WEEKLY, I THOUGHT THIS WOULD HELP ME MAXIMIZE THIS SCENE'S POTENTIAL.
ONE WEEK, AND YOU GIVE ME THE BOOT?
I WANTED TO PUT A LOT OF EMPHASIS ON MR. CREPSLEY AND THE FALSE VAMPANEZE LORD.
ぐすっ
GUSU (SNIFF)
I EVEN WISHED I COULD JUST TAKE DARREN'S FANTASIES AND USE THEM AS THE BASIS FOR THE REST OF THE STORY...
GEH-HEH-HEH! IT'S ALL REAL...
ガリ
GARI
I WAS SORELY TEMPTED.
ガリガリ
GARI (SCRIBBLE) GARI
BUT, OF COURSE, I COULDN'T SPOIL THE UNIQUE SHOCK THAT THIS SEQUENCE OF EVENTS CARRIED IN THE ORIGINAL NOVEL...
RAHHHH!!!
...SO I TOUGHED IT OUT AND STAYED TRUE TO THE TEXT.
HOW DID YOU READERS FEEL ABOUT THIS?
BY THE WAY, IN THE COURSE OF READING THE SERIES, I NEVER HAD MY EXPECTATIONS SHATTERED THE WAY I DID IN THIS SCENE.
SMASH HIT BESTSELLER PUBLISHED IN 26 COUNTRIES WORLDWIDE!!
DARREN-SAN, YOU ARE AMAZING. THERE'S A REASON THAT PEOPLE LOVE CIRQUE DU FREAK AROUND THE WORLD.

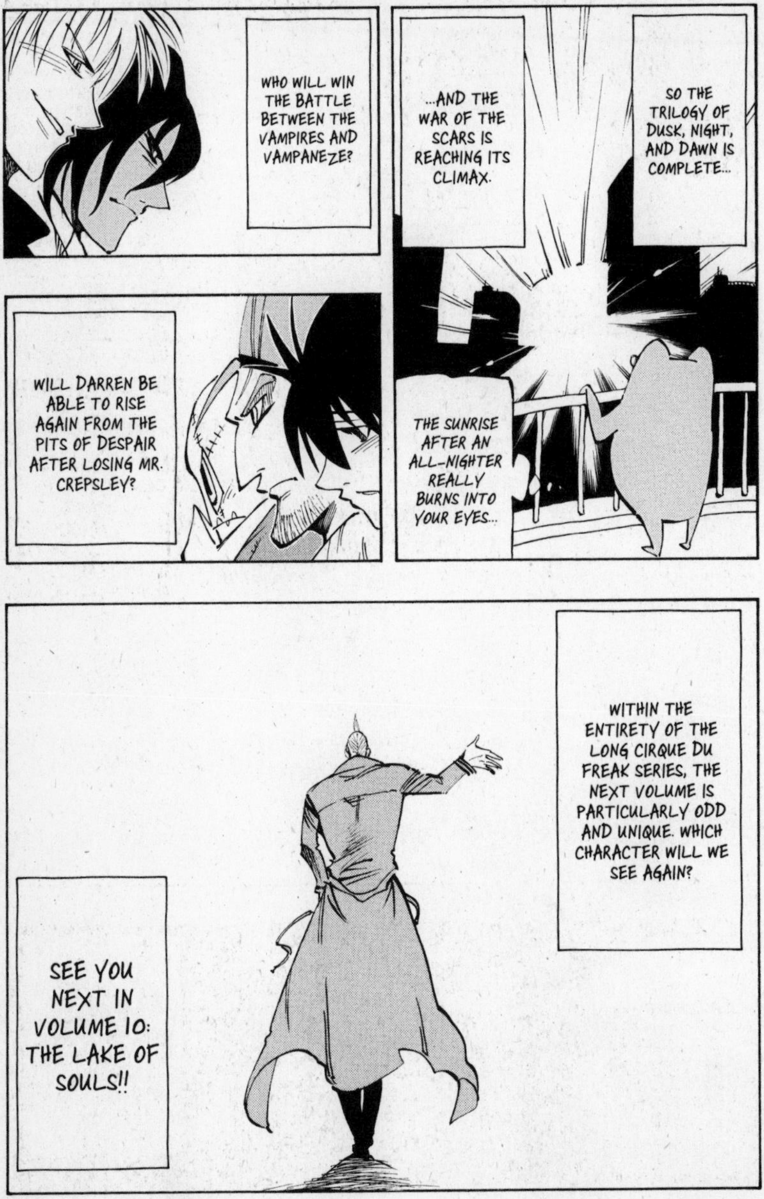
SO THE TRILOGY OF DUSK, NIGHT, AND DAWN IS COMPLETE...
...AND THE WAR OF THE SCARS IS REACHING ITS CLIMAX.
THE SUNRISE AFTER AN ALL-NIGHTER REALLY BURNS INTO YOUR EYES...
WHO WILL WIN THE BATTLE BETWEEN THE VAMPIRES AND VAMPANEZE?
WILL DARREN BE ABLE TO RISE AGAIN FROM THE PITS OF DESPAIR AFTER LOSING MR. CREPSLEY?
WITHIN THE ENTIRETY OF THE LONG CIRQUE DU FREAK SERIES, THE NEXT VOLUME IS PARTICULARLY ODD AND UNIQUE. WHICH CHARACTER WILL WE SEE AGAIN?
SEE YOU NEXT IN VOLUME 10: THE LAKE OF SOULS!!

The End

MESSAGE FROM
TAKAHIRO ARAI

THE MANGA VERSION OF *CIRQUE DU FREAK* HAS FINALLY REACHED THE TURNING POINT OF ITS LATTER HALF. I HOPE YOU ENJOYED THIS VISUAL TELLING OF "KILLERS OF THE DAWN," JAM-PACKED WITH AUTHOR DARREN SHAN'S MOST BRILLIANT STORYTELLING YET.

CIRQUE DU FREAK

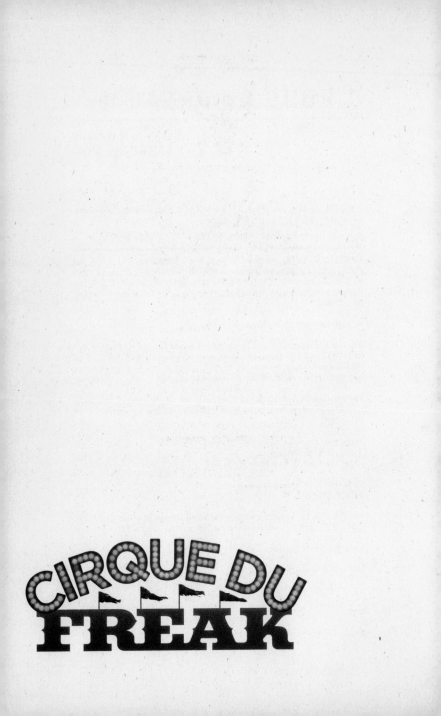

CIRQUE DU FREAK ⑨

DARREN SHAN
TAKAHIRO ARAI

Translation: Stephen Paul　　•　　Lettering: AndWorld Design
Art Direction: Hitoshi SHIRAYAMA
Original Cover Design: Shigeru ANZAI + Bay Bridge Studio

DARREN SHAN Vol. 9 © 2008 by Darren Shan, Takahiro ARAI. All rights reserved. Original Japanese edition published in Japan in 2008 by Shogakukan Inc., Tokyo. Artworks reproduction rights in U.S.A. and Canada arranged with Shogakukan Inc. through Tuttle-Mori Agency, Inc., Tokyo.

English translation © 2011 Darren Shan

Yen Press
Hachette Book Group
237 Park Avenue, New York, NY 10017

www.HachetteBookGroup.com
www.YenPress.com

Yen Press is an imprint of Hachette Book Group, Inc. The Yen Press name and logo are trademarks of Hachette Book Group, Inc.

First Yen Press Edition: May 2011

ISBN: 978-0-316-17606-4

10　9　8　7　6　5　4　3　2　1

BVG

Printed in the United States of America

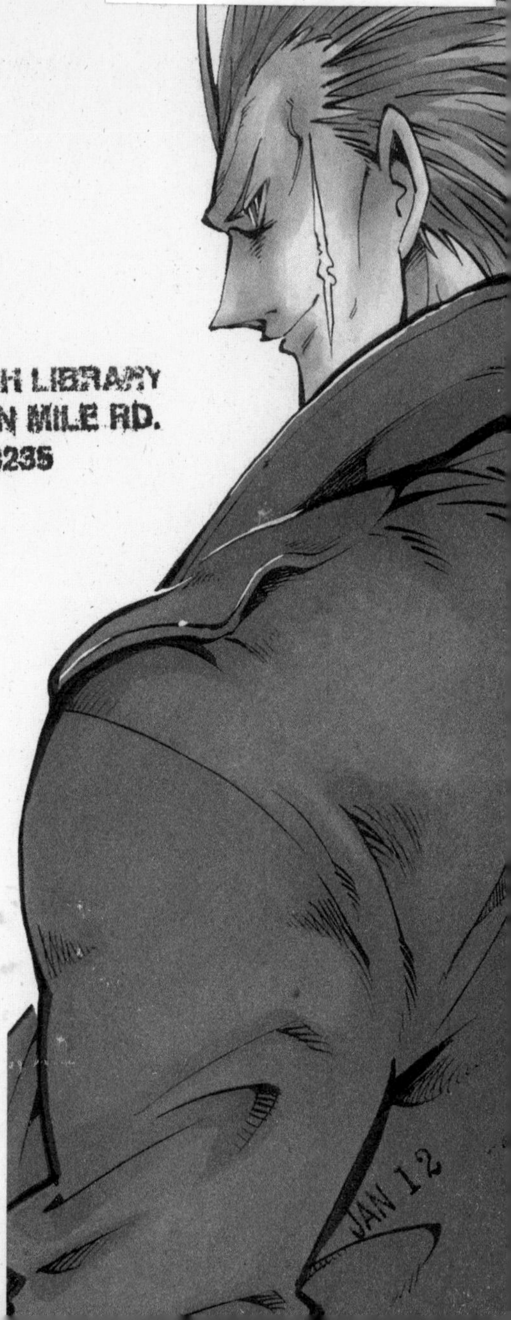